"Fleming Rutledge's Advent preaching bursts upon us with the same elemental force as the preaching of John the Baptist. Rutledge's fine crafting of language may be subtler than John's, but she carries forward his incisive, apocalyptic message of judgment and hope. This is essential preaching for a church wallowing in self-referential sentimentality and caught in captivity to the compromises of the present political order. This is preaching that tells the truth about the world's suffering and proclaims that God *acts* to rescue us. Do not drift anesthetized through another season of Advent; read this book."

—Richard B. Hays
George Washington Ivey Professor of New Testament, Duke University

"When it comes to preparing a congregation to observe the Christian season of Advent, no one should enter a pulpit, prepare worship, or teach a class without first reading this book. Biblically grounded, theologically centered, homiletically effective, and spiritually uplifting, this collection of writings and sermons by one of the church's great preachers is a winner on every front."

—Eugene Taylor Sutton
Bishop of the Episcopal Diocese of Maryland

"My not-so-secret hope is that Fleming Rutledge's *Advent* would become required reading in our seminaries and the focus of vestry book clubs, elder retreats, and worship leader workshops. Because that would give me hope for an apocalyptic renewal in the church—that we would learn again how to live as an Advent people, hoping in a God who acts and is making all things new. Taking this book to heart would teach us how to live wisely, faithfully, and prophetically in the Time Between."

—James K. A. Smith
Calvin College; author of *Awaiting the King* and *You Are What You Love*

"This compelling book of Advent sermons from Fleming Rutledge represents a masterclass in homiletics with a delightful array of biblically grounded, historically aware, theologically informed, and deeply relevant offerings. The bass note of the collection is the prophetic quest to recover the true meaning of Advent: far from simply marking the last, chaotic run-up to Christmas, it is a season that encapsulates the fundamental dynamic of the Christian life in this time between the times, in which the church both hastens and waits

W9-AEB-976

in hope for the promised return of its Lord. Written with bracing realism and deep compassion, yet also with verve and humor, this work once again confirms Rutledge's status as one of the leading preachers of our times."

—Paul T. Nimmo
King's Chair of Systematic Theology, University of Aberdeen

"What a treasure chest Fleming Rutledge has provided for us! In this volume, the apocalyptic turn in contemporary theology takes on liturgical and homiletical flesh: Christ is the One who came, who comes, and who will come again, each time breaking into the strong man's house to bind him and plunder his goods. The Advent preaching here on display communicates this incision, that we watch and wait and hope as Israel in the Lord."

—Paul R. Hinlicky
Tise Professor of Lutheran Studies, Roanoke College; Docent, Evanjelicka Bohoslovecka Fakulta, Univerzita Komenskeho, Bratislava, Slovakia

"This is a fascinating book. Rutledge's characteristic elegance and erudition are apparent throughout. But these graceful skills serve a deeper agenda, which is an interdiction into the rising sentimentality of Christianity through the beachhead in the church calendar which is the season of Advent. . . . To experience Rutledge's deep grasp and subtle, repeated evocation of Advent realities is not just to experience again the importance and wonder of preaching done well; it is not just to realize a searching depth in this liturgical time: it is to be strengthened, encouraged, and, in a word, reshaped."

—Douglas Campbell
Professor of New Testament, Duke Divinity School

"Advent is the most complex of the church's seasons, with its remembrance of God's former mercies and its looking forward in trust in God's promises. Fleming Rutledge's wonderful sermons on Advent are more than individual gems (though they are that): collectively they provide a rich and full exploration of the season in all its manifold moods and themes. This book is the perfect companion to the beginning of any church year."

—Alan Jacobs
Distinguished Professor of Humanities in the Honors Program, Baylor University

"This beautifully written book provides a wonderful example of how theological, exegetical, pastoral, and devotional wisdom are united in service of the church's witness as a pilgrim people who walk by faith, trusting in the sure and certain promises of God."

—Michael Pasquarello III
Lloyd J. Ogilvie Professor of Preaching, Fuller Theological Seminary

"My fellow Anglo-Catholics will prize this book, elegantly written with intelligence and clarity, for its rich resources in history, theology, and, yes, liturgy."

—Andrew C. Mead
Rector Emeritus, Saint Thomas Church Fifth Avenue, New York City

"Fleming Rutledge is a faithful guide in bringing the scriptural and theological motifs of Advent together with many of the customs and practices we associate with the season. The balance she brings to Advent—not simply a preparation for the Christmas feast but also the church's proclamation of the Second Advent of our Redeemer—is a particular strength of this book."

—J. Neil Alexander
Dean and Professor of Liturgy, School of Theology,
University of the South, Sewanee

"Whatever you previously thought or said about Advent (and 'pre-Advent'), this book will both challenge and deepen your understanding in ways never anticipated. For Fleming Rutledge, Advent is not merely preparation for Christmas, much less 'the most wonderful time of the year.' It is, rather, the season of difficult yet hopeful watching, waiting, and participating—the season that encapsulates the Christian life between Christ's first and second comings. Like Scripture itself, these are words to read and inwardly digest."

—Michael J. Gorman
Raymond E. Brown Chair in Biblical Studies and Theology,
St. Mary's Seminary & University, Baltimore

ADVENT

The Once and Future Coming
of Jesus Christ

Fleming Rutledge

WILLIAM B. EERDMANS PUBLISHING COMPANY
GRAND RAPIDS, MICHIGAN

Wm. B. Eerdmans Publishing Co.
4035 Park East Court SE, Grand Rapids, Michigan 49546
www.eerdmans.com

27 26 25 24 23 22 21 20 19 18   1 2 3 4 5 6 7 8 9 10

ISBN 978-0-8028-7619-5

Library of Congress Cataloging-in-Publication Data

Names: Rutledge, Fleming, author.
Title: Advent : the once and future coming of Jesus Christ /
    Fleming Rutledge.
Description: Grand Rapids : Eerdmans Publishing Co., 2018. |
    Includes bibliographical references and index.
Identifiers: LCCN 2018018269 | ISBN 9780802876195 (pbk. : alk. paper)
Subjects: LCSH: Advent.
Classification: LCC BV40 .R88 2018 | DDC 263/.912—dc23
    LC record available at https://lccn.loc.gov/2018018269

Dedicated to the saints of the congregation
of Grace Church in New York City
1981–1995

and in loving memory of parishioner Walter Parker
who well understood and well lived the Advent message
at the frontier of the ages

The watercolor-and-ink drawing by William Blake called *The Parable of the Wise and Foolish Virgins* is at the Metropolitan Museum in New York. It illustrates the story told by Jesus in Matthew 25:1–13. The parable, with its arresting depiction of a wedding party at night, is particularly suited for the season of Advent, especially when Advent is understood as the seven weeks between All Saints' and Christmas Eve. The passage from Matthew is appointed as the Gospel reading during this period in Lectionary Year A. Notable Advent hymns are based on the imagery of the bridegroom appearing at midnight ("Rejoice, rejoice, believers, and let your lights appear!," "Sleepers, wake!").

Blake's originality is on display here. The impending arrival of the marriage procession is heralded by an angel sounding a trumpet overhead. That detail is not in the biblical text, but by adding it, Blake focuses attention on the central imagery of the parable—the final day of judgment and the second coming of Christ the Bridegroom. The theme of preparation is powerfully illustrated by the contrast between the despairing agitation of the maidens on the right and the stately calm of the five on the left, whose lamps glow as one. The wise maidens exhibit varying individual facial expressions of awe, wonder, shock, and resolve as they collect themselves for what is about to happen, but the columnar relationship of their bodies displays their communal commitment. The central figure directs the improvident five on the right to go to a shop and buy more oil for their burnt-out lamps, but it is too late. Those who have kept their lamps in readiness will be recognized by the Bridegroom and swept up into the joy and movement of his lighted procession as the dawning City of God appears on the horizon.

The sermon in this collection, "What's in Those Lamps?," is based on this parable.

What other time or season can or will the Church ever have but that of Advent?

—Karl Barth, *Church Dogmatics*

Early Christian writing has the ends of the world upon it, hence its emphasis on fulfillment, fullness of time: the shape of the world-plot can now be seen.

—Frank Kermode, *The Literary Guide to the Bible*

Our lives are eschatologically stretched between the sneak preview of the new world being born among us in the church, and the old world where the principalities and powers are reluctant to give way. In the meantime, which is the only time the church has ever known, we live as those who know something about the fate of the world that the world does not yet know. And that makes us different.

—Will Willimon, *Conversion in the Wesleyan Tradition*

Is Advent a preparatory fast in preparation for the liturgical commemoration of the historical birth of Jesus in Bethlehem, *or* is Advent a season unto itself, a sacrament of the end of time begun in the incarnation and still waiting on its final consummation at the close of the present age? Is the content of Advent's proclamation centered in eschatological dread, judgment, and condemnation *or* eschatological hope, expectation, and promise? Is Advent really the beginning of the annual cycle *or* does Advent bring the year to a conclusion? The fact is that each of these "either/ors" are really "both/ands." And it is precisely because we cannot eliminate one or the other but must hold them in tension that we have inherited "a season under stress" [Richard Hoefler] . . . shaped by darkness *and* light, dread *and* hope, judgment *and* grace, second *and* first comings, terror *and* promise, end *and* beginning.

—J. Neil Alexander, "A Sacred Time in Tension," in *Liturgy*, vol. 13, no. 3

There is a birth from God before the ages, and a birth from a virgin at the fulness of time. There is a hidden coming, like that of rain on fleece, and a coming before all eyes, still in the future.

—Cyril of Jerusalem, Catechetical Lecture 15.1

Darkness—night—these are always symbols for the God-forsakenness of the world . . . and for the lostness of men and women. In the darkness we see nothing, and no longer know where we are. There is an apt passage in the book of Isaiah: "Watchman, what of the night?" . . . The watchman answers: "The morning comes, but it is still night. . . ."

But Paul, Christ's witness, proclaims, "The night is far gone, the day is at hand. Let us then cast off the works of darkness and put on the armor of light." So it is time to get up from sleep, to forget the dreams and the night terrors, and to experience life in the light of God's new day, which is now dawning. . . .

"Get up," says Christ to the benumbed disciples, "let us be going." So let us also go with eager attentiveness to each new day. We are expected.

—Jürgen Moltmann, *In the End—the Beginning*

Almighty God, give us grace that we may cast away the works of darkness, and put upon us the armor of light, now in the time of this mortal life in which thy Son Jesus Christ came to visit us in great humility; that in the last day, when he shall come again in his glorious majesty to judge both the living and the dead, we may rise to the life immortal; through him who liveth and reigneth with thee and the Holy Spirit, one God, now and for ever. *Amen.*

—The Collect for Advent I, Book of Common Prayer

Contents

The Universal Grip of the Enemy (Pre-Advent)

Justice and the Final Judgment (Pre-Advent)

God's Apocalyptic War (The Feast of Saint Michael)

The Coming of the Lord (Last Sunday of the Church Year: The Feast of Christ the King)

Advent Begins in the Dark (Advent I)

The Armor of Light (Advent II)

Bearing Witness on the Brink (Advent III)

King of the Last Things (Advent IV)

A SERVICE OF LESSONS AND CAROLS FOR ADVENT

Acknowledgments

This book was put together in summer 2017 under the pressure of a deadline, because there was no time to waste in getting it ready for publication in time for Advent 2018. Without my freelance literary editor Adam Joyce, working with me in the Berkshires online from Chicago, it simply would not have been possible. This is the second time I have worked with Adam against a deadline, and I cannot say enough good things about his contributions. His palpable support, endless good humor, and rare talent for arranging, paring away, and enhancing was indispensable. I give thanks to God for him and his gifts.

Many other people have helped me over the years, far more than I can list here. I would particularly like to thank James F. Kay, academic dean of Princeton Theological Seminary, who for over forty years has been my companion in a deep affinity for the Advent season. Professor Karl Froelich, who has been called "the man who knows everything," filled in some blanks for me concerning the four last things, and I am grateful for his generous help. During my residence at the Center of Theological Inquiry, David Tracy once said of me, "She should be called St. Fleming of Advent." He won't remember that, but it significantly boosted my enthusiasm for this project.

Paul Rorem of Princeton put me in touch with Mary Anne Haemig of Luther Seminary, whose work on Advent in Lutheranism was very useful. I very much appreciate the open-hearted support of Neil Alexander, dean of the School of Theology, Sewanee, who responded to my requests with rare immediacy; his Advent scholarship has been particularly helpful. The work of putting the eschatological nature of Advent into liturgical practice has been significantly enhanced by William H. Petersen's Advent Project.

Among supporters and encouragers, my friend Joe Mangina of Wycliffe in Toronto has been for many years—since he and his family were my next-door neighbors at the Center of Theological Inquiry—indefatigable in his ever-present help, always accompanied by his extensive knowledge and alert imagination. His emails to me over the years should definitely go into the archives; I'm keeping most of them.

Over the past twenty-three years since my first book, the good people at Eerdmans Publishing have become friends. I had the pleasure of meeting some of them in person for the first time last year at the AAR-SBL convention in Boston. Others I know only through email, but all of them have been not only professional and knowledgeable, but also kind and supportive. James Ernest has stepped into the demanding leadership position of editor-in-chief with singular grace and skill; he has been tremendously encouraging, as has David Bratt. Linda Bieze and Laura Bardolph Hubers have fine minds and a feel for literature. Amy Kent continues to be the indispensable person; as far as I can tell, she holds all the reins at once and never drops any of them. Once again, I've been most grateful to Tom Raabe; he was peerless in helping me through the last stages of my previous book *The Crucifixion*, and, with Linda, brought this new manuscript into shape.

At the very last stage, I called in my proofreader *extraordinaire*, my sister Betsy McColl. Long ago she was a grader at the Harvard Business School, and I imagine that some of those students had never before met anyone with her skills. She'll ask me to remove that, but I'm not going to. I want to say publicly that her keen eye, her knowledge of all the fine points, and her sheer stamina for the painstaking task have made this a much better book—not only because of the mistakes she caught, but also for her suggestions for stylistic improvement. In this as in so much else, I am endlessly grateful to her and for her.

Margaret Lee, of Grace Church in New York, typed most of the sermons from the original pulpit copies—an essential but laborious task. She is not only a willing helper but a family friend, and a member of Grace Church in New York for many years. A significant proportion of the sermons collected here were preached at Grace Church to a remarkably expectant congregation. In addition, for thirteen years I edited and wrote editorials for the Grace Church bulletin, which was beautifully set in "hot" type by a printer of the old school in Brooklyn. The weekly copies went out from the US Post Office not only to members in New York, but also to a small but devoted band of readers all over the country. During these years I honed my presentations about Advent. There were large numbers of these editorials; only a small number of them are included here. It would be hard to overestimate the depth and strength of the congregation at Tenth and Broadway during those years; much of what is in these pages would not have been possible without the enthusiastic support of so many of those beloved fellow pilgrims. To those saints of the church militant and the church expectant, this volume is dedicated.

Introduction

This volume of Advent sermons, writings, and other resources contains bold claims that may be new to some readers. Since the Advent season has been so closely linked to Christmas over the years, it may be startling to hear that Advent is not simply a transitional season but in and of itself communicates a message of immense, even ultimate, importance. Of all the seasons of the church year, Advent most closely mirrors the daily lives of Christians and of the church, asks the most important ethical questions, presents the most accurate picture of the human condition, and above all, orients us to the future of the God who will come again. The material collected in this book is intended as witness to those claims.

The Advent season has always had a particular resonance for Episcopalians. We can be a bit snooty about it; our tradition of withholding the poinsettias, the crèche scenes, and the Christmas carols until Christmas Eve itself has been a point of pride for many of us. Ever since I was a very young child, this way of observing Christmas by delayed gratification has meant much to me, and I find it disappointing when "Christmas creep" intrudes upon Advent Sundays. As I have grown older, my love of Advent has deepened and broadened into a strong commitment to its particular theological and liturgical character. I have long wished to share my lifetime love of the season with Christian believers in other traditions, with the hope that I might contribute to a wider interest in the profound themes and emphases particular to Advent.

The season has long been important to Episcopalians, and to some extent to Lutherans and Moravians, but after the Reformation the churches in the Reformed tradition and most other Protestant denominations abandoned the church calendar altogether, except for Christmas and Easter; nor does the Roman Catholic Church pay as much attention to Advent nowadays as one might expect, given its ancient roots.[1] Most of the numerous churches with no particular denominational allegiance broadly identified in America as "evangelical" have had little or no experience with Advent and its special character, and the same is true of the Pentecostal churches.

A few decades ago, however, a greater interest in the liturgical seasons began to develop among Methodists, Presbyterians, and others. This has enriched us all. There is a caution, however, lest enthusiastic new supporters of the calendar without deep roots in it will appropriate it without sufficient understanding, and this is true of Advent in particular; I have seen some curious examples in my visits to the Christian education wings of various churches where the pictures and fliers on the bulletin boards suggest that the season is another opportunity for playtime: "Advent is a red balloon!"[2]

The recent emergence of Advent wreaths and Advent calendars throughout churches of all denominations has had its own effect. I love them both; I give calendars to all the children in my life every year, and I brought up my own children with an Advent wreath. It must be said, however, that neither of these charming customs—which do not date back very far in church history—adds a great deal to our understanding of the season. There is a great deal of misinformation in circulation about the wreath custom. It is remarkable how frequently "ancient" (and even "pagan"!) origins are cited, without evidence, in support of such recent innovations.[3] A curiosity of our time is that we want to be progressive, forward-looking, unencumbered, even "emergent" in our liturgical observances, and yet we persist in harking back to "early" customs even when they are demonstrably not early at all. In fact, the Advent wreath originated in the middle of the nineteenth century as a custom in small Protestant communities in northern Germany.[4] It was unknown in the Episcopal

1. The liturgical observance of Advent in the Eastern Orthodox churches is not without its own importance, but lies beyond the scope of this project.

2. "Christmas creep" is beginning to infect even the Episcopal Church. William H. Petersen, the director of the Advent Project, reports being in an Episcopal parish for services on the *First* Sunday of Advent when the choir anthem was "Mary Had a Baby." *The Living Church*, October 21, 2012.

3. Other notable examples found in the churches of today would be the widespread contemporary use of a "labyrinth" and the current enthusiasm for all things "Celtic." The claims that have been made for these fashionable practices often do not stand up to serious historical investigation, and they tend to have a marked syncretistic or pantheistic character more in sync with the enthusiasms of the day than with biblical faith.

4. A Lutheran historian, Mary Jane Haemig, has written a brisk takedown of the relatively recent, romanticized mythology of the supposedly "ancient" custom of the Advent wreath: "The Origin and Spread of the Advent Wreath," *Lutheran Quarterly* 19 (2005): 332.

Church of my childhood, but it had become ubiquitous by 1970.[5] When the Advent wreath is used to distinguish Advent from Christmas, that is useful; but when it is taught and understood almost entirely as a way of preparing for Christmas, it loses any relationship to the eschatological, future-oriented nature of Advent that is the principal emphasis of this book.

Advent as the Season of the Second Coming

The origins and development of the Advent season are less well understood than we might wish.[6] There were varying emphases and customs in differing parts of Christendom in the fourth and fifth centuries, leaving us with a mixed picture that continues today. It has been tempting for local churches in recent times to seize upon notions of Advent observance in the early centuries to support the idea that it has always been essentially a season of preparation for Christmas. However, there is evidence to show that as late as the fourth century, a December season of penitence and fasting had no clear relationship to Christmas, at least not in Rome.[7] By the seventh century, however, the Advent-Christmas connection was well established, and Advent has been observed as a penitential season, not unlike Lent, in preparation for Christmas up until the very recent past. Older Episcopalians who grew up in the '40s and '50s will still remember Advent as a "purple" season like Lent—although it must be said that the supposed "penitential" aspect left very little mark in actual practice!

For this volume, we can state that by the medieval period the essentially eschatological nature of the Advent season was fully established. Martin Luther, in particular, was remarkably attuned to the apocalyptic Advent language.[8] In the time of the Reformation, there was a marked departure from the

5. Advent wreaths are now habitually sold in nurseries and florist shops to Roman Catholic customers (and, increasingly, others as well), with a "pink" candle, even though few realize that it should be "rose" to denote *Gaudete* (rejoice!) Sunday, an observance of relief from fasting that no longer makes sense since the Roman Church has largely abandoned the penitential character of the season.

6. For those who wish to pursue this interesting but complex subject, the first chapter of J. Neil Alexander, *Waiting for the Coming: The Liturgical Meaning of Advent, Christmas, Epiphany* (Portland: Oregon Catholic Press, 1993), is an excellent introduction.

7. A series of sermons during the December fast in fourth-century Rome by Leo the Great do not mention Christmas at all.

8. One need look no further than the words of his hymn "Ein' feste Burg" ("A mighty fortress") to see this. "And though this world with devils filled / should threaten to undo

3

customary Advent preaching in the Roman Church. As one might expect, this was particularly noticeable among Lutherans, who, unlike the Reformed, continued to observe the church calendar but with a dramatically different focus. Whereas Roman Catholic preachers continued to exhort those attending Mass to double up on their penitential practices during Advent, Lutheran preachers focused on proclamation of the undeserved grace of God—evangelistic sermons rather than hortatory ones.[9] Martin Luther himself, in his typically earthy and worldly-wise way, poked fun at the Roman focus on preparation, saying Jesus might very well return while people were "drinking fine wines . . . and not praying a word."[10] Paul the apostle might well approve of such an observation, for in his letter to the Galatians he exclaims, "Let me ask you only this: Did you receive the Spirit by works of the law, or by hearing with faith? Are you so foolish? . . . I am afraid I have labored over you in vain!" (3:2–3; 4:11).

Luther is still known for his grasp of the Advent scenario. However, his Pauline passion has faded among his heirs. The eschatological note of Advent, focusing on the second coming of Christ—the principal subject of this book—has been largely ignored even among the most enthusiastic Advent-lovers of late. However, with the transition to a new standard lectionary in the 1970s, now used in many denominations, the clear focus on the coming consummation of the kingdom of God in the day of the Lord has been recovered. Recovered, that is, among liturgists, trained musicians, and church historians—in actual practice, this recovery has occurred precisely at the time when the cultural Christmas craze has so overwhelmed the church's ancient understanding of Advent, that nothing short of a full-court press could bring it back into the worship of the church. The dissonance between the culture and the church's mission in the Advent season has been widely noted, but not until recently has heightened Advent observance been called upon as a countermeasure.

---

us, / we will not fear, for God has willed / his truth to triumph through us. / The Prince of Darkness grim, / we tremble not for him; / his rage we can endure, / for lo! His doom is sure: / One little Word shall fell him."

9. Mary Jane Haemig, "Sixteenth-Century Preachers on Advent as a Season of Proclamation or Preparation," *Lutheran Quarterly* 16 (2002): 125–52. "Implicitly or explicitly, Roman Catholic preachers emphasize what the season demands from their listeners rather than what the advent of Christ gives to them" (141). Put another way, they focused almost exclusively on human preparation, whereas most Lutherans followed Luther in proclaiming the justifying grace of God in coming to an *unprepared* world. I will not deny that the contents of this book favor the sixteenth-century Lutherans.

10. Quoted by Haemig, "Sixteenth-Century Preachers," 126.

William H. Petersen, the founder of the Advent Project, has written, "While there is scant hope of changing the culture around us, the Church need not be a fellow traveler. The call is for the Church to reclaim for the sake of its own life and mission Advent's focus on the reign of God and, in so doing, to hone once again the counter-cultural edge of the Gospel at the very beginning of the liturgical year."[11]

And so, to understand the truly radical nature of Advent, it is necessary to get its relation to Christmas in perspective. In the medieval period, the Scripture readings for Advent were well established, and they were oriented only secondarily to the birth (first coming) of Christ; the primary emphasis was his second coming on the final day of the Lord. Because the church in modern times has turned away from the proclamation of the second coming, an intentional effort must be made to reinstate it. Related to the second coming, which Jesus repeatedly says will come by God's decision at an hour we do not expect, is the Advent emphasis on the agency of God, as contrasted with the "works" of human beings. An exclusive emphasis on Advent as a season of preparation risks putting human endeavor in the spotlight for all four weeks of the season. All the Advent preparation in the world would not be enough unless God were favorably disposed to us in the first place. This will be a principal theme in many of the sermons collected here, which emphasize the theme of *watching* and *waiting*.

It would generally be agreed that Advent celebrates three "advents." This version, from early Lutheran preaching, will serve as well as any:

Adventus redemptionis: the incarnate Christ "born of the Virgin Mary, crucified under Pontius Pilate"
Adventus sanctificationis: the presence of Christ in Word and sacrament
Adventus glorificamus: the coming in glory to be our judge on the last day[12]

All of this is part of the Advent message. However, what has been largely lost to us since the eighteenth-century Enlightenment is the *primary* focus on the second coming of Christ, who will arrive in glory on the last day to consummate the kingdom of God. That is the special note of Advent—its orientation toward the promised future. The other seasons in the church calendar

---

11. *The Living Church*, October 21, 2012. The Advent Project online is highly recommended: http://www.theadventproject.org/.

12. Haemig, "Sixteenth-Century Preachers," 135. To fit my own project, I have omitted one "advent" without, I think, doing harm to the concept of three.

follow the events in the *historical* life of Christ—his incarnation (Christmas), the manifestation to the gentiles (Epiphany), his ministry and preaching (the season after Epiphany), his path to crucifixion (Lent), his passion and death (Holy Week), the resurrection (Easter), the return to the Father's right hand (Ascension), and the descent of the Holy Spirit (Pentecost)—with Trinity Sunday to round it off doctrinally.[13] Advent, however, differs from the other seasons in that it looks *beyond history* altogether and awaits Jesus Christ's coming again "in glory to judge the living and the dead."[14] In the cycle of seasons and festival days that takes the church through the life of Christ, it is Advent that gives us the final consummation; it is the season of the last things.

The traditional Scripture readings for the Advent season have preserved this emphasis, but most clergy in the pulpits of the mainline denominations have employed many stratagems to avoid expounding them in their full provocation. The revised Book of Common Prayer presently used in the Episcopal Church contains the eucharistic acclamation "Christ will come again," but this has not led to a noticeable increase in the preaching or teaching of this article of faith. During much of the twentieth century, the second coming of Christ was considered in the mainline churches to be an obsolete if not downright embarrassing topic for preaching, and the subject of the divine judgment that was so familiar to medieval and Reformation-era congregations fell into disfavor with the ascendancy of liberal theology. However, with the increasing interest in apocalyptic theology in the twenty-first century, the subject has increasingly been reopened and its central position in the New Testament reaffirmed by surprisingly sophisticated thinkers, if not by the rank and file of churchgoers.

Even more important, though, is the potential growth of appreciation for the special significance of the Advent season as a symbol of the church's life *in the present*. Here is another way of charting the trajectory of Advent, arguably the richest of the seasons because it celebrates three dimensions at once, embracing themes from the other highlights of the liturgical calendar. Note the order of the three, with the present last:

13. The churches of the Reformation are divided on the observance of the liturgical year. The Lutherans continued it, whereas the Reformed churches largely abandoned it. This pattern continues to this day; however, many Presbyterians, Methodists, and others have begun to return to the seasonal calendar, which affords a fresh opportunity to teach about the themes of Advent. One reason that Lutherans continued the tradition after the Reformation was that of catechesis; they believed that the progression of the church seasons made teaching the faith easier and more memorable, a factor that was certainly very important to me growing up (see Haemig, "Sixteenth-Century Preachers," 131).

14. The Nicene Creed.

1. The past: God's *initiative* toward the world in Christ (Christmas)
2. The future: God's *coming victory* in Christ (second coming, or parousia, made present by the power of the Spirit at Pentecost)
3. The present: a *cruciform* (*cross-shaped*) life of love for the world in the present time (Epiphany, Lent, and Holy Week)

Karl Barth exclaimed, "What other time or season can or will the Church ever have but that of Advent!"[15] This illuminates the *present* dimension of the season. It locates us correctly with relation to the first and second comings of Christ. Advent calls for a life lived on the edge, so to speak, all the time, shaped by the cross not only on Good Friday but wherever and whenever we are, proclaiming his death to be the turn of the ages "until he comes" (I Cor. 11:26). The gospel is incarnate in our lives in "this present evil age" (Gal. 1:4), not in a faraway empyrean but in "the sufferings of this present time," which are endured (*hupomone*) because of the promise that they "are not worthy to be compared with the glory which shall be revealed in us" (Rom. 8:18).

This more rigorous understanding of the church's location can be embraced without reserve today in the Northern Hemisphere as the church becomes less comfortable, less "established," and more marginalized in a society full of "nones." In that respect, as is increasingly being recognized, the life of the Christian community will come to resemble that of the early church rather than the boom years of the last midcentury.

In a very real sense, the Christian community lives in Advent all the time. It can well be called the Time Between, because the people of God live in *the time between* the first coming of Christ, incognito in the stable in Bethlehem, and his second coming, in glory, to judge the living and the dead. In the Time Between, "our lives are hidden with Christ in God; when Christ who is our life appears, then we also will appear with him in glory" (Col. 3:3-4). Advent contains within itself the crucial balance of the now and the not-yet that our faith requires. Many of the sermons in this book will explore this theme in relation to the yearly frenzy of "holiday" time in which the commercial Christmas music insists that "it's the most wonderful time of the year" and Starbucks invites everyone to "feel the merry." The disappointment, brokenness, suffering, and pain that characterize life in this present world is held in dynamic tension with the promise of future glory that is yet to come. In that Advent tension, the church lives its life.

---

15. Karl Barth, *Church Dogmatics* IV/3.1 (Edinburgh: T. & T. Clark, 1961), 322.

W. H. Auden's work is prominent in many of these sermons. His long poem *For the Time Being: A Christmas Oratorio* has been beloved by Christians throughout the English-speaking world since the 1950s. Written in the dark early days of World War II, it has not been cherished by secular readers as much as his undeniably Olympian prewar poetry, but for many discerning Christians it would rank among the great poetical works of the twentieth century. It embraces liturgical time from Advent to the Epiphany, but one can argue that it is actually an *Advent* oratorio because it not only begins with an extended Advent section but also ends with the return to "the time being."[16] The title, *For the Time Being*, is profoundly suitable for the Advent season, as is the phrase I will be using, "the time between." The Lord has come, the Lord will come. The subtitle of this present volume is *The Once and Future Coming of Jesus Christ*, the intent being to capture the dual nature of Advent's location in human and universal history. Auden is a supreme poet of the Advent atmosphere in his more secular work as well. In his celebrated poem written at the outset of World War II, "September 1, 1939," he captures the universal human tendency to cover up our unease and estrangement with sentimentality and denial. The poet knows better:

> Faces along the bar
> Cling to their average day:
> The lights must never go out,
> The music must always play.
> All the conventions conspire
> To make this fort assume
> The furniture of home;
> Lest we should see where we are,
> Lost in a haunted wood,
> Children afraid of the night
> Who have never been happy or good.[17]

16. The long poem was originally intended to be the libretto for a musical composition analogous to the oratorios of G. F. Handel. Auden intended the composer to be Benjamin Britten, but that never came to pass. Several composers have tried their hand, but none of their efforts have stuck. Carl Bricken, resident professor of music at my college, Sweet Briar in Virginia, set the whole thing to music, and it was spectacularly produced and performed at the college in 1958, but unfortunately was thereafter lost to posterity as far as I have been able to find out. Bricken's biography in the *Dictionary of American Classical Composers* does not mention it.

17. W. H. Auden, "September 1, 1939," in *The Collected Poetry of W. H. Auden* (New York: Random House, 1945), 57.

Auden identifies our defenses as a "fort" that we have made as comfortable as possible in order to fend off our fears. The Advent season encourages us to resist denial and face our situation as it really is.

Looking into the "Heart of Darkness"

It might be said of Advent that it is not for the faint of heart. To grasp the depth of the human predicament, one has to be willing to enter into the very worst. This is not the same thing as going to horror films, which are essentially entertainment. Entering into the very worst means giving serious consideration to the most hopeless situations: for instance, a facility for the most profound cases of developmental disability. What hope is there for a ward full of people who will never sit up, walk, speak, or feed themselves? Tourists go to the site of Auschwitz-Birkenau and take pictures, but who can really imagine the smells and sounds of the most depraved of all situations? The tourist can turn away in relief and go to lunch.

Some of the greatest novelists have attempted to portray the very worst. It was Joseph Conrad who gave us the phrase and the novella *Heart of Darkness*—which in turn gave T. S. Eliot the epigraph for his profoundly pessimistic, even hellish preconversion poem "The Hollow Men."[18] The esteemed writer Cormac McCarthy has always written about the darker side of life in gorgeous biblical language, but his masterpiece *Blood Meridian* is the one that presents the greatest challenge for the reader.[19] It is a very long novel, mesmerizing in its power, containing not a single hint of redemption. A narrative about a gang of bounty hunters in the Southwest, based on an actual historical gang, it is pure madness and evil from beginning to end. Eliot's lines in "Hollow Men" well describe the landscape in *Blood Meridian*:

18. T. S. Eliot, "The Hollow Men," in *The Complete Poems and Plays* (New York: Harcourt, Brace, and Co., 1952), 55–59. The epigraph is "Mistah Kurtz—he dead." It is the ignominious epitaph for the central figure who represents humanity in the grip of demonic impulses. (I have considered, but do not agree with the postcolonial objection to Conrad's representation of Africa as the heart of darkness. It is a universal parable about the grip of Sin and Death.)

19. The word "apocalypse" used in this way (as in *Apocalypse Now*) does not mean the same thing as "apocalyptic" when used to denote a type of literature or a theological position. The Greek word *apokalypsis*, meaning "revelation," refers to the utterly new thing that comes into being with the future advent of God and the new creation. "Apocalypse," taken from the same biblical root, refers to a much simpler multipurpose notion, that of a cataclysmic event that threatens our understanding or control of the world.

This is the dead land
This is cactus land

There is a satanic figure in *Blood Meridian* called "the Judge" who presides over everything, and every road leads to violence of the most extreme sort followed by death. There is not a single sign of hope at the end; indeed, there is a resolute refusal to offer any.[20]

The most overtly theological of McCarthy's books is one of his lesser novels, *No Country for Old Men*. Sheriff Bell is fighting a losing war with drug dealers on the Mexican border and is wondering if there's a God at all—the Advent question. The overall question articulated by Sheriff Bell seems to be, is the world overrun forever by demons (incarnated in the man he is hunting)? Is there a demonic new type of man, typified by the drug dealers? Is there a new generation coming who is the grandchild of the grandparents but who is unrecognizable, with green hair and nose bones, who was raised by grandparents who in turn have no grandparents and whose grandchildren may want to euthanize them?

He stops in a restaurant for lunch (McCarthy typically omits punctuation, and uses misspellings to convey the sheriff's accent and affect):

> When the waitress came with more coffee he [Sheriff Bell] asked her what time they got the evening paper.
>
> I dont know, she said. I quit readin it.
>
> I dont blame you. I would if I could. . . .
>
> I dont know why they call it a newspaper. I dont call that stuff news.
>
> No.
>
> When was the time you read somethin about Jesus Christ in the newspaper?
>
> Bell shook his head. I don't know, he said. I guess I'd have to say it would be a while.
>
> I guess it would too, she said. A long while.[21]

Then the sheriff, musing, wonders about an old man that he knows: "You'd think a man that had waited eighty some odd years on God to come into his

---

20. Movies have been made of McCarthy novels, and there has been much talk online of a movie of *Blood Meridian*, but one doubts if it will ever come to pass. A movie without even a tiny hint of redemption would be a tough sell, and if such a hint were inserted, it would be a complete rejection of the novel's essential force.

21. Cormac McCarthy, *No Country for Old Men* (New York: Vintage, 2005), 246–47.

life, well, you'd think he'd come. If he didn't you'd still have to figure that he knew what he was doin. I dont know what other description of God you could have."[22] This remarkable utterance gives us the Advent picture straight up. Even if God does not seem to be coming, he would not be God if he himself did not prepare the time and the manner of his own coming. And, being God, he knows what he is doing.

Most of McCarthy's novels are soaked in biblical themes and deal with ultimate questions—Advent questions. Since *Blood Meridian* depicts a world entirely given over to a "Judge" who is in every way the satanic opposite of Jesus Christ, the Judge who is to come in the last day, this book tells us the true story of who we are under the reign of Sin and Death. This, indeed, left to itself, would be the world under the curse of God. And so, for those who can stomach it, *Blood Meridian* takes us into the Advent darkness where there is no human hope whatsoever and the only possibility is the impossibility of the intervention of God. That is the apocalyptic invasion of the world announced by John the Baptist—precisely because "nothing can save us that is possible."[23]

Location as the Central Criterion of the Advent Life

"Location, location, location" is the time-honored slogan of the real estate business. The idea of *location* is central to this collection of Advent resources. The sermon entitled "On Location with John the Baptist" is therefore perhaps the best introduction to the collection, even though it is not placed at the beginning. John, the central figure of Advent, is the herald of the turn of the ages. He arrives announcing the opening event of the end-time. He is the herald of the age to come, as prophesied by Malachi at the very end of the Old Testament. It is the coming of the Lord that will lift the "curse" from the world. This placement of John at the heart of the season is the key to Advent's theological, liturgical, eschatological, and above all ethical meaning. To use a phrase from the great collect for the first Sunday of Advent, it is *"now in the time of this mortal life"* that we are seized by the announcement that the kingdom of God is at hand.[24] Thus, in our present

---

22. McCarthy, *No Country for Old Men*, 283.

23. From the Advent section of Auden's *For the Time Being*.

24. For hundreds of years, Anglicans (Episcopalians) heard this resonant collect, closely based on Rom. 13:11–14, every Sunday in Advent, so that it became very familiar to us. It is a loss to the church that the revisers in their wisdom have reduced its use to the first Sunday only.

lives we are both *bearing witness to* and *waiting expectantly for* the coming of the Lord. Bearing witness is an active stance; waiting is a passive stance. *Both* are part of the message of the herald of the age to come. In a notable verse from II Peter, the Time Between is characterized by "waiting and hastening the coming of the Day of God" (II Pet. 3:12).

Indeed, this passage from the little-read and somewhat difficult second letter of Peter is suffused with Advent atmosphere: "Since all these things are thus to be dissolved, what sort of persons ought you to be in lives of holiness and godliness, waiting for and hastening the coming of the day of God, because of which the heavens will be kindled and dissolved, and the elements will melt with fire! But according to his promise we wait for new heavens and a new earth in which righteousness dwells" (3:11-13).

The passage *locates* the Christian community precisely in "the time between" the old age[25] and the age to come. The appearance of the Messiah in the world has already fulfilled the promises of God in the prophetic and apocalyptic literature of the Old Testament. New Testament writings such as the Fourth Gospel and Ephesians emphasize the "already" aspect of the gospel ("the hour cometh, and now is"—John 4:23 KJV). But at the same time, it is "not yet." It is both "once" and "future."

It is challenging to hold two ideas in mind simultaneously: once and future, now and not-yet, but this is the summons of the gospel. We are citizens of two worlds, or ages: "this present evil age" and the age to come, the commonwealth of heaven (Phil. 3:20). Our true home is in the future, but it is made present reality to us by the Holy Spirit, the guarantee of our redemption (Eph. 1:14 NRSV).

This makes all the difference in the way the Christian community conducts itself in this present age. We live not according to the reign of Satan, but as those who know that "the ruler of this *kosmos*" is already doomed—in spite of all appearances to the contrary. The church is not called to be a "change agent"—God is the agent of change. The Lord of the *kosmos* has al-

---

25. Paul calls it "this present evil age" in Gal. 1:4. The newer translations are a definite advance on the King James Version in this instance. "This present evil *age*" (*aionos*, "aeon") is far more faithful to Paul's worldview than "this present evil *world*." It is important to hold on to this idea of two ages throughout the New Testament. For instance, when we encounter the "world" in the Fourth Gospel, we find that when Jesus speaks of the "world" (*kosmos*), he does not mean planet Earth. John's Gospel is not unlike Paul's letters in this respect. It is not a "world" that is meant, but rather a *régime*, so that Jesus can call Satan "the ruler of this world (*archon tou kosmou*)" and declare his coming downfall as the purpose of his own coming (John 12:31; 14:30; 16:11).

ready wrought the Great Exchange in his cross and resurrection, and the life of the people of God is sustained by that mighty enterprise.[26] The calling of the church is to place itself where God is already at work. The church lives, therefore, without fear, in faith that the cosmic change of regime has already been accomplished. Marilynne Robinson has written that "fear is not a Christian habit of mind."[27] The sermons gathered here attempt to offer examples of fearless living, life in which radical forgiveness is offered, divine justice is no respecter of persons, and nonviolence is a weapon of God's apocalyptic warfare.

Speaking of *location*, here is a story that brings the matter into the foreground. In 2017, Yemen, the poorest country in the Arab world, was suffering from a prolonged crisis as a result of civil war. The government and all its agencies had ceased to operate. All services—medical care, sanitation, food supply, factories, airports, seaports, bridges—everything was collapsing. Parents were desperate as their children began to die of cholera, a disease that is easily treated in the developed world. A man named Muhammad Nasir waited outside a primitive cholera clinic as his son Waleed hung by a thread. Even if he recovered, his father had no money to return home. Another poor man, Saleh al-Khawlani, had fled from bombing with his wife and six children from one side of Yemen to another. He said, "The war haunts us from all directions." A third man, Yakoub al-Jayefi, a Yemeni soldier, had not been paid anything for eight months, and his six-year-old daughter was in dire condition from malnutrition. Waiting by her side in a clinic, he said, "We're just waiting for doom or for a breakthrough from heaven."[28]

This is precisely the Advent situation: doom on one hand, deliverance on the other. The fact that the Yemeni are Muslims opens up a universal dimension to the description of a world poised on the brink of "a breakthrough from heaven." When the prophet Isaiah cries out, "O that thou wouldst rend the heavens and come down!" (Isa. 64:1), it is with just such a sense of desperate knowledge that nothing short of divine intervention can arrest the ever-recurring cycle of human misery.

This understanding of the placement of the church *in between* the first and second comings can be further understood as a life lived on the frontier of the turn of the ages. This is a key to the season of Advent—the concept of two ages, which collide in the cross of Christ. Advent binds Lent and Easter

---

26. I stole that phrase "mighty enterprise" from Christopher Smart, one of the greatest of all hymn writers. See "Alleluia, alleluia! Hearts and voices heavenward raise" (#191 in the 1982 Episcopal Hymnal, second verse).

27. Marilynne Robinson, "Fear," *New York Review of Books*, September 24, 2015.

28. "'A Slow Death': The Brutal Toll of Yemen's War," *New York Times*, August 24, 2017.

together. The motif of eschatological tribulation (*thlipsis*) is inextricably linked to bearing the cross of "the Lamb who was slain" (Rev. 5:12). The book of Revelation, always read during the Easter season, is marked from one end to the other by the promise of the imminent coming of the victorious Christ, but the "call for the endurance of the saints" is addressed to Christians who find themselves placed at the collision of the two ages—the place where the Enemy is most active and most malevolent.

The Advent Cosmology

All the New Testament writers share the same presupposition about the status of the world (*kosmos* in New Testament Greek) as occupied territory.[29] It is very obvious in Mark, the Johannine literature, and the letters of Paul and Peter, less so in James, Hebrews, the Pastorals, and Acts, but it is there in all of them and is taken for granted by all of them. This scenario was lost to academic biblical scholarship and mainline pulpits after the Enlightenment, but in our time it is making a strong reappearance as a result of the genocidal twentieth century. To this day, the facts on the ground continue to present probing moral and theological thinkers with a dilemma: How do we account for the fact that evil has not been conquered by the Enlightenment?

Many people who will be reading this introduction have grown up assuming that there are two actors on the biblical stage: God and the human being. The presenting symptoms of injustice, corruption, rapacity, exploitation, oppression, "battle, murder, and sudden death" are owing to the failures of the human being to live up to his or her potential.[30] In such a picture it is easy enough to introduce the idea of free will that is so beloved by Americans. But this is not the biblical picture at all. The New Testament presents us with not two but *three* agencies: God, the human being, and an Enemy who is variously called Satan, the devil, Beelzebul, "the ruler of this world," and "the prince of the power of the air," among other biblical designations. It has been given to this Enemy to enslave humanity, and indeed all of creation, until such time as God sees fit. When Jesus appears, the time is at hand; we are those "upon whom the end of the ages has come" (I Cor. 10:11).

---

29. I am setting aside the question of whether there are other planets that have not experienced the Fall. There is no better imaginative treatment of this matter than that of C. S. Lewis in *Out of the Silent Planet* and, especially, *Perelandra*.

30. "From plague, pestilence, and famine; from battle, murder, and sudden death, Good Lord, deliver us." From the Litany in the 1928 Book of Common Prayer.

A case in point may be made by the story of the Gerasene demoniac in Mark 5:1–20. If we read this pericope without "eyes to see," we will think it is about the healing of a man who is seriously mentally ill—schizophrenic, we would probably say. Even on those terms, Jesus's intervention is a remarkable event, since such a grave disorder is not curable, and was certainly not in the days before psychotropic drugs. Mark, however, is not telling us a story of simple one-on-one healing. In Mark's very deliberate telling, the event is *an exorcism*. The sufferer is "possessed" by a demon who is independent of him. It is important to note that the demon is so powerful that it is able to break any chains that are forged by human skill. We read that the man fell on his knees before Jesus, but the demon imprisoning the man is the one who speaks directly to Jesus, overwhelming the man's response. The demon recognizes his superior; in a Gospel that famously keeps the "messianic secret," this is the first entity to identify exactly who Jesus is: "What do you want with me, Jesus Son of the Most High God?" A direct confrontation between God and Satan is being described here. The immediate, absolute sovereignty of Jesus over the demon(s)—their name is Legion—is the point of the story. After the "evil spirits" have been driven over the cliff in a herd of pigs, the man is found quietly sitting and "in his right mind." Quite understandably, the people standing round are terrified of such powers and beg Jesus to leave them. Such is the unnerving authority of the man, even though, in Mark, no human being has yet recognized him as the demons have.

This is one particularly striking illustration of the New Testament panorama of cosmic conflict. Centuries of academic biblical interpretation have unfolded without recognition of this three-part New Testament scenario, and most seminary-trained clergy, until recently, had never heard of it. Now that it has been recovered, we can no longer ignore it. No one has summed it up more succinctly than Dostoevsky in *The Brothers Karamazov*: "God and the devil are fighting there, and the battlefield is the human heart."[31] Expanding that to display the whole apocalyptic panorama, we can say that the entire *kosmos*, the world God loves (John 3:16), is the scene of the struggle between God and the devil. When Jesus says to Pilate, "My kingdom is not of this *kosmos*" (John 18:36), his meaning is clear: the sphere of power belonging to God, who created the universe out of nothing (*ex nihilo*), has invaded the

---

31. Carl Braaten has pointed out that another novelist, the French Roman Catholic Georges Bernanos, makes precisely the same point in expressly the same terms. "The Recovery of Apocalyptic Imagination," in *The Last Things*, ed. Carl Braaten and Robert Jenson (Grand Rapids: Eerdmans, 2002), 19.

sphere of the Enemy, and in the most inconceivable way possible—the willed self-offering of God the Son to human wickedness in a scene of barbaric execution.[32] Therefore, far from escaping the world, the Christian disciple finds his or her vocation precisely here: at the collision of the ages where the struggle of the Enemy against God continues, making a space for the conquering love of God for the world.

The Apocalyptic Season

The groundbreaking New Testament scholar Ernst Käsemann referred to apocalyptic as "the mother of Christian theology."[33] Of all the seasons and holy days in the church year, Advent is the one most obviously grounded in apocalyptic theology, especially since it is most attuned to the apocalyptic passages in the Bible. These writings begin to appear during and after the exile. The exilic and postexilic parts of the book of Isaiah (40–66) are not only splendid, memorable poetry, but also the most influential writings displaying the theological turn to apocalyptic.

"Behold, I will create new heavens and a new earth" (Isa. 65:17). Before the exile and the destruction of all of Israel's hopes, there was no need for this kind of promise; the work of God would proceed in the land shown to Moses from afar and given to the descendants of Abraham, with Jerusalem and its temple as the constant sign of God's presence and favor. When the temple was destroyed and the people carried off to mighty, ultra-pagan Babylon, it seemed to signal the departure of God, the breaking of the promise, and the end of hope. When, therefore, the unknown prophet of the exile began his long prophetic poem with "Comfort ye, comfort ye my people," a new note was sounded and a completely different basis for hope was proclaimed. It was no longer possible to project a future with God out of the experiences of the past. The apocalyptic outlook that arose during the time of the exile was disjunctive in character; it looked, not to Israel's past glo-

32. The tragic (in the true sense of that word) moral failings of John Howard Yoder cannot erase the lasting importance of his groundbreaking book *The Politics of Jesus* (2nd ed. [Grand Rapids: Eerdmans, 1994]). In this remarkable volume he shows how the apocalyptic orientation of the New Testament shapes the conduct of the Christian community in the world.

33. Käsemann, "Die Anfänge christlicher Theologie," *Zeitschrift für Theologie und Kirche* 57 (1960). Published in English in *Journal for Theology and Church* 6, ed. Robert W. Funk (New York, 1969), 40.

ries and expectations, but to a completely new, unexpected, and most of all *undeserved* movement of God from the future. Thus, a "breakthrough from heaven."

It is the breakthrough from heaven that is foreseen in Isaiah's cry for help. The heavens are understood not as a place far off in the empyrean, but as the domain of God's power.[34] This desperate cry is that of those who recognize that they have come to the end of human resources. They cannot feel God's presence, but they continue to cling to the thought that he is there nonetheless, and that they have no other help.

Even when God seems hidden, his power is operative whether we recognize it or not. It is "from heaven" that the Son of God comes incognito, having "emptied himself" of his eternal glory (Phil. 2:7). Jesus brought the reign of heaven to earth, but in a guise so humble and lowly that it knocked the ruling powers—both church and state, so to speak—entirely off balance, causing them to react against their own best interests.[35] The strange, virtually invisible way in which God made his appearance in the world is the guide to the Christian life: "Have this mind in you which was also in Christ Jesus . . ." (Phil. 2:5–8).

The way that Jesus interacted with the powerful is the template for Christian political action. There is nothing more urgent for the Christian community in the present time than communal study of the politics of Jesus, who stood before the Roman procurator and declared, "My kingdom is not of this *kosmos*" (John 18:36). Does that mean that the followers of Jesus are to have nothing to do with the world? That is a tricky question. To get a grip on it, we need to know more about the New Testament scenario, presupposed throughout all its books.

---

34. Some major theological and exegetical work has been done in recent years, emphasizing that the biblical picture is not of "heaven" as a place to which individual Christians will go one by one, leaving the world behind, but as a completely new arrangement *upon earth*, depicted in Revelation as the city of God "come down out of heaven" (Rev. 21:2) and established "among human beings," that is to say, a new realm in which God will be all in all and the ills of the *ancien régime* will be obliterated forever along with the demonic powers. Christopher Morse and N. T. Wright have mounted strong arguments along these lines, albeit from differing perspectives.

35. The story of the Grand Inquisitor in *The Brothers Karamazov* duplicates this dynamic. The religious establishment must reject Christ all over again.

Advent and the Essential Components of Apocalyptic Theology

Advent is *the apocalyptic season par excellence* because it is grounded in this essential affirmation: God is the active agent in creation and redemption.[36] Here, in brief, is a summary of the essence of apocalyptic theology.[37]

God as the Acting Subject. Apocalypsis in Greek means disclosure or revelation. The central revelation in apocalyptic theology is the action of God. Specifically, God has revealed Jesus Christ as the One who has come to reclaim for God's self the territory now occupied by the Enemy. This is what John the Baptist refers to when he says, "Even now the axe is laid at the root of the trees" (Luke 3:9). That is what Jesus is announcing when he says, "Today, this scripture is fulfilled in your hearing" (Luke 4:21). The active agent here is God.

The Three Agencies. There are not two active entities in the New Testament but three, as mentioned above: God the creator of the world, the Enemy who has invaded and occupied the world, and the human beings and other creatures who are held in captivity by the demonic occupier. Those are the three agencies in the New Testament scenario. In Christian proclamation, there can be no suggestion that the outcome hangs in the balance, dependent upon how human beings behave. Rather, the way that human beings behave is determined by the mysterious grace of God that justifies the ungodly (Rom. 4:5).

The Controlling Concept of Two Ages. Advent is not about two *"ways"* between which autonomous human beings can freely choose. The gospel presents a crucial contrast with Hellenistic culture in this regard. The typical message in the cultic and religious milieu of the Roman Empire offered two alternative ways (not unlike today's enthusiasm for religious "journeys"). The New Testament, in contrast, was written against the backdrop of the two *ages*, each with its *cosmokrator*, its ruling Power. Two world orders are opposed to one another (Paul calls them flesh [*sarx*] and Spirit [*pneuma*]). This represents a break with any idea that human beings can make progress toward bringing the kingdom of God to pass. Only God can do that, by inaugurating a wholesale change of regime. This is what he has done in the invasion (not too strong a word) of the *old order* by the *new* in Jesus Christ. The New Testament

36. There will always be resistance to this. It is human nature to insist that nothing can happen unless we have a part in it. It is a lasting gift of the Reformation to reclaim the essential gospel, that God prepares his own way in his own time. We contribute by being faithful disciples, discerning what God is already doing on the frontier of the ages, and placing ourselves alongside him in harm's way, so to speak, "until he comes again."

37. I don't pretend that this is a definitive list. I have made several slightly differing lists myself. However, I believe this one covers a lot of the most important territory.

speaks of our citizenship in either one sphere of power or the other, baptism being the passage "from the dominion of darkness" into "the kingdom of his Son" (Col. 1:13).

Struggle and Conflict at the Turn of the Ages. "The style of the Bible is of the battlefield rather than the cloister," wrote Northrop Frye in *The Great Code.* The age to come has invaded "this present evil age" (Gal. 1:4) and has undermined its foundations. This invasion has been compared to D-Day, which marked the turn from defeat to victory in World War II, though final victory is still a long way off, with many battles yet to be fought.[38] The definitive invasion has occurred, but the occupying Enemy and his forces will not give up their territory without a fight. This will define the struggles of the church in "this present evil age." Participants in the most-noted nonviolent protest movements have often described themselves as combatants.

The Apocalyptic Role of the Church. Continuing the metaphor of the battlefield, the church is analogous to paratroopers who secure a place behind the enemy lines. We are God's commandos, guerrillas, and resistance fighters in the territory occupied by the enemy, who participate in establishing "signs and beachheads" signifying ultimate victory.[39] Insofar as is possible in "this present evil age," the form of this resistance will be nonviolent.

The Armor of Light. God's apocalyptic war is fought with different weapons than those of violent earthly wars. *Hupomone* is particularly important as a gift of the Spirit. Often translated simply "patience," *hupomone* can also mean "long-suffering," "endurance," or "perseverance." Eugene Peterson's phrase is apt: "a long obedience in the same direction." Dorothy Day wrote that the word "patience" meant suffering. Paul writes, "Love is patient and kind. . . . Love endures all things" (I Cor. 13:4, 7). The armor of light is described in Ephesians 6:10–17, concluding in verse 18 with *prayer* as perhaps the most powerful weapon of all.

The Stance toward the Enemy. This is at the heart of apocalyptic ethics. The great Enemy (Jesus calls him "the ruler of this world" in the Fourth Gospel) is the personified demonic power of Sin and Death (as Paul identifies it). No human being is born free of bondage to the Enemy. As one of Shakespeare's

38. This analogy, like all human analogies, has its perils. The American invasion of Afghanistan in 2001 was in no sense a victorious enterprise, resulting in a stalemate at best, a reversal at worst. A better analogy than D-Day may be "Aslan has landed!" (C. S. Lewis, *The Lion, the Witch, and the Wardrobe*).

39. J. Christiaan Beker, *Paul's Apocalyptic Gospel: The Coming Triumph of God* (Philadelphia: Fortress, 1984), 110.

characters puts it, "The web of our life is of a mingled yarn, good and ill together; our virtues would be proud, if our faults whipped them not."[40]

The gospel is the great equalizer; we are all in some degree or another enslaved by the malign forces that are set against God. Therefore we regard human beings as enemies only in a provisional, penultimate sense.

The Justification of the Ungodly. There is no biblical proclamation more central than this. "There is no distinction" between human beings in terms of our situation before God (Rom. 3:22–23). None of us deserves God's favor. The very definition of grace is that it is undeserved and unearned. Therefore the door is always open to the possibility that God will do something unexpected. This governs the Christian's stance toward others.

The Future of God. The Christ event inaugurated the reign of God, but the consummation is yet to come. In the Time Between, the characteristic stance of the Christian and of the church is continual vigilance (*Watch!*) for signs of the kingdom. God's future determines the present, rather than the other way round. The age to come is determinative of "this present evil age."

Suffering and Hope. The end-time exerts pressure on the present, creating an unbearable tension. The sign that God is near is marked by suffering. The book of Revelation is particularly oriented toward a Christian community undergoing tribulation. Apocalyptic literature, understood imaginatively, is therefore above all intended for the encouragement of the church, a reaffirmation of the promises of God and of the return of Christ to make all things new.

Apocalyptic Transvision. The gifts of the Spirit permit discernment of God's actions behind and beyond current events. The Christian community sees *through* the darkness of the present into the light of the coming kingdom. All the apocalyptic literature of the Bible, Old Testament and New alike, seeks to demonstrate this. A notable biblical illustration (though not from the apocalyptic literature per se) is in II Kings 6:15–19, where "the Lord opened the eyes of the young man" to see the chariots and horses of fire that protected Israel.

Continuity and Discontinuity. This is one of the most contentious aspects of apocalyptic theology. When we insist that apocalyptic—and particularly that of Paul—is *discontinuous* with what went before, it may sound as if we are rejecting the history of Israel and the role of the prophets. On the contrary, the apocalyptic way of thinking arose specifically out of the postexilic period, making its striking appearance in the later Old Testament prophets (Second Isaiah, Zephaniah, Daniel). The important thing to understand is that apocalyptic discontinuity does not mean severance from the Old Testament

---

40. William Shakespeare, *All's Well That Ends Well*, act 4, scene 3.

witness. What it does mean is a rereading of the Old Testament in light of the first and second comings of Christ. It means that the hope of redemption and the advent of the age to come no longer seeks evidence of the promise from present circumstances, but only in terms of the promised future of God. This is the radicality of a statement like Paul's, that Abraham "hoped against hope" (Rom. 4:18). This offers the Christian community a path through the most complete defeat and the most hopeless situations, still trusting in the Lord who makes a way out of no way (as the African American church is fond of saying). Hoping against hope means trusting in "the God who raises the dead and calls into existence the things that do not exist" (Rom. 4:17). This is the truly radical nature of the Advent promise, which sweeps away cheap comforts and superficial reassurances and, in the midst of the most world-overturning circumstances, still testifies that "Behold, I am coming soon! . . . I am the Alpha and the Omega, the beginning and the end" (Rev. 22:12, 13).[41]

Judgment Taken Up into Promise and Hope

The central drama of Advent is that of judgment and redemption, and yet we live in a time of wholesale reaction against the notion of judgment. I wouldn't want to try to pinpoint exactly when this trend began, but in my experience of a lifetime of churchgoing in various denominations around the country, most mentions of judgment condemn it as "judgmental" and therefore unsuitable for Christian discourse. "Justice," on the other hand, has been enshrined along with peace (as in "peace and justice issues") at the heart and center of enlightened Christian activity.

The concept of justice is indeed central to the biblical portrait of the God who has revealed himself in his written Word and in the incarnate Word who is his Son. However, the current use of "justice" as a rallying cry for the church is reductive, because it is limited to particular political and economic issues without reference to the righteousness of God. A key to the biblical meaning of justice is found in the fact that the word translated "justice" and "righteousness" is the same word in Hebrew and in Greek. The root of the word becomes, in both Testaments, both a noun *and* a verb, so that "justice" or "judgment" is the same thing as "righteousness" or "recti-

---

41. Parts of this section on discontinuity (disjuncture) were suggested by an essay by James F. Kay, "Proclaiming the Promise at Advent," part of an issue of *Perspectives* called "Advent and Apocalyptic" (December 1990).

fication" (making right). The Christian hope is founded in the promise of God that all things will be made new *according to his righteousness*. All the references to judgment in the Bible should be understood in the context of God's righteousness—not just *his being righteous* (noun) but *his "making right"* (verb) all that has been wrong. Clearly, human justice is a very limited enterprise compared to the ultimate making-right of God in the promised day of judgment.

Promise is a key concept in understanding Advent. We are all familiar with broken promises; indeed, it sometimes seems that broken promises are the only promises there are. This is a sign of the old age. The gospel announces the promise of *God*, which has an entirely different character from human promises because it is anchored in the very nature of the righteous God with whom "all things are possible" (Matt. 19:26). Therefore, the principal defining characteristic of the Christian community, along with faith and love, is *hope* (I Cor. 13:13).

I walk through cemeteries whenever I can, heading for the oldest parts because that is where one finds biblical inscriptions on the gravestones. "In thy presence is fullness of joy," "My soul waits in hope," and, marvelously, in Latin, *Qui credit in me, etiam si mortuus ferit, vivet*:[42] these are some of the soul-strengthening words I've seen on tombstones in my cemetery explorations. Even if we cannot be buried in a churchyard because of lack of space, we can continue to cherish the idea of a community of the living and the dead awaiting the coming of the Redeemer of the world. Advent faces into death and looks beyond it to the coming judgment of God upon all that deceives, twists, undermines, pollutes, contaminates, and kills his beloved creation. There can be no community of the resurrection without the conquest of death and the consummation of the kingdom of God. In those assurances lies the hope of the world.

Judgment Is Not the Same Thing as Condemnation

Judgment seen in this way, as God coming in his righteousness in the last day to reclaim his creation for himself, loses its fearsome aspect for those who trust in the promise of God to redeem humanity and the *kosmos* despite all appearances to the contrary. The word "justification" is the right one here. In his *righteousness*, God will *justify*—he will make right—all that is wrong. This

---

42. "I am the resurrection and the life; whosoever believes in me, though he were dead, yet shall he live" (John 11:25).

will cost something. Since it is an ultimate promise, it was made at an ultimate cost. Jesus Christ gave his life for it, but not only his life—the Son of God himself underwent the ultimate judgment of God upon the cross. He absorbed God's eternal rejection of Sin even though, as Paul says, "he knew no sin." In one of the most astonishing sentences in all Scripture, God "made him to be sin" so that we are "made the righteousness of God" (II Cor. 5:21). This is the way to understand the judgment of God in the ultimate sense. Mysterious as this verse is, it carries the crucial message that the righteousness of God was made manifest in the judgment upon Sin that Jesus bore and carried away from us in the ultimate Great Exchange. Therefore, as Paul further declares in ringing tones, "there is therefore now no condemnation for those who are in Christ Jesus" (Rom. 8:1).

The fundamental difference, then, is that between *judgment* and *condemnation*. The Advent season helps us to understand this, but we need to be intentional about facing up to the way that the season locates us. There have been many attempts, in recent years, to soften the message of Advent, and not just in the commercial world where Advent calendars are sold. I have personally been present when new names for the candles of the four Sundays of Advent have been proposed along the lines of Peace, Joy, Love, and Hope. This presents quite a contrast with the medieval Advent themes of death, judgment, heaven, and hell—in that order! As we have seen, hope is a central key to the meaning of Advent, but hope is a very meager concept if it is not measured against the malevolence and godlessness of the forces that assail the creation and its creatures every day in "this present evil age" (Gal. 1:4). The New Testament cosmology will orient us properly in our conflict with these forces.

The very familiar John 3:16 verse is constantly quoted apart from its context, which is misleading: "God so loved the world (*kosmos*) that he gave his only Son, that whoever believes in him should have eternal life. For God sent the Son into the world, not to condemn the world, but that the world might be saved through him."

The reference to condemnation is significant. The Son comes to *judge* the world, but not to *condemn* it. The implication is clear: the world deserves condemnation, but will be saved instead, through the Son. Therefore it is not accurate simply to say "God so loved the world . . ." without reference to the full context with all its implications. An uncritical love of the world as it is, a common problem with "creation theology," is not what is envisioned in this discourse with Nicodemus. Finding the balance, in proclamation and in conduct, between an uncritical love of the world and the fierce love of God that comes to purge and cleanse is part of the Christian vocation.

Now and Not-Yet

It can't be said too often: the life of the church is poised in the Time Between. The time of the coming of Christ is now, in the Word preached and in the sacraments of baptism and the Lord's Supper. But the time of the coming of Christ to consummate all things is not-yet, and there is nothing whatever that human beings can do to hasten that coming. The command to "prepare ye the way of the Lord" in the opening section of the apocalyptic announcement of Isaiah 40–55 is given not in order to entice the Lord to come, but to expect him imminently, for he is already on his way.

That is a delicate balance. Ever since Paul wrote to the Galatians, the church has constantly had to be on guard against the ever-present human wish to take the reins back into our own hands. It is a daily temptation to think that we and our works are going to supply something that God does not already have. The key word here, perhaps, is "participation" in what God is already doing. This is where *apocalyptic transvision* comes in. Jesus himself calls for this sort of discernment: "He also said to the multitudes, 'When you see a cloud rising in the west, you say at once, "A shower is coming"; and so it happens. And when you see the south wind blowing, you say, "There will be scorching heat"; and it happens. You hypocrites! You know how to interpret the appearance of earth and sky; but why do you not know how to interpret the present time?'" (Luke 12:54–56).

Reading the signs of the times is one of the most important of all the gifts given to the church. How often we have failed! We have remained silent when we should have spoken; we have retreated into our churches when we should have acted; we have mistaken a worldly cause for the cause of God. We asked earlier concerning the relationship of the gospel to the "world" that is so often referred to negatively in the New Testament. The nature of apocalyptic transvision is to perceive where *in the world* the activity of God can be discerned.

The constant temptation, given the self-centeredness of the human person under the sign of Sin and the specific individualism of Americans, is to think entirely in terms of each person's individual death and individual passage into heaven. But even if we do think that way, we must already notice that no one lives entirely alone. Even the most confirmed hermit in the mountain wilderness of Montana has been shaped by contact, for better or worse, with other human beings. Even the lack of meaningful contact with others has an effect on an individual. The biblical worldview has no place for the autonomous individual. The human *community* is always the focus. And so, when we think in terms of now and not-yet, it is the destiny of all humankind that is envisioned.

"Comfort ye my people" is not a message for a solitary self-determined person. It is addressed to all of God's people in exile, and the original setting in Babylon is widened and expanded to include all the descendants of Abraham (Gen. 12:3) who are no longer Jew nor Greek, slave nor free, male nor female, for all are one in Christ Jesus (Gal. 3:28). Paul's apocalyptic vision of the future of God is the most expansive of all, rising to a peak never before scaled in Romans 11:32—"God has consigned all human beings to disobedience, in order that he may have mercy upon all."

Living between the times requires not only *trans*vision (seeing across, through, and beyond) but also a kind of *double* vision. The life of each individual Christian will be shaped and formed by her identity as part of the body of Christ, but at the same time and *through the same lens* she will see the whole of humanity and all of creation as the great theater of the activity of the living God. The acts of God are often hidden and must be discerned by faith; in the now, we may often feel that we are stumbling in the dark. But in the not-yet, ahead of us, shines the Light of the World, the Daystar from on high, the "light to lighten the gentiles." He comes to us from the future that belongs only to God, a future guaranteed by the One who created the world *ex nihilo*—out of nothing—in the beginning.

The hope that we meet coming toward us in Advent, then, is the hope that lies beyond any possible good news that could arise out of the human situation. It must come to us out of the future of God or not at all. Such is the background of the Advent announcement that bursts upon a world in captivity. "Comfort ye, comfort ye my people."

> Hark! a thrilling voice is sounding,
> Christ is nigh, it seems to say;
> "Cast away the works of darkness,
> O ye children of the day." (Latin hymn, sixth century)

> Sleepers, wake! A voice astounds us,
> The shout of rampart guards surrounds us;
> "Awake, Jerusalem, arise!" (Reformation hymn, sixteenth century)

> Rejoice, rejoice, believers, and let your lights appear!
> The evening is advancing, and darker night is near. . . .
> Our hope and expectation, O Jesus, now appear,
> Arise, thou Sun so longed for, o'er this benighted sphere!
>   (Lutheran hymn, eighteenth century)

Lo, he comes with clouds descending,
Once for our salvation slain;
Thousand thousand saints attending
Swell the triumph of his train.
Alleluia! Alleluia!
Christ the Lord returns to reign. (Charles Wesley, eighteenth century)

A Word to Preachers

As this book goes to the publisher, my thoughts are often with the young preachers who have been given to me as friends, colleagues, and, dare I say, students (not to mention Twitter followers!). This is less through personal contact now than through my books and the Internet. If I have a regret in life, it's not being able to do more hands-on teaching of homiletics. In a sense, this book is intended as a sort of valedictory message to serious young preachers, who exist in far greater numbers today than I realized when I first turned to Twitter!

When I began as a preacher forty-five years ago, I tried out various styles that I had admired in other preachers (to some extent this can be observed in the differences between my sermons in the 1970s and those that came later). This was an essential exercise, perhaps, but in the end I had to find my own way. This will be true for all young preachers. There is one injunction, however, that can be universally employed. The great error that lies treacherously before us all, especially as we feel we are growing stale, is the temptation to lose sight of the text itself. My esteemed homiletics professor, the Lutheran preacher Edmund Steimle, cautioned his students in no uncertain terms: never fail to do a searching exegesis before you begin. I have found this to be profoundly important advice. If the preacher has not been seized by the text, the sermon will be a collection of merely human thoughts. However well these reflections may be put together, they will lead the hearers *away from* the Word of God unless the preacher can get herself out of the way. That, too, was important advice I received: take yourself out of it!

I make no attempt to conceal my commitment to apocalyptic interpretation of the Bible. This volume is an effort to model it in the pulpit. If there is one foundational truth that I have learned from apocalyptic theology, it is this: God is the subject of the verb. God doesn't need us to help him make his "dream" come true; God is on the march far ahead of us, bringing his purposes to pass, and if we don't run to catch up with him, he will commandeer someone else. If God is not the acting agent, the subject of the sentences in the sermon, then it's not the gospel. If the sermon is an exhortation to us to help out a "dreaming" God build the kingdom, as if he couldn't do it without our efforts, it's not the gospel. As a member of the African American congregation shouted out in a mass meeting during the civil rights movement, "We're not doing this! *God is doing this!*"[43] The right word for the connection between the purpose of God and human activity is "participation." We are participants in what God is already doing, but this is by grace alone (*sola gratia*); we should always beware of sermons that sound as if God is standing back waiting for us before anything can be accomplished.

Hope and *promise* are at the center of the Advent proclamation. A great many sermons are essentially exhortations, and exhortation ("Let us . . .") is powerless unless the hearers are already on their feet doing whatever it is. As I have tried to pass along to young preachers, every biblical sermon should give a reason for hope, and every biblical sermon should contain a promise. Sermons that end with statements like "we are called to . . ." (feed the hungry, celebrate diversity, build shelters for the homeless, and so forth), or questions asking "will we" (seek justice for the poor, fight against racism, march for various causes, etc.), are self-defeating. When sermons end that way, the hearers feel defeated and powerless—except, of course, for the few who are already doing whatever it is, who then can feel superior. For that reason, hortatory sermons are divisive. Sermons in the mode of promise, however, are uplifting and empowering for everyone. Every person in the congregation should feel that a promise has been made to him or her by the God who, unlike human beings, keeps his promises.

No Apologies for Repetition

When one has been preaching Advent sermons for more than forty years, there is bound to be some repetition. The most obvious one, perhaps, is the theme of the apparent absence of God—classically known as *Deus absconditus*. Most of the sermons address this existentially agonizing question in one way or an-

---

43. This often-told true story is recounted in full in the chapter called "Discerning the Mighty Acts of God" in my book of Old Testament sermons, *And God Spoke to Abraham* (Grand Rapids: Eerdmans, 2011), 199.

other. The suffering of believers whose prayers seem to go unheard is a central problem only too familiar to anyone who is alive and alert and thinking. No serious Christian can be indifferent to this challenge. Unbelievers often appear to be congratulating themselves for forgoing the consolations of belief; their loss is minor indeed, compared to the struggle of the believer to hang on in spite of the silence of God.

There are many other notes struck during the season that are bound to be repeated in sermons because of the cyclical nature of the appointed readings in the Advent lectionary. One chapter from the so-called Synoptic Apocalypse (Matt. 24; Mark 13; Luke 21) is read just before Advent every year, and sets the tone. The parable of the ten bridesmaids, the prophecies of Isaiah and Malachi, the parable of the sheep and the goats—such passages recur in the cycle again and again as Advent approaches. Other themes also recur frequently in these sermons, which might be off-putting if the collection were examined as a whole, but most readers will not read all the sermons in succession. It is envisioned that most people will select sermons here and there from the table of contents. Since each sermon stands by itself, I am hoping that readers will be indulgent concerning certain repeated themes. Some of them are macro-themes, such as the necessity for facing into darkness, and a few are micro-themes, such as the customs of the Episcopal Church during Advent. Some of the sermons that I preached as a guest in different congregations in different locations begin more or less the same way, orienting the hearers to Advent motifs that they might not have known about, but after the introductions the sermons take off in varying directions. Since most readers will read only one or two sermons at a time, I hope that the repetitions serve a purpose. In any case, I have made a strenuous effort, with the help of my editor, to excise a good many of them.

Certain literary figures will appear regularly in these pages. W. H. Auden and T. S. Eliot are so central to Anglican worship and seasonal emphases, and so endlessly fecund a source for understanding the human condition revealed in the Advent message, that they can hardly be overused. Other repetitions are inevitable, and I make no apology for that. John the Baptist appears regularly, as he does in the Advent readings, and since Jesus himself said there was no man ever born greater than John the Baptist, we can hardly hear enough about him. The prophet Malachi and the figure of Elijah make a number of appearances, being conspicuously related to the motif of the last judgment and the age to come. Pascal is quoted more than once. I return often to Abraham Lincoln's Second Inaugural Address, one of the greatest theological meditations ever made by a public figure, and his struggle to understand what God might be up to is particularly attuned to the questions raised by the Advent scriptural passages and, especially, the primary theme of God's righteousness in judgment.

About the Advent Hymns

I have put a good deal of stress on the music of Advent. Only one or two of the Advent hymns—unlike the Christmas hymns and carols—are well known throughout the churches, which is a great pity, because many of them are very fine. The best-known one to the general public is "O Come, O Come, Emmanuel," but its origins and meaning require much explanation (see the Great "O" Antiphons of Advent toward the end of this volume). Probably the second-best-known Advent hymn within the church is "Wachet Auf!" ("Sleepers, wake!"). This magnificent German chorale tune was embraced by Johann Sebastian Bach, and his several settings of it are part of the glory of world music. The words have been variously translated and appear in many hymnals.

I have made use of the Advent hymns in the Episcopal hymnal because, all things considered, there are a good many of them, and they are mostly of the highest quality.[44] I am not alone in my concern that the church is in danger of losing its hymnody because of the widespread turn to contemporary, often inferior, music. The Christian songs that one hears so often in the services pitched to young people today present a problem; the endless repetition of banal phrases set to insipid tunes does not build up the mental furniture of newcomers to the Christian faith. The best of the older hymns (and by "older" I don't mean nineteenth century; I mean the whole sweep of hymnody from the patristic period to the Reformation and beyond) are rich with biblical quotations and references. They teach doctrine to those who think they don't care about doctrine. Many of the best hymns have plots: they begin with praise, then in the middle verse(s) evoke instability and danger, and finally in the last verse resolve into sheer affirmation, empowerment, and thanksgiving. A particularly good example of this is Charles Wesley's "Lo, He Comes with

---

44. The Moravians are known for their Advent emphasis, and I am sorry I have not done more research into their music. A quick look at some of their extensive recordings shows that there is overlap with the Episcopal Advent hymns, but the keen focus on the second coming is more obvious in the Episcopal hymnal (1982). An example of a fine Advent hymn not in the Episcopal hymnal is "Oh Lord, How Shall I Meet You?" with words by the prolific Paul Gerhardt, in the Lutheran hymnal. It evokes the second coming in the final stanza.

Clouds Descending"; its trajectory is described in detail in the sermon "Who Are Those Wailing People?"

Handel's *Messiah* also plays an important role in Advent proclamation. Many of the most important Advent texts appear in that enduring work, so often performed to enthusiastic audiences during Advent itself. For its popularity, we may thank not only the composer but also Charles Jennens, who compiled Scripture verses into a thrilling dramatic whole.[45] One of the reasons I often stay with the King James Version for certain texts is that they are so well known from *Messiah*: "Comfort ye my people" is an obvious example. An effective Advent study course might be based partly on the text of *Messiah*.

When hymns are chosen to accompany the sermon, the overall effect is greatly enhanced—particularly when the selected hymns follow immediately after the sermon.[46] Planning a worship service in which the theme of the sermon is followed throughout the Scripture readings and hymns is extra work, but the impact is exponentially greater—particularly if the preacher leads the congregation through parts of the hymn text.[47]

How to Make Use of This Book

I have envisioned specific groups of nonacademic readers for this book. These include (1) preachers and teachers of the faith; (2) people who plan liturgies; and (3) laypeople who want to live more deeply out of the gospel as it is dramatized in the church's year.

In a general sense, though, this book will be valuable to anyone who is interested in the second coming, the last judgment, the end of the world, *and especially* the ethical dimension of the life of waiting and watching while also seeking to live a life of meaningful action.

45. Charles Jennens is finally beginning to attract the notice he deserves: Maev Kennedy, "Handel House Honours Charles Jennens, Librettist of *Messiah*," *Guardian*, November 27, 2012, https://www.theguardian.com/music/2012/nov/27/handel-house-charles-jennens -messiah. When I visited Handel's house in London in 2017, I was happy to see a handsome portrait of Jennens hanging in a prominent location.

46. At Grace Church in New York, this was the practice for many years. It was easy to do, liturgically, because three Sundays out of four were Morning Prayer. The revised eucharistic liturgy now makes it more difficult.

47. I particularly recommend the comprehensive offering of suitable hymns and other music from various traditions on the Advent Project website: http://www.theadventproject .org/Documents.

Readers should not be daunted by the large amount of material in this collection. The sermons and essays, though arranged in a carefully planned sequence, are meant to be mined as needed; each individual contribution stands on its own. Readers can use the table of contents to find what interests them. The table of contents will also orient them to what they might find useful at a particular point during the unfolding of the season. It will be clear from the way the sermons have been arranged that the four actual Sundays of Advent are at the core of the season, but it is increasingly recognized that Advent is really a seven-week season beginning after All Saints' Day, so there are many sermons from this period as well.[48] I have even included the Feast of Saint Michael and All Angels, because of its relative proximity to the coming of Advent and its related themes.

Few people will want to read everything at once, or even in the sequence here presented—in fact, that might be counterproductive because of repetition within subheads. One possible strategy is to read one sermon from each subheading, rather than all sermons under a subheading at once. Others might want to get a grip on a particular Sunday or week in the season; the table of contents will be a guide for this plan of attack as well. Preachers may want to read for ideas; laypeople may be looking for daily devotions during the season, or for illumination about specific scriptural passages listed in the index. Some readers who are new to Advent might seek more information from the essays concerning the season, and some, I particularly hope, will be looking for help with challenging themes like judgment and suffering. Help for all of this can be found in the table of contents.

Advent is less well known and understood in some branches of the church than in others. This volume has a conspicuous Episcopal (Anglican) flavor, but my hope is that Christian believers of all persuasions will find that the depth of theological meaning in the observance of Advent holds inexhaustible significance for them as well in these days. No other season of the church year is more closely connected to the difficulties, perplexities, setbacks, and seeming dead ends that the church faces on a daily basis.

It will be obvious from even a superficial run-through that the material gathered here is not for the squeamish! I mean it as a compliment to those who pick up this volume when I say that a certain amount of mental and emotional stamina will be required to pursue its themes. Advent is definitely not for sis-

---

48. The Advent Project seeks to build support for a seven-week season: http://www.theadventproject.org/.

sies. Those who are willing and ready to face the special mood of the season will, I hope, find that it opens up the deep meaning of Christmas in a way that is simply not possible with a less rigorous approach.

The Sermons and Writings

These sermons were delivered in a wide variety of settings in the United States and Canada over a period of nearly forty-five years. Some were delivered to lay audiences, a few to clergy, and one or two in academic settings. This accounts for their difference in tone and, sometimes, in length. The sermons for clergy assume a certain amount of biblical knowledge and familiarity with languages that other sermons do not. Those preached at Grace Church in New York in the 1980s and '90s have a special character; the congregation had experienced dramatic growth as a result of vigorous biblical preaching, and its members, mostly young and well-educated New York strivers, were accustomed to long, demanding sermons and expected them.

The "writings" in this collection do not really qualify as essays. One of them is a presentation given as a lecture at a gathering in a church hall. The others are editorials or relatively brief reflections published as series. I have written extensively about Advent over the years, but upon examining my files, I realized that publishing it all here would not be necessary, since most of the content shows up in the sermons.

A Few Technicalities

Bible Translations

As in my other books, I have largely used the RSV, but here with many exceptions. The NRSV has its virtues, but in many cases the cadence has been unnecessarily spoiled in a misguided attempt to modernize. When I have quoted from time-honored passages such as those set to music by G. F. Handel in *Messiah*, or other texts set to early music, I have used the King James Version, or whatever translation the composer used, if in English.

Inclusive Language

The sermons preached in the 1970s and early 1980s are not attuned to this concern, and in many cases I have left them as they were. As in my other books, I have generally avoided the use of "man" and "him" in my more recent work, but I am not fanatical about it. If I value the cadence of a sentence, or the time-honored use of a term (for instance, "the old Adam"), I will retain the old form.

WRITINGS

A Five-Part Advent Series for
the *Christian Century*

"Royalty Stoops"
Matthew 25:31–46
Christ the King, Sunday next before Advent, 1999

Not long before the onset of the cancer that finally killed him, King Hussein of Jordan undertook a small mission. He paid a personal visit to the families of some Israelis who had been killed in an Arab terrorist bombing. There was no talk of money or reparations; instead, the king quietly sat with the mourners, and by his calm demeanor, unhurried manner, and undivided attention was able to convey a sense of solidarity with them across the Arab-Israeli divide. The reaction of the relatives was out of all proportion to the simplicity of the gesture. By all accounts, they were deeply moved by Hussein's expressions of personal involvement in their loss. Their grief had been acknowledged. More memorably still, it had been acknowledged and shared *by a king*.

The star of Diana, Princess of Wales, has faded a bit in the year since the first anniversary of the funeral that was watched by two billion people. Though it is improper and unprofessional to venture an actual diagnosis, it does seem that she was emotionally troubled in some way. As we have learned more about her obsessions and failings, many have felt a little embarrassed about their initial reaction to her death. Among media people, there has been a lot of second-guessing about excessive coverage. Still, in all the hundreds of hours of television

These five articles appeared in Living by the Word, *Christian Century*, November and December 1999. Copyright © by the *Christian Century*. Reprinted by permission. For each, the title of the article is followed by the related lectionary Scripture passage and the apposite Sunday in the church calendar.

and the thousands of words written, I never heard anyone specifically identify the factor that I believe accounts for much of the extraordinary public outpouring. The various talking heads spoke of her beauty, accessibility, modernity, vulnerability, compassion, and common touch—all correct so far as they went—but no one precisely identified the *combination* that made Diana exceptional.

Many famous people have engaged in charitable activities. Show-business figures such as Danny Kaye and Audrey Hepburn have made an impression with their commitment to various humanitarian causes. Other personages have elicited near-fanatical devotion because of their beauty, talent, personal chemistry, or skill in creating a media image—Marilyn Monroe, Elvis Presley, Jacqueline Onassis. Eva Peron comes to mind, another glamorous blonde who died young and was adored by the common people. None of these, however, were able to combine in one person what was given Diana to do. In the Princess of Wales, ***majesty stooped***. That was the key to her power. President Clinton, even in his heyday as empathizer in chief, could not convey what Diana could, because a president is not royalty. The *symbolism* of Diana was this: she was seen as one who was willing to lay aside her princely prerogatives to come alongside those who are downtrodden.

It may seem to be trivializing Hussein, a man of great accomplishments, to mention him alongside the unformed and often frivolous Diana; indeed, the two are not really comparable. I bring them together here simply to show that in spite of our democratic instincts, the royal archetype is undimmed in the collective unconscious. It is no denigration of Hussein to observe that Diana, because she bore the aura of the British monarchy along with her own, was uniquely able to put her *echt*-princess image together with a readiness to *come alongside* those who have no status in the world. Many who saw the video of her Angolan visit would agree that Diana's ability to communicate her concern for the wretched of the earth took the breath away. I read the testimony of an American physician who had accompanied her on hospital rounds where there were no cameras. He said she did not hesitate to caress and linger beside patients with disfigurements and symptoms that were distressing even to medical personnel. That capacity, the doctor emphasized, cannot be faked. When it is offered generously and unstintingly by a beautiful young woman who is the living embodiment of everyone's image of a fairy princess, the impact is astonishing.

Much of the grief for the princess was neurotic, like human behavior in general. I am making a different point, having to do with the power of symbols. Diana was certainly an instinctive media genius, as the first Queen Elizabeth might very well have been had she lived in our century. Elizabeth I was a great monarch in part because the people knew that she loved them, and her processions through the countryside were specifically designed to allow them to love her in return. In her limited way Diana also knew how to use her immense candlepower for the good of ordinary people. This is the right use of royalty.

These thoughts are meant to suggest that the feast day of Christ the King presents us with an extraordinary opportunity. We were speaking of archetypes; something greater than archetypes is here. We were speaking of the strength of symbolism; something stronger than symbolism is here. If it is true that there is unique power in the combination of royalty and stooping, then there has never been anything comparable to the errand of the Son of God. In Jesus Christ we see the One "who, though he was in the form of God, did not count equality with God a thing to be clutched at, but emptied himself, taking the form of a slave" (Phil. 2:6–7). The problem with much of our Christology nowadays, it seems to me, is that we have concentrated so much on the stooping that we have lost sight of the royalty. More than half of the biblical message is thereby eliminated, for it is the *combination* that counts. Thus we read in Exodus 3, "Moses hid his face, for he was afraid to look at God. Then the Lord said, 'I have seen the affliction of my people who are in Egypt, and have heard their cry because of their taskmasters; I know their sufferings, and *I have come down* to deliver them.'"

The God who is so terrifying that we must hide our faces from his resplendence is the same God who has *come down* to deliver his people in their extremity. That is the secret. The Son who "sits upon his glorious throne with all the nations gathered before him" (Matt. 25:31–32) is the same One who, at the very apex of his cosmic power, reveals that the universe turns upon a cup of water given to the littlest ones in his name. An outpouring of the love of our hearts toward this King will therefore transcend the merely neurotic. Acts of mercy toward his little ones are vindicated already in the court of heaven, because they are taken up into the divine life of the Son of God, who loved us and gave himself for us.

"Cover-Ups"
Psalm 85
Advent II, 1999

Blaise Pascal evokes a sense of existential dread in his famous line: "The eternal silence of these infinite spaces frightens me."[1] Three hundred years later,

1. Pascal, *Pensées,* no. 206, at https://www.gutenberg.org/files/18269/18269-h/18269-h .htm#SECTION_I.

W. H. Auden wrote in a similar vein in the Advent section of his long, dramatic poem *For the Time Being: A Christmas Oratorio.* He pictures the human being forsaken in a blank, fathomless universe:

> . . . We are afraid
> Of pain but more afraid of silence; for no nightmare
> Of hostile objects could be as terrible as this Void.
> This is the Abomination. This is the Wrath of God.

The wrath of God is a principal theme of the pre-Advent and Advent seasons in the church. There is no more challenging task in theology than interpreting it for today. Pascal and Auden both interpret it as silence—*Deus absconditus.* C. S. Lewis wrote, after his wife's death, "Where is God? When you are happy . . . and turn to him with gratitude and praise, you will be—or so it feels—welcomed with open arms. But go to him when your need is desperate, when all other help is in vain, and what do you find? A door slamming in your face, and a sound of bolting and double bolting on the inside. After that, silence."

The wrath of God can be viewed as silence from a quite different perspective. I have a newspaper clipping in my file, dating back to the apartheid era in South Africa, reporting that Desmond Tutu, then bishop of Johannesburg, had just returned from one of his trips abroad where he openly sought support for the fight against the racial policies of his country. At an airport news conference in Johannesburg, he declared that he was not at all worried about his passport being confiscated yet again. Having one's passport taken away is not the worst thing that can happen to a Christian, he said. Even being killed is not the worst thing. "For me, one of the worst things would be if I woke up one day and said to people, 'I think apartheid is not so bad.' For me, this would be worse than death." This is surely a clue to understanding the wrath of God. A god who remained silent in the face of atrocities would not be the God of Abraham, Isaac, and Jacob or the God and Father of our Lord Jesus Christ. It has been given to Bishop Tutu more than almost anyone else in our time to be the human voice and face of the God who has not remained silent.

Other governments, other voices have chosen silence. The Guatemalan Commission for Historical Clarification, for example, was given an insufficient mandate; it was hamstrung by the military into continuing the same policies of cover-up and denial at the highest levels that gave the Guatemalan civil war its sinister character in the first place. Likewise in Argentina and Chile, blanket amnesties permitted state-sponsored killers to pursue lives of comfort. General Pinochet was allowed to slip away to England to enjoy teas with Baroness Thatcher. Voices have been heard, however, from the underground. The Mothers of the Plaza del Mayo have not been silenced. The families of the Chilean "disappeared" are voiceless no longer. A retired Argentine captain confessed to dropping as many as two thousand political prisoners from airplanes. Argentine president Menem, clearly afraid of more revelations, has urged former military executioners and torturers to confess in private to priests, calling on the country not to look back, to "move forward."[2] It will not do. Bishop Tutu has shown the world that the only *way forward* is the *way through*. With all its faults and limitations, the South African Truth and Reconciliation Commission was able to demonstrate that although they were determined to seek reconciliation and move into the future, justice had not been abrogated. As Bishop Tutu said to the victims, "Something seriously evil happened to you, and the nation believes you." Thus the wrath of God against injustice has broken the terrible silence.

The lectionary designers lost their nerve when they appointed Psalm 85 for Advent II. They omitted its vital center, verses 3–7:

> Thou hast taken away all thy wrath:
> thou hast turned thyself from the fierceness of thine anger.
> Turn us, O God of our salvation,
> and cause thine anger toward us to cease.
> Wilt thou be angry with us for ever?
> Wilt thou draw out thine anger to all generations?
> Wilt thou not revive us again,
> that thy people may rejoice in thee?
> Show us thy mercy, O Lord, and grant us thy salvation.

A failure of imagination was at work in this excision. Jettisoning the references to God's wrath deprives us of the good news that his wrath has been turned away. The lovely verse 10 has naturally been retained ("Mercy and truth are met together; righteousness and peace have kissed each other"), but the prior omissions have robbed us of an opportunity to understand that righteousness and peace cannot kiss until "the wrath of God is revealed from heaven against . . . those who by their wickedness suppress the truth" (Rom. 1:18). Ask Bishop Tutu.

---

2. Pope Francis played his part in maintaining a public silence when he was provincial superior of the Jesuits in Argentina during the "Dirty War" (1974–1983).

The premier personage of Advent is John the Baptist. When he appears on the banks of the Jordan, the cover-ups come to their appointed end. Two thousand years before all the Watergates, Irangates, and other sordid "-gates," John came proclaiming God's imminent judgment on the venality of governments, the corruption of police departments, the greed of financiers, the selfishness of the rich, the self-righteousness of the religious establishment. In the end, he became one of *los desaparecidos* himself, executed without a trial in the dank dungeon of the local strongman, thus becoming truly the precursor of the One whose way he prepared, the One whose death at the hands of the political and religious ruling classes signified the final judgment of God on all the powers and principalities.

There are cover-ups of all sorts. There are families that will not acknowledge the alcoholism that is destroying them. There are people who are making their loved ones miserable but will not go to a therapist. There are secretaries who cover up for bosses, business partners who cover up for each other, colonels for generals, bishops for clergy, parents for children. Advent is the season of the uncovering: "Bear fruit that befits repentance. . . . Even now the axe is laid to the root of the trees"! This is the right time to root out the cover-ups in our own lives, as we wait with bated breath for the lights to come on and the announcement of the angel that God is not against us but for us.

"The Two Faces of Advent"
John 1:6–8, 19–28
Advent III, 1999

Who among us would tolerate John the Baptist for even a few minutes? I understand that there is a medallion called "Laughing Jesus" being handed around. We will wait a long time, I suspect, for an image of "Laughing John the Baptist." John is the principal personage of Advent, with two whole Sundays focused on his preaching, but for some years now I have been offering a yet-unclaimed reward to anyone who can find him on an Advent calendar. There is nothing in his message to correspond to the well-loved "Peace on earth." John is not wishing us good will; he is calling down judgment upon our heads.

In the late '60s, the Catholic Interracial Council of the Twin Cities produced some remarkable—quite shocking, actually—Christmas cards. In 1968 the outside of the card was red-orange, with the words of the Benedictus (Luke 1:78): "From on high our God will bring the rising Sun . . ." Then you opened the card to find a stark black-and-white photograph of a small African American child caught by a ray of sunlight as he sits listlessly in the shadows of a slum courtyard. Along with the photo is the rest of the verse: "to give light to those who sit in darkness and the shadow of death" (v. 79). The contrast between the outside and the inside caused heads to snap back. My husband and I still think it is the best Christmas card we ever received. The next year (remember, this is 1969) the card had some words of John the Baptist (John 1:26) on the front, in red: "There is One among you . . ." Opening the card, one sees another black-and-white photograph, this time of a young Vietnamese girl with the blank, stunned expression we recognize from so many pictures of children in wartime, and the rest of the verse: ". . . whom you do not recognize." Propaganda? Dubious Christology? Politically heavy-handed? Maybe. But even the relatively benign Baptizer of the Fourth Gospel lends himself easily to messages of startling currency. This year, the child would be a Kosovar Albanian, or East Timorese—or, yet again, an American child sitting in the shadows of poverty.

Advent has two faces. One of its faces is apparent in the first lines of Advent hymns: "Hark, a thrilling voice is sounding!" "Sleepers, wake! a voice astounds us!" "Rejoice, rejoice, believers, and let your lights appear!" This is the Advent mood of rapturous expectation as the time of fulfillment moves toward us. The other face is that of John the messianic herald who stands on the frontier as the ages collide, destined to bear the impact. This face of Advent is that of the apocalyptic woes, the tribulation that overtakes all who stand their ground in the place of greatest pressure as the age to come pushes against "the rulers of this age, who are doomed to pass away" (I Cor. 2:6). Thus John flings his accusation against the religious leaders: "Who warned you to flee from the wrath to come?" This is almost always read aloud with the emphasis in the wrong place; it should not be on "you," because that enables us to distance ourselves from the "you," as though we ourselves were not being addressed. Rather, the emphasis should be evenly divided between "flee" and "wrath to come," so as to indicate the gravity of the coming judgment upon the godly and ungodly alike. John himself stood under this sentence of wrath. He did not flinch from his vocation, even though the strange mission of this Messiah was hidden from him. We think, based on what we know from Matthew 11:2–3, that John was expecting the Avenger. He did not yet know the secret, that the Vindicator would take the place of those who stood under judgment and in the shadow of death. It was not shown to John in this life; nevertheless, he held the piece of ground that had been prepared for him and now appears together with Mary the mother of God at the side of the crucified Christ. Combined in

John is the paradox of Advent: the coming triumph of God is made manifest precisely in the darkness of this present evil age (Gal. 1:4).

As we make our choices about what to emphasize in Advent, we might reflect on our cultural situation. A rising chorus of voices identifies irony as the prevailing posture in our post-Seinfeldian times. For instance, Andrew Delbanco writes that the prediction of Jonathan Edwards has come true, that it is no longer clear that anyone is to be blamed or condemned for anything.[3] This in itself is ironic, because even as we rejoice to subvert bourgeois values, we have somehow managed to enshrine them at the same time. A culture that can exhibit sliced cows in formaldehyde (never mind Madonnas decorated with dung) on the one hand, and sentimental illustrators like Norman Rockwell and Maxfield Parrish on the other, in major museums at the same time with no sense of absurdity, can hardly boast of its refined sense of irony.[4] Given the choice between sentimentality and irony . . . well, let's go back to John the Baptist. Christianity is under attack from every quarter—not least from within its own ranks as we become more and more indistinguishable from everybody else—but the commanding voices of the prophets and apostles are still capable of lifting us out of the culture wars onto a plane that not even the most cynical Jesus-basher can successfully besiege. As secular critic Northrop Frye wrote appreciatively in *The Great Code*, "The simplicity of the Bible is the simplicity of majesty."

Advent has two aspects. The Advent critique of sentimentality is manifest in the season's refusal to let Christmas come too soon. Flannery O'Connor defined sentimentality as skipping lightly over the Fall into "an early arrival at a mock state of innocence." Those who station themselves in the Advent watchtower (Hab. 2:1) will be vigilant against that too-early arrival. As for irony, there is one thing that will speak to it, and that is personal witness at great cost. Bishop Carlos Belo of East Timor is an Advent witness, and, perhaps even more so, so is Bishop Basilio do Nascimento, who never left the country even at the height of the reign of terror. These are Christians who in one sense have already "come through the great tribulation" (Rev. 7:14).

As for nonsentimental, trans-ironic Christmas cards, the Interracial Council turned away from its own best product in the mid-'70s and started offering cards with smiling, beautiful white and black people celebrating peace and joy.

3. Andrew Delbanco, *The Death of Satan* (New York: Farrar, Straus and Giroux, 1999), 216.

4. The reference is to works by Damien Hirst and Chris Ofili. Hirst is the richest living artist in Britain, perhaps in the world. The Ofili painting of the Virgin Mary sold for $4.6 million in 2015.

As far as I know, the Christmas cards of the Interracial Council dropped out of sight after they made that disappointing change. Advent, however, remains, with its paradoxical combination of waiting and hastening (II Pet. 3:12), suffering and joy, judgment and deliverance, apocalyptic woe and eschatological hope. It is the *combination* that counts. This is the way Christians live now, for "the light shines in the darkness, and the darkness has never mastered it" (John 1:5 REB).

"God's Entrance"
II Samuel 7:1–6; Luke 1:26–38
Advent IV, 1999

How strange that in the space of just one recent week a book reviewer in the *New York Times* mentions the "frisson-inducing" discovery only nine years ago of a ninth-century BC stele referring to the "House of David," thus issuing "a stony rebuff to those who think that David is a mythical figure," while another reviewer, writing about Thomas Cahill's new book *Desire of the Everlasting Hills*, raises seriously the question of whether the historical person called Jesus of Nazareth ever existed. These are the challenges that Christian interpreters and believers must meet every day, now. Which of our Scriptures are to be regarded as "historical," and which as "mythical"? Raymond Brown wrote amusingly, in a footnote, of being called on the phone every Christmas by reporters who wanted to know "what really happened." Father Brown would reply, one imagines with some asperity, that they would do well to inquire concerning the real message of the stories.

Yet another reviewer (same week!), this time assessing a TV movie about Jesus, complains of the "greeting-card sentiment" that permeates the script. She writes that the movie is a lot "better when it sticks to Scripture." She cites the scene when John the Baptist "announces convincingly, 'Behold the Lamb of God who takes away the sins of the world.'" It's encouraging to get this kind of support for the unique simplicity and grandeur of the Bible. Even as the reviewer urges the writer of the teleplay to stick to the Script, however, the point is again being made: John and Jesus are purely literary presences. This could be worse—they could be ignored as having no presences at all—but it makes the job of the believing interpreter more difficult. How to distinguish between what the church says and what the literary critics say?

What really happened? Did the prophet Nathan really say to the "historical David" that his throne would be established forever? Shall we settle on David as a historical presence and Jesus as a purely literary one? Surely it would make more sense to have it the other way round. Isn't it easier by far to conclude that David is a mythical King Arthur type than to believe that the human religious imagination would dream up a crucified Messiah? This is not a rhetorical question. Perhaps one of the problems is that many people who are tossing off opinions about these matters do not realize what crucifixion was as a mode of execution. It is flatly inconceivable that anyone would invent a Son of God who was consigned by church and state alike to die the most extreme form of death by degradation and dehumanization known to the ancient world. We need not waste time debating Jesus's actual existence. The question that is up for grabs is, **Who** was "crucified under Pontius Pilate"? Everybody who speaks of Jesus of Nazareth, thinks of him, prays in his name, or (increasingly) uses his name as an expletive will be taking a position with regard to this, whether the person consciously realizes it or not.

The angel Gabriel, according to Saint Luke, burst into the life of an ordinary young woman without permission, terrifying her. Every angelic appearance in Scripture causes fear, because the angel mediates the searing intrusion of the living God. But the angel said, "Fear not, Mary, for thou hast found favor with God. And, behold, thou shalt conceive in thy womb, and bring forth a son, and shalt call his name Jesus. He . . . shall be called the Son of the Highest, and the Lord God shall give unto him the throne of his father David . . . and of his kingdom there shall be no end." Is this literary truth? mythological truth? historical truth? or no truth at all? What really happened, and does it matter?

The one thing that matters, I think, is that we should ask ourselves about the single most fundamental affirmation in the story. Did God act? That question has two facets: Did **God** act? and did God **act**? Do we see here an event set in motion by spiritually precocious human beings with divine aspirations? Or do we see the God of Abraham, Isaac, and Jacob at work? And second, do we see God at a remove, watching over events as they transpire, perhaps nudging them along here and there? Or do we see here the definitive entrance of God upon the world stage as he reclaims lost human nature for himself? If a stele were to be found in Bethlehem saying, "Here was born Jesus bar-Joseph . . . ," would that make a difference? Wouldn't most of us still want to convert the story into a pretty, painterly scene of an angel and a maiden, suitable for ornament?

Karl Barth wrote that the church's creedal affirmation of the virginal conception is the "doctrine on guard . . . at the door of the mystery of Christmas."[5]

---

5. Karl Barth, *Church Dogmatics* I/2 (Edinburgh: T. & T. Clark, 1956), 182.

Matthew and Luke have both posted guards at the entrances to their Gospels: "Danger: God at work." Are these purely literary devices? Did it "really happen"? If not, what do we need to know?

And the angel said, "The Holy Spirit will come upon you, and the power of the Most High will overshadow you; therefore the child to be born will be called holy, the Son of God. And behold, your kinswoman Elizabeth in her old age has also conceived a son. . . . For *with God nothing will be impossible*" (Luke 1:35–37). As the millennium turns, this Christmastide will be another blessed opportunity for bearing witness unashamedly to the church's ancient faith that very God of very God *really happened here*. "The Incarnation is like a dagger thrust into the weft of human history" (Edwyn Hoskyns). Let not the celebrated literary power of the stories themselves obscure this truth: "The Word was made flesh, and dwelt among us, and we beheld his glory, the glory as of the only begotten of the Father, full of grace and truth."

"For Grown-Ups"
Isaiah 52:7–10; John 1:1–14
Christmas Eve, 1999

The first three Sundays of Advent speak of an adult Christ and the future reign of God, not of an infant born in the past. Only on the fourth Sunday of Advent do we turn back to the event of annunciation, and then on Christmas Eve to the birth of the Christ child. It must have been like that for the earliest Christians: at first, they were entirely focused on the resurrection, the gift of the Spirit, and the eagerly expected second coming; then, as the time lengthened, they began to reflect with wonder and no little curiosity about the divine origin and human beginnings of their Lord. It may be helpful for us to remember this sequence as we try to make sense of Christmas in view of the multicultural "holiday" that now threatens to swallow up the Christian holy day altogether. The lectionaries for Advent and the Twelve Days reveal that the adult Messiah is primary. Thus the climactic reading for the three services of Christmas is not the nativity from Luke but the prologue of John: "The Word was made flesh and dwelt among us." The numinous quality of this text will not be lost on children as they grow, but clearly, it does not fit our idea of a reading designed for them.

Many Christians, especially those from a tradition like mine that observes Advent scrupulously, not decorating the church or singing carols until Christmas Eve, find themselves playing two games at once during this season. On the

47

one hand there is the usual frantic shopping, wreath hanging, tree trimming, party going, and overeating. On the other hand there is the deepening mood of Advent, which calls us to a mature, clear-sighted, and steadfast faith. A similar split in our sensibility is apparent in Christian bookstores and church gift shops where an austere Byzantine icon will be displayed next to an angel that looks like a Barbie doll. Christmas cards with medieval illustrations sit cheek by jowl with designs of Santas playing golf. Perhaps I am wrong, but it seems to me that this aesthetic confusion contributes to theological immaturity. Grown-up people seem to become addled at this season, trying to recapture their lost childhoods. One of our leading mail-order companies put this verse on their Christmas shipping boxes a couple of years ago:

> May you find among the gifts
> Spread beneath your tree
> The most welcome gift of all
> The child you used to be.

A typical greeting card says,

> Backward, turn backward, O Time, in your flight
> Make me a child again, just for tonight!

Harmless, you say. Maybe. But in a culture like ours, where parents have very little time to spend with their actual children, and where an obsessive pursuit of youth has caused an 800 percent increase in cosmetic surgical procedures in ten years, a focus on becoming childlike at Christmas seems guaranteed to skew the message of the incarnation.

One of the most dramatic changes in recent decades in my own Episcopal denomination is the shift away from the adult "midnight" service on Christmas Eve to an earlier, wildly popular "family" service that, by its very nature, cannot offer much in the way of a sermon or more challenging music. I do not want to be misunderstood here; Christmas ritual can indeed be beneficial for the developing faith of children. However, if the children get the idea that Christmas is entirely for them, that there are no privileges reserved for their maturity, it does not seem likely that their faith will unfold in the direction of Good Friday. A famous painting of the annunciation in the Cloisters in New York shows the embryonic Jesus slipping down a shaft of sunlight toward Mary—and he is *already carrying his cross.* This is the hidden message of the manger. A Christmas card that I have cherished for many years features a black-and-white woodcut showing Mary and the baby in the stable—and in the background the silhouette of a devastated city with the shell of a burned window, twisted and bent, but unmistakably shaped like a cross.

Reading familiar biblical passages in their context is sometimes startling. Such is the case with one of the three Isaianic texts appointed for Christmas: " How beautiful upon the mountains are the feet of the one who brings glad tidings. . . . Break forth together into singing, you waste places of Jerusalem; for the Lord has comforted his people." This rhapsodic passage moves directly without a break into the Suffering Servant text associated with Good Friday: "His appearance was marred beyond human semblance . . . he was despised and rejected." We may not linger at the crib.

It is not easy to grow up. Maturing as a Christian means making sacrifices, delaying gratification, setting the needs of others ahead of one's own, pursuing distant goals instead of temptations ready at hand. In these stress-filled times, virtually all of us, as we get older, will seek relief by visiting, in our imaginations, a childhood Christmas of impossible perfection. These longings are powerful and can easily deceive us into grasping for a new toy, new car, new house, new spouse to fill up the empty spaces where unconditional love belongs. Our longings are powerful, our needs bottomless, our cravings insatiable, our follies numberless. For those who cannot or will not look deeply into the human condition, sentiment and nostalgia can masquerade as strategies for coping quite successfully for a while—but because it is all based on illusion and unreality, it cannot be a lasting foundation for generations to come. Christmas, someone said, is "the feast of Nicene dogma." That concept is not easy to teach or warm one's hands over without considerable effort, but it is not impossible to convey even to young children the sense that the real meaning of Christmas lies precisely in the *combination* of magical ceremonies and the grown-up message that in the very midst of our human selfishness, the waylaying love of God has broken through to us unconditionally. We may therefore sing with indescribable joy,

> God of God, Light of Light,
> Lo, he abhors not the Virgin's womb;
> Very God, begotten, not created.
> O come, let us adore him.

Suffering and Hope

*An Advent Series for Grace Church, New York City, 1987
(These very short pieces were written for the weekly
Grace Church bulletin)*

A biblical theology of hope addresses the corporate dimension of human suffering and thus incorporates individual suffering into a final solidarity of all humankind. The Christian hope in the communal resurrection of the dead, when all humankind will celebrate together the messianic meal in God's presence, will turn the solidarity of suffering into a solidarity of joy and fulfillment. The specific content of Christian hope, therefore, forms an antidote to all Christian egoism and privatization of bliss so common in American celebrations of the instant immortality of the individual soul after death. Therefore it is wrong to make claims for the ultimate salvation and heavenly joy of separate individuals until such time when the power of death and its attendant sufferings, in accordance with the biblical perspective of hope, will be lifted from all God's creatures and all humankind can rejoice together in the defeat of suffering and death in God's kingdom.

—J. Christiaan Beker

J. Christiaan Beker was well known to many at Grace Church because of his leadership of one of our parish weekends at Incarnation Camp in Ivoryton, Connecticut. Beker was known largely within the academy; his presentation at the camp may very well have been the only speaking engagement he ever undertook in such a setting. It was unforgettable.

Part 1

Our Advent series this year is inspired by J. Christiaan Beker's new book, *Suffering and Hope*.[1] No season of the church year is more appropriate to this theme. Advent invites us to reflect on the anguish, pain, and hopelessness that are all around us. Sometimes it almost seems as though there is more bad news in the paper during Advent than at any other time of year, and the lectionary readings reflect this somberness. Beker makes the point that, because of mass media, we are more aware of the world's suffering than ever before in history. As New Yorkers, we have been forced to acknowledge, these past few years, that there are people living like animals on our very doorsteps, in our most affluent neighborhoods. The Advent season is designed to lead us into an ever-deeper awareness of the solidarity of all human beings in pain and darkness. No one can count himself exempt from the distress of others.

The Bible drives home this truth in many ways. In Isaiah 64:1–9, the Old Testament reading for the first Sunday of Advent this year, the whole world is depicted under the curse of sin and is lamenting the absence of God. The religious community does not stand aside in a protected spot; on the contrary, it indicts itself first of all ("all our righteous deeds are like filthy rags") and considers itself part of the general calamity. This is the mood of lament and repentance in which Advent begins.

As my husband was brooding over a recent horror story in the newspaper, he suddenly observed, as if out of the blue, "No wonder God had to send his Son into the world." Yes. Ultimately, this is the only hope we have. But where do we see Christ in the world? "Thou hast hid thy face," writes Isaiah. Where do we discover the hope that is the preeminent Advent theme? Is there any real basis for hope? This will be the subject of the Advent series.

Part 2

The particular attraction of J. C. Beker's quest for a definition of Christian hope lies in his refusal to blink at the question of disproportionate suffering. He simply will not acquiesce in easy answers. In *Suffering and Hope* he puts forth his belief that traditional answers can be inadequate and even cruel.

1. J. Christiaan Beker, *Suffering and Hope: The Biblical Vision and the Human Predicament* (Philadelphia: Fortress, 1987). The second edition was published by Eerdmans in 1994.

Two traditional responses to the problem of arbitrary suffering have been as follows: (1) hardship strengthens us and enables us to grow; and (2) God teaches us endurance and purifies us through suffering. These explanations are true enough in some cases where strong Christian faith carries the sufferer through. But in the larger, more universal sense, they simply won't suffice.

Take the case of six-year-old Lisa, for example, battered to death by her "father" only three blocks away from Grace Church. All New York has been cut to the heart. No amount of talk about how other children will be helped can make it right. Ivan Karamazov's famous question about the suffering of one innocent child never seemed more urgent. The thought of God subjecting Lisa to such indescribable torment for pedagogical reasons is monstrous, inadmissible. Who among us would agree to the brutalization and murder of a little girl in order to move the hearts of some New Yorkers toward possibly intervening on behalf of other children somewhere along the line? In view of Jesus's saying, "What father among you, if his son asks for an egg, will give him a scorpion? If you, then, bad as you are, know how to give good gifts to your children, how much more will the Father give?" (Luke 11:11–13), we cannot explain Lisa's suffering by saying that God is bringing good out of it. God may indeed do this, but that is in no way sufficient to answer the urgent accusation.

Advent is the right time for the asking of hard questions. Advent comes to a climax, not only on Christmas Day but also in the massacre of the innocents by Herod. The church has historically observed the Feast of the Holy Innocents on December 27, a remarkable conjuncture that remembers a massacre of infants in the same season that we rejoice in the birth of Christ. The great theme of Advent is hope, but it is not tolerable to speak of hope unless we are willing to look squarely at the overwhelming presence of evil in our world. Malevolent, disproportionate evil is a profound threat to Christian faith.

Advent, along with the weeks immediately preceding it, is preeminently the season of the second coming. Many of us, growing up in theologically liberal mainline churches, had the doctrine of the second coming trained out of us. "Nobody believes in it anymore," I was told more than once by clergy. The coming of Jesus into the individual heart was preached and taught as the substitute for the second coming.

As long as there are Lisas in the world, however, we cannot be content with Jesus in the private heart alone. The victory of God over evil and barbarity will not be complete until the promised last day. We continue to look forward to the promised day when Jesus will come again, not incognito as he did the first time, but "in glory," as the Nicene Creed puts it. At the time of the second coming, "every knee shall bow and every tongue confess that Jesus Christ is

Lord, to the glory of God the Father" (Phil. 2:10–11). Then and only then will God's whole work be done; this is the "not-yet" element in the Advent season and in the biblical proclamation.

It is God, not human beings, who will have the last word. God's final triumph over evil does not depend on our success in overcoming sin and death; if it did, we would truly have no hope. We have learned this in our time; now that the Holocaust has happened, it is no longer possible to speak of progress in human goodness. The tabloids, with their shrieking headlines, remind us of this every day. The way of Christian community is not, however, to retreat from horror into the solace of personal religion, but to proclaim Christ's hope to the world (the not-yet in the now) by involving ourselves in what Beker calls "strategies of hope," like the ministries being carried out in this parish and Christian communities around the world even now.

Part 3

In a letter written last year, John Bald, retired Presbyterian pastor, former professor at Pittsburgh Seminary and brother of Grace Church's Bob Bald, had this to say about the problem of indiscriminate suffering: "What we really need is not some intellectually acceptable answer to life's most mysterious conundrum about God's action or inaction. The need is for God and the nurture of the expectation of his coming to be coupled with the patience to wait for him to come in his own time. The waiting is not easy. In his reflection on the death of his first wife, Martin Marty wrote of waiting as a time of praying what he describes as the 'Cry of Absence' [protesting the apparent silence of God] found so often in the Psalms."

One can readily see the Advent themes here. Every year, Advent begins in the dark with lessons that, in various ways, pose the question of the *Deus absconditus*, the God who hides himself. Every year, the Advent-to-Christmas momentum proclaims the God who breaks his own silence by coming in person. In an important text, John the Evangelist tells us that "No one has ever seen God; the only Son, who dwells in the bosom of the Father, he has made him known" (John 1:18). Christmas is the breaking-in Word of the silent God.

But notice that the Word of God, his Son, comes incognito at Christmas. Brueghel's panoramic painting of the event in Bethlehem depicts it; the whole world is going about its daily business, unheeding, while Jesus is being born. Similarly, in another of Brueghel's works, the wise men and their retinue thread their way unnoticed through the crowds and hubbub of a market town, as though their passing signified nothing unusual.

53

In many ways, this is still the condition of Christ's body in the world. The church must conduct its ministry of expectant waiting in a largely heedless society. The fact of the Son of God is hidden. Sometimes it seems as if he is hidden even from his own people. It is easy to become discouraged.

The church needs to be reminded of the way it has itself become the manifestation of the hope of Christ's coming again in glory. We can take courage from the fact that God has actually willed us to be witnesses of the incarnation of Christ, the hope of the world. In the present, God's Word breaks the silence as his people bear witness to their hope. When the church does this, it impresses even the skeptics; in a recent issue of the *New York Review of Books*, the celebrated journalist Murray Kempton writes these striking words:

> In the thirteenth century, Catholicism was unknown outside Europe, but it is now a universal force. From Cardinal Sin down the hierarchy to the simplest nuns, the Philippine Church was a critical factor in the overthrow of Ferdinand Marcos.
>
> A Korean archbishop is changing the face of his country's regime. In Poland and Nicaragua, Chile and El Salvador, churchmen stand reproaching and resisting the excesses of the state. Even unbelievers like myself have to concede that the Catholic Church has become the steadiest, and in many places the only, defender of human rights the wide world can show.[2]

"Reproaching and resisting." This, surely, is at the heart of the church's life in Advent. We are called to a vocation of protest against suffering. Patience does not mean passivity. Believing that God will come does not imply inaction. Rather, it stirs up the church to hopeful enactments of the reign of Christ. Everything we do in this regard, however small, from AIDS ministry to overseas missions, strikes a blow against the usurping powers and principalities until Jesus comes again in glory.

Part 4

As sign of judgment,
the earth shall run damp with sweat.

2. Murray Kempton, "Cheer Up, John Paul II," *New York Review of Books*, October 22, 1987.

Out of the heaven shall come the King who shall reign forever:
in flesh truly present,
He shall judge the world.
The old law passes on, the old rites pass away.
A virgin has brought forth
and given us a new-born son,
a healing gift,
a King and priest,
who makes the rough places plain,
strengthens the bonds of peace,
and cleanses our sins.
The bonds of sin are broken, for born is the King of glory: the flow of
      death is swallowed up and the law of grace is given to us.
It is a day of joy:
light is shed on the yoke of sinners.
A feast is now kept: therefore let us rejoice, for forgiveness of sin is
      granted.[3]

The Waverly Consort version of the Christmas story is enormously popular; the recording continues to sell well and the concert performances at the
Cloisters this year are standing room only. Like Handel's *Messiah*, this work
is frequently relished for purely musical reasons. Today in this space, we call
attention to the *words*. The theological depths that are plumbed in these texts
simply take the breath away. They date from the Middle Ages but are profoundly biblical in spirit.

The Waverly Consort program begins with the procession of the prophets,
culminating in the words printed above (translated from the Latin). The climax
of the introduction comes with the proclamation of Christ the King. The genius of this arrangement is that, in the final analysis, the Christmas story makes
no sense unless it is set in its full context—Christ the Alpha and the Omega,
the beginning and the end. The overwhelming impact of the Waverly Consort
prologue is similar to that of Saint Luke's Christmas story: the fullness of time
has arrived, the Lord is about to act, the Judge is already present with power
to save; the chorus sings, "Behold, the King gives a new law unto all creation."

The sections that are most relevant to our Advent theme of suffering and
hope, however, are "Herod's Court" and "The Slaughter of the Innocents,"
with Rachel's lament for her children familiar to us from Jeremiah 31:15. The

---

3. Prologue of "The Christmas Story," as performed by the Waverly Consort.

Waverly Consort program vividly depicts Herod and his son as vainglorious empire-builders, as recognizable in their transparently self-aggrandizing tactics as the tycoons and tyrants of today. Profoundly shaken by the Magi's news of a rival on the horizon, they plot the extermination of all possible threats: "We hear of the birth of a greater king, whose power is over us. Truly we fear that we be taken from our throne. Against that petty king, give word that the battle be begun!" (The hearers, of course, are meant to understand who the petty king is, and who the real king.)

But the climax of the entire work (unfortunately not included on the recording) is as follows: Rachel, who is the collective embodiment of all the mothers of all innocent children who have been tormented and slain, sings an eloquent lament—"Alas, tender babes, such savage wounds we see! . . . How do we bear such deeds?"

So-called consolers then sing, "Rejoice now even in your mourning, for they live now as the blessed among the stars." Rachel, refusing to be comforted, just as in the Scripture, decisively rejects their consolation: "How to rejoice when I behold these lifeless limbs?" The Pollyannas persist: "Why do you weep for the child when he has gained the Kingdom of Heaven?"

Rachel's final word is, "Great is the anguish of my soul; my heart is troubled within me." This is the last human word to be heard in the text. Speak not to me of my dead, mutilated child as a star! When we are faced with the Slaughter of the Innocents, where is there any hope to be found? We can say, indeed, that this is the last human word, period.

The next word after Rachel's lament is not a human word. It is the electrifying voice of an archangel, in the upper register, repeating the words of Jesus himself: "Suffer [allow] the little children to come unto me, for such is the Kingdom of heaven."

And the chorus responds: "O Lamb of God, who takest away the sins of the world, have mercy upon us."

Humanly speaking, there is no answer to Rachel's lament and no hope for her children's future. The only word left is the Word of God. This is the proclamation of Advent and Christmas: "The bonds of sin are broken, for born is the King of glory; the flow of death is swallowed up and the law of grace is given to us." In the midst of the trials and sufferings of this world, may we believe this promise, trust this Word, and hold to this hope until the Lord comes again.

Expectation and Hope:
Advent in the Writings of Karl Barth

A Three-Part Reflection for Grace Church
in New York City, Advent 1986

Part 1

The confluence of Advent, Karl Barth's 100th birthday, and our Reformation theme presents us with a problem: How to combine the three? More and more, Advent is being recognized today as a seven-week season devoted to the celebration of our apocalyptic hope; the lectionary readings for the last Sundays of the Pentecost season and the early weeks of Advent set the tone. So far, so good; but the apocalyptic theology of the New Testament has been rediscovered only in our own century. The Reformers did not think apocalyptically, in a conscious way (although Luther had a strong sense of "this world, with devils filled"), and Barth was only peripherally affected by this aspect of what his New Testament colleagues were doing.

A way of proceeding with these themes, however, showed itself as I read the section on hope toward the end of Barth's *Church Dogmatics*.[1] Sooner or later, being a profoundly biblical theologian above all, Barth was bound to come upon the motif of apocalyptic hope. One of the chief characteristics of the Reformation is the emphasis upon Scripture as the source of theological understanding. It was Karl Barth's careful, lifelong search of the Scriptures that led him into a profound understanding of the tension between the already and the not-yet that is the characteristic focus of the Advent season. It is Barth who writes, "What other time or season can or will the Church ever have but that of Advent?" (IV/3.1, 322).

---

1. References to Barth's *Church Dogmatics* (hereafter *CD*) will be placed in parentheses in the text, in the traditional style used for these references: volume number, followed by part number, followed by page reference.

The church's life in Advent, Barth writes, is like that of the horseman drawn by Albrecht Dürer who must ride between death and the devil. He rides confidently, knowing "his defensive and offensive strength," but he must make "this perilous passage" (IV/3.2, 230). Christians are not lifted out of the world into a life free from pain and danger. "Jesus has not yet uttered his last Word," Barth writes, until he comes again "to complete his revelation" (IV/3.2, 218). Barth emphasizes that the Jesus who will come again is the very same One who already gives us his peace and righteousness; but he wants us to understand that there is a not-yet standing over against our present existence. Conflict and contradiction are part of our lives in Advent. Our hope is in the coming triumph of God in Jesus Christ.

Part 2

When I was a child, I always loved the Advent season. We didn't have Advent wreaths and Advent calendars in those days; it was the dark purple color in the church and a certain drama in the Bible readings that impressed me. Clearly, there was something expectant and portentous about those weeks. However, I misunderstood the meaning. For many years, I thought that, during Advent, one was supposed to pretend that Jesus hadn't been born, so that we would be more excited when Christmas came.

Needless to say, this stratagem didn't work. For me, it was a revelation years later to learn that the last weeks of Pentecost and the first weeks of Advent look forward to the second coming of Christ. Even a cursory look at the Advent hymns in the Episcopal hymnal will prove the point. In Advent, we don't pretend, as I once thought, that we are in the darkness before the birth of Christ. Rather, we take a good hard look at the darkness we are in now, facing and defining it honestly, so that we will understand with utmost clarity that our great and only hope is in Jesus's final victorious coming.

Barth, in his chapter on hope in the *Church Dogmatics*, identifies three forms of threat that oppress us in our Advent life:

- Christians are a relatively small, besieged minority in the world. (One might add that this is true even in America, where Christianity appears to be far more popular than in Europe, for instance; but often this is a prosperous, middle-class version of Christianity bearing little resemblance to the real thing.)

- We ourselves must live with constant reminders that even though we know Jesus to be ahead of us assuring our righteousness and holiness, nevertheless our own unrighteousness and unholiness are, as Barth writes, "still behind [us] in ever new forms and with only too powerful a grasp" (IV/3.2, 232).
- The judgment of Christ upon our witness as Christians still lies ahead. "It is an intolerably bitter thing for [the Christian] to be confronted by this limit. For what courage or confidence can he have in the execution of his service when . . . he can have no knowledge whether even that which he has done with the best intentions and in exercise of his finest powers will finally be approved as serviceable or rejected as worthless?" (IV/3.2, 234).

The emphasis here on human weakness and incapacity is characteristic of Barth and of the Reformation. The theological atmosphere in America at present is inimical to this position; we live in a culture that prefers to emphasize "the power of positive thinking." Human potential is the watchword today, and is touted as a hopeful, optimistic philosophy in comparison to gloomy old Puritan Christianity with its emphasis on sin and judgment.

What a terrible misunderstanding! For one thing, religious systems that ignore the dark side of life are fundamentally dishonest (all the great poets know this). But, even more important, utterly lacking in such points of view is the true joy and robust humor that lie at the heart of biblical faith (and the faith of the Reformation is, above all, biblical). Karl Barth's theology is best described, in fact, as a theology of joy and humor.

It is precisely the coming judgment of Christ, Barth writes, that is the sure foundation of our hope. We live "in expectation of eternal light." As we stand in the darkness of this present order, we look forward to the redemption of the whole creation, as Paul says in Romans 8. The Christian sees and acknowledges "the continuing sin of men and above all of himself among them," but "he expects the coming of Jesus Christ in glory. . . . This implies something forceful and decisive. . . . It means even for him, too, glory and reward and gain. It means pardon in the final and strictest sense. . . . It means his translation out of the darkness around into the great coming light" (IV/3.2, 244).

Christian hope, the Bible and the Reformation insist, is in God alone. "It is not the Christian trying to help out his feeble faith and love with a little hope, but Jesus Christ already present now as the One He will be in the consummation of His revelation, who actually makes his hope the power which sustains his faith and gives wings to his love to-morrow no less than to-day" (IV/3.2, 229).

Elsewhere Barth writes, "When . . . any one of us . . . looks up to him, to Jesus Christ, a momentous change takes place. . . . A great and enduring light brightly dawns on such a person. . . . Such a person experiences joy in the midst of his sorrows and sufferings, much as he still may sigh and grumble. Not a cheap and superficial joy that passes, but deep-seated, lasting joy. It transforms man in his sadness into a fundamentally joyful being. We may as well admit it; he has got something to laugh at . . . not a mockery, but an open and relaxing laughter . . . honest and sincere laughter, coming from the bottom of man's heart. Such light and joy and laughter are ours when we look up to him, to Jesus Christ. He is the one who makes us radiant."[2]

Part 3

Does Advent run backwards? The movement is from the second coming to the first coming; it doesn't seem to make sense. The season begins with the last things and ends with the nativity in Bethlehem. Shouldn't it be the other way round?

Not really. The rhythm of the church's seasons turns out, in this as in so many other ways, to be theologically profound. If we began with the nativity and then moved to the last judgment, we would be so softened up by that little baby in the manger that we wouldn't be able to take the second coming of Christ in power seriously. The solemnity and awe do not lie in the fact that the baby becomes the eternal Judge. What strikes us to the heart is this: the eternal Judge, very God of very God, Creator of the worlds, the Alpha and the Omega, has become that little baby.

We must, as Karl Barth writes, "pass into the burning, searching, purifying fire of the gracious judgment of the One who comes" (IV/3.2, 931). In Advent, we pause to take stock of this uniquely sobering fact. Only if we do so can we truly understand what it means to know that this very One has submitted himself to the ignominy, humiliation, and disgrace of human life on our behalf. In a sermon for the Christmas season, Barth proclaims,

> He does not need us. He could very easily do without us. [But] he is deeply moved by our need of him, our bitter, inescapable need. Is this perhaps the casualness and condescension of a great ruler, occasionally bending down to the man in the street? Not in the least. He takes

2. Karl Barth, *Deliverance to the Captives* (Eugene, OR: Wipf and Stock, 1978), 46–47.

our place and surrenders himself for us, thereby binding himself to us and compromising himself once for all. He is the God of Christmas of whom we sing: "A tiny child and poor he came To give us mercy's blessing." This is the height and depth, the ultimate and eternal power and glory of the almighty Lord; he has mercy on us.[3]

3. Karl Barth, "Remember the Lord," in *Deliverance to the Captives*, 112.

"Something Evil This Way Comes"

Many people are raised to believe in innocence. Their parents or families of origin tend toward optimism and the bright side of things. They are devoted to "all things bright and beautiful." They don't have much experience with all things negative and nihilistic. In their families, they were taught to "keep on the sunny side of life."

The Bible, however, is not a sunny-sided book. It is full of "plague, pestilence, and famine; battle, murder, and sudden death," as the older version of the Litany puts it. Here's what Jesus himself told his disciples:

> "When you hear of wars and rumors of wars, do not be alarmed; this must take place, but the end is not yet. For nation will rise against nation . . . there will be earthquakes in various places, there will be famines. . . . Take heed to yourselves; for they will deliver you up to councils; and you will be beaten in synagogues; . . . brother will deliver up brother to death, and the father his child, and children will rise against parents and have them put to death; and you will be hated by everyone for my name's sake. But he who endures to the end will be saved. . . . Take heed; *I have told you all things beforehand.*" (Mark 13:7–13, 23)

This was given as an evening address at Trinity Episcopal Cathedral, Columbia, South Carolina, for Advent 2015. The title is that of a book by Ray Bradbury. Much of this material can be found in more depth in the chapters "The Descent into Hell" and "The Apocalyptic War: Christus Victor" in my book *The Crucifixion: Understanding the Death of Jesus Christ* (Grand Rapids: Eerdmans, 2015).

"I have told you all things beforehand." The Master tells his disciples what they should expect from the world as they go out to preach the gospel. Here is something similar from the first epistle of Peter: "Be sober, be watchful. Your adversary the devil prowls around like a roaring lion, seeking some one to devour. Resist him, firm in your faith, knowing that the same experience of suffering is required of your brotherhood throughout the world" (I Pet. 5:8–9). And think of the Lord's Prayer: "Lead us not into temptation, but deliver us from evil."

Evil is everywhere present in the world of the Bible. In the New Testament, the devil is a leading character. The devil, of course, is not a man in a red suit with a pitchfork. We all understand that. What is he, then? We need to know.

People are—of course—different, and people are brought up differently. In any group, you will find some who are sunny-side people. Chances are they grew up in a family where negative thoughts and feelings were suppressed. Other families are willing to confront evil, but often without fully understanding what "evil" is. The natural human tendency is to project evil onto other people and other groups. I am focusing, this evening, not so much on "evil *people*" or even evil *deeds*, but on the theological discussion called "the problem of evil." This arises from the perpetual question: How can there be an all-powerful and all-loving God when there is so much evil in the world? And why doesn't God put a stop to it?

Let me say right here at the beginning: no one has ever come up with a satisfactory answer to the problem of evil. A lot of philosophers and theologians have tried, but none of the attempts have stood up to scrutiny. I'm going to give away my main points here, at the beginning: If you ask me how God can allow so much evil, here's the answer: We don't know. Nobody knows the answer to the problem of evil. And yet it is in a sense the most important of all theological problems, and we should never lose sight of it.[1]

The classic definition of evil is "the absence of good," *privatio boni* in Latin. I never liked that definition, because it sounded weak to me, lacking purpose and agency.[2] The Bible personifies evil in the figure of Satan, which

---

1. Many have praised David B. Hart's little book, *The Doors of the Sea: Where Was God in the Tsunami?* (Grand Rapids: Eerdmans, 2005), as the best treatment of the problem of evil that we have. It takes essentially the same position stated here.

2. Among the Greek fathers, Gregory of Nyssa makes the point well: "All wickedness is marked by the absence of good [*steresis agathou* in Greek]. It does not exist in its own right, nor is it observed to have subsistence. . . . Nonbeing has no subsistence; and the Creator of what exists is not the Creator of what has no subsistence" (*Address on Religious Instruction* 282). Gregory compares evil to blindness, which is a privation of light.

embodies purpose and agency. Jesus himself refers to this figure in several ways: Satan; the devil; "the ruler of this world" (John 12:31); Beelzebul, the chief of the demons (Luke 11:15). Flannery O'Connor had a particularly sophisticated understanding of the devil, whom she depicted in various disguises in her stories. She wrote that "Our salvation is played out with the Devil, a Devil who is not simply generalized evil, but an evil intelligence determined on its own supremacy."[3]

J. R. R. Tolkien did a good job of depicting evil as an active agency in *The Lord of the Rings* (the book, not the movie so much), and his friend C. S. Lewis wrote the best imaginative description of the devil that I have ever read, in *Perelandra*.[4] The main idea to hold on to is that there is an evil power loose in the world, independent of human beings, a power that has an agenda of its own, and this power can only be defeated by another power greater than itself. Unaided human beings can make no lasting headway against evil. Don't you think this is obvious by now? We have an example right in front of us. To try to get ahead of the Islamic state (ISIS), which is Sunni, we have to do business in Iraq with the Shiite militias from—of all countries—Iran. It would be a joke if it weren't so serious. All this is in the name of making a better world.

The last movie that the greatly beloved actor Philip Seymour Hoffman made before he died of a heroin overdose (speaking of evil) was *A Most Wanted Man*. I watched it last week on DVD. It takes place in the present time. Hoffman plays a German intelligence agent working to identify terrorist organizations. He is the hard-drinking, chain-smoking, disheveled, highly skilled leader of a team of operatives who have been recruiting young Muslims to penetrate the terrorist networks. Hoffman's character is decent but cynical. He wants

---

3. Flannery O'Connor, letter to John Hawkes, November 20, 1959, in *The Habit of Being* (New York: Farrar, Straus and Giroux, 1979).

4. "Some critics have suggested that Dante failed to produce as impressive a Devil as Milton later did, but this explanation misses his point. Dante specifically intended Lucifer to be empty, foolish, and contemptible, a futile contrast to God's energy. Dante viewed evil as negation and would have thought Milton's Devil much too active and effective. . . . [Dante agrees with] scholastic theology in limiting the Devil's role. . . . The lack of dramatic action on the part of Dante's Lucifer is a deliberate statement about his essential lack of being. Satan's true being is *his lack of being, his futility and nothingness*. There he is in the dark at the very dead center of the earth, where sins have sunk to their proper place" (Jeffrey Burton Russell, *Lucifer: The Devil in the Middle Ages* [Ithaca, NY: Cornell University Press, 1984], 225 [emphasis added]). In *Perelandra*, the second novel in his space trilogy, C. S. Lewis comes close to success in portraying the obscene, vulgar stupidity of evil. There is nothing magnetic or attractive in his devil; indeed, the reader experiences magnetic repulsion. Lewis's descriptions of the devil are memorable in this regard.

to do the right thing but fully understands the nature of the compromises he must make. (This is all based on a novel by John le Carré, and you know how his work exposes moral ambiguities.). It's been necessary for him to join forces with an American diplomatic attaché in Berlin (played by Robin Wright in her best *House of Cards* villainess mode). They have a conversation in a tavern. He asks her why she and he do what they do. She says (not without cynicism), "To make this a better world." He looks at her with an expression that silently conveys a mixture of incredulity and contempt. At the end of the movie we learn what kind of supposedly better world she has made.

Quite a few thinkers have reflected on the fact that we are indeed unable to make a better world because we cannot get a grip on evil. Andrew Delbanco, a professor at Columbia University, wrote a book called *The Death of Satan*. He is an antireligious unbeliever, and yet he writes this lament: "Our culture is now in crisis because evil remains an inescapable experience for all of us [and yet we have lost our] symbolic language for describing it."[5] But I'm arguing here that Christians do still have that symbolic language for evil, and it's the best and most robust account of evil that there is. I'm just trying to sketch it out here.

The horrors of World War II forced many to reach back for a stronger symbolism. Robert Coles of Harvard, for instance, wrote this: "[The twentieth] century has not treated [eighteenth- and nineteenth-century optimism] kindly. The Devil, has, in a sense, returned—our struggle, these days, is to find a way of thinking about the radical evil that lives all too comfortably in our communities. . . . our usual secular pieties don't quite work in the face of our recent dark past."[6]

Coles wrote that toward the end of the twentieth century. The terror attacks of September 11, 2001, and more recent events have had a similar effect in the twenty-first century. These phenomena have pushed us beyond the familiar, manageable categories of right and wrong. The essayist Lance Morrow writes about the difference between "evil" and mere "wrong." He would have trouble, he says, calling the Nazi "Final Solution" or the torture-murder of a child "wrong." "A crucial difference between wrong and evil is that people are implicitly in charge of the universe in which rights and wrongs are discussed; people have systems of laws to right wrongs. But *evil implies a different universe*, controlled by extra-human forces. Wrong is a human offense

---

5. Andrew Delbanco, *The Death of Satan: How Americans Have Lost the Sense of Evil* (New York: Farrar, Straus and Giroux, 1995), 223.

6. Robert Coles, "Eternally Evil and Never out of Work," review of *Mephistopheles*, by Jeffrey Burton Russell, *New York Times Book Review*, March 8, 1987.

that suggests [that] reparation is possible. . . . Wrong is not mysterious. [But] *Evil suggests a mysterious force that may be in business for itself* and may exploit human agency as part of *a larger cosmic conflict*—between good and evil, God and Satan."[7]

That precisely describes the symbolic universe of the New Testament Gospels, particularly found in the letters of Saint Paul. I think the best way to begin understanding this is to note that there are three actors, or forces, on the stage, not two. Most accounts of the Christian life refer to two actors: there's God, and there's the human being. The human being is pictured as making a journey to God. A great deal of what's being taught in the Episcopal Church and the other mainline churches is based on this idea of the spiritual journey we are supposed to be making. And yet there is remarkably little of this in the New Testament. The New Testament is not about our journey toward God. It's about what Karl Barth calls "the journey of the Son of God to the far country." And when the incarnate Son arrives in this far country, what does he find? He finds that it is occupied by a great Power. So in the New Testament story, there are not two actors, but three: God, humanity, and the great Enemy—Satan, the devil, or what Paul calls the Power of Sin and Death.

Why is there evil in the world? We don't know why, but we know that it is a terrible Power and that, against it, unaided human beings are helpless. The Power of Sin and Death is external to the human being, working on us from outside, so that, in the words of one of our great prayers, "we have no power of ourselves to help ourselves."[8] We are in bondage to Sin and Death. We are "tied and bound by the chain of our sins."[9] This is the subject of a good deal of the Epistle to the Romans: Paul writes that Sin is able to "work death in [us]" *even "through what is good"* (Rom. 7:13). You know the saying "No good deed goes unpunished." That's a helpful way of understanding what Paul is getting at. Good intentions get twisted. Attempts to help often turn out badly. Sin is able to "work death in [us]" even "through what is good." We have no control over this in and of ourselves, any more than we can stave off the approach of Death when the hour comes. Only God has the power to overcome the evil working of the Enemy. This is the message that is foreseen in the great story of Joseph, in the book of Genesis. Joseph's older brothers sold him into slavery in Egypt; imagine that, grown men selling their own little brother into slavery because they were jealous of him! Many years later, after many adventures,

7. Lance Morrow, *Evil* (New York: Basic Books, 2003), 51 (emphasis added).
8. Collect for the third Sunday in Lent, 1979 Book of Common Prayer, 167.
9. Penitential Office for Ash Wednesday, 1928 Book of Common Prayer.

Joseph is reunited with his brothers. When they fall on their knees to ask his forgiveness for what they did to him, he says to them, "It was not you who sent me here, but God. . . . You meant evil against me, but God meant it for good, to bring it about that many people would be kept alive, as they are today" (Gen. 45:8; 50:20).

So in the very first book of the Bible, we learn that God is able to overturn the forces of evil and bring good into being. In New Testament terms, Satan is a great enemy agent, but God is a greater agent for good. This is striking, since it's the book of Genesis that tells us how evil came to rule over the creation in the first place. Or, rather, how evil arrived in the *second* place—a far distant second place. The first place is always God's. In Genesis 1, we read that when God finished his work of creation, "God saw everything that he had made, and behold, it was very good" (Gen. 1:31).

Evil, therefore, is not part of the creation. That's why the definition *privatio boni*, the absence of good, is such an important idea, in spite of its apparent blandness. Although evil made its appearance in the creation, it possesses no existence or being of its own, but is rather a negation, or corruption, of being. Only God has Being, and only God can create Being. Evil therefore is a great nullity, an X factor, a parasite on the good.

Having said all this, we are still faced with the difficulty of describing evil as nonbeing; it seems to lack force and malignity. And, if evil was not created by God, how did the serpent get into the garden of Eden? Again, we don't know, and the book of Genesis does not tell us. My grandmother read me the story of the creation and the Fall to me when I was not yet eight years old, and now, after all these years, it seems to me deeper and wiser and more miraculous than ever. Saint Paul makes a great deal of the Adam and Eve story in Romans, but you don't get the feeling that he's talking about historical people. He's talking in mythic terms about a great primordial catastrophe, whatever it was, which admitted evil and godlessness into God's good creation. The story of the disobedience of Eve and Adam has never been fully plumbed; that is part of its surpassing greatness. It tells us what we need to know about ourselves, that we are "bent" (C. S. Lewis) out of shape from our conception because "in sin hath my mother conceived me" (Ps. 51:5). This has nothing to do with sex being sinful. It's about the fact that Sin is, as W. H. Auden wrote, "bred in the bone," or, as we would say less poetically today, it's in the DNA.[10]

---

10. Auden wrote that in September 1939, when Hitler invaded Poland. In doing so, he did not divide the good English people from the wicked German people. He identified the

The occasion for this presentation right now is the fact that I think most of us realize that in our time we have crossed some sort of boundary into new territory. The sunny-siders have been dragged willy-nilly out of their safe places. We are beginning to see more clearly now that no office, school, or church is truly safe; that the Internet has greatly increased our capacity to share lethal information; that terror is only a click away. Moreover, too many clergy have been arrested for child molestation, too many teachers have been caught sexually abusing students, too many supposedly upstanding citizens have downloaded too much child pornography. There is something ugly lurking in human nature.

This is the atmosphere of the Advent season. It's time to put away sentimentality and face up to the Enemy. The readings for the season speak of the final judgment of God upon the enslaving Powers. This is our great hope: that the cycle of evil and destruction will be broken and the creation will be set free and healed. This is the promise of the second coming of Christ. But, I don't need to tell you, this is not a call for us to be passive. On the contrary, Advent summons us to take a fearless inventory of our own hearts. No one is free from the Power of Sin and Death. No one has power in himself to help himself. No one can say to herself, well, I'm not a murderer, so I'm not so bad. The widely admired writer Primo Levi was a survivor of Auschwitz. He wrote that the Holocaust showed us that "Man, the human species—we, in short—[have] the potential to construct an infinite enormity of pain, and that pain is the only force *created from nothing,* without cost and without effort. It is enough *not to see, not to listen, not to act.*"[11]

There is no one in this room—including the speaker—who is not guilty of failing to see, failing to listen, failing to act. If there was no insatiable appetite for narcotics in America, there would be no murderous drug cartels in Mexico. If pornography was not a multibillion-dollar industry, young people's minds would not be full of distortion. If we did not put our prisons out of sight, out of mind, there would not be so much potential for inmates coming out worse than when they went in. If we had not abandoned our American standards out of fear, the CIA would not have created "dark sites" for torture.[12] And so on and so forth. Americans are complicit in many evils.

---

evil as the condition of all humanity. J. R. R. Tolkien did the same in his epic (which Auden admired) and in his private letters.

11. Primo Levi, *The Drowned and the Saved* (New York: Vintage Books, 1988), 86 (emphasis added). Only God can create something good *ex nihilo*, out of nothing.

12. Some of the best work on how the American government went over to what Dick Cheney famously referred to as "the dark side" was done by Jane Mayer, *The Dark Side* (New York: Doubleday, 2008).

Just preparing this talk has convinced me once again that the Christian account of evil is unlike any other. We do not and cannot know how and why evil happens, and why God lets it continue. None of the attempts to explain this have ever worked. But at every point along the way in the biblical story, evil is faced for what it is, taken with the utmost seriousness, identified as the ultimate Enemy not only of God but especially of humanity, bent on destruction, malevolent and determined. At every point in the New Testament, this Power is present and active and named: the Power of Sin and Death, Satan, the devil, "the ruler of this world" (John 12:31; 14:30; 16:11), "the prince of the power of the air who is at work in those who are disobedient" toward God (Eph. 2:2). The calling of the Christian is to resist this evil. To repeat what Peter says: "Your adversary the devil prowls around like a roaring lion, seeking some one to devour. Resist him, firm in your faith."

Resistance to the power of evil and Sin is central to Christian identity. It is crucial to discern those times when it is sinful "not to see, not to listen, not to act." Unfortunately, however, we so often cannot even agree on what to resist, because we find ourselves on opposite sides of so many issues. Abraham Lincoln found himself in that situation at the end of the Civil War. His famous Second Inaugural Address is widely recognized today as one of the greatest of all theological reflections on the mystery of evil and the universality of human failure. Lincoln knew that neither the South nor the North was free from blame for the terrible war, so that he was able to summon *both* sides to the work of reconciliation. The American civil rights movement is another case in point. Part of the greatness of Martin Luther King was that he recognized Sin in himself. That enabled him, like Lincoln, to be nonpartisan in his cause. He had a deep sense of the suffering love of Jesus for *all* sinful human beings.[13] Therefore, it can be said that both Lincoln and Martin Luther King raised resistance to a higher level. They were speaking and acting in the conviction that the work of reconciliation belongs to God and that God can, and will, work through profoundly flawed human beings to accomplish his purpose of defeating evil—the evil without, and the evil within.

The promise of the second coming tells us that God is Victor over Sin and Death. It tells us that evil is vanquished *now*, in suffering love, and *will be*

---

13. It is well known that Martin Luther King continually referred to the liberation of whites as well as blacks. The civil rights movement will always be known as one of the few moments in history when there was absolute clarity in a resistance movement. Most such movements are smaller, more conflicted, less world-historical; but each of us in our own lives needs to discern those moments when being a Christian requires us to identify and resist Sin when we see it, especially when it is within ourselves.

vanquished forever in the triumph of God. I cannot tell you why God delays that day, and neither can anyone else. I can only tell you that when we see the resistance of Christians, we see living witness to the hope that is in our Lord Jesus Christ. Those who believe in God hold to the biblical promise that some day we will know the answers in the kingdom of God—and at that point it will no longer make any difference, because *there will no longer be even a memory of evil*.[14]

> Then I saw a new heaven and a new earth; for the first heaven and the first earth had passed away, and the sea was no more. And I saw the holy city, new Jerusalem, coming down out of heaven from God, prepared as a bride adorned for her husband; and I heard a loud voice from the throne saying, "Behold, the dwelling of God is with men. He will dwell with them, and they shall be his people, and God himself will be with them; he will wipe away every tear from their eyes, and death shall be no more, neither shall there be mourning nor crying nor pain any more, for the former things have passed away." (Rev. 21:1–4)

Amen, come, Lord Jesus.

---

14. See Miroslav Volf, *The End of Memory* (Grand Rapids: Eerdmans, 2006).

THE SERMONS

Waiting and Hastening
the Kingdom Yet to Come (Pre-Advent)

Waiting and Hastening

Saint Michael and Saint George Episcopal Church,
Saint Louis, Missouri
Second Sunday of Advent 1999

II PETER 3:11-13

As a general rule, Americans are a people of action. We don't take long lunches like the French. We don't take siestas like the Spanish. We don't look forward to our pensions like the English. We don't wait for the crosswalk light to change like the Germans. We aren't fatalistic like the Bangladeshi. Is there anyone I haven't offended yet? All kidding and stereotyping aside, I think it's safe to say that we Americans think of ourselves as busy, busy, busy making things happen. We are the go-go people, and we are a bit impatient with those who aren't full of energy as we are. We don't like passivity. We don't like waiting around.

So the theme of *waiting and watching* that permeates the Advent season strikes a false note with us. We give lip service to it, but we don't take it very seriously. We don't want to sit around watching and waiting. We want to speed things up. We want to move things along. If God isn't going to bring the kingdom, we'll bring it ourselves. That's our American way. I don't mean this lightly; I think we need to ask ourselves seriously, what are we going to do with this tiresome Advent refrain about watching and waiting? Most of the readings at this time of the church year sound that note; you've heard it for three Sundays in a row, and we meet it again today in the Epistle from II Peter. The Bridegroom has been delayed. The Master is a long time coming, a lot longer than we expected.[1] Shouldn't we forget about the theme of the second coming of Christ and get on with the job ourselves? And isn't that a good reason for being Episcopalians instead of fundamentalists? We don't believe this business about a second coming, do we?

---

1. Read on the Sundays immediately preceding Advent were the parable of the wise and foolish virgins waiting for the Bridegroom, the parable of the talents in which servants wait for their master to return, and Jesus's description of the last judgment.

That is the question that the preacher must ask herself at this time in the church year, because Advent is not really the season of preparing for Jesus's birth, as though he had never come in the first place. Advent is the season of preparation for his coming again. Whenever I undertake a sermon on this theme, I must examine my own heart and mind. You may think that preachers just get up and say these things as a matter of course, but that's not so. I'm a modern, urban person like you; I don't want to be classified with the Christian Right or the sectarian fanatics. Do I really believe Jesus is coming back, not just coming to individual souls one by one in their own hearts, but coming to call the entire universe into judgment, coming to bring history as we know it to a close, coming to bring his everlasting kingdom to pass? That's what the New Testament sets before us—not a private, invisible, spiritualized coming of Christ but a cosmic event that will be visible to everyone. "Every eye will now behold him, robed in dreadful majesty."[2] This claim that the church makes is too serious to fool around with. If we don't mean it, we should put an end to Advent. We should take the phrase out of the Nicene Creed: "He will come again with glory to judge the living and the dead." We shouldn't say that every Sunday if we can't believe it.

The second epistle of Peter, appointed for today, is the last piece of the New Testament to be written, and it addresses several familiar questions. Why has so much time gone by? Why has Christ not come back? Is he really coming back? Isn't the creation going to just go along on its own (II Pet. 3:4)? "Mockers [scoffers] will come in the last days," writes the apostle, saying, "Where is the promise of his coming?" You Christians are absurd, say these scoffers; only the gullible and superstitious believe such things. So, you see, we are not the first to be skeptical about the second coming. I will tell you honestly, I very often ask myself, who am I kidding? An actual day of judgment? Jesus coming with the clouds of heaven? The kingdoms of this world becoming the kingdom of our Lord (Rev. 11:15)? The Bible offers no proof of this, and the entire apparatus of modern science would seem to undermine it so conclusively that we would be fools to go on believing in it.

Rereading II Peter, however, I was caught by surprise once again, as I have been so many times before by the Scripture. The writer who speaks for the apostle Peter says, "For we did not follow cleverly devised myths when we made known to you the power and coming of our Lord Jesus Christ, but we were eyewitnesses of his majesty" (II Pet. 1:16). Here, in just one verse, are the factors that keep me coming back again and again to a position of trust

2. Charles Wesley, "Lo, He Comes with Clouds Descending."

in spite of my many doubts. There is something different about the tone of the New Testament witness, something out of the ordinary. These men and women were staking their very lives, literally, on something that had been seen and corroborated by a large number of other witnesses whom they, in turn, trusted. It is not cult-like or weird, however; there is something sober, worldly, disingenuous about the New Testament. Its atmosphere is not what you would call "religious" at all. It is much more straightforward. It is full of real people with real faults, recognizably like ourselves, who nevertheless have a report to make: we are not following a myth, we were eyewitnesses of his majesty, we are testifying of his power and his future coming. The more I read the Bible, the more I trust the sobriety of these witnesses, their plainness, their lack of ostentation. It is a world away from the self-absorbed "spiritual" writers of today like Deepak Chopra and Marianne Williamson.

Trusting the apostolic testimony, then, means entering upon a life lived in the expectation of Christ's coming, and this brings us back to the very un-American idea of waiting. The first Sunday of Advent focuses on this theme. The Gospel lesson on that day always contains these words of Jesus: "Of that day or that hour no one knows, not even the angels in heaven, nor the Son, but only the Father. Take heed, watch; for you do not know when the time will come . . . and what I say to you I say to all: Watch. Wait! Keep awake!" (Mark 13:32–33, 37, also Matt. 24:42 and Luke 21:36). A related Advent image is that of the watchman who sits all night looking for the dawn. It all sounds very passive, as though there were absolutely nothing we can do to hasten things along.

And so, we come to our passage today from II Peter, with its fascinating pair of matched but opposing words; listen for them: "Since all these things [everything mortal and perishable] are thus to be dissolved, what sort of persons ought you to be in lives of holiness and godliness, waiting for and hastening the coming of the day of God, because of which the heavens will be kindled and dissolved, and the elements will melt with fire! But according to his promise we wait for new heavens and a new earth in which righteousness dwells."

Waiting and hastening! How can you wait and hasten at the same time? That, my fellow Americans, is the secret of the Christian life, knowing how to keep those two modes in creative tension, "*waiting for and hastening* the coming of the day of God . . . [the] new heavens and a new earth in which righteousness dwells." This is so typical of Advent, the time of contrasts and opposites: darkness and light, good and evil, past and future, now and not-yet. Finding the right balance between *waiting and hastening* is the challenge of our existence in the body of Christ until he comes again. We might call it "action in waiting."

The action part, the hastening part, is easy for us. That we understand. Tear down that old building, open up the new branch, build a new parking garage, start a new ad campaign, test the latest brand. "Move it!" we say. We're used to thinking in terms of hastening. The hard part is this waiting. What is the point of waiting? What are we waiting for? Why not get on with whatever it is?

Whatever it is, is this: "the new heaven and the new earth in which righteousness dwells"; and no one can bring that about except God. Every year the Christmas cards go out, "Peace on Earth," and maybe we Americans can fool ourselves that there can be such a thing, but that would be to ignore the fact that three-fourths of the world's population are living in misery. Maybe there are some people who still think that humankind can accomplish peace on earth, but I don't know who they are, not after the century we have just lived through. At the turn of the last century, plenty of people thought that an age of peace and harmony was just around the corner, but not any more, not after millions dead in the First World War, millions in the Holocaust, millions in Stalin's gulag, more millions in Mao's China, another million in Cambodia and another million in Rwanda—it is a commonplace now to hear the twentieth century described as the most violent and most murderous in history. As Jason Epstein points out in a compelling recent essay, "Always Time to Kill," there is no end to human wickedness and folly.[3] The waiting of the Christian church, therefore, is the waiting and longing and hoping expressed in the haunting cry at the very end of the Bible: "*Maranatha*: Come, Lord Jesus" (Rev. 22:20). Not until the final intervention of God in the last day will the true and lasting peaceable kingdom come. That is the not-yet of Advent. That is why we wait. "Thou must save, and thou alone."[4]

We come to our climactic question. If only God can bring peace and good will, if only God can create "a new heaven and a new earth in which righteousness dwells," then what is the point in our doing anything? If there's nothing we can do to improve the situation, then we really might as well withdraw into a private world of gated communities, exclusive clubs, and personal privilege and enjoy it as best we can before we are overtaken by cancer or senility.

Here's where the "action in waiting" comes in, the "hastening." It's all a matter of what we're pointing toward. Let's look for a moment at another section of II Peter. Speaking of the promises of God, the apostolic writer says, "We have the prophetic word made more sure. . . . Pay attention to this as to a

3. Jason Epstein, "Always Time to Kill," *New York Review of Books*, November 4, 1999.
4. Augustus Montague Toplady, "Rock of Ages."

lamp shining in a dark place, until the day dawns and the morning star rises in your hearts" (II Pet. 1:19). There's the Advent message, right there.

> Hark, a thrilling voice is sounding;
> Christ is nigh, it seems to say;
> Cast away the works of darkness,
> O ye children of the day![5]

The church responds to the "thrilling voice" by doing the works of the day, the works of the light, the ministry to the prisoners, the soup and sandwiches for the hungry, the houses for the low-income families, the birthday parties for the children who have no parties.[6] These are lamps shining in dark places. These are works that glorify Christ while we wait for him. This is action while waiting.

Just last Tuesday, here in Saint Louis, a plaque was unveiled to commemorate the *Dred Scott* decision of 1857, in which the US Supreme Court ruled that the slave couple Dred and Harriet Scott, being black, had "no rights which the white man is bound to respect." Those words are engraved on the bronze plaque, which has been installed at the Old Courthouse downtown where the Scotts first brought suit. The *Dred Scott* decision was one of the events that precipitated the Civil War. The Scotts' great-grandson, John Madison Jr., was in attendance at the unveiling, with his family, and he said, "We're extremely proud of our great-grandparents who were willing to stand up and say it was time to do something about slavery."[7] Thus, out of the courage of one slave couple and the most bloody conflict ever waged on American soil, God wrought a transformation resulting, almost one hundred years later, in the 1954 *Brown v. Board of Education* decision in which the US Supreme Court unanimously overturned "separate but equal." Did human beings do this, or did God do this? No one would be quicker to respond to that question than the black leaders of the civil rights movement, who never tired of saying that God had made "a way out of no way." Thus, the erection of a simple bronze plaque in downtown Saint Louis becomes a signpost on the way to God's kingdom, "a lamp shining in a dark place, until the day dawns and the morning star rises in the hearts of us all," black and white and brown alike.

5. "Hark! A Thrilling Voice Is Sounding," hymn by an anonymous hymn writer, sixth century, in Latin.

6. Various ministries carried out from Saint Michael and Saint George's parish.

7. Tim O'Neil, "Dred Scott Case Is Remembered with New Plaque," *St. Louis Post-Dispatch*, December 1, 1999.

Waiting and hastening the day of God. Here is one more story from the newspapers, an Advent story, a Hanukkah story, a little story about darkness and light. No Supreme Court decisions issued from it, no mighty movements came of it, no commemorative events have happened around it. Yet it, too, is a wondrous image of God's coming kingdom. Picture a tidy residential street in an American suburb, ending in a cul-de-sac, lined with ten or fifteen attractive houses. Most of them are gentile homes, but one is Jewish. It is December, and that house has a menorah in the window for the celebration of Hanukkah. One night, vandals smash the window, remove the menorah, throw it on the ground, and scribble a swastika on the side of the house. The next night—can you imagine it?—the next night, every house on the street had a menorah burning in its window, *lamps shining in a dark place, until the day dawns and the morning star rises in the hearts of us all.*

Now, that was all the information there was in the newspaper article about this event.[8] But we can read between the lines of that news story. Do you think each one of those non-Jewish families had a menorah sitting in their closet? Of course not. This could not have been an entirely spontaneous event. We may be certain that during the day following the anti-Semitic vandalism, there was one person who thought to himself or herself, "We need to do something." Maybe that person talked to a neighbor. Maybe a couple or a family at breakfast dreamed up the idea of the menorahs in every window. Then what? Somebody had to call everyone else on the street and get them to agree, then someone had to find out where to get a whole bunch of menorahs, then somebody had to collect the money and maybe take off from work to go buy them and take them to every house. A lot of little actions, little decisions, little sacrifices had to be made before all those menorahs went into those windows. Lots of different people had to make quick decisions to help or not to help. These kinds of things don't just happen.

Dear friends of Saint Michael and Saint George's parish, we all stand on the threshold of God's kingdom. We never know from moment to moment when an opportunity might be presented to us. The church in its sinfulness has done so much damage over the years, so much harm to blacks, Jews, foreigners, unbelievers of all sorts and conditions, but it is not too late. The Lord is still out in front of us. His future still approaches, his future in which all will

---

8. Later, I found a detailed story about the menorahs. Jennifer Preston, "Menorahs Bloom from Act of Vandalism," *New York Times*, December 13, 1996, http://www.nytimes.com/1996/12/13/us/menorahs-bloom-from-act-of-vandalism.html?mcubz=0. Later still, I discovered that there had been a similar action in Billings, Montana, seven years before.

be made new. His promise is sure; he will come. We make ready for him, this Advent season and every season, by lighting whatever little lights the Lord has put in front of us, no light too small to be used by him, action in waiting, pointing ahead, looking to Christ and for Christ. Even our smallest lights will be signs in this world, lights to show the way, beachheads to hold against the Enemy until the day when the great Conqueror lands with Michael the archangel at the head of his troops, the day that *shall dawn upon us from on high, to give light to those who sit in darkness and in the shadow of death, to guide our feet into the way of peace* (Luke 1:78–79).[9]

Amen.

9. On the previous day, many parishioners had attended an Advent Day that focused on the "signs and beachheads" that Christians hold in the world until the final victory of Christ. Saint Michael is especially mentioned as being the patron saint of the parish.

The End of the Ice Age

Grace Church, New York City
November 1986

MALACHI 3:13–4:6

W. H. Auden's long poem called *For the Time Being: A Christmas Oratorio* is beloved by many Christians. It begins, as the church year begins, with Advent. The first section of the poem has this refrain, repeated several times: "Winter completes an age."

In just a few days—this coming Sunday—the church year will come to an end. One week after that will be the first Sunday of Advent. It's a season of unique significance for the Christian community—a time of looking back and straining forward, a time of patient waiting and urgent watchfulness, a time uniquely designed to lift us out of our personal concerns onto the cosmic stage where God's purposes for the universe are being carried out. As the church year draws to its close, the Scripture lessons begin to exert an unmistakable pressure, as though the circumstances of our lives were becoming intolerable, as though everything was coming loose, as though all we were counting on was slipping from our grasp, as though all the losses and disappointments and betrayals were going to force themselves in upon us in spite of our frenetic efforts to hold them at bay.

For Christians, then, it is the approach of the New Year of the church, not the New Year of the secular calendar, that has implications both ominous and profound. As T. S. Eliot writes of it,

> Since golden October declined into sombre November
> And the apples were gathered and stored, and the land became
> brown sharp points of death in a waste of water and mud,
> The New Year waits, breathes, waits, whispers in darkness . . .[1]

1. T. S. Eliot, *Murder in the Cathedral.*

I have read that in Vermont, the process of nature shutting down for winter is called "the locking." That's the image I'm looking for—the closing of the door, the turning of the key, the sliding of the bolt, and silence. C. S. Lewis knew what he was doing when he made Narnia a cold and frozen place, ruled by a malevolent Snow Queen, a land where it was always winter and Christmas never came. In Dante's vision of hell, the lowest and darkest pit of all is not a circle of fire but a circle of ice, where the damned are frozen forever, where no light or warmth ever penetrates.

So, as winter approaches, the church intentionally contemplates—in her art, liturgy, symbols, and Scripture—the plight of the human race, the death of human hopes, and indeed, the continuing possibility of the end, not just of the year, but of the human story as we have known it, in the phenomenon known by two bone-chilling words: "nuclear winter."[2] The fact that the nuclear disarmament talks came to an abrupt halt in Iceland is only a coincidence, of course, but a suggestive one.[3] The approach of Advent is a reminder to us that we live on a planet that exists precariously under the righteous judgment of God, a bright but threatened globe poised in icy interstellar space, preserved from extinction by one factor and one only: not by "the triumph of the human spirit," but by the hand of God. We can't go on acting as if there were nothing in the Bible about the fate of the earth and the coming of God to be our Judge. The last weeks of the church year and the first Sunday of Advent are sharply focused on these motifs.

But these weeks are also a time to narrow the focus and admit that, as the last leaves are falling dispiritedly to the ground in Union Square and it gets dark at four-thirty, in many ways it is winter in our hearts. After all, what is winter if not a time to turn up our coat collars, lower our heads against the wind, and hurry through the streets and subways to our own hearths, shutting out our fellow human beings as we shut out the cold? The city streets feel very different in the November twilight; the expansiveness and latitude of summer evenings are gone, and we can't help being aware that the Christmas lights will not be around to cheer and warm us in comfortless January. At the time when the predicament of the homeless is at its worst, these fellow citizens become more isolated; no one wants to stop in the cold, no one wants to remove a glove to offer alms, no one wants to unbutton a coat to reach for a wallet. In this sense winter is a metaphor of human indifference. One thinks only of getting home.

2. Jonathan Schell's much-discussed *The Fate of the Earth* had come out in 1982.
3. This was the Reykjavik Summit, between Reagan and Gorbachev, October 1986. The talks collapsed at the last minute.

Perhaps, above all, winter symbolizes the silence, the absence, of God. Auden, in a similar vein, continues his Advent musing:

> . . . We are afraid
> Of pain but more afraid of silence; for no nightmare
> Of hostile objects could be as terrible as this Void.
> This is the Abomination. This is the Wrath of God.

Out of just such a fearful silence the children of Israel lifted up their voices and said, "It is vain to serve God. What is the good of our keeping his charge . . . ? Henceforth we deem the arrogant blessed; evildoers not only prosper, but when they put God to the test they escape" (Mal. 3:14–15).

It was a dark and cold time in Israel's history. It was the end of an age, the great age of prophecy. The book of the prophet called Malachi, from which today's text is taken, is the last book of the Christian Old Testament. The Scriptures of the church were designed to end that way. After the time of Malachi, there would be no further prophecy, no word from God—only silence. Religion thereafter would become repetition, with all the light and fire gone out of it. Auden again:

> As winter completes an age,
> The eyes huddle like cattle, doubt
> Seeps into the pores and power
> Ebbs from the heavy signet ring;
> The prophet's lantern is out
> And gone the boundary stone,
> Cold the heart and cold the stove,
> Ice condenses on the bone,
> Winter completes an age.

In such a time, the prophet Malachi is given a word to utter, a promise to bequeath to Israel, an electrifying vision that down the centuries and to this day has fired the imagination of the church:

> "For behold, the day comes, burning like an oven, when all the arrogant and all evildoers will be stubble; the day that comes shall burn them up, says the Lord of hosts. . . . But for you who fear my name the sun of righteousness shall rise, with healing in its wings. You shall go forth leaping like calves from the stall . . . on the day when I act, says

the Lord of hosts. . . . Behold, I will send you Elijah the prophet before the great and terrible day of the Lord comes. And he will turn the hearts of parents to their children and the hearts of children to their parents, lest I come and smite the land with a curse." (Mal. 4:1–6)

With these urgent and solemn words, Old Testament prophecy comes to an end. Malachi sums up all the warnings of the prophets before him that a final day would come, like a conflagration, a day of reckoning to clear the way for the definitive establishment of the reign of God.

This is a cosmic vision. Like all biblical apocalyptic, it embraces the universe. God's rule extends far beyond the boundaries of the visible church on earth. There is no one living or dead who exists outside his providential oversight. The passage envisions a time when every human being, past, present, and future, will have to answer to the Lord God. The appearance of the Sun of Righteousness (*solis iustitiae*) will envelop the entire created order.

But now notice an extraordinary thing. Just as Malachi reaches the climax of this extraordinary universal prophecy, he suddenly narrows the focus to the most homely, most personal, most intimate circle you could possibly imagine. The final words of the prophecy are these: "And he [God] will turn the hearts of parents to their children and the hearts of children to their parents, lest I come and smite the land with a curse."

That is how the Old Testament ends. This is amazing. The destiny of the universe is found in the destiny of families.

The most dreadful sign of culture in decline and the approaching judgment of God is rupture between parents and children. It is against nature and against heaven. Why has the whole city been so focused on the murder of Jennifer Levin?[4] Not just because it's a sensational story, but because we are afraid of a whole generation out of control, a whole city of parents who have abdicated their responsibilities. One journalist wrote, "The abandonment [of children by parents] was more than physical. It was emotional, spiritual, and complete." She gives an example of a Manhattan girl, a senior in a private high school, who arrived home on Friday afternoon to find an empty apartment, a hundred-dollar bill, and a note from her mother saying, "Away for a long weekend. Be good."

---

4. That summer in 1986, New York was convulsed over the murder of Jennifer Levin by Robert Chambers, called the "preppy killer." They met at Dorrian's Red Hand, a bar frequented by privileged, underage young people. After they left the bar, he killed her in Central Park near the Metropolitan Museum.

The Big Chill between parents and children works the other way too. Just this week I got a letter from an out-of-town friend who writes in despair about her teenaged daughter, "She is so angry—at God, at her father, at me." Their home is fraught with a silence that feels unbearable. Another friend told me that her son was full of inexplicable rage and that the family was in "a cold dark place." "Ice condenses on the bone; winter completes an age." There is no person here who has not experienced such moments of lonely, impenetrable, frigid silence and incomprehension.

Now. The season of Advent tells us where we are and what time it is. Saint Paul writes, "You know what hour it is, how it is full time now for you to wake from sleep. For salvation is nearer to us now than when we first believed." The Christian church is located at the very edge of Malachi's prophecy. We stand at the juncture of two ages: the old age of approaching winter where God's own people along with the world at large are frozen in sin, separation, and death—locked in a silent room where God speaks no word; and the age to come where the glow in the eastern sky announces the coming of the rising sun. That's why one of the principal images of Advent is that of the watchtower. Those who serve God still stand in a dark place, but we strain forward with expectation and an unconquerable hope toward the horizon where the Sun of Righteousness will appear someday with healing in his wings.

Malachi's unique contribution is his vision of the messenger who will precede the dawn. Elijah, who was taken up in a chariot of fire, will return to be the messenger of the age to come, and the sign will be the reconciliation of families. It is awesome and wonderful to know that our Bibles are arranged so that after Malachi, all is silent until suddenly there bursts upon the scene the last and greatest of the prophets of Israel, the "voice crying in the wilderness" that the kingdom of heaven is at hand. John the Baptist is the new Elijah, the leading figure of Advent, the herald of the One who comes to turn our cold and frozen hearts into flaming torches of his unquenchable love.

All human endeavor awaits its "great and final collapse . . . [in] the consuming fire that comes from God."[5] When the day of the Lord comes, the whole world will discover that the only thing that matters is the consummation of God's purpose, and the only things that are lasting are the things that are done in accordance with his will. This means that every human deed undertaken in love will be redeemed, however poorly it was executed and however much it may have seemed to fail. Every generous human action in every possi-

---

5. Gerhard von Rad, *Biblical Interpretations in Preaching* (Nashville: Abingdon, 1977), 117.

ble configuration of family, however flawed it may seem in the present, will be taken up into the depths of the love of God. "He comes to make his blessings flow / far as the curse is found."[6]

Thus we live in this world according to the promise, and in the sure and certain hope of the age to come, watching for and praying for and waiting for and hastening the coming of the Sun of Righteousness. When he comes, the ice age will be over forever. Understanding this is not an answer to the problem of pain and the silence of God, but it shows the way ahead, through the ice fields, to the aurora borealis.

May this be for you a deeply significant Advent season. If you recognize tonight a degree of winter in your life, that is a sign that the healing rays of the Son of God are already at work in you. For you, then, there will be special joy at Christmastime when you sing this verse from Charles Wesley's glorious hymn "Hark! The Herald Angels Sing":

Risen with healing in his wings,
Light and life to all he brings,
Hail, the Sun of Righteousness!
Hail, the heaven-born Prince of Peace!

Amen.

6. Isaac Watts, "Joy to the World."

Whispers in Darkness

Saint Luke's Episcopal Church, Darien, Connecticut
November 1999

AMOS 5:18–24; MATTHEW 25:5–7

That movie *The Ice Storm*, that was about Darien, wasn't it? Or was it New Canaan? I never got around to seeing it, but I read some reviews. I gather that it gave a pretty bleak picture of affluent suburbia. It's almost a cliché; inside those expensive houses with the manicured lawns you have bored, overprogrammed, emotionally neglected children and frustrated, dissatisfied, emotionally chilly parents. We all know, don't we, that just because our people sitting in the pews are slender, blond, and suntanned doesn't mean that there isn't also the usual lot of human unhappiness and venality.

For most of us, though, this is the time of year for the fading of the suntans. Responsibilities press upon us. Winter is coming. I wonder how many of you have noticed that something ominous is going on in the liturgy and the lectionary? After All Saints' Day, the tone of the Sunday morning readings begins to change. It happens every year, in all three lectionary cycles. Once you have learned to look for this shift, you can't mistake it; it's actually quite dramatic. We sense a note of urgency and danger in the texts. The heartbeat of the church begins to accelerate. The last Sunday of the Christian year, the Feast of Christ the King, is November 21; the first Sunday of Advent is only three weeks away. Many of us who occupy pulpits love this time of pre-Advent and Advent better than any other season. Millennium or not, it is the approach of the liturgical New Year that counts for Christians, not the secular New Year. In T. S. Eliot's *Murder in the Cathedral,* the chorus represents the working people who cluster around Canterbury Cathedral. Like all medieval people, they live by the church seasons. The Advent season is approaching, which means the New Year, but it is not a happy thought for them. The poet captures the atmosphere:

The New Year waits, breathes, waits, whispers in darkness. . . .
Some malady is coming upon us . . .
Ill the wind, ill the time, uncertain the profit, certain the danger.
O late late late is the time, late too late and rotten the year . . .
                                        . . . only is here
The white flat face of Death, God's silent servant,
And behind the face of Death the Judgement
And behind the Judgement the Void, more horrid than active shapes of
        hell;
Emptiness, absence, separation from God.[1]

This is the mood as Advent approaches. The world is full of danger and unpredictability. It is "late"—one of the themes of Advent is that of the Last Days. Even in privileged Darien, mortality is just around the corner. What do the "whispers in darkness" say? What lies ahead for us? Strange diseases brought from Africa by insects? Bacteria lurking in hospitals, impervious to antibiotics? Melting Antarctic ice caps? Biological terrorism? Hurricanes that come in twos and threes every single year? Dying crows, dying hemlocks, dying trout streams? What is happening to us?[2]

Governor Jesse Ventura says that religion is a crutch for the weak-minded.[3] Maybe that's why some of us love this most tough-minded of all the church seasons. It so clearly shows that our faith is not for sissies. Listen to the words of the prophet Amos in today's reading:

Why would you have the day of the Lord?
It is darkness, and not light;
        as if a man fled from a lion,
        and a bear met him;
or went into the house and leaned with his hand against the wall,
        and a serpent bit him.
Is not the day of the Lord darkness, and not light,
        and gloom with no brightness in it? (Amos 5:18–20)

These are frightening images. To go into one's own home, a place of rest and comfort, and be attacked by a poisonous, hidden enemy? To recover from

---

1. T. S. Eliot, *Murder in the Cathedral*, portions from parts I and II.
2. Even in 1999, these things were already happening.
3. Jesse Ventura, interview in *Playboy*, September 30, 1999.

cancer and then have a stroke? To lose your job and then have your child hit by a car? These are the thoughts of the season. Where is security to be found? Eliot captures this, too:

> A man may walk with a lamp at night, and yet be drowned in a ditch.
> A man may climb the stair in the day, and slip on a broken step.[4]

The world of Fairfield County testifies that security is found by making the very best use of the stock market. Then we can have six-foot stone walls and electronic gates and security guards. Then we can come to a nice church like this with other people just like ourselves. Then quietly and discreetly, as befits our Episcopal style, we can thank the Lord for all our advantages. The only trouble is, if we come to church, we might get hit over the head with one of the most challenging readings in the entire Bible. The Word of the Lord through the prophet Amos was originally spoken to prosperous people worshiping in the finest communities, just like me and you. I'm going to give you the King James Version (slightly modified) because it's so much more vivid: "I hate, I despise your feast days, and I will not smell in your solemn assemblies. Though ye offer me burnt offerings and meat offerings, I will not accept them. . . . Take thou away from me the noise of thy songs; for I will not hear the melody of thy viols. But let justice roll down like waters, and righteousness like a mighty stream" (Amos 5:21-24).

Here at Saint Luke's, you are familiar with these themes from the Hebrew prophets. Worship is empty, indeed it is offensive to God, where there is no concern for the poor and the defenseless. If you ever should go to Montgomery, Alabama, I hope you will make a point of going to see the civil rights memorial.[5] It was designed by Maya Lin, who also designed the Vietnam memorial in Washington, DC. The Montgomery monument has two components. The first is a waterfall rushing down over a nine-foot wall of black Canadian granite. Under the waterfall, clearly visible, are these words engraved on the stone:

> . . . Until justice rolls down like waters,
> And righteousness like a mighty stream.

The second feature of the memorial, below the wall, is a low round table of the same granite with a thin sheet of water flowing over it, but very slowly,

---

4. *Murder in the Cathedral*, part I. Compare Amos 5:19.

5. These details are taken from William Zinsser's book *American Places* (New York: HarperCollins, 1992), 90-104. I was able to visit the memorial in person a few years later.

so that visitors feel drawn to touch the names inscribed on the table under the water. They are the names of forty people who gave their lives during the civil rights movement. One of them is Jonathan Daniels, a young white Episcopal seminary student, shot dead in broad daylight in Hayneville, Alabama, as he tried to protect a young black woman.[6] He has his own day, now, in the Episcopal Church calendar—*August 11, Jonathan Myrick Daniels, martyr*. Right there you have the definitive answer to the charge of "weak-mindedness." The truth about God is written in the lives and in the deaths of those who have made a sacrificial commitment to God's justice and righteousness.

In the last week of his life, Jesus went to the temple every day to teach. He was engaged in a fight to the death, literally, with the religious leaders. This whole section of the Gospel of Matthew is always read toward the end of the church year; it projects an atmosphere of impending crisis. The parable of the ten virgins, or bridesmaids, is one of the very last that Jesus told.[7] We are meant to see ourselves in this story. Ten young women with lamps and oil are waiting for a wedding procession. It is midnight, and the bridegroom has not come. The lamps are burning low. Maybe he is never coming. Maybe the whole thing was a mistake.

Midnight is the time of the church year that we are in. This is the time for asking if there is some mistake, for, as W. H. Auden wrote, "Unless you exclaim—'There must be some mistake'—you must be mistaken."[8] In other words, if we are not willing to look at the hard questions, our faith is too shallow to survive. On Friday there was a scathing book review in the *New York Times* by the respected critic Michiko Kakutani. She delivers a withering blast at a new book by Neil Postman that proposes "transcendent narratives" as a basis for building a society in the twenty-first century. She heaps scorn upon him for failing to consider "the horrors of the 20th century [that] have undermined faith in . . . optimistic beliefs" and "the advances in science that have made us all too aware of the randomness and chaos in the world."[9] These are very serious charges that could equally well be brought

---

6. The young woman, Ruby Sales, was only seventeen at the time of Jonathan Daniels's death. She grew up to become an activist and well-known speaker. She later studied at the same seminary as Jonathan Daniels, and preached at the parish in New Hampshire where he had grown up.

7. I don't mean to imply that he told this parable in the temple. This was communicated privately to the disciples. Matthew sets it, however, during that last week.

8. Advent section, *For the Time Being: A Christmas Oratorio*.

9. Michiko Kakutani, "Looking Backward toward the Future," review of *Building a Bridge to the 18th Century: How the Past Can Improve Our Future*, by Neil Postman, *New*

against the church. If we have failed to consider these things, if we have not looked straight at them, now is the season to do it. "Optimistic beliefs" may be the very thing for Norman Rockwell's America, but they won't do for the church. All the evidence tells us that the world is indeed random and chaotic, and that the new millennium won't be any better.

The Old Testament scholar Ellen F. Davis recently wrote that the Christian church in America needs to rethink its situation because we are becoming a minority. We must learn, she writes, to understand and speak well for what we believe. "It is a call we cannot afford to ignore; nostalgia is not likely to carry the Western church beyond another generation or two. . . . Ordinary Christians must now practice talking about our faith, studying seriously, teaching our children just what it means" to be a Christian.[10] She has said something very important. We do have a "transcendent narrative," the story of Jesus the Son of God who gave himself up to be crucified in order to save the world from sin and death. But telling the story in a nostalgic way as though it were a nice fairy tale for the children won't work anymore, if indeed it ever did. Jonathan Daniels did not die for a fairy tale.

The church can't survive on sentiment and nostalgia. If we try to do that, we will wake up at midnight and discover that *our lamps are going out*. Sentiment, nostalgia, optimism: these are weak, thin fuels. We need premium oil for our lamps if we are to keep the light of the church burning in the time of trial. Christianity is not for sissies. We need to understand the difference between optimism and hope. Optimism often arises out of denial of the real facts; hope, however, persists in spite of the clearly recognized facts because it is anchored in something beyond. This time of the church year is about hope. We need to face up to the horrors of the twentieth century and the apparent chaos and randomness of life and then see if we can still say "Jesus is Lord."

This is the most serious matter that biblical faith confronts. Where is the evidence for the truth of our creeds in view of the senseless violence, arbitrary cruelty, and meaningless suffering in the world? Barry Bearak, a foreign correspondent for the *New York Times*, is doing his best to write straight reports about the catastrophic cyclone last week in India, but you can tell he has been deeply affected by it and is asking all sorts of questions. His first article said that the landscape looked as if a "malign giant" had stomped all over everything. In a way, that is a theological protest; he is personalizing the destruction and

---

York Times, November 5, 1999. Postman is not recommending the church's narrative, but that of the Enlightenment.

10. Ellen F. Davis, *Virginia Theological Seminary Bulletin*, July 1999.

asking the God question. This is much more obvious in his second piece. He describes the devastating losses of one homeless woman. She showed him the few objects she had managed to save, an umbrella and some children's books, stained with water. "But the dearest possession of all was a small painting of Lord Krishna, there in his legendary glory, dressed in gold finery. . . . A sea serpent's hood shielded Krishna's head from a storm, just as the Lord himself protected those below from the raging tempests loosed in their mortal midst."[11] I think this is meant to be bitterly ironic. Hundreds of people in just one small city were drowned, and countless thousands robbed of their homes and live-lihoods. Where was Lord Krishna?

These are questions for this season. Where is Jesus, the bridegroom? Who can believe in "transcendent narratives" when there is so much random suffer-ing? Isn't it more grown-up, more courageous, to accept the essential mean-inglessness of the universe? If religion is just a refuge for the weak-minded, then you and I are in the wrong place this morning.

If it weren't for one thing, I would join with those who say that we are in the wrong place. I would agree that religion is something that we cling to in order to feel better. With all due respect for other faiths, however, Christianity is different. Jesus was not sheltered from the storm. He did not sit on a throne high above the cyclones of this world in his divine finery.[12] The only begotten Son of God came down himself, and the storm broke over his head and swept him away, crying, "My God, my God, why hast thou forsaken me?" There is a unique paradox at the center of our Christian narrative. God submitted himself to the very worst that human sin could do; as our representative, he comes under his own judgment. And on the third day he was raised victorious over evil and death. This really happened. No one made it up. That is the only thing that keeps me believing. This is the only "transcendent narrative" that can stand up to the scrutiny of Barry Bearak's bitter challenge.

But now listen. If all we do is tell the story over and over and talk about how superior it is to other stories, that will convince no one. The one thing that impresses nonbelievers, the *only* thing that testifies to the truth of our narrative, is a Christlike life. The only thing that truly glorifies Jesus in this world is costly action in his name on behalf of those for whom he died. There is a sense of crisis at this time of year because the coming of Jesus calls every

11. Barry Bearak, *New York Times*, November 2, 1999, and November 4, 1999.

12. In fairness, it is said that Krishna came incarnate into the world also. But there are two major differences. *First,* Krishna came in mythological time; Jesus came into a real place at a real historical time. *Second,* Jesus died a shameful and godless death, identifying completely with our sinful condition in order to save us from it and make us new.

mortal arrangement into question. What should our loyalties be? Where is our ultimate security? What sort of witness do we want to make to our children and grandchildren? Jonathan Daniels's witness is already written in the stars of heaven; but what can you and I do, in the midst of our suburban routines, to keep our lamps burning? I know a mother and daughter who go to a spa together every year, but I know another mother and daughter who go together for two weeks to Central America to work in a Christian medical mission. I meet a lot of doctors who play a lot of golf, but last year when I was attending a church in Princeton, I met a plastic surgeon who spends two weeks every year in Africa performing surgery on children with cleft palates. These are lights to the world. Now, to be sure, not all lights are as dramatic as these. Not everyone can go to Africa or Central America. But everyone can contribute for someone else to go. Everyone can offer encouragement and prayer. Everyone can lend a hand to the needy in nearby communities. Not everyone can be a medical missionary, but everybody can do something. There is no one who is unable to offer a costly sacrifice of some kind. These actions glorify Christ. This oil will keep on burning past midnight.

The church keeps her lamps burning through the night because she still expects her Lord. Will the new year bring "brown sharp points of death in a waste of water and mud"? Yes, it will. Are we afraid to admit that? Yes, we are. Mere optimism cannot survive the brutal facts; but Christian hope is something else. Christian hope does not build a foundation on a new millennium. Christian hope builds its foundation on the promise of the living God that the random chaos of the world will be revealed one day to have been led and shaped by the same hand that reached out to heal the sick and make the blind to see, to raise the dead and "to call into existence the things that do not exist" (Rom. 4:17). In the midst of our fears and sorrows, even in the hurricanes and the ice storms, we have this hope. This is what the church "whispers in darkness": *Christ has died; Christ is risen; Christ will come again.*

Amen.

What's in Those Lamps?

Princeton Theological Seminary, Princeton, New Jersey
The Barth Conference 2015

MATTHEW 25:1–13

This sermon was delivered shortly after an event that shook America. A young man named Dylann Roof entered Emanuel AME Church in Charleston, South Carolina, and deliberately and fatally shot nine members of a Bible study group, including the pastor of the church.

Here in the middle of the so-called "long green season," or "ordinary time," here at the very moment of the summer solstice, this will be an Advent sermon. As Karl Barth wrote many times, the church has no other time in this world but that of Advent—"the time between," as he often called it. Advent is the time of both "waiting and hastening"; Barth loved to quote a verse from the second letter of Peter: "waiting for and hastening the coming of the day of God" (II Pet. 3:12). Advent is the dialectic between the waiting and the hastening, the faithful confidence that strains forward toward the day and the long endurance that's required to wait for it. There is no time given us in this life other than this time, the time between the first coming of our Lord in humility and his second coming in glory. This is a strong theme in the Gospel of Matthew.

Many things have changed. When I was a Sunday school student growing up, this parable was called "the wise and foolish virgins." Now it's called "the wise and foolish bridesmaids." I guess bridesmaids aren't virgins any more . . . fifty-something years ago when my classmates and I were getting married, quite a few of us actually *were* virgins (that was a good thing, in my opinion).

Many things have changed in the world of biblical interpretation, also. When you have preached largely from the Epistles and the Old Testament for the past twenty years, as I have, and you come back to the Gospels for the

95

first time in a while, you forget how disconcerting it can be to use some of the biblical commentaries. Take today's parable, for example. When you look it up in scholarly commentaries, you find all kinds of disputes: Who is meeting whom, and where? Were they lamps or torches? Would shops really be open at night? Does this parable actually go back to the historical Jesus? Etc. It is not to the point to be told that the bridegroom is late because he is haggling over the bride-price! Not only is this sort of thing very discouraging for the preacher, but it can actually lead *away from* the point of the parable. How refreshing it is for us preachers to turn to Barth's expository passages!

And there is yet another thing that's changed in the last fifty years. The creedal confession that "he will come again in glory to judge the living and the dead" used to be rejected out of hand by virtually all progressive American Christians when I was young. Today, the eschatological, even apocalyptic, atmosphere of the New Testament has finally begun to percolate down into the local congregations. Perhaps we're beginning to realize that if Christian faith is going to have any guts, it simply cannot be satisfied with exclusively human hope.

Two days ago, the principal of the Goose Creek School in Charleston, where one of the murdered churchgoers was an admired track coach, said, "Our society is broken, pretty much, but there will be a time when these times will be made right." Notice the use of the passive voice, "*will be made* right." There is a divine agency behind this making right, and that agency cannot be overcome by the principalities, or by the powers, or by things present or things to come (Rom. 8:38–39). That's what the twenty-fourth and twenty-fifth chapters of Matthew point to. They are oriented toward the triumph of God in the second coming of Christ.

The various parables and sayings of these two chapters offer a remarkably rich and varied picture. We have the long discourse that is Matthew's version of the Synoptic Apocalypse. Then we have the parables of the thief in the night, the faithful and unfaithful servants, the ten bridesmaids, the money in trust (the "talents"), and finally the last judgment. All these are appointed for the Advent season.[1] And then, "When Jesus had finished all these sayings, he said to his disciples, 'You know that after two days the Passover is coming, and the Son of man will be delivered up to be crucified'" (Matt. 26:1–2). Matthew has arranged this link between the last judgment and the crucifixion in a most artful and intentional way.

---

1. Increasingly, and rightly, the Advent season is being described as a seven-week period, beginning after All Saints' Day.

Now, about those ten young women. The reason it still makes sense, biblically speaking, to think of them as virgins is that Paul writes to the Corinthian church as follows: "I betrothed you to one husband, to present you as a chaste virgin espoused to Christ" (II Cor. 11:2). Virtually all interpreters agree that the ten bridesmaids represent the church—the community of professing Christians. That's why the bride doesn't appear in the story. If there was a bride, the symbolism would become bifurcated, with two different figures representing the church. In this parable, the *bridesmaids* are the virgin church, and the bridegroom, Jesus Christ, is arriving to sweep them up into his triumphal procession.

As we all know, the image of a wedding festival is a primary image—perhaps *the* primary image—of the kingdom of heaven (as Matthew calls it). Whatever the marriage customs may have been in first-century Judea, it's clear that the most important characteristic of the celebration is its untrammeled joyousness. In the story, the arrival of the bridegroom is intended to signal the beginning of the feast. Until he comes, it's all anticipation.

Anticipation is thrilling, for a while. The excitement about what is just around the corner heightens the sense of coming fulfillment. Everyone feels supercharged. This lasts for an hour, two hours . . . then the waiting becomes tedious. Why is he late? Three hours, and the nagging question arises, what if he doesn't come at all? Darkness has fallen. More hours go by. No one can stay at a pitch of anticipation forever. The young women begin to grow sleepy; their oil lamps begin to burn low. Suddenly the electrifying cry arises, "He's coming!" The lights of the procession approach in the night. The bridesmaids leap to their feet, grab their guttering lamps, trim them, and pour in their reserves of oil. Except that five of them have no extra; they wail, "Our lamps are going out!"

Some have suggested that the five wise virgins are selfish because they won't share. That's a moralistic reading of the story. As one interpreter says acerbically, "Better to greet the bridegroom with five lights than no lights at all."[2] The foolish five rush off to the shops, but it's too late. The five whose lamps are brilliantly burning go into the wedding feast with the bridegroom, and the five who were unprepared have the door shut against them.

We can be here for the rest of the day debating the ultimate destiny of the foolish five. Barth famously wrote that we are permitted to hope for a salvation that will reach to all. That's why one woman in Charleston—a woman

---

2. Francis Wright Beare, *The Gospel according to Matthew* (New York: Harper and Row, 1982), 482.

prepared—said directly to the killer, "May God have mercy on your soul." The important thing about this parable right now is to think about what it means for the church to be ready for the coming of her Lord. What does it mean for us, all these weary and discouraging hours, and days, and years that he does not come and it appears that he never will, and the church grows slack?

What's in those lamps? What does it mean to be ready at all hours of the night? What does it mean to be "the community of the last times"?[3] In Luke's Gospel, Jesus says, "Let your loins be girded and your lamps burning" (Luke 12:35). The emphasis is on being supplied and ready. On the night of the Passover, the children of Israel are commanded: "[Eat with] your loins girded, your sandals on your feet, and your staff in your hand; and you shall eat in haste" (Exod. 12:11). Does this mean we always have to gobble down our dinner standing up? Of course not. No one can be awake all the time. All ten of the bridesmaids went to sleep. Human frailty is accounted for; God understands our weakness. Perpetual alertness is not what's wanted; what's wanted is that stored-up emergency supply to last while "according to his promise we wait for new heavens and a new earth in which righteousness dwells" (II Pet. 3:13).

This confidence in the "great gettin' up morning" has strengthened the congregation of Emanuel AME Church in Charleston, South Carolina—known to many as "Mother Emanuel." When I started struggling with this sermon ten days ago, I wondered how in the world I was going to illustrate it. Little did I know that something would happen that would show forth the Advent church, assaulted by darkness, but rising up with all its lamps burning, and with plenty of extra oil for the long, long haul ahead.

When Eric Harris and Dylan Klebold shot up Columbine High School in 1999, there were some troubling stories about local Christian youth groups. Before the blood was even dry, it seemed, youth leaders began asking the traumatized students whose friends were dead, "Do you forgive Eric and Dylan?" This sort of premature, even invasive, call for forgiveness should never be inflicted on anyone, let alone young teenagers who have just experienced the unimaginable. It's very difficult even for much older Christian people to navigate the passage between justice and mercy. Ordinarily we might do well to mistrust such premature offers of forgiveness.

Last week in Charleston, however, was different. To be sure, it's important not to romanticize or idealize the black church, or any church. All Christian groups are riven by Sin, just like all other groups. But the black churches have suffered so extremely, and so unjustly, for so long, that they have achieved a

3. Karl Barth, *Church Dogmatics* III/2 (Edinburgh: T. & T. Clark, 1960), 508.

maturity that sometimes seems almost superhuman. The members of Mother Emanuel church who lost their pastor, their relatives, their friends in a bloody, hateful assault are not teenagers unaccustomed to suffering, crime, violence, and death. These are adults who have seen ugliness in human character that white people cannot even comprehend. Many of them have been learning "the mind of Christ" (I Cor. 2:16) for decades. They were being conformed, as a group, to his likeness. Therefore they had a readiness, as a *community* of believers, that can't develop the same way in isolated *individuals*.

I heard a long interview on NPR with an African American pastor in South Carolina. The interviewer simply could not comprehend what he was saying to her. She kept saying, "But how can you forgive? How can you be like this?" All weekend, the mystification of the reporters was notable. They kept asking the same question over and over: "How can you forgive Dylann Roof?" They couldn't understand it. The radio and TV people kept using well-worn phrases like "the triumph of the human spirit" and "the goodness of the American people." No, the pastor on NPR said, it is *our faith*. What we have seen in the members of Mother Emanuel church and the other black churches is neither the triumph of the human spirit nor the goodness of the American people. It was a cloud of witnesses to the victory of the limitless love of the One who will come again to set things right.

Barth testifies that the oil of the lamps is the witness of the Spirit in the waiting church.[4] That's what we're seeing in this response of the Mother Emanuel members. They are so practiced, through regular worship, Bible study, and prayer, that they don't need to run out to the store in the middle of the night to buy more oil. They've been in the middle of the night for a long time. They don't need any well-meaning, immature counselors to tell them to forgive Dylann Roof. It's part of their DNA as a Christian community. They have been storing up oil for generations. On Friday night, they were standing out in the courtyard of their horribly violated church, and they were singing "Let My Little Light Shine." When the church reopened for worship yesterday, one of the ministers said that people kept asking why, and how, but "those of us who know Jesus, we can look through the window of our faith, and we see hope, we see light."[5]

---

4. Barth, *Church Dogmatics* III/2, 505–6.

5. John Eligon and Richard Fausset, "Defiant Show of Unity in Church That Lost 9," *New York Times*, June 22, 2015. It is almost unknown for the *New York Times* to quote someone using the name of Jesus in a confessional context except when the speaker is African American. Sermons given at the funerals of well-known white people are often quoted, but the quotations are always generic. References to Christ are not included. I have noticed this for decades. Therefore the witness of the black church is all the more important to us all.

Maybe the best clue to the inner meaning of this parable of the lamps and the oil can be found in just two words. The parable tells us that when the bridegroom arrived, "those who were ready went in with him to the marriage feast." *With him!* The five who were prepared, who stored up a supply of oil in anticipation of the great banquet, see the lighted procession approaching them with the glorious Bridegroom at its head. "Come, good and faithful servants, enter into the joy of your Master." We *accompany* him, we enter his eternal wedding banquet *with him, at his side*, cleansed from all our accumulated misdoings, freed from our bondage to the power of Sin, in fellowship with the Lord Jesus in all his splendor, the one who has loved us even unto death and hell, who comes again to receive those who belong to him.

"With him!"

Beloved . . . it does not yet appear what we shall be, but we know that when he appears we shall be like him, for we shall see him as he is. (I John 3:2)

Amen.

The Hope of Heaven

Grace Church, New York City
November 1995

MALACHI 4:1–6; I CORINTHIANS 13; MATTHEW 5:3–11

We have just come through the Thanksgiving season. I am reminded of a great prayer of Thomas Cranmer, the General Thanksgiving. When I was a pious young girl, it used to bother me that the General Thanksgiving was so nonspecific. There was no reference to family or school, let alone boyfriends or dates. All it said was "we bless thee for our creation, preservation, and all the blessings of this life." That was not enough for me at that stage of my existence. Now that I am much older, however, I appreciate the General Thanksgiving as one of the Prayer Book's greatest treasures. It goes on to say that we thank God "above all for . . . the redemption of the world . . . , for the means of grace, and for the hope of glory." *There* is something, I now realize, truly to be thankful for when the boyfriends and the dates are barely even a dim memory.

"The hope of glory!" That is a wonderful phrase to introduce our four-part series about heaven. Why are we talking about heaven at this particular time of year?

The answer to that question lies in the word "hope." We are coming up on the season of Advent. I have noticed that for more and more people, Advent is becoming a very important time, even a favorite. This is partly because it is such a welcome contrast to the commercial madness outside the church doors. But it is also because Advent, more than any other season of the church year, is the season of hope. It is the season that is concretely oriented to the *future*. It grows out of the lessons for the last two seasons of the church year immediately preceding Advent, when we read of the final apocalypse: the

---

This was the first of a series of four pre-Advent sermons on the subject of heaven preached by the clergy of Grace Church at the Wednesday evening services.

second coming of Christ, the last judgment, the defeat of Satan, the triumph of God. Advent, therefore, summons us to what Saint Paul calls the "hope against hope" (Rom. 4:18)—the Christian hope that perseveres when human hope is at an end.

The Grace Church clergy have been asked to reflect upon heaven in four sermons, of which this is the first. The lessons that you have just heard are the ones I have chosen to illustrate heaven. If we had had three lessons, I would have chosen the fourth chapter of the prophet Malachi. These words are uniquely suited for this unique week in the Christian calendar, because they are the last words in the Old Testament. Let me read them to you now:

> "Behold, the day comes, burning like an oven, when all the arrogant and all evildoers will be stubble; the day that comes shall burn them up, says the Lord of hosts, so that it will leave them neither root nor branch. But for you who fear my name the sun of righteousness shall rise, with healing in its wings. You shall go forth leaping like calves from the stall. And you shall tread down the wicked, for they will be ashes under the soles of your feet, on the day when I act, says the Lord of hosts. Remember the law of my servant Moses, the statutes and ordinances that I commanded him at Horeb for all Israel. Behold, I will send you Elijah the prophet before the great and terrible day of the Lord comes. And he will turn the hearts of fathers to their children and the hearts of children to their fathers, lest I come and smite the land with a curse." (Mal. 4:1–6)

This passage is perfect for this week. It's a strange week; one hardly knows what color of stole to wear. It is not yet Advent, and yet we sense that the "long green season" has finally come to a resounding conclusion with the feast of Christ the King. The reading from Malachi is a little like that; it belongs not quite to the past, not quite to the future. It looks back to the law of Moses, but it looks forward to the coming of the last day. It is an in-between passage, just as this is an in-between week.

You know that Advent itself has been called the season in between, "the Time Being," as W. H. Auden wrote. It is a not-yet time, a time for "the hope of glory" that is yet to come. It is a time for looking toward the future kingdom of God in the sharp realization that the kingdom is not realized. We are still living under the sign of the wrath of God, as all good Advent reflections will tell you. I will give you a little example. This morning in the women's Bible study, we went around the circle and asked people to give snapshots of their Thanksgiving. Some said, "Peace and quiet"; some said, "Everybody together"; some said, "Great food." One honest woman said, "Family conflict." How my heart went out to her. This is what so many people fear about holidays: family conflict. This is an image, not of heaven, but of hell.

I don't think it's possible to talk of heaven without talking also of its opposite, of hell. Family conflict is hell. I would like to draw your attention to an aspect of the Malachi passage. It has all sorts of apocalyptic imagery. It depicts the coming of the Lord of hosts and the final judgment of the wicked. It also makes reference to Elijah, whose coming would be the signal for the end of the world. So the passage has a huge cosmic setting in view at first. Then, suddenly and unexpectedly, it narrows down to a very small focus: family conflict. This is the worst of all curses. If the hearts of the parents are not turned to the children and the hearts of the children to the parents, the result will be a permanent condition of living under the wrath of God. That's why the prophet Malachi speaks of the repairing of family relationships as the sign of the final triumph of God over the wickedness of the human race.

Up in the Berkshires, where we spend a lot of our time, members of a family who have owned a leading wallpaper-and-paint business have just broken up with great acrimony. I went into the store the other day. The atmosphere was so thick you could cut it with a knife. Up on the wall there was a sign that said, "J. J. Petricelli and Sons: Decorating the Berkshires for three generations."[1] Under the circumstances, the sign seemed like a mockery. Family conflict is hell. Divorce creates damage for generations. Parental neglect, fraternal strife, sibling rivalry, abusive behavior—these things are signs of the wrath of God.

"Behold, I will send you Elijah the prophet before the great and terrible day of the Lord comes. And he will turn the hearts of fathers to their children and the hearts of children to their fathers, lest I come and smite the land with a curse." This is the last thing our Bibles tell us before we read the opening words of the New Testament. This week, this space between the old liturgical year and the new, this winter evening with its gathering darkness, this Time Between is the time for looking back and looking forward, looking back at the mess we have made of our lives, looking forward to . . . well, to what? That is an Advent question.

---

1. Not their real name. A few months later the sign read, "J. J. Petricelli and Son," minus the *s*. The cast-off son had left town with his family, under a dark cloud.

The Advent world is a world without Jesus Christ. "Darkness shall cover the earth, and gross darkness the peoples," writes the prophet Isaiah in words set to music by Handel in *Messiah*. A world without God's presence is a world accursed, and the sign of God's curse is destroyed families and destroyed relationships.

The Old Testament ends with an evocation of the wrath of God combined with a powerful image of "the redemption of the world by our Lord Jesus Christ, the means of grace, and the hope of glory." I don't need to tell you that heaven is not a place. Heaven is not harps and wings and haloes and pearly gates. Heaven is restored relationships. The hope of this future is "the hope of glory." Heaven is seen in the face of Jesus Christ. Here is what Saint John says: "The Word became flesh and dwelt among us, full of grace and truth; we have beheld his glory, glory as of the only Son from the Father" (John 1:14).

And what, exactly, is his glory? What does it mean to look upon the face of the Lord who comes at Christmas? God is love. "Love is patient and kind; love is not jealous or boastful; it is not arrogant or rude. Love does not insist on its own way; it is not irritable or resentful; it does not rejoice at wrong, but rejoices in the right. Love bears all things, believes all things, hopes all things, endures all things" (I Cor. 13:4–7).

Biblical theologians have observed that we can substitute the name Jesus for the word "love" and the passage from I Corinthians makes even more perfect sense. I believe this is equally true of the Beatitudes. They are descriptions of Jesus. What does it mean to be blessed? It means to be like Jesus himself—"Blessed are the poor in spirit. . . . Blessed are those who mourn. . . . Blessed are those who hunger and thirst for righteousness. . . . Blessed are the merciful. . . . Blessed are the pure in heart. . . . Blessed are the peacemakers. . . . Blessed are you when men revile you and persecute you and utter all kinds of evil against you" (Matt. 5:3–11).

To be a disciple of Jesus is to be assimilated to him, to be grafted into him, to become part of God's plan for the perfecting of sinful human nature. Heaven means that the reality of God's perfect love in Jesus Christ will become a reality for all humanity.

From time to time I hear of people in our congregation whose relationships have been fractured, people in our midst who are not speaking to each other. These are signs of the wrath of God, signs of the times we live in. Heaven is not yet. Even in Saint Paul's favorite church, the one at Philippi, such things happened. Two leading women in the Philippian congregation were fighting. Paul is distressed about this. He writes, "I entreat Euodia and

I entreat Syntyche to agree in the Lord. And I ask you also, true yokefellow, help these women, for they have labored side by side with me in the gospel" (Phil. 4:2–3).[2]

We know from the Corinthian correspondence that nothing distressed Paul more than family conflict. Nothing brings dishonor to God more than division and disharmony in the body of Christ. Someone said to me recently that she had never experienced such unpleasant and judgmental attitudes as in the church. This is so sad; it breaks the heart. This tarnishes the name of our Lord and Savior. This is hell, a world without Jesus.

You and I cannot make heaven break in. Unassisted human nature cannot turn the hearts of the children to the parents and the hearts of the parents to the children. Only God can do this. This is a fundamental truth of the Advent message. Unassisted human nature is under the sign of the wrath of God. But light is breaking, brothers and sisters, the dawn is coming. As Malachi foresaw and Charles Wesley adapted in his famous hymn, "For you who fear my name the sun of righteousness shall rise, with healing in its wings."[3] Human nature is unassisted no longer.

In the words of another much-loved Christmas hymn, "Joy to the world, the Lord is come . . . he comes to make his blessings flow, far as the curse is found." As in the prophecy of Malachi, there is no promise of joy without reference to the curse. In our class this morning, there was a witness who reminded us of the wrath of God. In this world, there can be no talk of heaven without talk also of hell. But there is light ahead. In the collect that we will say together on Sunday, the great collect for the first Sunday of Advent, we will pray to "cast away the works of darkness, and put upon us the armor of light, *now in the time of this mortal life*" (emphasis mine). However dimly, however imperfectly, heaven is to be mirrored in our lives right now. Now in the time of this mortal life, now in the time of this present darkness, now in this time of deteriorating family relationships, now at this corner of Tenth and Broadway, take heart! "Look up! Raise your heads! Your redemption is drawing near!" (Luke 21:28).

Even the tiniest sign of reconciliation, the smallest hint of forgiveness, the most minuscule glimmer of kindness is a sign that God is with us, our Lord Emmanuel. In even our most seemingly insignificant moments of fellowship and renewal, God is at work. He can use you to make a little piece of heaven

---

2. By the way, this is an indication of the high status of women in Paul's churches.

3. "Hark! The Herald Angels Sing": "Risen with healing in his wings, / Light and life to all he brings, / Hail, the Sun of Righteousness! . . ."

come, if only for a moment, for someone, this very night. Never underestimate the power of a God who could have turned his back on us in wrath forever, but instead became Love incarnate, love that bore all things and endured all things, even to the cross, so that we might be restored to him and to one another. And so we may truly give thanks, tonight, for this "hope of glory" and, in so doing, rededicate ourselves to his service, "not only with our lips, but in our lives."

Amen.

The Voice of the Son of Man

Grace Church, New York City
Wednesday evening, ten days before Advent I, 1982

MARK 13; JOHN 5:25–27

If you know your Christian calendar, you're getting goose bumps. There is a great shift in the lectionary that begins after All Saints' Day. Last Sunday was a good example. The readings from Scripture start getting apocalyptic in November. This coming Sunday is the last Sunday of the Christian year, and the Sunday after that is the first Sunday of Advent, the season of the last things. The turn of the year is the church's way of looking backward and forward at the same time, and acknowledging the One who holds both the past and the future. "I am the Alpha and the Omega," says the Lord God, "the first and the last," the beginning and the end, "who is, and who was, and who is to come" (Rev. 1:8, 17).

The lessons are concerned with the great themes of the end of all things, the last judgment, the second coming, the consummation of history, the final intervention of Christ the King, the Son of Man who "is coming with the clouds of heaven . . . and his kingdom [is] one that shall not be destroyed" (Dan. 7:13–14). For many, this has always been a particularly dramatic and evocative season of the church year, but it's always a challenging time for preaching, because these apocalyptic themes are so strange to us.

The Gospel for this week, Mark 13, speaks of wars, earthquakes, eclipses, people running for their lives, demonic figures appearing in the murky light, cosmic cataclysm, and then the Son of God riding in on a cloud with an army of angels and archangels. It really is quite thrilling in some ways, but utterly alien and baffling in others, especially the parts about how there is going to be more suffering and more calamity than the world has ever known.[1] On the

---

1. Readers of this sermon in this volume published in 2018 may feel that these apocalyptic phenomena do not sound as far-fetched as they may have in 1982.

whole, we feel more comfortable talking about the love of God, the joy of Christian fellowship, the justification of the ungodly, even the management of prayer groups, than we do the second coming and the end of the world. Nuclear catastrophe is, in a real sense, almost literally unthinkable.[2]

It's interesting to note that the apocalyptic message of Scripture has become the focus of so much attention in recent years. When I was a child in Episcopal Sunday school in the 1940s, the ideas of the end of the world and the second coming were regarded as an embarrassment, not to be taken seriously. Several things have happened since then, though. First of all, the easy humanism and optimism of the early years of the twentieth century caved in with the two world wars. Concepts of moral progress collapsed, or should have collapsed, in the face of the Holocaust. And, of course, the prospect of nuclear annihilation has caused many biblical scholars to rethink the whole apocalyptic worldview that, many now believe, was taken for granted by the writers of the New Testament.

So this is the time, historically speaking, to talk about the big picture, the global issues, the world-historical significance, the cosmic Christ—and the end of the church year is the time to talk about it in the context of the coming of the Lord in power and glory to gather in his kingdom from the ends of the universe. And, as always, the big question is, *What has it all got to do with us, personally?*

One part of Mark 13 that jumps out at me is that "in those days there will be such tribulation as has not been from the beginning of the creation until now, and never will be." Isn't this a rather morbid exaggeration, as if we are supposed to take some delight in hearing about it? It seems almost pathological. And yet the question that we all ask, if we are serious about faith and life, is, "Why are things so bad in the world? Why is there so much evil and suffering?" In particular, when violence and cruelty are visited upon trusting and helpless children, we simply *must* ask questions about it. If we do not, it must mean that we are only half alive.

One of the reasons that the Christian gospel makes sense is that it takes fully into account the sadness and brokenness and downright wickedness of this life. Suffering and distress are inescapable in a world fallen away from God. We have been warned: "Behold, I have told you all things beforehand" (Mark 13:23). Disease, loss, suffering, and death are inescapable in the Christian life. We have been warned. If we continue to speak only of peace and love when

---

2. Jonathan Schell has thought about it more than most. See *The Fate of the Earth* (New York: Knopf, 1982).

Jesus has predicted conflict and catastrophe, then we have simply refused to hear a substantial part of his message. You see, there is a link between suffering and the kingdom of God—a close connection. That's what the readings about the end of the ages tell us.

"Tribulation" (*thlipsis* in Greek) is a word that the New Testament uses to describe the signs of the coming kingdom. It's not just ordinary suffering. *Thlipsis* is a revelatory word; it points beyond itself to the coming triumph of the Lord. "I have said these things to you," says Jesus Christ in the Gospel of John, "that in me you may have peace. In this world, you will have tribulation (*thlipsis*); but be of good cheer, I have overcome the world" (John 16:33). Jesus says these words an hour before he goes to be betrayed and given up for torture and execution.

The curious and paradoxical thing about the New Testament teachings concerning the last things is that they produce hope, not despair; confidence, not fear. *Hope* and *confidence*—those are the key ideas. Look, says Jesus as he stands with his little group of disciples overlooking the city of Jerusalem, the transition from this world to the coming reign of God will not happen without a fight to the death. That's why there's so much military imagery in both the Old Testament and the New Testament. The "ruler of this world," as Jesus calls Satan in John's Gospel, will not go down without a battle. He is a foe too powerful for unaided human beings; but, as in the story of the servant of the prophet Elisha in the book of Kings, there are unseen horses and chariots of fire guaranteeing the promise of God (II Kings 6:17).

The Christian life is not a pleasure trip and never was. Perhaps people used to understand this better than we do now. It is characteristic of our own time to retreat from a realistic assessment of the reign of Death. In earlier times, people lived closer to suffering than we do today. People were sick at home, and they died at home. When there was war, and there usually was, it was waged hand to hand in one's own street and on one's own farm, not far off in a remote land where bombs can be dropped from great heights. For Christians in earlier times, and for Christians in our own time who live in conditions of "battle, murder, and sudden death," the apocalyptic Scriptures that we read approaching Advent have brought hope, encouragement, confidence.

Now here is the part of the story that has to do with you and me, now in our own lives in the city of New York in a time of uneasy discontent when nothing seems to be radically wrong with the American project but there is a mood of dark uncertainty, not only about our personal careers, our relationships, our place in the world, but also about the stability and safety of our city. As you know, my husband and I live in a house in the suburbs where I never gave a thought to pickpockets or muggers, but recently I went out and bought a little purse with a cross-body strap that might foil a thief—something I would never have thought of until I came to work in the city. I'm glad to be here. I'm glad to have a place to stay in the city where I can share in the uneasy mood. I'm glad to be reminded of the precariousness of human life by the presence of extremely needy people that are hidden in the suburbs.

There is such a thing as apocalyptic ethics. Advent is the time to think about that. Advent does not mean that we can sit back and ignore the predicament of humanity because God is going to come in on a cloud and clean it all up. The nature of God's future is that it impinges on our lives right now. God's future exerts a pressure upon us. That's what the apocalyptic New Testament language of this season really means when it tells us that the time is short. In each life, in each action of a Christian believer, we act as if it were our last act. This is somewhat tricky to talk about because we don't mean that every moment has to be a crisis—that would be an intolerable way to live. Perhaps the best way to think about it is that the knowledge of the coming of the Lord gives a significance to each act of mercy that it would not otherwise have, and a confidence that God will fit it all into his great purpose.

Tonight, as every Wednesday night, we will have dinner and then split up into our small groups. Have you ever thought of your small group, with all its peculiarities and challenges, as a sign of the coming kingdom of God? Well, that's what it is. The people who come to us at Grace Church, representing as we do the aspirations and struggles of the young strivers of our city, find that here, meeting regularly in the context of worship, Bible study, and a shared meal, we are experiencing the work of God through the sometimes humdrum, sometimes raucous, sometimes revelatory work of being a disciple of Jesus Christ in a great city. But this is not like any other type of small group, because all the pleasure and all the pain of tight association with a mixture of one's fellow human beings to whom one is accountable is taking place as part of God's project of redemption and re-creation. Yes, you! That is, after all, the way it began: with Jesus of Nazareth gathering a small group around himself to be the messengers of the age to come.

"And behold, I have told you all things beforehand." Why do we believe that what an itinerant preacher said to a few fishermen and tax collectors in occupied Judea two thousand years ago should guide us in all things in this life of ours today? Isn't that quite ridiculous on the face of it? Your nonbelieving friends and coworkers might be too polite to say so, but they most likely think it's absurd. It's far easier to defend Jesus's role as a teacher of generic peace and love than it is to explain what the second coming means for our lives now. In

Mark 13, we hear the voice of Jesus as one who tells of great suffering for the sake of the age to come when God will reign supreme over Death and destroy every form of evil.

Why should anyone ask you to believe this? The preacher tonight is not "asking you to believe it." The gospel of Jesus Christ is not a list of things to believe. The preaching of the gospel today, just as it was two thousand years ago, is a summons to hear the voice of the Son of God and to let his Holy Spirit do the work of convicting, converting, and consecrating our lives to our great good and to his great glory. The voice of Jesus is not like any other voice ever heard. That's one of the reasons I believe in him. There is this note of command over all that is, or was, or is to come. It's a voice of authority, cosmic, universal authority, proclaiming the destiny of the world. "Truly, truly, I say to you, the hour is coming, and now is, when the dead will hear the voice of the Son of God, and those who hear will live. For as the Father has life in himself, so he has granted the Son also to have life in himself, and has given him authority to execute judgment, because he is the Son of man" (John 5:25–27).

Who talks like that? What other voice has ever been heard claiming such things? This is the voice that has given confidence, courage, and hope to oppressed and subjugated peoples all over the world, and that reaches into the depths of every single human heart afflicted with anxiety, or pain, or confusion, or hopelessness. "We believe that he will come to be our Judge." That means that the destiny of the whole world is in the hands of a Savior and Redeemer whose name is *Emmanuel*: meaning, *God for us.* Not against us. For us and with us, forever and ever.

Yes, there will be suffering. Yes, there will be horrible, inexplicable violence, and much of it will seem utterly without any redemptive meaning. But there is nothing that can happen that is not subject to the sovereignty of God. This was the faith that electrified the ancient world when people heard the preaching of the apostles and evangelists—many of whom would die violently at the hands of the occupying oppressors. No suffering can be properly understood until the Lord comes—but he will come. God is accomplishing his purposes in spite of all appearances to the contrary. Nothing can lie beyond the power of God to redeem and transform. We believe this because we have been seized by the unique authority of the voice of Jesus Christ.

When you know that our Redeemer has warned you that his kingdom will arise out of great suffering, then you will not be taken by surprise if your faith costs you something. What you will have, however, throughout it all, are *faith* and *hope*. If you know that God the Creator and Judge of all things is truly sovereign over all of human and cosmic history, then your small concerns will begin to become part of a great pattern, and they will worry you less as your commitment to your fellow Christians means more and more. If you know that the reconciliation of all things is the grand design of the Creator of the universe, then your own individual and communal acts of faithfulness to one another become signs in this world of the world to come. If you know that "the one who endures to the end will be saved" (Mark 13:13), then you will be given courage and strength to meet whatever happens. Even though the apocalyptic language of Advent is grand and cosmic, nevertheless it is in the daily round of small but self-forgetful actions of faithfulness that the future of God is made present.

Many Episcopalians before the Prayer Book revision knew the collect for the first Sunday of Advent by heart, because we heard it every day of the season. It superbly locates the life of the Christian community here and now, in the sure and certain hope of the day of the Lord. The prayer is based on Paul's words in Romans 13:11–12. Let us pray it together:

> Almighty God, give us grace that we may cast away the works of darkness, and put upon us the armor of light, now in the time of this mortal life in which thy Son Jesus Christ came to visit us in great humility; that in the last day, when he shall come again in his glorious majesty to judge both the living and the dead, we may rise to the life immortal; through him who liveth and reigneth with thee and the Holy Spirit, one God, now and for ever. *Amen.*

The Universal Grip of the Enemy (Pre-Advent)

When God Is Silent

Montreat Conference Center, Montreat, North Carolina
2013

For Pat and Mary Ann Miller

ISAIAH 45:15; DEUTERONOMY 29:29

I wonder how many of you *Downton Abbey* fans out there noticed when Dame Maggie Smith quoted from the hymnbook (for her, it would have been the Church of England hymnal). With Lady Violet's trademark grandeur, she said, "God works in mysterious ways his wonders to perform." She quotes it ironically, but the original text is anything but ironic. William Cowper, the eighteenth-century English poet who wrote the poem, suffered from suicidal depression for most of his life. He knew a thing or two about the mysterious and often impenetrable ways of God.[1]

The prophet Isaiah wrote, "Truly, thou art a God who hidest thyself" (Isa. 45:15). This verse has had a lot of attention over the centuries. Throughout Christian history, the question has always been asked: "When terrible things happen,

---

1. Cowper's poem, "God Moves in a Mysterious Way" (1774), continues:

Deep in unfathomable mines
Of never-failing skill,
He treasures up his bright designs
And works his sovereign will. . . .
Judge not the Lord by feeble sense
But trust him for his grace;
Behind a frowning providence
He hides a smiling face. . . .
Blind unbelief is sure to err
And scan his work in vain;
God is his own interpreter
And he will make it plain.

This was not an Advent sermon, but there is no theme more suited to the Advent season than the silence of God.

where is God?" My sister Betsy, who lives in Columbia, South Carolina, recently sent me some clippings about a terrible airplane crash in Alaska. I'm sure most of you know all about this calamity. Two sets of parents, five teenagers, prominent and devoted members of Christ Church, Greenville. One father, a beloved physician. All the young people, leaders of one sort or another—valedictorians, student presidents, athletes—and all of them committed Christians. Enjoying a wonderful two-family outing, all the sights of Alaska . . . all dead.

When terrible things happen, where is God? Throughout Christian history, this question has always been asked. It becomes more urgent and more agonizing when something happens to children. When the news of the massacre at the Newtown, Connecticut, elementary school came through, there wasn't, or shouldn't have been, a Christian believer in this country who didn't ask, "Where was God? Why does God permit these atrocities?"

This is the question that Christian faith must ask. It's a very shallow faith if it does not ask. Unfortunately, many people have been conditioned *not to ask* these kinds of questions—as though they were disrespectful, or intrusive, or dangerous. There's even an idea that asking such a question is like opening a door to not believing in God at all. But the people of the Bible *do* ask, directly and bluntly. The questions are asked over and over again in the Psalms. The wonderful little book of the prophet Habakkuk asks it this way: "Oh Lord, how long shall I cry for help and you will not hear? Why are you silent when the wicked man swallows up the one more righteous than he?" (Hab. 1:2, 13).

The silence of God, the absence of God, is a major theme of Scripture and the Christian life. Habakkuk's questions are part of every believer's struggle for faith. I suspect that many of you seasoned Montreat people have had occasion to ask yourselves why God so often seems to be absent. Anyone who has not asked this question hasn't been fully tested yet.

Today's text: "Truly, thou art a God who hidest thyself" (or, "Truly, you are a God who hides himself"). Why is the King James Version better? Because when we say "thyself," we are still addressing God in the second person. When we say "himself," we are moving into the third person, distancing ourselves. "Truly, you are a God who hides *yourself*" sounds a bit flip to me. So I'm sticking with the King James. "Verily thou art a God that hidest thyself."

Today's hymn says this:

Immortal, invisible, God only wise,
In light inaccessible hid from our eyes,
Most blessed, most glorious, the ancient of days,
Almighty, victorious, thy great name we praise.

The idea that God lives in "light inaccessible" is an ancient one. When Moses came down from speaking with God on Mount Sinai, his face reflected God's light so brightly that he had to wear a veil over it so as not to blind the people (Exod. 34:29–35). When Moses asked God to show him his glory (*shekinah*), God placed him into a cleft in a rock and covered him with his hand to protect him from seeing the glory directly (Exod. 33:21–23). Hymns from older times refer to these biblical stories in a way that assumes the congregation will know them and make them their own. One hymn has these words, "He shelters me [me! you!] in the cleft of the rock and covers me there with his hand." It's a tender personalization of the story about Moses, but I don't think the average churchgoer today would recognize the connection. Our hymn today makes a biblical reference to God as "ancient of days"; that phrase comes from God's appearance in the book of Daniel (Dan. 7:9, 13).

God dwells in inaccessible light—light that we can't directly look at. This is *uncreated* light that emanates from God's very being. This light was already there *before* God created the light that we see. "In light inaccessible hid from our eyes." This, also, is a basic biblical idea. God isn't a product of human imagination. God isn't a human wish raised to the nth power. God isn't a projection of human hopes and fears. God is outside and beyond *our ideas* of God, so we can't see God from a human point of view at all. Let me say that another way. God is invisible not only to our eyes; God is also invisible to our imaginations. That ought to raise a question in your minds: How do we know who God is, then? How do we even know if there is a God?

"Truly, thou art a God who hidest thyself." Maybe some of you like Latin—it seems to be back in vogue in some high schools. The name for this idea in Latin is *Deus absconditus*, the hidden God. But that doesn't quite get at what Isaiah is saying, because we need to understand that God is not just hidden on general principles. If God is hidden, it is because he hides *himself*. He *means* to be hidden. It is God's nature to be out of the reach of our senses. There is a distance between God and ourselves that cannot be bridged from our side.

One of the main reasons we need to know the Old Testament intimately is that the God revealed in it—the God who is the father of Jesus Christ—is huge and elusive. One of the great biblical theologians of the past century (Samuel Terrien) wrote a book called *The Elusive Presence*, in which he argued that the most important unifying factor in the Old Testament witness is God's absence-in-presence, or presence-in-absence. Similarly, the important French thinker Blaise Pascal wrote that "A religion which does not affirm that God is hidden is not true . . . and a religion which does not offer the *reason* [for this hiddenness] is not illuminating." Let us try very hard, this morning, to be *illuminating*—that is, to shed God's illumination into the darkness of this world.

The saying of Isaiah—God hides himself—is remarkably set into a passage of rapturous praise of God's mighty deeds of salvation for his people. It's the same with our hymn: God is hidden in light inaccessible, and yet he is most blessed, most glorious, ancient of days, almighty, victorious. These two statements seem to cancel one another out. How do we know that God is gracious and almighty and so forth if God is hidden and inaccessible?

The only way to respond to questions like these is to learn what God has told us about himself. That is to say, to immerse ourselves in the Holy Scriptures. This may seem obvious, but one of the most familiar laments that I hear from seminary professors is that the students who come to study for the ministry arrive without knowing anything about the Bible. One hopes they know something by the time they graduate, but there isn't any substitute for being immersed in the Bible from earliest childhood. One way to become thus immersed is to know lots of hymns. They are full of Christian teaching and biblical doctrine. I commend to you the full text of William Cowper's poem. His life was a torment to him in many ways. And yet he had known the love of God and would not give up his hold upon it.

There are two different ways of asking "Where is God? Why does God hide himself?"

One way is scornful, hostile, and truly *God-less*, like the abuse and mockery hurled at Jesus on the cross: "He trusted in God to deliver him, so let God deliver him!" The people who yelled that insult thought they knew who God was and what God would and would not do (Matt. 27:43; also Ps. 22:8).

But the *other way* of asking, like the poet Cowper's way, comes from deep faith. It comes from having at least a partial knowledge of God and of the darkness that opposes God. This is a thread that runs through the whole discussion of the hiddenness of God. Anyone who has received even a tiny glimpse of the majesty, holiness, and righteousness of God will have an increased sense of the darkness, disorder, and malevolence that's loose in the world. These forces would swallow us up had not God set in motion his great plan to reclaim his creation. This is what Isaiah celebrates above all.

The verse "Truly, thou art a God who hidest thyself" is curiously placed because it comes in the midst of a passage of ecstatic praise.[2] In fact, almost

---

2. Claus Westermann suggests that this verse is an "amen gloss" (an exclamation of affirmation by someone editing the passage) (*Isaiah 40–66: A Commentary* [London: SCM, 1969], 171).

all of Isaiah 40–55 is ecstatic. It's the longest, most sustained hymn of praise to the power and purposes of God in the whole Bible. Yet the conditions in which those chapters were written were literally hopeless by any ordinary standards. The people of God had been dragged off to Babylon, where the colossal Mesopotamian gods dominated everything. They were forced to ponder the fact that their God had apparently abandoned them, along with his promises to them. When we remember that, it makes Isaiah's prophetic work seem truly miraculous. He writes that God is not dependent upon circumstances. God creates his own circumstances. God is not located simply within Israel. His power and promises encompass the entire created order. The chapter continues, mocking the gods of Babylon:

> "They . . . carry about their wooden idols,
> and keep on praying to a god that cannot save. . . .
>> There is no other god besides me,
> a righteous God and a Savior. . . .
> Turn to me and be saved,
>> all the ends of the earth!
> For I am God, and there is no other. . . .
>> From my mouth has gone forth in righteousness
>> a word that shall not return:
> 'To me every knee shall bow,
>> every tongue shall swear.'" (Isa. 45:20–23)

If we understand the context of this—a minuscule band of captive Hebrews dwarfed by the mighty empire of Mesopotamia—we can begin to grasp the audacity of the prophet of the exile. It's the most advanced portion of the Old Testament. In the unexcelled proclamation of Isaiah, we look ahead to the proclamations of the apostle Paul, who picked up the universal theme: "At the name of Jesus every knee [will] bow, in heaven and on earth and under the earth, and every tongue confess that Jesus Christ is Lord, to the glory of God the Father" (Phil. 2:10–11).

It was widely noted, and noted with skepticism and even disdain by some, that every one of the funerals for the children of Sandy Hook school was held at a church. This does not answer the question of why God did not stop the shooter, that inexplicably damaged and lost young man, when he opened fire at the school. We do not know why God appeared to be absent. What we do know is that God was present in this way: he was, and is still, present in the coming together of those who grieve with the families, to bring small lights into the blackness of their grief. They were not alone. There was something or Someone that drew the bereaved families deeper into the midst of the communities that continue to trust God even when he has hidden himself. Incomprehensible as it may seem, God is alive in the faith of his people wherever they are and in whatever condition.

The fact that God hides himself in the midst of revealing himself is paradoxically a testimony to his reality. Presence-in-absence is the theme of his self-disclosure. God isn't hidden because we are too stupid to find him, or too lazy, or not "spiritual" enough. He hides himself for his own reasons, and he reveals himself for his own reasons. If that were not so, God would not be God; God would be nothing more than a projection of our own religious ideas and wishes.

The Lord *hides* himself from us because he is God, and God *reveals* himself to us because *God is love* (I John 4:8). Does that make sense? Probably not . . . but sometimes Christians must be content with theological paradox. To know God in his Son Jesus Christ is to know that he is unconditionally Love unto the last drop of God's own blood. In the cross and resurrection of his Son, God has given us everything that we need to live with alongside the terrors of his seeming absence. Many churches do not use the phrase "he descended into hell" in the Apostles' Creed, but for many who have pondered its meaning, it is a central affirmation. In his death on the cross, Jesus descended into the hell of the absence of God. That's what the cry of dereliction on the cross means. "My God, my God, why have you forsaken me?" He experienced the absence of God his Father as no one else ever has, not even in the greatest extremity, because he experienced it for all of us. The Son of God underwent the opposite course: he came out from the light and went into the darkness . . . to be himself the light in our darkness.

Toward the end of World War II, during the liberation of Europe, Allied troops found a crudely written inscription on the walls of a basement in Cologne (Köln), Germany, by someone who was hiding from the Nazi Gestapo. Here's what it said:

I believe in the sun even when it is not shining.

I believe in love even when feeling it not.

I believe in God even when God is silent.[3]

---

3. This was set to music by Michael Horvit, for the fiftieth anniversary of Kristallnacht.

The silence of God descended upon the cross on Good Friday.
And on the morning of the third day the sun rose upon the empty tomb.
Hear now the word of God in the book of Deuteronomy:

> The secret things belong to the Lord our God; but the things that are revealed belong to us and to our children for ever. (Deut. 29:29)

Amen.

The Enemy Outvoted

Trinity Episcopal Church, New Orleans
2003

EPHESIANS 2:1–10

You may have noticed that ever since 9/11 President Bush has been saying emphatically that events would unfold "at a time of *our choosing.*" This is the way that powerful people tend to speak. It is also the way that nonpowerful people sometimes speak in order to gain a taste of power. We lay out our plans, we talk about our choices, we throw our weight around, we declare what we believe is going to happen and what we intend to do. The Pentagon is talking this way at the daily press conferences. On Friday, Brigadier General Vincent Brooks declared, "*The coalition is setting the conditions* for future operations."[1]

As everyone knows by now, however, the field commanders in Iraq are giving reports that differ from those coming out of the Pentagon. While I was reading a whole bunch of articles about how the war in Iraq is going, one sentence caught my eye. It was in a story about the way the coalition forces are attempting to adapt to unexpected setbacks. The sentence reads, "In carrying out any military plan, commanders here like to say [that] it is important to remember that *the enemy has a vote.*"[2] In other words, there is more than one army on the field. There is *another, opposing force* to be reckoned with.

Very often—more often than not, in fact—the Christian faith is presented as a rather static two-party transaction in which God presents himself to us and then stands back and lets us decide what choices and responses we're

1. John M. Broder, "Two Views of War: On the Ground and at the Top," *New York Times*, March 29, 2003.
2. Michael R. Gordon, "Allies Adapt to Setbacks," *New York Times*, March 27, 2003.

This sermon, preached when the Iraq War was in its early months, is not specifically an Advent sermon but is included because it quite explicitly expounds the Advent scenario and its relation to human behavior.

going to make. The emphasis is on *us—our* projections, *our* strategies, *our* decisions. God may be looking on as an interested, caring, and, indeed, loving spectator, but still a spectator, observing us as we work out our jobs and our lives and our wars but withholding his involvement, allowing us our "free will" and watching to see how well we perform.[3] Again, we typically think of this as a reciprocal two-party arrangement. If we make the right choices, God will then approve.

But that's not what the New Testament shows us, and in particular it is not what the epistle to the Ephesians dramatizes. The New Testament story is not a two-party transaction; it is a *three*-part *cosmic drama* in which not only does the "enemy get a vote," the enemy plays a colossal role—indeed, a very nearly dominant role. To see this, we look at our reading from Ephesians for today. As always in the Bible, the bad news about our condition is preceded by the good news. Here are the first words of the chapter: *And you he made alive.* God has already come to us with his gift of new and eternal life. That precedes everything else.

But then the apostle continues, laying out before us the true state of things in the world. Until God intervened with his gift of life, he writes, *you were dead.* "You [and I] were dead through the trespasses and sins in which [we] once walked, following the course of this world, following the prince of the power of the air, the spirit that is now at work in the sons of disobedience. Among these we all once lived in the passions of our flesh, following the desires of body and mind, and so we were by nature children of wrath, like the rest of mankind."

The basic scenario here is that there is an Enemy arrayed against us, and I do not mean Saddam Hussein. The "prince of the power of the air" is called *Satan* in Scripture. The figure of Satan is symbolic; this symbolism functions to show us that the Enemy of God is a personal intelligence possessed of an implacable will and an unrelenting purpose, far stronger than the will or purpose of any human being, far stronger indeed than the wills or purposes of all human beings put together. Matthew's story of the temptation of Christ dramatizes the unique power of the incarnate Son of God, the only human being able to go head-to-head against this Enemy and confound him.

Americans like to think of themselves as innocent and good. But this is dangerous, as we should have learned by now. For example, the superb movie

---

3. "Free will" is in quotation marks to indicate that in the biblical view, human beings unaided by God have very little of it, because we are in bondage to the Enemy forces (called by Paul Sin and Death, or the principalities and powers).

The Pianist is being advertised not as a movie about the Holocaust but as "an experience of the triumph of the human spirit." This is false to the film and false as an assessment of human nature. The movie dramatizes the moral chaos and loss of context that occur when evil runs rampant, so that people who were friends or neighbors or even blood relatives turn against one another, and *who among us*, however "good," can say what he or she would have done under such circumstances?[4] In Graham Greene's novel about Vietnam, *The Quiet American*, the British journalist says wearily, "God save us always from the innocent and the good."[5]

In his thousand-page epic *The Lord of the Rings*, J. R. R. Tolkien has replicated the three agencies in the biblical drama in an astonishingly complete way. It is commonly believed that his story is about good versus evil. It is not.[6] It is about the way that the independent power of evil can corrupt *anybody*, even the "good" (and in his letters, Tolkien often put "good" in quotation marks). Evil is personified in the story as Sauron, but is more often called simply "the Enemy." This Enemy is capable of taking up residence in anyone. The ring, which represents pure unadulterated power of the sort that everyone would like to have, is the symbol of the way this happens. Power is most dangerous in the hands of the strong and well meaning, those who are sure that they can use it for good purposes. Evil is loose in the world and can take over anyone, anywhere, at any time—but the proud and the self-righteous are especially vulnerable.

Opposed to this Enemy is another force. Tolkien never names this force, never identifies it, never calls attention to it—and you certainly won't see it in the movie—but it is there on almost every page. This other Power (which Christians have often called Providence) is ceaselessly working to defeat the enemy, but it is an indirect, often invisible kind of working. This Power can work through anyone, and there are plenty of grand and glamorous figures in Tolkien's story, but it prefers to operate through people the Bible calls "those of low degree." When the angel came to Mary the mother of Jesus, she said,

---

4. In my judgment, this is by far the best of Roman Polanski's films, and many have called it the best of all films about the Holocaust. It is firmly based in a true story splendidly well told in the book *The Pianist*, by Władysław Szpilman (1946).

5. Jesus says something like this in his parable of the Pharisee and the publican—it is the self-satisfied "good" person, the person who is sure that God is on his side, who is in the most peril (Luke 18:9–14)

6. A careful reading shows that it is not, and moreover, Tolkien explicitly says in his letters that it is not. For a full treatment of this, see my *Battle for Middle-Earth* (Grand Rapids: Eerdmans, 2004).

"[God] has put down the mighty from their seats and has exalted the humble and meek" (Luke 1:52). *The Lord of the Rings* is also about the way that God is able to accomplish his purposes through the smallest and the least, those who have no standing in the world.

The story told in Ephesians, and indeed in all the New Testament, is that there are three active agencies, not two—and the three are (1) God, (2) *all* (not just *some*) of humanity, and (3) the Enemy. As we have seen, the Enemy is called in Ephesians "the prince of the power of the air." This prince—this formidable ruling power—is also called (in Eph. 6) "the devil" who commands "principalities and powers," who leads the "rulers of this present darkness," who marshals the "spiritual hosts of wickedness in the heavenly places."

So Saddam Hussein is not the Enemy at all, except in a very limited sense. Rather, he is in the grip of the greater Enemy. But here is the point: we are just as susceptible to the real Enemy as he is. All of us, I think, are genuinely enraged by the things that the Iraqi forces seem to be doing to POWs. But it is precisely in our righteous outrage that we ourselves become vulnerable. Push us just a little bit more and a little bit more and we too are capable of mistreating prisoners and killing children—as former senator Bob Kerrey discovered in Vietnam.[7] Three days ago one of the reporters "embedded" with the marines wrote a dispatch in which he observed that at first the American troops were scrupulous about civilian casualties, but as they saw more and more of the battle, they were becoming less and less careful.[8] The end of that story is that we *all* end up as "children of wrath."

But God . . . says Ephesians, and when you hear those two words, "but God," in the New Testament, tune in, because you are about to hear the good news: "But God, who is rich in mercy, out of the great love with which he loved us, even when we were dead through our trespasses, made us alive together with Christ (by grace you have been saved), and raised us up with him, and made us sit with him in the heavenly places in Christ Jesus. . . . For by grace you have been saved through faith; and this is not your own doing, it is the gift of God."

The Enemy, you see, is too strong for us. Only by the grace of God are we brought "out of error into truth, out of sin into righteousness, out of sin into

7. He wrote later, "I did not recognize the person I had become." A year after this sermon was preached, the graphic photographs from Abu Ghraib prison were released to the public, showing ordinary American soldiers unleashed to abuse the prisoners in any way they chose.

8. I have mislaid this article.

life."[9] We cannot do it for ourselves. It is "not our own doing, it is the gift of God. . . . It is not because of works, lest any man should boast."

Now, the question always arises at this point in the gospel story: If God has done it all for us, what is there for us to do? The very best answer is in the next verse of our text. "For we are [God's] workmanship, created in Christ Jesus for good works, which God prepared beforehand, that we should walk in them." God has already prepared our good choices for us, and he has guaranteed that what we do *in Christ Jesus* cannot be undone by the Enemy.

But what does it mean to act *in Christ Jesus*? Here are two stories from the war, told by two embedded reporters, side by side on the front page of yesterday's *New York Times*. Let's listen to these two stories with our three-part drama in mind.

At the base camp of the Fifth Marine regiment in Iraq, two sharpshooters traded war stories as a reporter listened. "We had a great day," said one. "We killed a lot of people." They talked about the difficulty of deciding what to do when Iraqi soldiers were standing close to noncombatants. "We dropped a few civilians," said one of the Americans, "but what do you do?" Another acknowledged killing a woman. "I'm sorry," he said, "but the chick got in the way."[10]

The second story comes from the Third Infantry Division. Sergeant Mark N. Redmond is troubled. He and his comrades have spent three days and nights fighting to secure one bridge, and they have succeeded. But Sergeant Redmond is reflective. "I mean, I have my wife and kids to go back home to," he said. "I don't want them to think I'm a killer." He had not expected the Iraqis to resist so strongly, he said; he had thought they were going to surrender. "When I go home," he continued, "people will want to treat me like a hero, but I'm not. I'm a Christian man. If I have to kill the other guy, I will, but it doesn't make me a hero. I just want to go home to my wife and kids."

The final words in the second story come from an army chaplain. The young men brag among themselves, he said, but then they come to talk to him. "It bothers them to take life," he said. "They want to talk to me so that they know that I know they are not awful human beings."[11]

None of these young men are either "evil" or "good." They are neither "guilty" nor "innocent." They are neither "awful" nor "saintly." Maybe it is more accurate to say that they are hovering on the brink of both, and could go either

9. 1979 Book of Common Prayer, 368.

10. Dexter Filkins, "Take a Shot or Take a Chance," *New York Times*, March 27, 2003.

11. Steven Lee Myers, "Haunting Thoughts after a Fierce Battle," *New York Times*, March 27, 2003.

way, like all the rest of us. One striking difference, perhaps, is that the hardened elite warriors—the snipers, the bomber pilots, the special ops—may be less aware of what the Enemy might be doing to their souls (and I don't mean the Iraqi enemy). This particular sergeant, however, is gifted with remarkable insight. He knows that being acclaimed as a hero is dangerous. He's afraid of that kind of power. As a confessing Christian, he knows he has been given a job to do and he is doing it, but he claims no merit for it.[12] He does not want to divide up the world into good guys and bad guys. In that respect, he is closer to being *in Christ Jesus*.

The story told to us in Ephesians is above all a universal story. It is not the story of Americans or even the story of Christians. It is the story of the whole of humanity in all its unacknowledged inner conflicts, moral ambiguity, mixed motives, and uncontrollable passions. All human beings are "children of wrath." Unaided human beings cannot free themselves from the Enemy. As Paul exclaims in Romans, "Who will deliver us from this body of Death?" (Rom. 7:24). It has been done for us by God through Jesus Christ, who was triumphant over Satan on Satan's own turf. The Enemy has a vote, all right, but his vote has been invalidated, annulled, canceled. It has been overridden by the greater Power. God has accomplished something that we could never have accomplished. Sin and Death, those cosmic Powers of the Enemy of God, no longer have any final hold upon us. The One who holds the future of the human race is God, and God alone.

And therefore, as Winston Churchill said to the English in the Battle of Britain, "Let us brace ourselves to our duties." Let us confidently go forth to "do all such good works as God has prepared for us to walk in." Tolkien called God "the Writer of the Story." The time of choosing is not ultimately within the president's power to decide. The One who is setting the ultimate conditions is God. The One who has sent his Son to rescue the "children of wrath" is God. And the ultimate outcome, for *all* of us warring human beings, belongs to God. Thanks be to God. "We are his workmanship, created in Christ Jesus for good works, which God prepared beforehand, that we should walk in them."

Amen.

12. In our Rite One eucharistic prayer we speak of God "not weighing our merits, but pardoning our offenses."

The Call to Resistance

Wycliffe College, Toronto
Preaching Day, October 5, 2011

I PETER 5:8–11

The Canadian theologian Douglas Harink, whose commentary on I Peter I commend to you, writes these words that are almost like a prayer for the preaching and the hearing of a sermon: "'Theology begins . . . with the opening of the scriptures by the risen Lord.' The messianic 'time of legibility' of the scriptures is inaugurated wherever the risen and reigning Messiah is present and active, himself interpreting the scriptures 'where two or three are gathered [together].' When the scriptures are heard and preached in the congregation, and the same Holy Spirit who was sent from heaven upon the apostles comes again upon the church, we are enabled also, through the stories, patterns, and types of scripture, to read our present time."[1]

May it be so.

Let us therefore listen once more to a portion of the reading from the first epistle of Peter: "Be sober, be watchful. Your adversary the devil prowls around like a roaring lion, seeking some one to devour. Resist him, firm in your faith, knowing that the same experience of suffering is required of your family of brothers and sisters throughout the world. And after you have suffered a little while, the God of all grace, who has called you to his eternal glory in Christ, will himself restore, establish, and strengthen you. To him be the dominion for ever and ever. Amen" (I Pet. 5:8–11).

---

1. Douglas Harink, *1 & 2 Peter* (Grand Rapids: Brazos, 2009). I have altered the word order for the purposes of this sermon. The opening quotation is from John Behr, *The Mystery of Christ: Life in Death* (Crestwood, NY: St. Vladimir's Seminary Press, 2006), 141. "Opening of the scriptures" alludes to the episode where Jesus met the believers on the road to Emmaus.

Another sermon not specifically for Advent, but strongly focused on the Advent theme of resistance to the Enemy.

Here's a story about the devil. A Scottish professor who was a militant, outspoken atheist was out fishing on Loch Ness. He was enjoying the peace and serenity when suddenly an enormous, ravening creature reared up from the deep. The terrified professor cried out, "Oh, Lorrrd God, save me!"

A mighty voice rumbled down from the heavens: "I thought you didn't believe in Me!"

The trembling professor responded, "Aye, Lorrrd God, but until a minute ago I didn't believe in the Loch Ness monster, either!"

Now on this same subject, here is a very much more serious reflection from Canada's own senator Roméo Dallaire, who is known throughout the world for his confrontation with the powers of evil during the genocide in Rwanda. Sometime after his return to Canada and his struggle to come to terms with what had happened, a Canadian padre asked him if it was still possible for him to believe in God. This is what he said: "I answered that I know there is a God because in Rwanda I shook hands with the devil. I have seen him, I have smelled him, and I have touched him. I know the devil exists, and therefore I know there is a God."[2]

The New Testament does not present arguments or explanations for the presence of Satan. The presence and power of the demonic are simply assumed. The great Adversary is part of the New Testament cosmology, and although many have tried to tell the story without him, it really can't be done. As Stanley Hauerwas puts it, "No Enemy, No Christianity."[3]

Therefore Peter urges the Christian community: "Be sober, be watchful. Your adversary the devil prowls around like a roaring lion, seeking someone to devour. Resist him, firm in your faith." The Christian life is a call to resistance.

One of the great commentaries on I Peter was written in England by E. G. Selwyn during World War II. He does not refer often to the circumstances in which he writes, but you can tell that he has it in his mind all the time. About the image of the "roaring lion" who is "prowling around" (RSV), he writes,

2. Roméo Dallaire, *Shake Hands with the Devil: The Failure of Humanity in Rwanda* (Toronto: Random House Canada, 2003). Speaking strictly in theological terms, we do not say that the devil "exists" in the same way that the created order exists. God made the world and pronounced it good; God did not create evil. Nevertheless, evil appeared. This paradox is expressed when we say that the devil, or devils, lacks existence (hence the well-known definition of evil as *privatio boni*, the absence of good). Any account of evil, however, must take into account its rampaging malignity and power, however its lack of created existence is technically defined.

3. This is the title of an essay in Hauerwas's *Sanctify Them in the Truth: Holiness Exemplified* (London: Bloomsbury T. & T. Clark, 2016).

"[this] graphic simile depict[s] the strength, ubiquity, and destructiveness of evil . . . the picture of the lion ranging at will for his prey suggests the action of swirling tides of irrational prejudice used by a Gestapo rather than [a] deliberate imperial law." Peter's picture of the lion "expresses the fell and deliberate purpose of the malignant Power of Evil."[4]

Understanding the Christian faith and being the Christian church require imagination. If we want to raise children as Christians, it's important to exercise their imaginations. I've always remembered something that a former colleague said one Christmas. He said he didn't mind his children believing in Santa Claus, because it was "training for transcendence." Similarly, when children hear Bible stories in early childhood with a sense of wonder, before they start asking, "Did that really happen?," it makes a difference that lasts all their lives. It makes it so much easier for them to enter "the strange new world of the Bible" (Barth).

This sermon is about a month ahead of its time. It's best suited for the Sundays just before Advent, when we are thinking about the apocalyptic collision between God and the powers of the Enemy. I have often recalled the cover of *Time* magazine during the Rwandan horror. Against a black background with hints of corpses, these words appeared in large letters: "There are no devils left in Hell; they are all in Rwanda."[5] That was spoken by a worker with one of the humanitarian agencies. He had a sense of the cosmology of the New Testament. Roméo Dallaire also had this sense. This sort of imagination needs nurturing in the church.

Resist him, says the apostle. This is a clear command. But how are we to resist the devil? I am tempted to say simply, go home and read *The Screwtape Letters*.[6] I particularly remember one bit of that book where Screwtape urges his young trainee to keep his charge's attention focused exclusively on the

---

4. E. G. Selwyn, *The First Epistle of St. Peter* (London: Macmillan, 1964; original 1946). The capitalization of "Power" and "Evil" are Selwyn's own.

5. *Time* magazine cover, May 16, 1994.

6. In the preface to the revised edition of *The Screwtape Letters*, Lewis gives us a further glimpse of the New Testament cosmology: "Now, if by 'the Devil' you mean a power opposite to God and, like God, self-existent from all eternity, the answer is certainly No. There is no uncreated being except God. God has no opposite. . . . The proper question is whether I believe in devils. I do. That is to say, I believe in angels, and I believe that some of these, by the abuse of their free will, have become enemies to God. . . . Satan, the leader or dictator of devils, is the opposite, not of God, but of Michael [the archangel]" (preface to the 1960 edition of *Screwtape*; original preface written in 1941). This does not perfectly account for the existence of evil (nothing does, this side of the kingdom of God), but it has a certain power.

mundane aspects of church life: the irritants, the bad music, the unattractive people, the tasteless architecture, and so forth. Don't let him see the church as we see it, says Screwtape, "spread out through all eternity, terrible as an army with banners." That, Screwtape confesses, is a sight to make even the most experienced tempter quake. But fortunately for Wormwood, the man in the pew can't see that. Only through the Word of God is the human being enabled to see what God sees.

The first epistle of Peter is a letter from a God's-eye view, and the view it gives is of the church. We can never say it often enough: the Bible is addressed, for the most part, not to *individuals*, but to the *people* of God.[7] We need to say still more. As Peter puts it in various ways over and over throughout the letter, the people of God have been constituted, not by their *own* preferences or choices, but by *God's prior* choice, first of Israel, and then, through Jesus Christ, of the church. The church resists, endures, and conquers not through its own efforts, let alone its merits, but because of the call, the commission, and the continuing presence of God. "The God of all grace, who has called you to his eternal glory in Christ, will himself restore, establish, and strengthen you." The church lives out of (not "into" but "out of") its foundation upon the "living stone" (I Pet. 2:6), which is Christ, out of its baptism into his death and resurrection, out of its promised future guaranteed by his Holy Spirit. It is this certainty that gives courage for resistance.

But how are we to resist evil? Most of us are so taken up with our own little lives that we have no vision of a resistant church. We have been fooled by a veneer of generic, bland "spirituality" that has no devouring enemies. Some of our most thoughtful Christian leaders are saying that we now live in a post-Christian culture and must begin to act like the church in the Roman Empire before Constantine. I can't speak for you here in Canada, but this is going to be very, very difficult for the American church because we are so accustomed to thinking of America and Christianity as almost synonymous, especially in the South, where I was raised. It was idolatrous for us to think that in the first place, and now we must pay for our mistake. We must pay for it by learning to resist the lies of the enemy and the false gods that the enemy celebrates.

7. The theme of Peter is the church among the nations as the people of the crucified, risen, and reigning Christ. Therefore resistance is not largely a matter of individuals but of the corporate body. "Peter does not issue a general call to become a Christian and then, as a subsequent and perhaps optional move, for individual Christians to join together into a voluntary association that might serve our projects of being individual Christians." God precedes the people; the people precedes the person; the person is constituted by being incorporated into the people (Harink, *1 & 2 Peter*, 73).

The foremost way of resistance is, of course, the worship of the Christian community—*true* worship, that is, that "ascribes to the Lord the honor due his name." Judging from my experience going to church in the States, it isn't all that easy to find true worship—but you know it when you see it. As the African Americans say, "We had *church* today!" The presence and power of God take over. True worship isn't focused on exhortations to do better, or lessons about inclusivity, or instructions about "spirituality," or even one-dimensional repetitions about how "God loves you just as you are," which shifts the emphasis away from God to our own little selves. The *first* order of worship is the triune God alone, God as he is in himself, "the God of all grace"—and only then ourselves because *he* "has called us to his eternal glory in Christ."

The "eternal glory" of God is a very strong theme in I Peter. I don't know how much we think about the glory of God, even though church memorials are usually dedicated to it. The glory of God is so resplendent that it should cause us to forget about ourselves for a brief space as we behold his surpassing majesty, his everlasting dominion, his "uncreated light," his ineffable holiness, his triumph over evil, his power "that raises the dead and calls into existence the things that do not exist" (Rom. 4:17). It is the glory of God that raises us out of our preoccupations to see the promised future that is guaranteed to us through our incorporation into Christ. We know this future by faith, and we are secured in God's glory through baptism.

That brings us to a corresponding theme in I Peter, which would seem to cancel out the glory of God, and that's the theme of *suffering*. "Resist [the devil], firm in your faith, knowing that the same experience of suffering is required of your family of brothers and sisters throughout the world." *Resistance* requires *suffering*. No book of the New Testament emphasizes suffering as much as I Peter, and yet it has always been a beloved book because of its reassurance.

The church is called into the way of Christ. This is the road we walk, the race we run. When the church is truly being the church, it imitates our Lord by setting its face like flint toward Jerusalem, toward the sacrifice of itself. As the epistle to the Hebrews puts it unforgettably, "Let us run with perseverance the race that is set before us, looking to Jesus the pioneer and perfecter of our faith, who for the joy that was set before him endured the cross, despising the shame, and is seated at the right hand of the throne of God" (Heb. 12:1–2).

Because our Lord is the "pioneer and perfecter," the church is able to bear its burden, endure its humiliation, despise its shame, and enter into the glory of God.

The great question then presents itself: What should the church be resisting right now?

John Stott entered into glory a few weeks ago, ending an earthly life that was untouched by scandal and single-mindedly devoted to the glory of God and the spread of the gospel. One of the people who knew him best reported that his last years were clouded by disappointment that the church has been so riven with inner conflict that it has little energy for tackling the great problems of the world—poverty, hunger, natural calamity, corporate rapacity, environmental degradation, greed, violence, war. It seems so very sad that this towering figure in worldwide Christianity should feel these wounds so acutely as he lay dying. The resistance of God's people should be directed outward, not consuming itself with its own inward quarrels. Such is the power of Sin, the handmaid of Satan, who ranges as freely through the church as he does throughout the world.

We have a battle on two fronts—not only *without* but also *within* the church. This visiting preacher tonight has no way of knowing what your warfare will be as members of this Christian community in Ontario. Your calling is to discern the place of resistance that the Lord has set before you. You will recognize it by the temptation to avoid it. It will be way out of your comfort zone. It will be characterized by pressure, by disturbance, by antagonism, by pain, by humiliation. But remember that you are part of the great company of witnesses and that Satan has no chance against the Lord of hosts.

Remember also that there is one thing the devil cannot abide, and that is being ridiculed. Here's a little story from the American civil rights movement, told by Bayard Rustin, one of the movement's most effective leaders: "When the Ku Klux Klan marched into Montgomery [Alabama] and we knew they were coming, Dr. King and I sat down and thought it over. And we said, 'Ah! Tell everybody to put on their Sunday clothes, stand on the [church] steps, and when the Ku Kluxers come, applaud 'em.' Well, they came, marched three blocks, and . . . [departed]. They could not comprehend the new thing. They were no longer able to engender fear."[8]

Remember that, when you are called to the barricades. And remember most of all these words of Peter: "And after you have suffered a little while, the God of all grace, who has called you to his eternal glory in Christ, will himself restore, establish, and strengthen you. To him be the dominion for ever and ever. Amen."

8. Howell Raines, *My Soul Is Rested: Movement Days in the Deep South Remembered* (New York: Putnam, 1977), 56.

Righteous Deeds Like Filthy Rags

Little Trinity Anglican Church, Toronto
November 2008

ISAIAH 64:6; JEREMIAH 33:14–16

These weeks preceding Christmas are the best time in the whole liturgical year for the church to be introspective—even more so than in Lent. In Lent we are attending to the Lord's journey toward his crucifixion, but in the seven-week season that incorporates Advent, beginning after All Saints' Day, we are summoned as the people of God to come before his judgment seat. That was the theme of last Sunday night's sermon. We heard the call from the first letter of Peter: "The time has come for judgment to begin with the household of God" (I Pet. 4:17); and we were comforted and established by the promise given by Saint Paul: "God has not destined us for wrath, but to obtain salvation through our Lord Jesus Christ" (I Thess. 5:9).

The Hebrew prophets are crucially important at any time of year, but especially during this time. They address the household of God from the edge, from the frontier, from the place where expectations and hopes are dashed by "the facts on the ground." Let's attend carefully to a classic Advent reading from the prophet Isaiah; in this passage, the people continue to speak to God even though he is either silent or hostile or both: "Behold [O Lord], you have been angry . . . in our sins we have been a long time, and shall we be saved? We have all become like one who is unclean, and all our righteous deeds are like filthy rags. We fade like a leaf, and our iniquities, like the wind, take us away. . . . You have hidden your face from us, and have delivered us into the hand of our iniquities" (Isa. 64:5–7).

All our righteous deeds are like filthy rags. I won't go into detail from the pulpit, but these filthy rags are not just dirty cloths, as if they had been used to wipe up the marks of muddy boots from the kitchen floor. These filthy rags, or "a polluted garment" (RSV), are not just gross; they are ritually unclean—contaminated, desecrated, unholy, unfit for any use at all except to be burned up. That's what our righteous deeds are worth.

What does *that* mean?

I've been reading a lot of books about genocide, especially the genocide in Rwanda. Several of them have been scathing in their indictment of the humanitarian organizations that went to Rwanda to help.[1] The aid organizations are variously described as being starry-eyed, bumbling, uninformed, self-righteous, interfering, competitive, and in the way. Worse—much worse—it is now widely known that the inability or unwillingness of the nongovernmental organizations (NGOs) to make distinctions between authentic victims and hardened killers resulted in the reconstitution of the Hutu Power movement in the refugee camps, which in turn has led directly to the present horrors in the Congo, the worst human rights disaster in the world today.[2] It makes you wonder if you should ever send another cent to a humanitarian agency. *All our righteous deeds are like filthy rags.*

On election night in the United States, the chief pastor of an African American congregation in Springfield, Massachusetts, went to bed late, having spent the evening celebrating and rejoicing in the victory of Barack Obama. He had only slept a few hours when he was awakened by the telephone. The brand-new church building of which he had been so proud was burning to the ground. The fire had been deliberately set.[3] CNN reported a few days later that since the election there had been a significant increase in racial incidents directed against blacks. Osama bin Laden lost no time, either; the front page of the *New York Times* showed a frame from his latest incendiary video showing Barack Obama at the Western Wall in Jerusalem with a yarmulke on his head, so that the cross-cultural gesture of solidarity by the young black candidate was transmuted into an incitement to greater hatred of Jews. One step forward, two steps back, it sometimes seems: *Even our righteous deeds are like filthy rags.*

After the American invasion of Afghanistan in 2002, two young American Christian women, barely into their twenties, traveled to Afghanistan full of zeal to convert Afghans by showing them a movie about Jesus. They were promptly seized by the Taliban and held for several weeks. When they got

---

1. Roméo Dallaire, *Shake Hands with the Devil* (Toronto: Random House Canada, 2003); Philip Gourevitch, *We Wish to Inform You That Tomorrow We Will Be Killed with Our Families* (New York: Farrar, Straus and Giroux, 1998).

2. Philip Gourevitch, in his prize-winning book about Rwanda, can hardly contain his rage and contempt, calling the Western NGOs "criminally irresponsible" and "mindless" (*We Wish to Inform You*, 325).

3. Actually, the new church building was still under construction, about 75 percent finished. I omitted that detail for simplicity's sake. Dan Barry, "A Time of Hope, Marred by an Act of Horror," *New York Times*, November 17, 2008.

home, they were immediately canonized by various evangelical churches and were asked to speak all over the place. Back in Afghanistan, however, the seasoned Christian missionaries who had been there for years were furious with the two of them for being so reckless and presumptuous. *Even our righteous deeds are like filthy rags.*

I haven't been in Canada long enough to be able to comment on the churches here, but in the States, it is not untypical for churches to brag about themselves. Very often, on the signs in front, or on the websites, or at the top of the church bulletin, you will see something like this: "We are a friendly, welcoming, warm, inclusive, embracing, Bible-based, Spirit-filled, Christ-centered fellowship doing all sorts of great things in our community." I have become somewhat jaundiced about all this. I could tell you story after story of troubled people who have sought friendship and community from those welcoming, embracing churches, only to meet with disappointment and rejection. Someone told me recently that some insurance companies won't even insure churches anymore because of all the sexual exploitation and abuse. Maybe we should try putting up a different kind of sign: "This congregation is a bunch of sinners and hypocrites, misfits and marplots, Pharisees and tax collectors, and all our righteous deeds are like filthy rags."

Have you ever done something that was meant to be kind, only to have it blow up in your face? Have you ever had someone turn on you angrily when you were only attempting to help? Have you seen a carefully tended project undermined by someone's jealousy, or derailed because of your own mistakes? Have you poured yourself into a community, or a marriage, or a friendship, only to be rejected or abandoned? Then you know what it means to be aware that the very best we can do often ends in failure. Even our righteous deeds are like filthy rags.

After God's people Israel were defeated, overrun, and humiliated by the Babylonian Empire, they had plenty of time for introspection. In the capital city of Babylon, they were surrounded by colossal statues of the Babylonian gods. It appeared that the honor of Israel's God Yahweh had been ground into dust. As the captive Israelites languished in Babylon, they had to admit that the calamity was their own fault. A realistic assessment of their past performance in the role of God's elect community could only result in profound repentance and lamentation. As we enter the season of Advent, this is our condition also. Sin and Death, those twin Powers, continue to do their annihilating work. Together with the Hebrew people in exile, we acknowledge that "there is no one that calls upon thy name . . . for thou hast hid thy face from us, and hast delivered us into the hand of our iniquities. . . . We have all become like one who is unclean, and all our righteous deeds are like a polluted garment."

But now let me ask you another type of question. Have you ever had someone thank you profusely for some little thing you did that you do not even remember? Have you ever been praised to the skies for something that you just happened into, by chance, as it were? Has something you ventured succeeded in spite of your mistakes? Has an employee been loyal to you even when you have not been the greatest boss? Have you ever experienced someone saying in front of a whole group of people that you saved his sanity, or his job, or his very life, when you know you did no such thing? Have you ever prayed a little perfunctory prayer for someone and had it answered on the spot? Have you ever been forgiven for something you did that was really destructive? Has someone continued to love you even though you have been beastly to him or her? If any of these things, or anything like them, has happened to you, then, beloved of God, you have been granted a clue to the Lord's grace and mercy.

Let us now turn to another Hebrew prophet, Jeremiah, who saw the ruins of Jerusalem and the exiles carried off into pagan Babylon. In the book of Jeremiah, the themes of judgment and salvation are all mixed up together, more than in any other Old Testament book. You can't disentangle them; you can't have salvation without judgment. That's an Advent message, in case you hadn't noticed. Few prophets are more scathing and more pessimistic about what Israel deserves, but few prophets make more radical promises than Jeremiah. I'm going to read one of these promises, but first, in order to understand it in the context of Advent, we need to remember some biblical symbolism. One of the names that the church gives to our Lord Jesus Christ is "the righteous Branch." This symbol refers to the green shoot that springs forth from the dead stump of the destroyed royal house of David. One of the verses of "O Come, O Come, Emmanuel," a favorite Advent hymn, refers to Christ as "the Rod of Jesse's stem," Jesse being the father of David. Here is the word of the Lord spoken through the prophet Jeremiah: "Behold, the days are coming, says the Lord, when I will fulfil the promise I made to the house of Israel and the house of Judah. In those days and at that time I will cause a righteous Branch to spring forth for David; and he shall execute justice and righteousness in the land. In those days Judah will be saved and Jerusalem will dwell securely. And this is the name by which [the house of Israel] will be called: 'The Lord is our righteousness'" (Jer. 33:14–16).

The Lord is our righteousness! Do you see? Our own righteousness, such as it is, is so corrupted and distorted by the sinful nature, that we cannot make things turn out right to save our lives. Even our righteous deeds are like filthy rags. But we are not saved by our own righteousness. *The Lord is our righteousness!* God has done and will do what his people cannot do for themselves. What did Saint Paul say? The elect community was ignorant of the righteousness that comes from God and sought to establish its own righteousness, but the heathen who did not pursue righteousness have attained righteousness through faith (Rom. 9:30–10:4). And what else did he say? "If a law had been given which could make alive, then righteousness would indeed be by the law. But the scripture consigned all things to sin, that what was promised to faith in Jesus Christ might be given to those who believe" (Gal. 3:21–22). Truly, righteousness is by grace through faith. And so, we pray, in the beautiful words of Thomas Cranmer in the old Prayer Book, that God will receive us "not weighing our merits, but pardoning our offenses."

The pastor of that African American church in Massachusetts is praying the words from Isaiah, "Our holy and beautiful house . . . has been burned by fire, and all our pleasant places have become ruins. Wilt thou restrain thyself at these things, O Lord? Wilt thou keep silent, and afflict us sorely?"

God willing, the white people of Massachusetts (I am one of them) who were proud of themselves for voting for Barack Obama will now step forward and help. There will be contributions and a new bridge between the congregation and the wider community. These deeds will not be righteousness according to the law. These deeds will be not be weighed into a treasury of merit. These deeds will not be attempts to establish our own human righteousness. These deeds will be signs—signs that God is not silent, signs that God is not impotent, signs that our God reigns even in the midst of arson, fear, and hatred. And it will be said with joy that "this is the name by which our house is called: 'The Lord is our righteousness.'"

Amen.

The Line Runs through Each Person

Saturday Night Tent Meeting,
Saint Michael's Church, Charleston, South Carolina
On the Eve of the Feast of Michael the Archangel 2000

II KINGS 6:11–17; DANIEL 12:1; MARK 13:7–9;
PHILIPPIANS 1:29–30

Well, here we are, south of Broad in gorgeous Charleston, the epicenter of living tradition, effortless social superiority, and not-so-shabby gentility. What an unlikely spot to be talking about Good and Evil! No wonder your planning committee included lots of refreshments and other enticements under this probably very expensive tent to lull you into thinking this would be a "fun evening." Give yourself a pat on the back for being here on a Saturday night to hear a very long recruiting speech, because that's what this is going to be. Tonight and tomorrow, you get an opportunity to enlist in God's army.

Saint Michael's Church has put together a beautiful Christian formation booklet for this event. On the cover is a handsome illustration showing the archangel Michael in full flight with his spear, striking at the Adversary. In art history, Michael is ordinarily depicted with *one dead* dragon at his feet; this picture, however, shows him battling *four live* dragons, one for each point of the compass. Both these ways of illustrating Michael are valid. The traditional version shows how the victory of Christ, with the archangel at the head of his forces, has already been accomplished in the cross and resurrection. In this depiction, the war against the demonic powers has already been decisively won. The picture on the Saint Michael's booklet, however, suggests that Satan still rampages around the world, coming at us from all sides. This is true too; Satan has been at work setting in motion the terrible events that have caused the twentieth century to be called the most murderous in human history,

---

This sermon illustrates how the themes of Advent start to make their mark in the church calendar as early as the Feast of Saint Michael. A month later, after All Saints' Day on November 1, the Advent motifs begin their seven-week progression.

and Christians need to be prepared for him to mount the same attacks in the twenty-first century.

Both of these scenarios are faithful to the biblical testimony. The dynamic between the victory already won and the victory yet to come was vividly illustrated fifty years ago by a European New Testament scholar when he compared the timeline of the gospel with that of World War II. The cross and resurrection, he said, are like D-Day, and the second coming is like V-E Day. When the Normandy invasion took place, everyone knew that the Allies had won, that Hitler's game was finished. However, the Allies had to recapture Europe bit by bit, so there was still more than a year of bloodshed to come, including the intensely fought Battle of the Bulge with tremendous Allied losses. The end *had come*, yet it was *still in the future*.

We can find another illustration of this same dynamic in the children's book by C. S. Lewis, *The Lion, the Witch, and the Wardrobe*. The frozen kingdom of Narnia is in the grip of a wicked queen who turns all her enemies into ice and rules with terror. There is a rumor, however, that there will be an invasion from outside, led by a great lion named Aslan. One night the kingdom of Narnia is set abuzz with the rumor of great news: "Aslan has landed!" From that moment on, everything in Narnia changes. The little creatures who inhabit Narnia are emboldened by what they have heard. They are seized by hope. They know that the queen's days are numbered. They feel themselves becoming valiant for the struggle that still lies ahead. We can give many examples from modern life. Recollect, for example, the events in Poland on December 11, 1981. The Solidarity strikers at the Gdansk shipyard had pushed the Communists beyond the breaking point. The government cracked down with brutal repression. I was working in New York City at the time; that evening, a friend and I drove through the Polish neighborhoods of the borough of Queens, just wanting to share in the trauma. We did not know that at that very hour, Lech Walesa, the head of Solidarity, was saying to the Communist authorities, "Right at this moment, you have lost. The last nails are driven into your coffin."

How did Walesa know that? Sustained by his Catholic faith, he understood the dynamic of Christian warfare. Tyranny and oppression appear to have the upper hand; the dragons seem to be in control at every point. In such a time the Lord spoke to the prophet Daniel, in exile in pagan Babylon: "At that time shall arise Michael, the great prince who has charge of your people. And there shall be a time of trouble, such as never has been . . . but at that time your people shall be delivered" (Dan. 12:1).

Whenever Christians are under siege, we take heart when we think of Saint Michael at the head of the legions of Christ, for we know that he is going to win. However, we also know that here on earth, *we* are the legions. Jesus warns his disciples that they will be the ones in the line of fire:

> "And when you hear of wars and rumors of wars, do not be alarmed; this must take place, but the end is not yet. For nation will rise against nation, and kingdom against kingdom; there will be earthquakes in various places, there will be famines; this is but the beginning of the birth-pangs. But take heed to yourselves; for they will deliver you up to councils; and you will be beaten in synagogues; and you will stand before governors and kings for my sake, to bear testimony before them. . . . You will be hated by all for my name's sake. But he who endures to the end will be saved." (Mark 13:7–9, 13)

Jesus's disciples, in other words, are going to be his troops here on earth. We are the counterparts here below of the angelic army of the Lord on high. I love that hymn (not in the Episcopal hymnbook), "Let the Lower Lights Be Burning," with its evocation of two levels of reality. You and I are the lower lights. The upper lights are invisible to us, but we see by faith that they are the angelic armies that fight for us on high. The torches of Gideon's small band here below are the "lower lights" of a greater host above. Now, there are certain people in the church who ridicule this kind of talk about "above" and "below." They say that we have come a long way from the old flat-earth days. Well, we can just ridicule them right back for not understanding metaphorical language. "Above" and "below" language has always been more poetic than literal. It doesn't mean anything as elementary as "up there" and "down here." It refers to dimensions of reality: one dimension is transitory, the other is eternal; one is bound by sin and death, the other is free for blessedness and joy; one is clouded and torn by unending strife, the other is bright with the glory that fadeth not away.

Do you know the story about these two dimensions in II Kings? Many have seen the movie *Chariots of Fire*, but not everyone knows the Old Testament reference. The scene opens with the king of Syria demanding to know who it is from Israel who is spying on him.

> And the mind of the king of Syria was greatly troubled . . . and he called his servants and said to them, "Will you not show me who of us is for the king of Israel?" And one of his servants said, "None, my lord, O king; but Elisha, the prophet who is in Israel, tells the king of Israel the words that you speak in your bedchamber." And

he said, "Go and see where [Elisha] is, that I may . . . seize him." It was told him, "Behold, he is in Dothan." So the king sent horses and chariots and a great army; and they came by night, and surrounded the city. When the servant of Elisha, the man of God, rose early in the morning and went out, behold, an army with horses and chariots was round about the city. And the servant said, "Alas, my master! What shall we do?" Elisha said, "Fear not, for those who are with us are more than those who are with them." Then Elisha prayed, and said, "O Lord, I pray thee, open his eyes that he may see." So the Lord opened the eyes of the young man, and he saw; and behold, the mountain was full of horses and chariots of fire round about Elisha. (II Kings 6:11–17)

This is the story that forms the background for many other hymns, such as this one:

Go forward, Christian soldier,
Fear not the secret foe;
Far more o'er thee are watching
Than human eyes can know.

Those who are with us are more than those who are with them. No one in our time has illustrated this faith more than Bishop Desmond Tutu of South Africa. In the darkest days of apartheid, the state system that divided blacks from whites and robbed them of both civil rights and human rights, this small black man insisted on living as though he had an invisible army. I'll give you an example of the kind of speech he was giving back in the '80s and early '90s when he was constantly having his visa revoked and when no one thought that apartheid could ever be dismantled without a bloody revolution. You will see how he combines the story of the chariots of fire with visions from the book of Revelation:

I am a bishop in the Church of God, I am 51 years old, yet I don't have a vote. . . . Well, they can remove Desmond Tutu. They can end the South African Council of Churches. But the Church of God goes on. The government must know that the Church is not frightened of any earthly power. . . . More are for us than can ever be against us. A vast throng no one could ever count, from every nation and every tribe, standing before the throne and before the Lamb, robed in white and bearing palm branches in their hands, shout together, "Victory to our God!" We are joined with angels and archangels and the whole company of heaven.

This was a man who knew that Aslan had landed.

In the New Testament, the basic imagery of this world is that of a country occupied by the enemy forces—like most of Europe occupied by the Nazis. It is not that the world *itself* is bad, for as we know, the world is God's good creation; but since the fall of Adam and Eve, the world is occupied by Satan. That's why Jesus, in the Gospel of John, three times calls Satan *the ruler of this world* (John 12:31; 14:30; 16:11). As long as the occupying troops are firmly in power, the only way to resist is by underground action. As I don't need to tell you, this too is a metaphor; "underground" action is not necessarily happening in caverns and catacombs. The nineteenth-century Underground Railroad that assisted runaway slaves was never literally underground. During the Solidarity strikes in Poland, when the Communists closed all the newspapers, the resistance network was kept informed by the "underground" presses. Today in China, there are two churches: the one sanctioned by the Communists, and the resisting church that meets in people's houses and is called the "underground" church. It is the members of the underground Chinese church who are under surveillance, who are being arrested and imprisoned, and who need our special prayers.

The imagery of occupation is important for us to keep in mind. We Southerners have lived in a Christian, or supposedly Christian, culture for so long that we forget that Christians are, as the New Testament repeatedly tells us, perpetually under siege in this world even when we think we are secure. Up in New York and New England, where I spend most of my time, indifference to Christianity is much more advanced than it is here. Yet the "Christ-haunted South" has produced writers who understand evil. Flannery O'Connor is among the best. She wrote, "My subject is the action of grace in territory held largely by the Devil." Explaining her stories, she wrote further: "Our salvation is played out [in opposition to] the Devil, a Devil who is not simply generalized evil, but an evil intelligence determined on its own supremacy."

Tomorrow at the Saint Michael's Sunday school class, we will talk more about how evil is directed by that personal intelligence bent on defeating the purposes of God, but tonight we are going to speak more about what it means to live in between the resurrection of Christ and the second coming. We're going to talk tonight not so much about good and evil as abstract entities, but about the struggle that you and I are caught up in—whether we know it or not. If you

143

live in occupied territory, you can be a collaborator or you can be in the underground resistance, but you can't just be neutral. And so, Saint Paul wrote to his favorite church, the one in Philippi: "It has been granted to you that for the sake of Christ you should not only believe in him but also suffer for his sake, engaged in the same conflict which you saw and now hear to be mine" (Phil. 1:29–30).

Let's look at that verse carefully. Notice that Paul gives just two criteria, two essential characteristics of being a Christian—"you should *not only* believe in him *but also* suffer for his sake, engaged in the same conflict [that I am engaged in]." Every television evangelist will summon us to believe in the Lord Jesus Christ, but not many will tell us that this means suffering for Christ. It isn't so easy to explain this; people who are psychologically healthy are not going to go out and seek to suffer. What Paul means, though, is that once you believe in Jesus, you are going to be drawn into his battle. Before the Prayer Book was modernized, we used to welcome the newly baptized baby with these great words: "We receive this child into the congregation of Christ's flock, and do sign *him* with the sign of the cross, in token that hereafter *he* shall not be ashamed to confess the faith of Christ crucified, and manfully to fight under his banner, against sin, the world and the devil; and to continue Christ's faithful soldier and servant unto *his* life's end."[1]

When we enter upon the Christian life, we are already enrolled in the battle against the devil. That's a pretty big order. If we take it seriously, we will recognize that it means suffering sooner or later. We are all thinking about athletes right now because of the Olympics; Saint Paul combines his battle imagery with that of the gymnasium or sports arena. He speaks of the punishing discipline that an athlete must undergo: "Every athlete exercises self-control in all things. They do it to receive a perishable wreath, but we [Christians, to receive] an imperishable. Well, I do not run aimlessly, I do not box as one beating the air; but I pommel my body and subdue it, lest after preaching to others I myself should be disqualified" (I Cor. 9:25–27).

Paul lets his churches see him struggle, lets them know that the new life in Christ is not a carriage ride around the Battery.

There seem to be two sets of values at war within our society; we are thrilled by athletic accomplishment and we are obsessed with winning, yet surveys show that Americans are more sedentary and out of shape than ever

---

1. The gender issue is awkward today. In the 1928 Prayer Book the words "him" and "he" were used throughout, but italicized to indicate that "she" and "her" may be substituted. I proclaimed this welcome over many a baby girl, proud to think of her as fighting manfully against evil.

before in our history. The image of today's children sitting around, playing computer games, surfing the Internet, and watching television for hours on end, day after day, is truly disturbing, yet many parents are unwilling or unable to put in the time and energy to guide their children toward family activities and goal-oriented pursuits. I mention this because it is an example of the sacrifice required of Christian parents. This is one of many forms of Christian warfare today—the battle for our children's bodies and minds. Christian communities can band together in these struggles to offer support to parents and children. There is no more important form of resistance to the devil than that.

Here in the South, here in Charleston, you have a strong military tradition, and I am respectful of that. Because of this tradition, however, it is difficult sometimes to remember that the battle imagery of the New Testament is not about conventional warfare. When we sing hymns like "Onward, Christian Soldiers," we tend to think of actual, literal war. Indeed, the hymn is often sung at the funerals of military men. In the New Testament, however, it is clear that the battle imagery was never about nuclear subs, stealth bombers, and Kalashnikovs. The New Testament speaks of spiritual and moral warfare, as in the words of the hymn:

> For not with swords' loud clashing,
> Nor roll of stirring drums,
> But deeds of love and mercy,
> The heavenly kingdom comes.

Tomorrow morning the sermon will go further into the matter of Christian warfare. Tonight, we are going to focus on the nature of evil.

What is evil?

I watched an episode of CBS's *Sixty Minutes* on January 18, 1998. The distinguished journalist Christiane Amanpour reported on massacres in Algeria. It was the single most harrowing story about barbarous inhumanity that I have ever seen. Only hours and days after the events, the camera recorded the blood and body parts of whole families with their throats slit, while a young girl, still in shock, reported the murder of her parents and siblings before her eyes while Algerian troops quartered close by did nothing to prevent it. Amanpour was more shaken as she reported than I have ever seen her. Later I found a newspaper clipping, "More Than 400 Die in Latest Massacres in Algeria" (January 3, 1998). One horrific sentence read, "In violence that lasted for hours, they [the insurgents] killed 412 people, slitting throats, cutting off heads and beating children to death." *Evil.*

145

All over the world, children are being trained to bear arms in civil wars. In Cambodia, during the Pol Pot regime, the most feared soldiers were the ones between twelve and fifteen. One man wrote that of all the Khmer Rouge fighters, the youngest ones were "the most completely and savagely indoctrinated. The [Khmer Rouge] took them very young and taught them nothing but discipline. Just take orders, no need for a reason. . . . They have killed their own people, even babies, as we might kill a mosquito. I believe they did not have any feelings about human life because they were taught only discipline." *Evil*.

But those examples are from countries far away. Here is something closer to home. Just a few weeks ago in an upstate New York town, a group of teenagers, several boys and one girl, ordered seventy dollars' worth of Chinese food to be delivered to a house that they knew was isolated. When the delivery man arrived, they threw a sheet over him, hit him with a brick until he was dead, then ran off with the food and ate it. The dead man, the owner of a small takeout restaurant who did all his deliveries himself, had a wife and young children. As for the young killers, all of them were from hard-working, intact families. Later they "explained" that they wanted a Chinese dinner but did not want to pay for it. *Evil*. Incomprehensible.

The shootings last year at Columbine High School rocked America as few things have. The soul-searching is still going on. One columnist, who happened to be black, wrote an arresting newspaper piece in which he said that "they" had finally become "us." For years, he said, young black men had been shooting each other and very little attention had been paid. The overwhelming nationwide anguish in reaction to Columbine, where young white men did the shooting, offered a striking contrast. The time has come, said the journalist, to speak "not simply of black poverty but of the nation's poverty, not the pathologies of privileged white teenagers but . . . of all our . . . alienated young men."[2]

Now we are moving closer to the real subject of the preaching tonight. When we think of evil, we *all* tend to think of something "out there," separate from us and our kind. Evil is something Algerians and the Khmer Rouge do. Evil is something that happens in Sierra Leone or Rwanda or East Timor. When it comes closer to us, we cannot comprehend it. We never thought it would touch us. We have ways of dealing with it, of course. We can build more and more prisons and execute more and more people. Evil is something that Susan Smith did, so we lock her up where she can spend the rest of her life

---

2. Orlando Patterson, "When 'They' Are 'Us,'" *New York Times*, April 30, 1999. Actually, Patterson is not a journalist but a professor of sociology at Harvard; I say "journalist" for the sake of simplicity.

luring her jailers into temptation. We will come back to Susan Smith shortly, but here we are approaching something near to the heart of each and every one of us here tonight. Evil is not far off. Evil is not "out there." Evil does not always wear a mask of barbarity; sometimes it smiles. Sometimes it has beautiful manners. Sometimes it looks like your neighbor. Sometimes it looks like the face in the mirror. You know the saying of the Pogo character in the comic strip: "Yep, son, we have met the enemy and he is us."

I have in my files a clipping about a young woman who has the elephant man disease. Her face is disfigured beyond description. The newspaper story tells how her doctors first met her when she was four years old. She won them over completely with her wonderful personality. "She had a profound effect on me," one of them said. He wanted to help her, because of the terrible suffering she endured from being ridiculed in public. Her sister testified that she is insulted everywhere she goes. Grown men and women abuse her in front of their children, as though that would somehow protect their children from a similar fate. She is verbally assaulted in shopping centers, at her university, even on the quiet woodland path where she likes to walk.

Are these evil people, or are they just ordinary people, neighbors that we see in the supermarket every day? Also in my file is a famous photograph. It shows a group of beautiful girls, about sixteen or seventeen, dressed impeccably in the fashion of the early sixties, with gleaming hair, flawless makeup, and fresh, pretty dresses. They look like debutantes. They look like daughters we would be proud to have. But something is wrong with the picture. The faces of the girls are contorted. They are screaming something. They look as though they are consumed with anger and hate. The caption on the photograph is "Montgomery, Alabama, 1963." It is the time of the Montgomery bus boycott, and the young women are screaming at black people.

Were these girls evil, or were they just young people who didn't know any better? Forty-five years ago, I can assure you, one of them might have been me. There is a saying that you have all heard: "There but for the grace of God go I." It is attributed to a seventeenth-century English Puritan, John Bradford. He was watching some convicts led through the streets of London to be executed, and he said, "There but for the grace of God go I." It isn't in the Bible, but it is a profoundly biblical idea; think, for instance, of Psalm 130:3,

> If thou, O Lord, shouldst mark iniquities,
>> Lord, who could stand?

In other words, if God were to count up our sins, we would all be condemned.

In our own time, Václav Havel, the anti-Communist dissident who was put in prison for his activities, has constantly stressed these points. Now president of the Czech Republic, Havel has been conspicuously forgiving toward his former enemies and other collaborators. In the central European regimes of the seventies and eighties, Havel said, "The line [between good and evil] did not run clearly between 'them' and 'us,' but through each person. No one was simply a victim; everyone was in some measure co-responsible.... Many people were on both sides. Society was kept down by millions of tiny Lilliputian threads of everyday mendacity, conformity, and compromise.... If that is true," he continued, "it is much less clear who, if anyone, should be put on trial."[3]

The line between good and evil runs through each person. Listen to Saint Paul:

Sin came into the world through one man and death through sin, and so death spread to all men because all men sinned. (Rom. 5:12)

There is none righteous, no, not one; no one understands, no one seeks for God. All have turned aside, together they have gone wrong; no one does good, not even one. Their throat is an open grave [think of those screaming debutantes, and the parents who tormented the disfigured young woman! Their throat is an open grave].... There is no distinction; all have sinned and fall short of the glory of God. (Rom. 3:10–13, 22–24)

The line between good and evil runs through each person.

Two weeks ago, the front page of the *New York Times* featured two stories. One headline said, "Documents Indicate Ford Knew of Engine Defect but Was Silent."[4] I used to drive a Ford that was always stalling in the middle of intersections, so I knew what that was all about. "In spite of repeated internal company studies, consumer complaints, numerous reports of deadly and other serious accidents ... Ford continued to deny there were problems for nine years." Yet this is a company that recently, and voluntarily, announced its plans to redesign their Explorers to be more environmentally sensitive. The line runs through each company. The other headline on that same front page

3. Quoted by Timothy Garton Ash in "The Truth about Dictatorship," *New York Review of Books*, February 19, 1998, 36–37. The resistance leader and former Solidarity spokesman Adam Michnik, in Poland, has taken much the same position since 1989. Alas, as this book goes to the publisher, Poland seems to be going in the opposite direction from what Michnik and Lech Walesa envisioned. Such is the grip of Satan still in our world.

4. *New York Times*, September 12, 2000.

said, "Violence in Media Aimed at Young, FTC Study Says. Denial from Hollywood." Reading on, we see that various entertainment officials deny that their companies deliberately direct their advertising toward children, but "studio executives acknowledged privately that the reports had some validity. 'Everyone's hands are dirty,'" said one executive who chose to remain unidentified.

All of you will remember the murder of Matthew Shepard, a young gay man in Laramie, Wyoming, a couple of years ago. Matthew, who as a teenager had been an acolyte at his Episcopal church, was savagely beaten by two other young men and tied to a fence to die in near-freezing weather. The man who found his body thought at first that he was a scarecrow. His face was covered with blood except for the tracks made by the tears running down his cheeks as he hung on the fence. A play called *The Laramie Project* was written about this event and was received with high praise from the very demanding New York critic John Simon. These words that he wrote about the play are quite remarkable:

> You will be held in rapt attention by this in-depth examination of just about every aspect of the background and foreground of the event. . . . In a little over two and a half hours we get to know every nook and cranny of Laramie before, during, and after the Shepard tragedy, and so much more besides: how smart or stupid, compassionate or cruel, noble or ignoble some very ordinary—as well as some extraordinary—people can be. And beyond that, how closely compounded and confused the ordinary and the extraordinary can be **within a single person**. . . . Guilty of this murder is a large portion of humanity. . . . For which of us in one way or another, has not been [beastly] to his fellow man?[5]

"Everyone's hands are dirty." *If thou, O Lord, shouldst mark iniquities, Lord, who could stand? There is none righteous, no, not one.*

So tonight, we are placing the emphasis on the predicament that you and I share, every single one of us in this tent. "Evil lies close at hand." Who said that? Well, actually, it was Saint Paul—he's talking about his own hand:

> I find it to be a law that when I want to do right, evil lies close at hand. (Rom. 7:21)

5. John Simon, "Broken Heartland," *New York*, May 29, 2000.

I do not understand my own actions. For I do not do what I want, but I do the very thing I hate. . . . I can will what is right, but I cannot do it. For I do not do the good I want, but the evil I do not want is what I do. Now if I do what I do not want, it is no longer I that do it, but sin which dwells within me. (Rom. 7:15–20)

Is there anyone in this tent who does not recognize this?

The human being is in the grip of impulses that are more powerful than our wish to do good. A poignant story was told me just recently about a much-beloved and very distinguished man, the head of a prominent institution and a deeply committed Christian. After his wife died, it became obvious that he was sinking into the morass of alcoholism. (This was in the fifties, before we knew what we know now about alcoholic intervention.) Three colleagues of equal stature made a formal call on their friend. They told him in some detail what his drinking was doing to him, his work, his relationships, and his legacy. They poured out their souls into this difficult confrontation, and it left them emotionally exhausted. At the end of the call, the man who was the object of their concern thanked them for their godly visit and solemnly promised them that he would stop drinking. They went away grateful, feeling that their mission had been accomplished, because, as one of them told me, "we knew John to be a man of his word." It seems incredibly naive now, doesn't it? Great was their disillusionment when it became clear that he was not going to stop, could not stop, and in fact, in the end, drank himself to death. The three friends had disastrously underestimated the power of the forces holding him in thrall.

Our Lord wants us to know of the power of these forces. In the words of Jesus in the Gospels, in the writings of Saint Paul, we are told over and over in various ways that the powers we face are powerful, malevolent, and extremely clever. "Put on the whole armor of God, that you may be able to stand against the wiles of the devil. For we are not contending against flesh and blood, but against the principalities, against the powers, against the world rulers of this present darkness, against the spiritual hosts of wickedness in the heavenly places" (Eph. 6:11–12).

Therefore our Lord warned his disciples not to be alarmed: "This must take place, but the end is not yet . . ." And then he says, "I have told you all things beforehand" (Mark 13:7, 23). Jesus wants us to know ahead of time that the Christian life is going to be one long struggle against evil, sin, and death— and no one, absolutely no one, is going to be exempt. You can try to opt out, but if you do, you will find yourself caught up on the side of the enemy.

The line runs through each of us. That is what we are admitting in every worship service when we say the General Confession. The older form is the stronger one: "Almighty and most merciful Father, we have erred, and strayed from thy ways like lost sheep. We have followed too much the devices and desires of our own hearts. . . . We have left undone those things that we ought to have done, and we have done those things that we ought not to have done . . ." (and there is no health in us!).

The use of the word "we" in the General Confession is important in community worship. When we say "we have erred and strayed from thy ways like lost sheep," the "we" points toward our solidarity in the sin of Adam. The clearest exposition of this solidarity is found in Romans 5:12–21. Paul gives all humankind the name of Adam. The fraternity of Adam is the most comprehensive community of all, for it is universal. In the 1980s, when the foreign service officer Moorhead (Mike) Kennedy was released from his long ordeal as a hostage in Tehran, he was invited to give speeches about his experiences. Mr. Kennedy, an Episcopalian, began these speeches by addressing his audiences as "fellow hostages." This was both amusing and pointed. He was echoing Paul: "Sin came into the world through one person and death through sin, and so death spread to all humanity because all humans sinned" (Rom. 5:12). This is repeated in I Corinthians 15:22: "In Adam all die." *Human solidarity in bondage to the power of sin* is one of the most important of all concepts for Christians to grasp.

At the same time, though, saying the words of the General Confession by memory in church does not always cause us to appropriate their truth deep in our being. All of us need to say also, "*I* have erred and strayed from God's ways like a lost sheep. *I* have followed too much the devices and desires of *my own* heart." This is not so easy for us. All of us, to one degree or another, participate in that psychological phenomenon famously called *denial*. Denial, or avoidance, is a way of keeping consciousness of sin at bay. We think we can make sin go away by pretending it is not there; we are like the little girl who says, "I've got my eyes closed so nobody can see me." Many parish clergy will tell of the frustration they feel when attempting to counsel parishioners with stubborn problems when there is no willingness to acknowledge any fault, accept any blame, or acknowledge any need for change. I think of one churchgoing couple in particular. The wife was dying inside because the husband would not accept his part of the struggle to hold the marriage together. He did not think there was any problem. He did not see that there was anything he needed to do differently. He said, "If Janet would just let go of all these complaints, everything would be fine." I asked him what he had in mind when he confessed his sins in church. He was unable to give any answer.

The universal human tendency is to blame someone else. As Adam said to God, *"This woman made me do it."* In fact, he said, this woman *that you gave me* made me do it, thus managing to blame Eve and God at the same time. This is the way we project evil onto someone else. Let us return for a moment to Susan Smith. I think all of us have probably wanted to throttle our children at some point, but we don't give in to the impulse, so we consider ourselves a great many steps up the moral ladder from Susan Smith. In case there is someone here who doesn't know, she is the young mother who drowned her two young sons in John D. Long Lake near their home up in Union. A recent novel called *Freedomland*, which I highly recommend to you, is loosely based on the Susan Smith case. The author, Richard Price, said in an interview, "I wanted to create people who wind up tripping all over themselves because they have unexpected empathy for the other. I just wanted to do a story where people cannot hold to their sides." He wants us to see ourselves in all the characters, instead of setting ourselves over against the "bad" ones.

Freedomland is set not in South Carolina but in Newark, New Jersey. The main character is a black police detective, Lorenzo. He is assigned to the case of a young woman, Brenda, who says she has been carjacked by a black man and that her child was in the car. Lorenzo is suspicious of the story but has no proof. He befriends Brenda and spends countless hours with her visiting the site, canvassing the neighborhood, and just talking. Lorenzo himself is a fascinating character. Everything that we see him doing in the book makes us like him tremendously; he is hard-working, conscientious, smart, tough—and gentle. He talks to Brenda in explicitly Christian terms: "You got to draw strength from God. . . . See, you can think of people as good, bad, guilty, innocent, but whatever *we* do, whatever mistakes *we* make in life, He don't make mistakes, and me, you, everybody out there, we're nothing more than His agents. You see what I'm saying?"[6] As the story unfolds, we discover that this likable detective is a recovering alcoholic and one of his sons is doing time in prison. The other son, a good citizen and schoolteacher, won't have anything to do with his father. So we can see that Lorenzo is talking about himself as well as Brenda when he says, "Let me tell you something. . . . With kids? No matter what you did, how badly you messed up, God will find some way of letting you get up to bat again. You see, Brenda, God's grace? It's, like, retroactive."[7]

There could be nothing more biblical than that. But that's not all he says. Trying to coax Brenda into a confession, he talks to her about a song by Mary

6. Richard Price, *Freedomland* (New York: Broadway Books, 1998), 202.
7. Richard Price, *Freedomland*, 327.

Wells called "Two Lovers." "I got two lovers and I ain't ashamed," she sings. It turns out that the two lovers are, as Lorenzo puts it, "the same guy split into two, kind and loving, and the other person, when he was treating her bad, messin' around on her, like, a split personality. But you know, I swear, the older I get the more I think that song is about everybody, you know what I'm saying? . . . *I mean we're all two people.*"[8]

The line between good and evil runs through each person. The tragedy, the true tragedy, is not to see it in oneself. The truly tragic person is not the one who commits a crime or causes harm to others; the truly tragic person is the one who causes harm and never repents of it, never admits it even to himself. The gospel of Jesus Christ is that "God's grace is, like, retroactive." If it weren't, the promise it holds out to us would be empty. The promise of God is that we sinners will not only be forgiven, we will be *justified*, which means that we will be set right by the power of God, and all who have suffered as a result of our faults will be restored. If you ask me how that can be, I will have to say that I do not know; but it is the promise of God himself, who says in the book of Revelation that the redeemed "shall hunger no more, neither thirst any more."

> "For the Lamb in the midst of the throne will be their shepherd,
>   and he will guide them to springs of living water;
> and God will wipe away every tear from their eyes." (Rev. 7:16, 17)

This is the announcement of God's good news.

In the twelfth chapter of John, we find Jesus preparing for his final combat with the powers of Satan. Speaking to the inner group of his disciples, he says: "'The hour has come for the Son of man to be glorified. . . . Now is my soul troubled. And what shall I say? "Father, save me from this hour"? No, for this purpose I have come to this hour. . . . Now is the judgment of this world, now shall the ruler of this world be cast out; and I, when I am lifted up from the earth, will draw all men to myself.' He said this to show by what death he was to die" (John 12:23, 27, 31–33).

This is Jesus's own announcement of the beginning of the last act in the drama of salvation. Matthew, Mark, and Luke tell the same thing in another way; they describe how Jesus falls to his knees on the ground in the garden of Gethsemane, praying in agony on the night before his death. The Lord does

---

8. Richard Price, *Freedomland*, 322.

this in full knowledge that the final battle is at hand.[9] It is not death in the usual sense that the Lord fears. It is the knowledge that he must face—alone and abandoned—the full, naked onslaught of the great enemy powers: Sin, Death, and the devil. "The Son of God goes forth to war," yes, but it is like no warfare ever seen before. He will be unarmed. He will be beaten. He will be stripped and spat upon. His face will be swollen and bloodied *beyond human semblance*, as the prophet Isaiah wrote (52:14). He will be pinned up, naked and helpless, to face the obscene mockery of the kinds of people who like to watch executions, the kinds of people who scream insults at those who are disfigured. What kinds of people might they be? Under certain conditions, they might very well be you and me. "There but for the grace of God go I."

The grace of God became incarnate in Jesus of Nazareth. Now he enters his last battle. "Now is the judgment of this world, now shall the ruler of this world be cast out" (John 12:31), he says, and again, "The ruler of this world is judged" (16:11). Those who do not know him as Savior and Lord will see nothing happening on Calvary except an ugly scene of human cruelty and the hideous end of a Jewish prophet. The eyes of faith, however, see what is occurring on both the human level and the cosmic level. As Jesus is crucified, the ruler of this world is being judged, not in some abstract sense, but in Jesus Christ's own person. Saint Paul explains: Christ "became a curse for us" (Gal. 3:13). He placed himself under the curse of God upon sin, and he did it *for us*, on our behalf and in our place. It is the central event of human history; at the same time, it is the decisive battle in the cosmic war between God and the Enemy. One of our Palm Sunday hymns captures both dimensions for us:

> Ride on, ride on in majesty!
> In lowly pomp ride on to die.
> The angel armies of the skies
> Look on with sad and wond'ring eyes
> To see th'approaching sacrifice.

The sacrifice of Jesus our Lord is this: he has gone into the day of judgment utterly alone, separated from the Father, taking the sentence of condemnation upon himself, and that means he is being judged in our place. As Christ hangs upon the cross, he himself is absorbing the final judgment of God upon every form of evil—including the evil that is lodged in every human heart. The un-

---

9. Raymond E. Brown develops this theme at some length in his magisterial work, *The Death of the Messiah*, 2 vols. (New York: Doubleday, 1994, 1998).

aided human tongue is inadequate to the terror and wonder of this once-for-all event; may God give grace to these words and to the ears that hear.

Saint Paul puts it all together: "Sending his own Son in the likeness of sinful flesh and for sin, [God] condemned sin in the flesh," that is, the flesh of the Son himself. "There is therefore now no condemnation for those who are in Christ Jesus" (Rom. 8:3, 1).

This is the gospel. This is the good news of the Christian faith. There has been an invasion from on high. The landing troops have arrived. Neutrality is no longer possible. Satan is slashing and burning, but he is in retreat. Saint Michael the archangel awaits his orders from the Lord. There is no longer any room for self-deception, excuses, denial, or evasion, for, as C. S. Lewis puts it, "Fallen man is not simply an imperfect creature who needs improvement; he is a rebel who must lay down his arms."[10]

Now let each person present think upon his or her own situation at the foot of Christ's cross, as he is lifted up before us. What do we see within our own hearts as we contemplate his sacrifice? If we really understand what is happening there, we will no longer be able to hide behind our own defenses. In light of the cross of Christ, it just isn't possible anymore to fall back on "Nobody's perfect," or "I misspoke," or "We all make mistakes." It just isn't possible to continue to act as though nothing has happened to us and to the world.

This is a tent meeting tonight, which suggests some sort of call to commitment. We're not going to ask you to stand up. We're not going to ask you to come forward; but we are going to ask you this:

Will you lay down your arms tonight?

No, you won't—but God is going to do it for you. He will take those weapons of self-destruction away from you. Tonight, you can come to Christ with all your defenses put aside. This very night, you can acknowledge your need for his intervention in your life. This very moment, you can say to him, Lord, I know that without you I am powerless over my harmful habits and traits. You can say, Lord, I need you and my family needs you. And all together tonight we can give him thanks for his invasion of the enemy's territory, for in this gospel we can live victoriously here in this present time, in sure and certain hope of his eternal victory.

Let us bow our heads in prayer.

Lord Jesus Christ, you promised that whenever two or three were gathered together in your name, you would be present in the midst

---

10. C. S. Lewis, *Mere Christianity* (New York: Macmillan, 1943), 59.

of them. Tonight, you have drawn many more than two or three to hear the preaching of your holy and gracious Word. You come into our gathering with the wounds in your hands and side to show us once again the price you paid for our redemption from sin, evil, and death. Each one of us, preacher and people alike, is in need of your help in overcoming the battles that rage within our own souls. We know that there are many times that we have collaborated with the Enemy. We know ourselves to be deeply enmeshed in structures of sin and death. We ask you to abide with us, that we may receive your life and your Spirit for our warfare against all evil.

Lord, there are those here tonight who have known you for many years. Deepen their faith and strengthen them for more years of service in your army of witnesses. Give them discernment to see where the battle lines are drawn and to go forward dauntlessly in your name to join the battle for justice, freedom, and peace. Grant them an abundant measure of the gifts of your Holy Spirit so that they may not only believe, but be enabled to bear suffering for your sake.

And Lord Christ, perhaps there are people here tonight who have not really known you before. By your own initiative you have opened their hearts tonight. Let them know that it is really you and not any human preacher. Show your face to them as surely as you did by Galilee so long ago. Draw them into your presence and clothe them with their Christian armor. Defend them, O Lord, in all assaults of their enemies, be now and evermore their rock and shield. We lift up these imperfect prayers, Lord Jesus, knowing that by the power of your Holy Spirit they are made acceptable in your sight. To you with the Father and the same Holy Spirit be all glory, might, majesty, dominion, and power, now and forever.

Amen.

Justice and the Final Judgment
(Pre-Advent)

The Consuming Fire

Christ Trinity Church, Sheffield, Massachusetts
August 22, 2010

HEBREWS 12:18–29

A couple of years ago, when I was teaching homiletics in Toronto during the Advent season, I was invited to preach a series of Advent sermons in a local church. One of my students asked me what my theme would be. I said, "Wrath and judgment!" He laughed. He thought I was kidding.

You can't have Advent without the full biblical picture of God. In the reading today from the epistle to the Hebrews, there are two word pictures. One is from the old covenant and one from the new. The first scene shows the children of Israel gathered at the foot of Mount Sinai. The mountaintop is blazing with volcanic fire, so that even the redoubtable Moses is fearful of the manifestation of the power, majesty, wrath, and judgment of God. The celebrated American writer Annie Dillard loved passages like this. She wrote one like it herself: "Why do we people in churches seem like cheerful . . . tourists on a package tour of the Absolute? . . . On the whole I do not find Christians, outside of the catacombs, sufficiently sensible [aware] of conditions. Does anyone have the foggiest idea what sort of power we so blithely invoke? It is madness to wear ladies' straw hats and velvet hats to church; we should all be wearing crash helmets."[1]

The second word picture painted by the biblical writer shows us a different mountain, Mount Zion, the coming kingdom of God. He envisions the celestial city where "the angels and archangels and all the company of heaven" are gathered around the throne of the Son of God: "You have come to Mount Zion . . . the city of the living God, the heavenly Jerusalem, [with] innumerable angels in festal gathering, and to the assembly of the first-born who are enrolled in heaven, and to a judge who is God of all, and to the spirits

---

1. Annie Dillard, *Teaching a Stone to Talk* (New York: Harper and Row, 1988), 40.

of the righteous made perfect, and to Jesus, the mediator of a new covenant" (Heb. 12:22–24).

At first glance, these two pictures might seem to be contrasting the God of the Old Testament with the God of the New Testament. A lot of good church members make that mistake. But notice how the author of Hebrews links the two visions, first, by referring to God as "the judge who is God of all," and then by the last sentence of the passage: "Our God is a consuming fire." It's the same God. The God of Abraham, Isaac, and Jacob (the God of the Old Testament) and the God and Father of our Lord Jesus Christ (the God of the New Testament) are not two gods, but one God. There are not two gods, one wrathful and one loving, but one God who is Judge of all. "Therefore," says Hebrews, "let us offer to God acceptable worship, with reverence and awe" (12:28). The writer wants his readers to know "what sort of power they so blithely invoke." That's really the thrust of the passage; we are to understand that the God who has promised to gather his people into a great "cloud of witnesses" through the blood of Jesus is the same God whose judgment upon sin and death is felt as a consuming fire.

You see, the world was not created to be the way it is. We are not supposed to be reading and hearing bad news every day. The world is not supposed to be filled with earthquake, fire, and flood, with plague, pestilence, and famine (to use the language of the older Book of Common Prayer). Oil spills were not part of our Creator's plan for our planet. Cancer was not part of his plan for humanity. It was not God's plan that humanitarian aid workers should be shot point-blank by the Taliban.[2] Murderous drug cartels were not part of his plan, and the rapacious American appetite for cocaine that keeps the cartels in business was not part of his plan. Is it not good news that God will judge all of this?

One of my favorite cousins died a month ago. She was only fifty-four. It will give you an idea of how respected and loved she was when I tell you that there were seven hundred people at her funeral. She had a melanoma that spread to her brain. There was nothing her doctors could do. What do we make of this? It is one sign among a trillion others that the creation is bent out of shape. Melanoma was not part of God's good creation.

Not long before he died, the great twentieth-century theologian Karl Barth wrote a letter to a friend:

> Somewhere within me there lives a bacillus with the name *proteus mirabilis* which has an inclination to enter my kidneys—which would then mean my finish. I am certain that this monstrosity does not be-

long to God's good creation, but rather has come in as a result of the Fall. Like sin and with the demons, it cannot simply be done away with but can only be despised, combated, and suppressed. That [is] the task of the doctors [and] good nurses. . . . Apart from this, however, I am getting along remarkably well. The main thing is the knowledge that God makes no mistakes and that *proteus mirabilis* has no chance against him.[3]

Barth's *proteus mirabilis*, my cousin's melanoma, the afflictions of our own parishioners, of which we have seen a great many in recent years—none of this is part of God's good creation. Like sin and all the other manifestations of the demonic, it can only be despised and resisted.

But the Hebrews passage gives us a more complete picture of the wrongs that need to be made right. On Mount Zion, we see Jesus, now reigning from heaven, "the mediator of a new covenant, [with his] sprinkled blood that speaks a better word than the blood of Abel" (12:24). Let's look at that. What's Abel got to do with this? This reference to Abel reminds us of what happened immediately after the fall of Adam and Eve, the "first disobedience."[4] Just in case we might think that being kicked out of the garden of Eden wasn't necessarily the worst thing that could happen, we are told that Cain killed his own brother, Abel, for no reason except jealousy. Rembrandt made a drawing of this murder, and an art critic wrote, "The drawing establishes that murder requires concentration, a sure method, and sudden energy, and that it hurts. Of course, this isn't just any homicide. It's the first—a cosmic disaster."[5] Ever since that cosmic disaster, the blood of Abel has cried out for justice. The blood of the martyrs of Afghanistan just two weeks ago cries out for justice.

But where is that justice to come from? Where is the power that *not only* can defeat cancer, heal the planet, and overcome our murderous instincts *but also* is able to make everything right again and restore what was lost?

Let's take a look at the psalm we just read, the first two verses:

In thee, O Lord, do I take refuge;
    let me never be put to shame!

---

3. Karl Barth, *How I Changed My Mind* (Edinburgh: Saint Andrews Press, 1969), 86. Letter to John D. Godsey, January 25, 1966. I have simplified the syntax somewhat in a couple of places.

4. John Milton's phrase in *Paradise Lost*.

5. Peter Schjedahl, "Story Line: Rembrandt in Boston," *New Yorker*, November 10, 2003.

In thy righteousness deliver me and rescue me;
    incline thy ear to me, and save me! (Ps. 71:1–2)

Throughout the Psalms it is continually repeated: God is the One who saves, the One who is powerful to deliver. God alone can make right what is wrong. God alone can overcome death and the demons.

It's typical of human beings to think of the demonic in terms of something external to oneself, something that afflicts others but not us. I was reading a review of a new reassessment of the theologian Reinhold Niebuhr. It noted Niebuhr's insight that humans become self-destructive when they define themselves as sinless and manifest arrogance toward others. That's the danger of losing sight of the theme of divine judgment. Part of being a Christian is understanding that we are *all* in need of the divine judgment. Look again at the Hebrews passage. It says that the city of God will contain "the souls of the righteous made perfect." That's suggestive. If someone is righteous, then why does he need to be made perfect? Maybe it means that good people need just a little fixing up to be perfect, just a little nip and tuck here and there. But that isn't what the biblical story tells us. As the fire-breathing writer Robert Farrar Capon says, God did not come to improve the improvable, but to raise the dead.[6] Every one of us, every single one of us in church this morning, including the person in the pulpit, is far gone in unrighteousness; but God is able to create something that does not yet exist—a perfected humanity. He will judge and destroy those aspects of ourselves that, if we are repentant Christians, we want never to see again.

Listen further to Hebrews: "You have come to Mount Zion and to the city of the living God, the heavenly Jerusalem . . . and to a judge who is God of all, and to the souls of the righteous made perfect, and to Jesus, the mediator of a new covenant, and to the sprinkled blood that speaks more graciously than the blood of Abel."

The blood of Abel has been crying out for justice and righteousness from the first day until now, but that cry has been answered. It has been answered by the blood of Christ.

The psalmist says,

In thee, O Lord, do I take refuge;
    let me never be put to shame!

---

6. "For Jesus came to raise the dead. He did not come to reward the rewardable, improve the improvable, or correct the correctable" (Robert Farrar Capon, *Kingdom, Grace, Judgment* [Grand Rapids: Eerdmans, 2002], 317).

I don't think people experience shame today in the same way they used to. I don't think many parents tell children they ought to be ashamed of themselves when they do something wrong, the way my parents did. Today, shame seems to mean something more like being humiliated or embarrassed or disgraced. Either way, however, the letter to the Hebrews makes an essential connection. We have to go back a few verses to see it.[7] Here is what it says: "Therefore, since we are surrounded by so great a cloud of witnesses, let us also lay aside . . . sin which clings so closely, and let us run . . . the race that is set before us, looking to Jesus the pioneer and perfecter of our faith, who . . . endured the cross, *disregarding its shame*, and is seated at the right hand of the throne of God" (Heb. 12:1–2).

Can you see how this all hangs together? The Bible interprets itself. Jesus is the one who took our shame upon himself on the cross, on our behalf and in our place. He is the pioneer who has run the race ahead of us, who perfects our faith, and—from his seat at the right hand of God—will come in glory to be the Judge of this whole world of sin and death. It is his blood that speaks more graciously than the blood of Abel or even the blood of the martyrs—more graciously because God alone is able, through Christ, to make right everything has been wrong.

The third part of today's reading brings us back to our Advent theme of God's wrath and judgment. The God who shook the mountain with his mere voice has promised to give a kingdom that cannot be shaken. God is an awesome God. He is not awesome in the way my grandchildren say that movies and fashions and soccer games are "awesome," but in the real sense of the word—causing fear and awe by power. Only a truly awe-inspiring God is able to shake the earth and the heavens in order to defeat evil and cause a new kingdom to come into being, a domain that cannot be shaken. "Therefore let us be grateful for receiving [this unshakeable] kingdom . . . and thus let us offer to God acceptable worship with reverence and awe, for our God is a consuming fire" (12:28–29).

And so, our great and unconquerable hope is this: sin and the demons will be judged and consumed by the Lord himself. That will happen in his time, which is not ours to know. But in the meantime, the powers of death will be judged a little bit at a time as God works through the deeds of love and mercy done by his people, not only by doctors and nurses but also by

---

7. It's so important to read biblical passages in their context. The little printed sheets used by many churches have the effect of disconnecting the readings from their place in the Bible, and people are not learning how to handle the Bible and find passages.

all who stand alongside others in suffering and who work for justice and righteousness.

Let us close in confident hope by reading together the great words of the ancient canticle called the Te Deum:[8]

> Thou art the King of glory, O Christ,
> thou art the everlasting son of the Father. . . .
> When thou hadst overcome the sharpness of death,
> thou didst open the kingdom of heaven to all believers.
> Thou sittest at the right hand of God. . . .
> We believe that thou shalt come to be our Judge.
> We therefore pray thee, help thy servants
> whom thou hast redeemed with thy precious blood.

Amen.

8. Book of Common Prayer, Rite One, pp. 52–53.

Save Us in the Time of Trial, and Deliver Us from the Evil One

Grace Church, New York City
1993

LUKE 21:10–19, 26–28

The *New York Times* Sunday magazine had a story last week that brought me up short. The subject was political conditions in Egypt today. It is no light thing to be a Christian in that country under the present regime. The article contained a number of stories about Egyptian Christians who have been tortured. This started me thinking. What would I do if I were a Christian in that country? Would I have the courage to attend worship, knowing that I might be arrested? Would I have the strength of character to continue my ministry of preaching and teaching the Bible? Would I be able to muster the bravery to speak of the Lord Jesus Christ? I have always been pretty sure that I could do the right thing if I were faced with quick extinction, by a bullet, say, or maybe a speeding subway train, but I can assure you that my courage fails utterly at the thought of days or weeks—or even a few minutes—of torture in unspeakable prisons by human beings bent on doing me harm. That is what Christians in various parts of the world have faced over and over again since the time of Jesus.

There are portions of the New Testament that deal directly with this prospect. The Synoptic Gospels, Matthew, Mark, and Luke, each have a section (called the Synoptic Apocalypse) in which Jesus himself envisions a time when Christians will be dragged before governors and rulers and made to testify:

> Then Jesus said to them [his disciples], "Nation will rise against nation, and kingdom against kingdom; there will be great earthquakes, and in various places famines and pestilences; and there will be terrors and great signs from heaven. But before all this they will lay

---

This was originally part of a weeknight sermon series on the Lord's Prayer.

their hands on you and persecute you, delivering you up to the . . . prisons, and you will be brought before kings and governors for my name's sake. This will be a time for you to bear testimony. . . . You will be delivered up even by parents and brothers and kinsmen and friends, and some of you they will put to death; you will be hated by all for my name's sake. But not a hair of your head will perish. By your endurance you will gain your lives." (Luke 21:10–13, 16–19)

These words are a portion of the long passage in the Synoptic Apocalypse of Luke.[1] With this teaching, Jesus seeks to prepare his disciples for the great time of testing, when the powers of darkness will be arrayed against them personally as the people of God. Traditionally, in both Testaments, this time of trial will come just before the end. It will be the last thing that happens before the final, conclusive appearance of God in human history. In the book of Revelation, this time is called *the great tribulation*. On All Saints' Day, we read the passage in Revelation where John sees the great company of the redeemed in their white robes, and is told, "These are they who have come out of the great tribulation."

In the early church, this teaching of Jesus about the last days was understood to be the crisis facing Christians as they were persecuted. As Christians were brought before their accusers, they knew that they faced death, often by torturous means.[2] In that hour, it was their confidence in the promise of their Savior and Redeemer that gave them superhuman strength. In the earliest years, the certainty of his coming again was the most powerful of all motivations.

Over the years, as we know, the expectation of the early Christians that the second coming of Christ and the last judgment would take place in their lifetimes was replaced by the hope of it coming in the far distant, unforeseeable future. After the Enlightenment, and in the twentieth century, mainline Christians ceased to believe in it coming at all. In the early decades of the twentieth century, virtually no one in the mainline churches was thinking seriously about a final day of the Lord. I remember going to a church conference in the early

---

1. The Synoptic Apocalypse is found in Mark 13; Matt. 24; and Luke 21.

2. One of the reasons that we may believe in the resurrection is that, against all reason, there were so many people willing to die for their faith in a Messiah who had been shamed, tortured, abused by all the best people, utterly dehumanized and erased from the human record—so it was thought—by suffering the most disgusting and despised possible method of publicly and officially executing a person. When Jesus spoke of taking up the cross, it was not necessarily a figure of speech.

1960s where leading clergy and seminary professors dismissed the idea as a relic of an unenlightened mind-set.

This is now changing, however. The events of that most murderous and violent of centuries caused a rethinking. The apocalyptic ideas of the New Testament seem more relevant than they used to, and I don't mean David Koresh.[3] I mean that it makes more sense these days than it did before World War II to think in terms of a cosmic battle between good and evil, light and darkness. Evil is more than the sum of individual misdeeds. Evil has a life of its own. It is not enough to stand aside from it. If it is not actively resisted, it sweeps all before it. Part of a Christian's calling is to resist evil, and in doing so, to endure to the end. "To him that overcometh, the crown of life shall be."[4] The hymns that we are singing in this service reflect this idea of a battle in which all Christians are soldiers.

With the reintroduction of apocalyptic theology and biblical interpretation in our own day, it is now generally agreed by biblical interpreters that the Lord's Prayer has an apocalyptic context. That's why some of the modern translations of the prayer, instead of "lead us not into temptation," have "save us in the time of trial," and instead of "deliver us from evil," have "deliver us from the evil one"—meaning Satan. Don't worry, we're not going to change the words here at Grace Church any time soon. However, this translation does give a greatly enhanced understanding of our calling to locate the prayer at the frontier, so to speak—the frontier where the ages meet, where the Christian community faces the powers of evil and is called to bear its witness in the face of all that "the ruler of this world" can do (that's what Jesus calls Satan in the Gospel of John). That's why the epistle to the Ephesians says we need armor. In the passage that you heard tonight, the apostle writes:

> We are not contending against flesh and blood, but against the principalities, against the powers, against the world rulers of this present

3. At the time of this sermon, David Koresh was still in the news, with his apocalyptic cult of Branch Davidians.

4. The hymnal revisers changed this wonderful phrase derived from the King James Version of the book of Revelation to the much less resounding "to valiant hearts triumphant the crown of life shall be." The idea of *overcoming* is central to the New Testament scenario because it refers to a life-and-death struggle with the cosmic Enemy. The civil rights anthem "We Shall Overcome" preserves this sense. So many testimonies from that time speak of the opposition in these larger terms; this made it possible for the soldiers of nonviolence to think of their enemy as the Evil One, not as individual white people or even groups of white people. The leaders of the movement knew that the Klan members—for instance—were in the grip of a demonic Power from which they needed to be released. The best literature of the movement preserves this biblical sense.

darkness, against the spiritual hosts of wickedness in the heavenly places. Therefore take the whole armor of God, that you may be able to withstand in the evil day, and having done all, to stand . . . having girded your loins with truth, and having put on the breastplate of righteousness, and having shod your feet with the equipment of the gospel of peace; besides all these, taking the shield of faith, with which you can quench all the flaming darts of the evil one. And take the helmet of salvation, and the sword of the Spirit, which is the word of God. (Eph. 6:12–17)

World War II was an apocalyptic time for the world and for Christians. Here at Grace Church this fall, we have a class on Sunday mornings where we've been talking about the widespread failure of the Christian churches during the period of the Nazi extermination of the Jews. Only a small number of Christians were willing to risk imprisonment, torture, and death to save Jews. Some of those who did are now remembered gratefully at Yad Vashem in the Garden of the Righteous in Jerusalem. They are the ones who wore the armor of God in the time of trial. Corrie ten Boom, a Dutch Christian watchmaker, together with her whole devout family, successfully hid many Jews in a little closet in their tiny house in Haarlem before the Nazis came for them. Corrie was the only member of the ten Boom family to survive the camps. To them, we may be sure, has been awarded the crown of life. They passed through the great tribulation and have overcome.[5]

Another apocalyptic time and place for the church, another "time of trial," has been South Africa under apartheid. The book of Revelation played an important role in that struggle. Allan Boesak, one of the theologians of the antiapartheid movement, wrote a commentary on Revelation. In it he tells how Bishop Desmond Tutu, later archbishop of South Africa, stood face-to-face with Louis Le Grange, Minister of Law and Order, and said, "Mr. Minister, you are not God. You are merely a man. And one day your name will only be a faint scribble on the pages of history while the name of Jesus Christ, the Lord of the Church, lives forever."[6]

5. The notable story is told in the book *The Hiding Place*, an account of the ten Boom ordeal. It was made into an impressive movie in 1975, starring Julie Harris as Corrie's saintly sister Betsie, who died in the camp.

6. Allan A. Boesak, *Comfort and Protest* (Philadelphia: Westminster, 1987), 107. When the episode that Boesak described took place, the struggle against the regime was still going on and Nelson Mandela was still in prison. (Boesak was later disgraced by financial and other improprieties, which was a great pity because he had been one of

Now, all of this has been very dramatic, very world-historical. We don't think in these terms 99 percent of the time, if at all. I look out at you, and I don't think you're worrying about being dragged before "kings and governors" any time soon. Mostly we're worrying about such things as our workplace, or our love affairs, or our lack of love affairs, or our aging parents, or the escalating cost of everything. Nevertheless, you come faithfully to these Wednesday night services—partly because you care about the people here, partly because of habit, partly as a refuge from the city, but mostly, I think, because you are sincerely seeking to know and to follow Jesus Christ. It is his prayer that you say every Wednesday and Sunday. If you're like me, however, most of the time you're just rattling off the words without thinking. It's a common undertaking for all of us, not just the preacher, to rethink the Lord's Prayer.

I realize that the interpretation of the prayer that I'm offering tonight is not a familiar one to most people, even though it's been accepted in scholarly circles for some time. I realize that it's not practical, perhaps not even desirable, to change the translation to read "Save us in the time of trial, and deliver us from the evil one."[7] But I wonder if we, together, in our worship and in our prayer groups, might begin to think afresh about ways in which the church can bear its witness in the cosmic battle that Jesus and the apostolic writers of the New Testament have in mind all the time. Surely we can offer ourselves in new and more intentional ways to stand at the battle line and not to retreat. That is what the armor of God is for, as Ephesians says: to enable us to stand, to hold our ground. Maybe this means something that does not sound very dramatic or courageous. Maybe it simply—or not so simply!—means not betraying our vocation to be disciples of Christ. I'm thinking of a passage from the first epistle to Timothy. Much of this letter is rather didactic and even pedestrian—like many of our encounters in life—but toward the end it suddenly reveals itself to be set in the apocalyptic framework we've been invoking. After many chapters of counsel about various rather humdrum matters, we come upon this bracing passage:

> But as for you, man of God, shun all this; aim at righteousness, god-liness, faith, love, steadfastness, gentleness. Fight the good fight of the faith; take hold of the eternal life to which you were called when

---

the strongest of the antiapartheid leaders and had also done much excellent theological work.)

7. This was preached in the early 1990s. The new translation is more widely used now.

you made the good confession in the presence of many witnesses. In the presence of God who gives life to all things, and of Christ Jesus who in his testimony before Pontius Pilate made the good confession, I charge you to keep the commandment unstained and free from reproach until the appearing of our Lord Jesus Christ; and this will be made manifest at the proper time by the blessed and only Sovereign, the King of kings and Lord of lords, who alone has immortality and dwells in unapproachable light, whom no man has ever seen or can see. To him be honor and eternal dominion. Amen. (I Tim. 6:11–16)

In this charge to Timothy, we see how even in the Pastoral Epistles the call to be faithful in the daily grind is set into the cosmic panorama of the coming of the Lord of the universe in glory and power. In his "eternal dominion," the time of trial will be over, and the evil one will be not only conquered but obliterated forever.

The genocidal history of the past century, beginning with the genocide of the Armenians in 1915, has shown that the New Testament language of "principalities and powers" and "the world rulers of this present darkness" is not at all far-fetched. But this language, when found in the Lord's Prayer—"save us from the time of trial, and deliver us from evil"—brings it home to us sitting in these pews tonight. For each of us, it is always the apocalyptic time, the time of crisis. Some of us are conflicted about unfair treatment of colleagues. Some are trying to decide whether and how to get out of a relationship. Some are seeking reconciliation with their parents. Some are wondering how long we should "go along to get along" in various situations. In every such situation, whether minuscule or world-historical, it will be a time for us to "make the good confession," to "bear testimony" to the Lordship of Christ. In a sense, every time is an apocalyptic time because every time brings trials in which we may or may not glorify our Redeemer by our actions.

"Here is a call for the endurance and faith of the saints" (Rev. 13:10). What endurance and faith are called for in your life? in our life as a community of faith? When we pray to the Lord, "Lead us not into temptation, but deliver us from evil," what are we asking for? I believe we will know it when we see it, for the Lord gives us the gift of sight. Perhaps the first stage of endurance is the willingness to see. Look around you! Where is the Lord's work being undone, and where is it being built up? "Aim at righteousness, godliness, faith, love, steadfastness, gentleness. Fight the good fight of the faith; take hold of the eternal life to which you were called." Aim at righteousness! Isn't that encouraging? Look for it, and aim for it! We'll miss the target many times, but we'll keep on aiming. And all the while we will be upheld by the Savior who has taught us to pray to be saved in the time of trial, and to await the kingdom of God.

"By your endurance you will gain your lives."

We shall overcome . . . because our Lord has overcome.

Amen.

Loving the Dreadful Day of Judgment

Little Trinity Anglican Church, Toronto
November 16, 2008

ISAIAH 57:17; I PETER 4:17; I THESSALONIANS 5:9

My family, like most families, loves to tell and retell certain stories. One of our most beloved stories concerns some favorite New England cousins, some years ago, whose daughter was to be married. She'd been raised as an Episcopalian and wanted the Episcopal service, but her grandfather, who was a prominent minister in the Congregational Church, was asked to conduct the ceremony. My cousin and her grandfather sat down together to go over the service from the 1928 Episcopal Prayer Book. Now you need to understand that this grandfather was a Congregationalist of the theologically liberal Harvard variety, who made it a point of honor to distinguish himself from his Puritan ancestors. He and his granddaughter began to read through the traditional Anglican marriage service, and they quickly got to the place where the minister is supposed to say, "I require and charge you both, as ye will answer at the dreadful day of judgment when the secrets of all hearts shall be disclosed . . ."

"Well!" said the grandfather. "You certainly don't want to use *that*. We'll just leave that part out."

"No, Grandpa!"[1] exclaimed the bride-to-be. "I *love* the dreadful day of judgment!"

The approach of the Advent season sets before us the question, *How shall we love the dreadful day of judgment?*

As a good many commentators have noted, the Advent season actually begins *before* the first Sunday of Advent. It's a seven-week season, beginning af-

---

1. Actually she called him "Père," but I have simplified it for retelling. The veracity of this story was vouched for by the bride's mother, who was present for the conversation and greatly relished telling about it. The bride, clearly a feisty and perspicacious sort, later became a well-known travel writer and radio personality.

ter All Saints' Day. In the Northern Hemisphere, the weather cooperates with the change in the lectionary readings. Have you noticed? When the change from daylight time to standard time takes place, when the darkness comes on so abruptly, that's when the lectionary begins to take on a note of foreboding. Prophecies of doom from the Old Testament begin to appear. From the Gospels, we get parables about the coming judgment. Last week we had the parable of the bridesmaids who ran out of lamp oil in the middle of the night, and tonight the parable of the judgment upon the man who wasted his investment. "Cast the worthless servant into the outer darkness; there men will weep and gnash their teeth." Jesus said that! Did we know that Jesus said things like that?

Advent begins in the dark. Saint Paul writes, "As to the times and the seasons, brothers and sisters, . . . the day of the Lord will come like a thief in the night. When people say, 'There is peace and security,' then sudden destruction will come upon them . . . and there will be no escape" (I Thess. 5:1–3).

The intended effect of the readings at this time of year is to disturb our peace and security. The purpose of this seven-week season is to take an unflinching inventory of darkness. That's why the Anglican tradition refuses to celebrate Christmas until Christmas Eve. It's one of the very best things about us, one of the things we really do well. Our liturgy is designed to show that we are willing to refuse the easy comforts of the commercial Christmas. Advent is an exercise in delayed gratification. One of the classic readings for the season, a lament from Isaiah, expresses the mood:

> Behold [O Lord], you have been angry . . .
>> in our sins we have been a long time, and shall we be saved?
> We have all become like one who is unclean,
>> and all our righteous deeds are like filthy rags.
> We fade like a leaf,
>> and our iniquities, like the wind, take us away. . . .
> You have hidden your face from us,
>> and have delivered us into the hand of our iniquities. (Isa. 64:5–7)

When we observe the seven-week season of Advent, we ponder these things. Like the falling leaves and the early darkness each year, the twenty-four-hour news cycle performs on cue. I have never had any trouble finding Advent messages in the newspapers.

Here is the front page of the *Globe and Mail* two days ago. At the top of the page, the latest incarnation of James Bond minus his wit and easy charm—he is grieving, depressed, and angry, more disposed than ever to use his license

173

to kill. Just below, "Faces of Suffering in Afghanistan." Afghan girls, blinded and disfigured by an attack of acid sprayed in their faces because they had the temerity to go to school. Advent begins in the dark.

Exhibit number 2: a three-part article for Remembrance Day, also from the *Globe*, about the problem of remembrance in three countries where people died at the hands of their own governments—the Soviet Union under Stalin, Spain under Franco, Germany under the Nazis. According to the article about fascist Spain, more than 130,000 people disappeared during the regime of Franco (this era is vividly portrayed, by the way, in the remarkable movie *Pan's Labyrinth*, which shows how the church supported Franco). A leading Spaniard is quoted: "We [the Spanish people] need to condemn the fascist period, but we haven't." According to the article about the Soviet Union, a movement to memorialize the millions who died in Stalin's Gulag is "being opposed by the [Russian] Orthodox Church and its highly placed friends in Putin's new Russia"—the church cooperating with repression yet again.[2] Here perhaps is a place to listen carefully to the announcement of the first epistle of Peter: "The time has come for judgment to begin with the household of God" (4:17).

Exhibit number 3: Stephen Lewis, that admirable Canadian, is collecting testimonies from women who have survived politically motivated gang-rapes in Zimbabwe. These women were deliberately chosen for rape because they have been active in the MDC (Movement for Democratic Change), seeking the overthrow of the tyrant Mugabe. I can't give you the details from the pulpit, but they are beyond horrifying. Let me just quote one woman, who said that after the assault she could not stand or walk, so she had to crawl away. The leader of the team who attacked her told her repeatedly, "You deserve this, this is your punishment for daring to support the MDC. We have a list and everyone on it like you will receive a punishment."[3]

My students ask me: How do we preach about judgment when there is so much resistance to the topic? It would be hard to exaggerate the degree of this resistance throughout the church, even though it is one of the most important and pervasive themes throughout the Bible—not only in the Old but also in the New Testament. A student in one of my classes bravely chose to preach about judgment even though one of her Christian friends scolded

2. "The Power of Memory," *Globe and Mail*, November 8, 2008, in three parts: "The Value of Shame" (Spain), "The Battle over Russia's Gulags," and "A Kristallnacht Exile Back in Berlin."

3. Stephanie Nolen, reporting from Botswana: "The Politics of Terror: Lewis Reaches Out to Women Raped for Supporting Zimbabwe's Opposition," *Globe and Mail*, November 10, 2008.

her for it. "Why do you want to focus on all that sin and judgment?" Last year a well-known Canadian biblical scholar and his wife were visiting my husband and me, and we took them to one of our local Episcopal churches. The Gospel lesson was one of Jesus's teachings that prominently featured judgment. The preacher—who was a recent graduate of a distinguished American theological college that shall remain nameless—announced that he would not preach on the Gospel that morning because "we don't believe in a God of judgment." The visiting theologian and his wife were, shall we say, appalled—and I wanted to crawl under the pew in mortification.

How shall we love the dreadful day of judgment? One woman working with Stephen Lewis to collect testimonies said, "We are exposing the fact that [Zimbabwe] is a terrorist state and the entire country is either living in a culture of complete terror or a culture of complete impunity." This is an important concept, *impunity*—Latin, *im-punitas*: without punishment. When a culture of impunity is present, so that one can do whatever comes to hand with no fear whatsoever of consequences, human beings become bestial toward one another. That's not an opinion; that's a fact. We know this now. Even the nicest American boys and the sweetest Canadian girls, under certain conditions, will turn on other people with ferocity. That's what produced the conditions in the Abu Ghraib prison. Imagine a world without judgment. That's impunity. Is that what we want?

How shall we preach judgment? If we are unable to live with the thought of the judgment of God because we don't want to allow it into our tidy concept of God as loving, forgiving, and accepting, then what we need to do is envision those Afghan girls whose only crime was to seek education. The resurgence of the Taliban in Afghanistan is so threatening right now, despite the excellent efforts of the Canadian soldiers, that many girls are now quite literally unable to attend their classes. If we are reluctant to think about judgment, we need to call to mind the Spanish *desaparecidos*, the people who wrote editorials or joined political groups in opposition to Franco, who were taken from their families under cover of darkness and never seen again. If we remember them, and the violated women of Zimbabwe, and the young Canadian journalist Melissa Fung, who was kept in a hole for a month because she wanted to tell the truth, then let us ask ourselves, do we want a world without the wrath of God? If we summon these examples, the words of God to the prophet Isaiah seem more suitable: *I was angry, I smote [Israel], I hid my face and was angry.* In such circumstances, we can understand that the judgment of God upon all evil is good, right, and necessary. A culture of impunity is nothing less than hell.

The trouble is, as I am sure you have already figured out, that we don't mind God being wrathful against somebody other than us. The difficulty comes when judgment draws close to *us*, to *our* friends, to *our* group, to *our* favorite cause. How are we to understand the words of Peter? How shall the church stand first in line for the dreadful day of judgment?

We begin to do this by remembering that the church is not a collection of autonomous individuals, but a family, brothers and sisters of Christ by adoption and grace, "fellow citizens with the saints and members of the household of God, built upon the foundation of the apostles and prophets, Christ Jesus himself being the cornerstone, in whom the whole structure is joined together and grows into a holy temple in the Lord" (Eph. 2:19-21). When we reflect upon *that* gospel truth, doesn't it become clear that there is nothing, not even God's own judgment, that can destroy a structure built upon the cornerstone that is God's only begotten Son? In that sense, truly the fellowship of the baptized has already passed through the judgment, as John says.[4] In that sense the words of Paul in our reading from First Thessalonians are also true: "God has not destined us for wrath, but to obtain salvation through our Lord Jesus Christ" (5:9). This is true security, a security that the empires of the world with all their might cannot pretend to convey.

But this true security does not simply lift us clear of this world. We must live this perilous existence along with everybody else. This is a world where cancer strikes the just and the unjust indiscriminately, where punishment is meted out to those who do *not* deserve it while those who *do* deserve it go free, where the poor get poorer and the rich, even in this financial crisis, are only a little bit less rich than they were but a whole lot less inclined to be generous this Christmas. This is the world of Advent, a world that makes no moral sense to the unaided eye. Advent begins in the dark. Anyone that tells you otherwise is living in denial.

"But you are not in darkness, brothers and sisters," continues the apostle Paul. "You are not in darkness for the day [of judgment] to surprise you like a thief. For you are all children of light and children of the day; we are not children of the night or of darkness. So then let us not sleep, as others do, but let us keep awake and be sober" (I Thess. 5:4-6).

As children of the day, we stand first in line at the bar of judgment by repenting of our sins and the sins of the whole church and the sins of the whole world. We are involved in each other because God was first involved in us. The

---

4. "Truly, truly, I say to you, he who hears my word and believes him who sent me, has eternal life; he does not come into judgment, but has passed from death to life" (John 5:24).

wrath of God and the love of God are two faces of the same thing. The world will be purged of its iniquity in the consuming fire of the second coming of the Lord Jesus Christ. That is the Advent theme. He will come again to set all things right. In the meantime we take up the weapons of his warfare: "Since we belong to the day, let us . . . put on the breastplate of faith and love, and for a helmet the hope of salvation" (I Thess. 5:8). Anything we can do—anything at all, however small or large—any deed of kindness or generosity or courage that eases the load of someone else or brings truth and justice to light—is a sign of the advent of the One who is and who was and who is to come, the Almighty (Rev. 1:8).

"The time has come for judgment to begin with the household of God," but "God has not destined us for wrath, but to obtain salvation through our Lord Jesus Christ, who died for us so that whether we wake or sleep we might live with him. Therefore encourage one another and build one another up, just as you are doing," and the power of the Ruler of the universe will be your strength and your shield, your rock and your fortress, your shepherd and your judge, your Savior and Redeemer, your Lord and your God.

Amen.

The Great *BUT*

Trinity Presbyterian Church, Cherry Hill, New Jersey
The Sunday next before Advent 2016

ISAIAH 54:7–8; 57:15–19; MALACHI 3:1–3

Advent is on the horizon. That means that the theme of judgment is going to come up, and that makes most of us uneasy. We've devised all sorts of stratagems to avoid this subject, cutting it out of liturgies, skipping over it in the lectionary, frowning upon it if it comes from the pulpit. All the same, there it is. The Holy Scriptures of the Christian church—the Bible—contain a great many passages about judgment. I'm the guest preacher, so I can get by with telling you this since I'm leaving town this afternoon. A major theme of the Bible is the righteousness of God and his judgment upon unrighteousness. A lot of people think that this theme of judgment is all in the Old Testament, not the New, which is a serious mistake leading to all kinds of problems in our understanding of our own Scripture. There's a very significant amount of judgment in the New Testament, most of it, to tell the truth, in the teachings of Jesus himself. Try this, for example: "Woe to you, scribes and Pharisees, hypocrites! . . . You serpents, you brood of vipers, how are you to escape being sentenced to hell?" (Matt. 23:29, 33).

It's easy for us to scoot out from underneath this, since we are not Pharisees, or hypocrites, are we? I heard a joke once about two men. One of them invites the other to attend worship at his church. The other man said he never went to church because it was full of hypocrites. That's OK, said his friend, there's always room for one more.

Most of us figure out ways to excuse ourselves from whatever it is that Jesus is condemning. Our friends are not broods of vipers. Judgment is for some other group. Certainly it isn't for the most prominent leaders of our community, those who exceed everyone else in righteousness—oops, that's a description of the Pharisees. The prophets of Israel and Jesus himself repeatedly declare that it is the most "successful" people who are apparently going to be judged ahead of everyone else.

It's remarkable how much Jesus refers to hell. Whether this is a literal concept of hell or not can be debated. The point is this: Jesus the Messiah was dead serious about pronouncing the judgment of God upon idolaters—upon those who oriented their lives upon false gods and ignored the reality and righteousness of the God who is really God. In the Old Testament and in the New, one of the subjects to be taken most seriously is idolatry. John Calvin famously said that the human mind was a perpetual factory of idols, which has been true from the days of the golden calf in Moses's time up until our own time. And one of the idols of our own time is the idol we have made of a God who never judges anyone or anything. We have created a God who accepts everyone "just as they are" and never says anything against us, because that would be "judgmental."

In our time, one of the worst things that can be said about anybody is that he or she is "judgmental." It's remarkable that this word, "judgmental," is a relatively new word. It doesn't appear in the authoritative *Oxford English Dictionary* until the twentieth century. Prior to that, judging something was considered a positive thing, meaning to discern its truth, or its value. The capacity to judge accurately was a form of exercising wisdom. I'm not sure how "judgmental" entered the language, but it must have been related to our contemporary attitude of "whatever works for you." The god of "whatever works for you" is certainly one of the idols of our era.

At the same time, sniping at other people has never been more common-place. We may be seeing the end of "political correctness," which has been one of the favorite targets of criticism in the campaign just ended, but I remember political correctness very well from my first days in seminary in 1972, when the reading list for Systematic Theology 101 was bitterly attacked for not including any female theologians. Well, although there are several world-class female theologians now, forty years ago there were none, so the agitators really had no recourse.[1] Still, the wrath that descended on the heads of the designers of the course was considerable. I got very caught up in this and narrowly escaped, by the grace of God working through some remarkable people, including one very brave faculty member, a Jewish woman who taught Hebrew. She was

1. Katherine Sonderregger and Sarah Coakley would head this list now. In 1972, Mary Daly was the best that anyone could come up with. Whatever one might say about this formidable personality, a systematic theologian she was not.

utterly disgusted by the idea that women students were supposed to read only works by feminists. I still remember her with fondness.

The real theological problem here is that we have lost sight of the fact that an act of judgment may very well be an act of liberation. The difficulty we have with the idea of making judgments speaks largely to our insecurity. When we feel judged by someone, it seems fearful to us, a threat to our existence even. I remember how much my mother hated the famous mosaic in the dome of the church in Daphni, in Greece. It was the typical image of Christ as Pantokrator, the judge of all things, seen everywhere in Greek churches, but unlike some of the more benign images of the Pantokrator, this one is really ferocious. My mother had nerves of steel intellectually, but she was unnerved by the looming presence of the image. I, on the other hand, loved it. More about that in a minute, but I knew the reason that my mother felt that way. I was very close to her and knew that she suffered somewhat from feelings of unworthiness, therefore she experienced Christ as Judge in a very negative way, as if he were coming after her personally.

At the close of the Te Deum we sing, "We believe that thou shalt come to be our Judge." Everything depends on what we know of Jesus Christ and his second coming in glory as ruler of all things. What sort of Judge will he be? When we look at images of Christ in majesty, what sort of ruler do we imagine him to be?

This is an Advent question. We've been speaking at some length during the past two days about the nature of the Advent season. Over the centuries, as the church's liturgical calendar developed, the identity of Advent took on a particular shape that is not so well understood today. The season was not intended to be the run-up to Christmas in the sense that we think of today. It was designed to be the season that looked forward, not to the birth of the baby Jesus in Bethlehem, but to the second coming of Christ. Advent locates the church properly, in between the times, the time of waiting through the night for the Bridegroom to come. The parable of the wise and foolish bridesmaids is a quintessential Advent reading; the foolish young women who are supposed to greet the bridegroom when he arrives have allowed their lamps to run out of oil (Matt. 25:1–13). This is an image of the church when she lets her lights burn low. The time of waiting is long; it is hard; it is extremely dispiriting much of the time; but the promise that the Lord will come sustains the church throughout the night. Keep the lower lights burning!

The coming of the Lord will be accompanied by the final judgment over all things—over the waste we have made of God's creation by wars and greed and rapacity and cruelty and self-aggrandizement at the expense of the poor and needy whom God loves. How are we going to survive this judgment? Listen again to the prophecy of Isaiah:

> For thus says the high and lofty one
>> who inhabits eternity, whose name is Holy. . . .
> I will not continually accuse,
>> nor will I always be angry. . . .
> Because of [the] wicked covetousness [of my people] I was angry;
>> I struck them . . . but they kept turning back to their own ways.
> I have seen their ways, *but* I will heal them;
>> I will lead them and repay them with comfort, . . . says the Lord;
>> and I will heal them. (Isa. 57:15–19)

Did you hear that "but"? The name of this sermon is "The Great *BUT*." Here again is part of today's reading from I Thessalonians: "You yourselves know well that the day of the Lord will come like a thief in the night. When people say, 'There is peace and security,' then sudden destruction will come upon them. . . . **But** you are not in darkness, brothers and sisters, for that day to surprise you like a thief. For you are all children of light, children of the day; we are not of the night or of darkness" (I Thess. 5:2–5).

We are all children of light! We, here in this space today! Paul says so! Does that mean that we are good people who have done good things and will therefore be rewarded as we deserve? We know better than that, don't we? Even our righteous deeds, writes Isaiah, are like filthy rags (64:6). In my Episcopal church we used to say, in the General Confession, "We have left undone those things that we ought to have done, and we have done those things that we ought not to have done, and there is no health in us." We stopped saying all that about forty years ago, along about the time that we decided that "judgmentalism" was the worst thing in the world. But it is still true that we have done what we should not, and that we have not done what we should, and that even our best efforts often turn to ashes. Isn't that true? It surely is true of me, anyway. I've done things that I meant to be helpful, and they turned out to be exactly the opposite. It is only as God inhabits our efforts and turns them to his purposes (sometimes in a different direction than we intended!) that our deeds find their place in his great plan for each of us.

The joke on us is that quite often our worst failures turn out to be not so bad after all. The setbacks become lessons that build us up; the rebukes that we suffer turn out to be strengthening and correcting. It all depends on the context in which the rebuke occurs. When it occurs in the context of unconditional love, judgment has a redemptive effect:

> Because of their wicked covetousness I was angry [says the Lord];
>> I struck them, I hid and was angry;
>> but they kept turning back to their own ways.
> I have seen their ways, **but** I will heal them;
>> I will lead them and repay them with comfort.

Yesterday at our retreat gathering I mentioned something that I think is worth mentioning again. I was privileged to learn from two superb psycho-analysts who were very much in tune with each other. From them I learned this: "The negative moment is in the service of the positive moment." In other words, there are times in the therapeutic relationship when the therapist must challenge the patient in a way that may seem confrontational, hostile, "judg-mental." But if the patient can receive this in the context of an ongoing and affirming therapeutic relationship, it will lead to a breakthrough, and the pa-tient's life may take a decisive turn for the better. A professor at Princeton Seminary, Charles Bartow, wrote something very similar. He wrote of "the God who is against us in order to be for us."[2]

I'd like to try putting it another way. The overall testimony of the Old and New Testaments is that God will save us *from* the judgment, but he will not save us *without* judgment. I'm sure many of you have heard the famous saying of H. Richard Niebuhr about American Christianity: "A God without wrath brought men without sin into a kingdom without judgment through the ministrations of a Christ without a cross."[3] So let me say it again: **God will save us *from* the judgment, but he will not save us *without* judgment.** God being who he is, he cannot allow evil to exist forever. Something has to be done about the human heart, which constantly misleads and deceives. Something has to be done about the rule of Sin and Death in the world that God made, the world that God still loves in spite of everything. The secret of being a faithful follower of the Lord Jesus is that we know that *he* is the one who will judge the living and the dead, and that we will be saved from ourselves by the one who has loved us to the last breath of his own life.

2. Charles L. Bartow, *God's Human Speech: A Practical Theology of Proclamation* (Grand Rapids: Eerdmans, 1997), 99 and elsewhere.

3. H. Richard Niebuhr, *The Kingdom of God in America* (New York: Harper and Row, 1937).

This, then, is the place for the great BUT, from Isaiah 54:

For a brief moment I forsook you,
   but with great compassion I will gather you.
In overflowing wrath for a moment
      I hid my face from you,
but with everlasting love I will have compassion on you,
      says the Lord, your Redeemer. (vv. 7–8)

So it is for our ultimate redemption that God will judge us. In the surpassing Advent passage that ends the Old Testament,

> Behold, I send my messenger to prepare the way before me, and the Lord whom you seek will suddenly come to his temple; the messenger of the covenant in whom you delight, behold, he is coming, says the Lord of hosts. **But** who can endure the day of his coming, and who can stand when he appears? For he is like a refiner's fire and like fullers' soap; he will sit as a refiner and purifier of silver, and he will purify the sons of Levi and refine them like gold and silver, till they present right offerings to the Lord. (Mal. 3:1–3)

If you're alert, you saw that in that passage the BUT plays the opposite role. To those who think the coming of the Messiah will be a picnic, the prophet says absolutely not, because we are not worthy to stand before him when he appears. *But* we will undergo the refiner's fire, and will emerge as new people, remade in his image and fit for his eternal company. We will enter into the wedding feast *with him* to rejoice for ever.

Only a very great and mighty Judge is able to do what is promised us in Jesus Christ. He has promised us that he will do away with Sin and Death forever. The face of the frightening Pantokrator is turned against everything that reduces us, that imprisons us, that distorts us, that annihilates us. It is our redeemed self that he loves and promises to make whole in us, but not without judgment upon all that is crippling and destructive.

I wonder if you, like me, have grown weary of patterns in your own life. As I have grown older, I have recognized that there are certain impulses and tendencies in my personality that I have worked very hard to overcome, but they are still there, causing me—and others—no end of trouble. I am looking forward to passing through the refiner's fire. I am so joyful to know that those traits will be judged and gone forever. I hope that's true for you too. We rejoice to know that it is the Lord himself who will come to be our Judge.

Saint Paul writes to us about this in one of the great passages appointed for Advent. Let us gladly hear his words: "So then . . . since we belong to the day, let us be sober, and put on the breastplate of faith and love, and for a helmet the hope of salvation. For God has not destined us for wrath, **but** to obtain salvation through our Lord Jesus Christ, who died for us so that . . . we might live with him. Therefore encourage one another and build one another up, just as you are doing" (I Thess. 5:6–11).

Amen.

Good Works and Words: Signs of the End

Grace Church, New York City
Pre-Advent Season 1983

II THESSALONIANS 2:1–8

After All Saints' Day, the tone of the lectionary readings speeds up considerably as we approach Advent. From the second epistle to the Thessalonians, written by Saint Paul to one of his favorite churches, the second chapter, beginning with the eighth verse: "The lawless one will be revealed, and the Lord Jesus will slay him with the breath of his mouth. . . . The coming of the lawless one by the activity of Satan will be with all power and with pretended signs and wonders. . . . Now may our Lord Jesus Christ himself . . . comfort your hearts and establish them in every good work and word" (II Thess. 2:8–9, 16–17).

A lot of talk has been going around during the last few weeks about the end of the world. Carl Sagan and Paul Ehrlich have been associated with a recent scientific conference that stated that the effects of even a moderate-sized nuclear exchange would be infinitely worse than hitherto believed, because the world's climate would be altered to such a degree that we would all die in the cold and the dark.

On November 20, as all of you must know by now, there will be a program on ABC, in the evening, called *The Day After*. Many groups have released study sheets and practical guides about how to watch this program and how to cope with it afterward. We are going to make some of these guides available. This one is called "Watch 'The Day After,' but Don't Watch It Alone." All of this reminds me of a quotation from Jonathan Schell's well-known book of a couple of years ago, *The Fate of the Earth*, a quotation I published in the bulletin in 1982 that has stayed with me daily ever since. I can't shake it off. It goes like this: "Extinction by nuclear arms would not be the day of judgment in which God destroys the world but raises the dead, and then metes out perfect justice to everyone who has ever lived. It would be the utterly meaningless and completely unjust destruction of mankind by man. Extinction by nuclear arms would not be the perfect justice of God. It would be the ultimate injustice of mankind."[1]

I cannot forget that balance, that contrast that he has struck, between the last judgment of God and the annihilation of mankind by mankind. We don't want to think about these things, but we must. It is that time of year in the church.

Now a lot of church people around the nation, upon hearing someone say in November that it is "that time of year," immediately think, "They are going to ask me for my money." Fall is, indeed, stewardship time everywhere, and it is stewardship time at Grace Church. However, when I say, "It is 'that time of year' in the church," I'm not referring directly to stewardship (although, as you will see, I hope to refer to it indirectly). I am referring directly to the fact that the end of the Christian year is November 20 (Stewardship Sunday at Grace Church), the Feast of Christ the King, the last Sunday before the first Sunday of Advent.

The lectionary takes on a new and portentous note every year at this time. As the year turns from the closing of the old year to the beginning of the new, the readings from the Old and New Testaments have an urgency about them, a note of warning, coming directly from the Lord himself, who said, "Watch and pray, for you do not know when the Son of Man will appear" (Mark 13:33; Matt. 24:42).

The note of judgment and the announcement of the imminent arrival of God are appropriate to this time of year. That's one of the reasons for reading the second epistle to the Thessalonians, with its powerful note of apocalyptic urgency, in this pre-Advent season. The Thessalonian community is characterized particularly by two things: first, they are full of enthusiasm about the second advent, the second coming of Jesus Christ, and second, they are suffering from unnamed persecutions and afflictions. We don't know exactly what the identity and nature of the sufferings and persecutions and afflictions are, but Paul refers to them quite specifically, and encourages the little body of Christians to persevere in the face of hardship and pain. And so, in the letter to the Thessalonians, we have a combination of themes: (1) the end of the world; (2) the second coming of Jesus Christ; and (3) the question: How shall we live? or, How shall we conduct ourselves?

Those are the Advent questions in distilled form.

The Thessalonian correspondence is concerned in part with such mundane topics as sexual behavior and earning a living, so it is a most unexpected

---

1. Jonathan Schell, *The Fate of the Earth* (New York: Knopf, 1982), 127.

mixture of themes—the end of the world, the second coming of the Lord God, sex, and money!—this is so wonderfully typical of our Scriptures, this connection of ethics and apocalyptic. Very Advent-ish.

Much of today's text is bewildering, if not downright off-putting for contemporary people. Paul speaks of "the lawless one" who will be revealed (the lawless one is sometimes called the antichrist, a strange and malevolent figure who appears at the end of time). Much foolishness has been spoken about the antichrist—attempts have been made over the centuries to equate him to every kind of historical phenomenon: the Roman Empire, the pope, the Ottoman Empire, Nazis, Communism—but what's important here is the clear picture of a Power of Evil (Paul typically identifies this as the Power of Sin and Death) who actively works to subvert the purposes of God. This Power is personified in the New Testament under various names (Satan, the devil, Beelzebub), not because anyone either then or now should conceive of him in reductive, cartoonish terms, but because Paul and the other New Testament writers want us to understand that God has an active, personal Enemy who works tirelessly to distort, contaminate, and destroy God's plan for salvation. This apocalyptic scenario takes radical evil very seriously, and so should we. It is this "lawless one" who will be conquered once and for all in the last day when "the Lord Jesus will slay him with the breath of his mouth."

The apostle writes that the end of the world as we know it will not come until archetypal evil is banished, and archetypal evil is represented by this curious figure of the lawless one, the son of perdition. We don't entirely understand Paul's references here, and no scholars have been able to plumb the depths of these symbols, but perhaps it is enough to say that when this ultimate figure of wickedness does appear, it will appear, as Paul writes, with pretended signs and wonders that will fool many. Perhaps the pretended signs and wonders will be nothing more than dollar signs, perhaps the sign of a mushroom cloud; I do not know. As with many biblical images, the meanings are manifold. But here is the point of Paul's letter: the end of the world has not yet come upon the Thessalonian Christians, as they apparently were tempted to think it had. No, the end of the world will not come until archetypal evil is banished forever; but in the meantime—in the meantime—*good works and words* are signs of the victory of the Lord Jesus Christ.

There are two women in this congregation who, this week, have suffered manifold hardships and misfortunes. Just to give one illustration, a young woman who has already had much affliction in her life was pushed down the subway steps this afternoon, and her friend who was with her at the time of this mugging received the news a few hours later that her mother had died this morning. This is just one of any number of examples I could give of the way in which evil seems to pile up. It seems to pile up on specific people sometimes, in a way that we cannot understand.

Well, in the case of both of these women, whose stories I really have only told in the most sketchy way—some of you will recognize them—in the past week each of them has done something extraordinarily kind to another member of this congregation, and I have been privileged to hear about this through the grapevine. In the midst of their suffering and pain, in the midst of what Saint Paul calls in this text "the mystery of lawlessness," each of these women has found her own way to act out the victory of Jesus Christ over every form of evil and pain. The reason that Paul writes to the Thessalonian Christians about Jesus's second coming on the one hand, and mundane topics like Christian sexual behavior and earning a living on the other hand, is that in tiny little human acts, like kindness to a fellow parishioner, like giving money away, like self-control in the middle of every kind of pagan temptation, in these small ways, Christians act out signs of the victory of Jesus Christ.

"May our Lord Jesus Christ himself comfort your hearts and establish them in every good work and word." By our faith and by the living of our faith, we signify our trust that the end of the world belongs to God. The end of the world is not the wicked end of man, which we so justly deserve, but God's end, God's purpose. "The lawless one will be revealed, and the Lord Jesus will slay him with the breath of his mouth. So may our Lord Jesus Christ himself comfort your hearts, and establish them in every good work and word."

Attempts to identify the antichrist are misleading at best, and dangerous at worst. The point is this: the great and terrible enemy of God is real; he seeks to overthrow God's handiwork; and he lies behind all the accumulated evil and wickedness in the world; *but!* he will ultimately be wiped out, obliterated, like a puff of smoke. "The Lord Jesus will slay him with the breath of his mouth."

But the Jonathan Schell quotation keeps coming back to me: "Extinction by nuclear arms would not be the day of judgment in which God destroys the world but raises the dead, and then metes out perfect justice to everyone who has ever lived. It would be the utterly meaningless and completely unjust destruction of mankind by man."

The distinction that he makes between the injustice of man and the justice of God is a central theme of the coming season of Advent. But what's particularly important is that these global, indeed cosmic, themes are acted out in the humble details of everyday life. The good work and the good words that are given to us in our time are the acting out, in our own lives and in our own community, of the victory of Jesus Christ over every form of evil. However small, however insignificant, our works of resistance to every kind of idolatry and violence are signs of the coming triumph of Jesus Christ. Resistance to frantic consumerism by committing a proportion of our income to the Lord's work; resistance to the sexual anarchy in America today by self-control; resistance to the nuclear arms race in whatever ways one finds suitable to one's own calling—these good works and good words are given us to perform as signs of Jesus's second advent.

In one of the brochures that has been put out about the TV program *The Day After*, there is this statement: "It is important to remember that the future is not some place we are going to, but something we are creating every day." Not quite right from the Christian point of view! You and I are not creating the future. The future is coming to us, from God. God is creating the future. That is our only hope. Let us not deceive ourselves that we are creating our future, because if we are, there is no hope. We need to think about the nuclear arms race from God's point of view. It is not God's will that his people should perish. The day of judgment in the Bible is ultimately for God's people a day of hope, and not of despair, a day of restoration and not a day of doom, a day of judgment, yes, but a day of purification, a day of new life, where sin will be no more. "The lawless one will be revealed, and the Lord Jesus will slay him with the breath of his mouth. . . . The coming of the lawless one by the activity of Satan will be with all power and with stupendous signs and wonders. . . . May our Lord Jesus Christ himself comfort your hearts and establish them in every good work and word."

Please join with me in opening your prayer books to the collect for today, and in reading it again, all together this time. It is on page 236 of the Book of Common Prayer.

Let us pray: "Oh God, whose Blessed Son came into the world that he might destroy the works of the devil, and make us children of God and heirs of eternal life, grant that having this hope, we may purify ourselves as he is pure, that when he comes again with power and great glory, we may be made like him in his eternal and glorious kingdom, where he lives and reigns with you and the Holy Spirit, one God, forever and ever. Amen."

God's Apocalyptic War
(The Feast of Saint Michael)

Silver and Gold on the Last Day

Grace Church, New York City
November 20, 1990

ZEPHANIAH 1:14–18; MATTHEW 25:14–30

Every year, as the last leaves drop from the trees and we start hunkering down for winter, the church's theological clock starts to tick faster. Beginning after All Saints' Day, the Scripture readings build to a tremendous crescendo. There is nothing else like it in the church calendar. We might imagine a movie camera mounted on a crane; at first the lens is focused on a small local happening in the streets of first-century Jerusalem; then the camera pulls back and the crane swings away so that the scene before us becomes all Jerusalem, then all Judea, the entire Mediterranean, and finally the whole world, seen through the lens of scriptural prophecy. That is what happens in the church's liturgy in November, in the readings on the Sundays just before Advent. In the oracles of the Hebrew prophets, in the letters of Saint Paul, in the parables told by Jesus in the week before his death, the message is the same: the last things are at hand.

"The dreadful day of judgment" . . . do you who are over fifty remember that phrase? It used to be the first thing that the minister said to the man and woman in the marriage ceremony, if you can imagine it. "I require and charge you both as you shall answer at the dreadful day of judgment when the secrets of all hearts shall be disclosed. . . ." Those words were said at our wedding, and it never occurred to us that there was anything we should change.

God has had a little joke on the Episcopal Church. In 1976, we adopted a new Prayer Book from which all phrases like "dreadful day of judgment" were diligently expunged. At the same time, however, we also adopted a new lectionary. I don't know how many of you remember the old lectionary, but it was the exact same every year, year in and year out, so that we were reading

---

This sermon was delivered on "Pledge Sunday," but the scriptural context is the coming of the Advent season.

very much less Scripture than we are now. The joke is that while the Prayer Book revisers were busy pushing the dreadful day of judgment out of camera range, the lectionary committees were bringing it back in by many degrees of magnification, through the lens of God's Word.

The great challenge of the season of Advent and the theme of the last judgment is to show why, in light of the promises of God, the coming of the Lord in judgment is not bad news but the best possible news. This is not the easiest thing in the world to explain, but it is that time of year, and we are looking at the world through a wide, wide-angle lens. In the words of the prophet Zephaniah, appointed for today, we are seeing nothing less than the end of the world as we know it.

> Be silent before the Lord God!
>> For the day of the Lord is at hand. . . .
> A day of wrath is that day. (Zeph. 1:7, 15)

There is a stunning thirteenth-century Latin poem based on this text from Zephaniah.[1] It's really fun to read because of the amazing multisyllabic rhymes, but its content is anything but fun. Music lovers will recognize this poem as the *Dies Irae* (Day of Wrath) section of the Requiem Mass, which called forth powers of expression from such composers as Mozart, Verdi, and Berlioz.

Dies Irae, dies illa	The Day of Wrath, that day
Solvet saeclum in favilla,	shall dissolve the world in ashes,
Teste David cum Sibylla.	as witnesseth David and the Sibyl.
Quantus tremor est futurus	What trembling there shall be
Quando judex est venturus	when the Judge shall come
Cuncta stricte discussurus!	who shall thresh out all thoroughly!
Mors stupebit et natura	Death and Nature shall be astounded
Cum resurget creatura	when the creatures shall rise again
Judicanti responsura.[2]	to answer to the Judge.

This theme of the day of the Lord, a future time when God will arrive to set things right once and for all, increases in importance throughout the pro-

---

1. There were quite a few people who knew Latin in the congregation of Grace Church in New York City.

2. This was not read when the sermon was actually delivered, but was inserted in the written copy for later distribution.

phetic books of the Old Testament, coming to a climax in the book of Daniel with the appearance of the Son of Man descending with the clouds of heaven.[3] This motif reaches its apex in the New Testament with Jesus referring to *himself* as the Son of Man, and the book of Revelation bringing the whole thing to a stupendous apocalyptic climax with the words of the risen and reigning Christ coming to us, not from the past, but *from the future*:

> "Behold, I am coming soon. . . . I am the Alpha and the Omega, the first and the last, the beginning and the end." (Rev. 22:12–13)

> Behold, he is coming with the clouds, and every eye will see him, every one who pierced him; and all the tribes of the earth will wail because of him. (Rev. 1:7)

You see what I mean about the wide-angle lens. The entire universe is taken into this picture. The whole of history is taken into this picture. This is the day of reckoning for all peoples, tribes, nations, and tongues; and the One who does the reckoning is Jesus Christ. It is hard to stand here and even try to put this staggering claim into words. That's why the books of Daniel and Revelation describe it in imagery, in word pictures. It's described in various ways: we hear of the sky darkening and the stars falling; we hear of a great book opened, a mountain split in two, a conflagration that consumes everything that is wicked. We recoil from most of this. And yet, you know, many Americans rejoiced without reservation when Dresden was bombed into oblivion, when Tokyo was carpet-bombed, when the atomic bomb was dropped on Hiroshima. Why do we become finicky when we hear of God destroying the wicked and their works? Is it because we are afraid we might be among the wicked? Or is it some sort of tender-mindedness that we have suddenly developed about being merciful to evildoers? Somehow I doubt it. I don't really understand why we are able to be of two minds about these things.

It gets worse. From Jesus himself we hear of alarms and battles, angels and trumpets, false messiahs and the Son of Man himself coming to divide the sheep from the goats (Matt. 24–25). In Revelation, we learn of generals and kings running for their lives, to hide in caves and hills, asking the mountains to fall on them to save them from the wrath of the Lamb of God (Rev. 6:15–17).

---

3. Charles Wesley's hymn, "Lo, He Comes with Clouds Descending," picks up this imagery from Daniel. A choir anthem by Palestrina has become traditional for the first or second Sunday of Advent: "Tell us . . . ," with its repeated references to the "cloud covering the whole earth." (The full text can be found in the Advent liturgy at the back of this volume.)

All these images have their significance, but one in particular seems fitting for
the great city of New York:

> "On that day," says the Lord,
>> "a cry will be heard. . . .
>> For all the traders are no more;
>> all who weigh out silver are cut off.
> At that time I will search Jerusalem with lamps,
>> and I will punish those . . .
>> who say in their hearts,
> 'The Lord will not do good,
>> nor will he do ill.'
> Their goods shall be plundered,
>> and their houses laid waste." . . .
> Neither their silver nor their gold
>> shall be able to deliver them
>> on the day of the wrath of the Lord. (Zeph. 1:10, 11–13, 18)

In case this isn't clear enough, we read the same thing in various other
parts of the Bible. For example: "'Fallen, fallen is Babylon the great!' . . . 'Alas,
alas, the great city. . . . For in one hour your judgment has come.' . . . And the
merchants of the earth weep and mourn for her, since no one buys their cargo
anymore, cargo of gold, silver, jewels and pearls . . . all articles of costly wood,
bronze, iron, and marble, wine and olive oil . . . cattle and sheep, horses and
chariots, *slaves—and human lives*" (Rev. 18:2, 10–13).

So this is the first part of the sermon this morning. Where do we go from
here? Clearly we are all implicated in a sickness unto death that afflicts the entire human race, and we are without excuse because we stood by and watched
while *human lives* were being destroyed all around us—and the usual ways in
which we protect ourselves will not work anymore. An end has come upon
those who say, "The Lord won't do anything, neither good nor bad." The message of the coming season of Advent is: oh, yes, he will; and whoever you are,
whoever I am, we are going to be caught up in the judgment of God. And the
vividness of the language, for better or worse, tells us that gold and silver and
the piling up of worldly possessions and status symbols will be of no use to us
whatsoever when God's final reckoning comes. Money and wealth and possessions and commerce will count for nothing. Indeed, they will be a minus.

Now for a change of pace—sort of. What, in everyday terms, does all this
mean for the way we live our lives? Some individuals and sects have taken

these matters so seriously, even literally, that they have divested themselves of all personal property. This is by no means as heedless as it sounds. The more responsible among such groups—ranging from Catholic monks and nuns to Protestant communities like the Bruderhof—set a remarkable example for us all. For most of us, though, the handling of money is and will continue to be a significant part of life. The question then becomes, how do we handle our money in such a way as to indicate that money has no lasting significance?

The answer to this question is surprisingly simple. We bear witness to our allegiance to the kingdom of God by giving away a lot of our money. When we do this, we are acting out our calling as the people of the age to come. This is not just a message for our stewardship season. This is a message for eternity. Saint Paul, in an exceptional passage from First Corinthians, puts it like this: "I mean, brothers and sisters, the appointed time has grown short; from now on, let even those who have wives be as though they had none, and those who mourn as though they were not mourning, and those who rejoice as though they were not rejoicing, *and those who buy as though they had no possessions, and those who deal with the world as though they had no dealings with it.* For the present form of this world is passing away" (I Cor. 7:29–31).[4]

Here's where the Gospel reading for today comes in. In the famous parable of the talents, Jesus illustrates with a story about the use of money. Let's get one thing out of the way from the outset. This is not a parable about people who have talent. It's unfortunate that the English word "talent" is also the name of a coin in Roman times. Jesus is not talking about people being talented at drawing, or piano playing, or football, or foreign languages. He's talking about money: shekels, francs, yen, marks, dollars—the green stuff. It's remarkable how the parable has been watered down to mean that we should be generous with our "talents," like offering to design a poster for the Pecan Festival. Not that there's anything wrong with that! But the proper name of the parable is the parable of the Money in Trust.

It has often been pointed out that Jesus of Nazareth had a surprisingly sophisticated understanding of finance and business. He uses images having to do with money more than any other single motif in his parables and teachings. He would say, "The kingdom of God is like a merchant searching for fine pearls," or "There was once a landowner who let out his property to tenants," or "What man would set out to build a tower without first calculating the cost?"

---

4. Students of Paul's letters call this the "as though not" passage (or, in Greek, the *hos me* passage). There is no portion of Scripture that more precisely locates the Christian community on the frontier of the ages.

The parable of the so-called talents, the parable of money in trust, does not work unless we grasp the idea that an absentee investor has every right to expect that his property will be managed imaginatively while he is away. He gives various sums of money, quite large ones, to his agents. If we think of this as "talents," in the sense of individual abilities like singing or acting or carpentry, the parable makes no sense at all; it only works when we understand that the master has invested *money* and expects a good return. When he discovers that one of his agents has squirreled the money away so that it has not brought in a single penny of interest, let alone doubled or tripled in value, he takes away every cent and gives it to the one who was most successful in increasing what was entrusted to him.

Now I'm going to confuse you because, although the parable is indeed about money and nothing but money on the surface, it's about something else on the deeper level, and that brings us back to the Advent theme. On the deeper level, the parable of the money in trust is about the second coming and the stewardship and mission of the church. It's about money, but it's also about something greater than money. How are we going to work this out?

"Deal with money as though not dealing with it." Make money, spend money, invest money, put money in the bank, take money out of the bank, buy mutual funds, give some of it to the church and get a tax deduction—but do it all with the sure and certain knowledge that silver and gold will not help us in the last day, that there will be no traders in the house of the Lord on the last day, that the merchants of the earth will wail when no one buys their wares on the last day.

"How hard it will be," said Jesus, wonderingly, "for a rich man to enter the kingdom of heaven! It is easier for a camel to go through the eye of a needle than for a rich man to enter the kingdom of God" (Matt. 19:23–24). Money is a problem for us. That's why Jesus invited the rich young man to give away his wealth to the poor. He was offering the young man his freedom. Jesus knows we have trouble with money; that's why he brings us a new life, free from greed and acquisitiveness, a life in which we are able to stand back from our small preoccupations in order to see what God is up to in the world. And when we begin to see it, we will begin to be liberated, like the faithful servants in the parable—liberated "into the joy of our Master." What a surpassingly wonderful thought that is! We will be thrilled to be pried loose from our money, because we will be so excited about the return on his investment—his investment *in us.*

One of the most celebrated camera shots in the history of film occurs in *Gone with the Wind* when Scarlett O'Hara goes to the Atlanta depot to find the doctor to deliver Melanie's baby. All the wounded and dying soldiers have been brought there from the battlefields. At first we see Scarlett's figure filling the picture as she picks her way along. Then the camera slowly pulls back and pulls back, until she is almost lost to view as the screen fills with one vast panorama of human suffering and death—the cost of war.

As the Advent season approaches, the lens of Holy Scripture pulls all the way back. The entire spectrum of human folly and duplicity is in view. Into "such a world as this," the Lord is coming—not as a baby this time, but with glory and majesty to judge the living and the dead.[5] Silver and gold will have no purpose in that last day; the time for using money is *now*, in *these* days, using it to testify to his coming deliverance, using it up as if it were going out of style—as, indeed, it is. The purpose of Sundays like today is for us, the people of God, to practice taking the long view, in preparation for the day of his coming. We need to catch the larger vision of God's plan for the church, set in the world not to clutch, conserve, and hide its treasure in the ground, but boldly to invest it in *God's* "futures."

The world as God sees it is a panorama of deprivation and exploitation and death. The history of the world has shown over and over again that it is incapable of rescuing itself from forces too strong for mere human nature. The great good news of the last judgment is that "on that day" God will set everything right, once and for all. He will end war forever. "He will put down the mighty from their seat, and exalt the humble and meek."[6] He will overthrow the pride of the smug and arrogant. He will touch your heart and he will touch my heart with a blaze of righteousness that will consume everything in us that is unworthy of himself. As you sign your pledge card today, the overarching vision is to signify that great day to come, when there will be no traders or merchants in the house of the Lord, for we will have received as a gift everything that we will ever need for the life of the age to come—because we will have the Lord himself, for ever and ever.

"Well done, thou good and faithful servants; you have been faithful in a little; I will set you over much. Enter into the joy of your Master."

Amen.

---

5. "Such a world as this" is marvelously slipped into an otherwise somewhat anodyne Christmas carol ("See amid the Winter's Snow"), lifting us into a God's-eye perspective of the desperate plight we have gotten ourselves into.

6. From the Magnificat (Luke 1:46–55).

The Army of Saint Michael

Saint Michael's Church, Charleston, South Carolina
The Feast of Saint Michael the Archangel 2000

REVELATION 12:7; PHILIPPIANS 1:29–30

Just for fun, let's take another look at the first verse of the hymn we sang as our service began, "Ye Watchers and Ye Holy Ones" (#618).[1] This is a favorite hymn in the Episcopal Church because it has a great tune and lots of alleluias, but I've discovered that many people don't really know what it's all about. Generally speaking, it's about praising the Holy Trinity in song. In the first verse, the angels lead the singing; in the second, the leader is the Virgin Mary ("O higher than the cherubim, more glorious than the seraphim . . . thou bearer of the eternal Word, most gracious, magnify the Lord"); in the third, it is the prophets, apostles, and martyrs of the church; and in the final verse, the singers are you and me. Wonderful!

But who are the "watchers and holy ones" and all those other characters in the first verse? Well, to begin with, we find them in the apocalyptic book of Daniel. The pagan king of Babylon, Nebuchadnezzar, has a dream. "I saw in the visions of my head as I lay in bed, and behold, a watcher, a holy one, came down from heaven." The watcher angel delivers a decree against Nebuchadnezzar, that he should go mad and live with the beasts of the field and eat grass. "The sentence is by the decree of the watchers, the decision by the word of the holy ones, to the end that the living may know that the Most High rules the kingdom of men, and gives it to whom he will" (Dan. 4:13, 17); that, essentially, is the message of the book of Daniel, that the Most High God of Israel, in spite of all the appearances to the contrary, is in charge of the world, and none of this world's rulers have a chance against him or his purposes.

But what about all these "thrones, dominions, princedoms, powers, virtues"? Well, those are the ranks of angels. There are nine ranks: seraphim

1. Text by John Athelstan Laurie Riley (1858–1945).

at the top, then cherubim, thrones, dominions, virtues, powers, principal-ities, archangels, and then just plain angels at the bottom of the heap. Your patron saint, Michael, is a mere archangel. Okay, that's all you're going to hear about the ranks of angels. A lot of it isn't in the Bible anyway, so you can just set it aside.

We move now to what *is* in the Bible. You have heard it read in today's lessons for the Feast of Saint Michael and All Angels, which actually was two days ago, September 29. Strictly speaking, we shouldn't be celebrating Saint Michael today, because his day is not a Feast of Our Lord—but the link be-tween Michael and Christ is so total that we are taking a liturgical liberty. In fact, in this age of angel-mania in America, you can administer a simple test: If the supposed angel glorifies Christ, then it's a real angel. If not, then it isn't.

There is great reticence about angels in the Bible. Seraphim and cheru-bim appear only at rare moments of supreme epiphany—manifestations of God's very presence. Only two angels are actually named in canonical Scrip-ture—Michael and Gabriel—and they, too, are surrounded by mystery. They appear only four times apiece (Gabriel in Dan. 8:16–17; 9:21–22; Luke 1:11–20; 1:26–38; Michael in Dan. 10:13 and 21; 12:1; Jude 9; Rev. 12:7).[2] It seems that God in his Word does not want us to know very much about these fascinating creatures. Having drawn back the curtain briefly, he drops it again.

The word "angel" means "messenger," but that's not the whole story. An-gels, in Scripture, are living embodiments of God's powerful presence and activity in the world. When the biblical writers speak of angels, they mean that God is present and at work, shaping events according to his purpose. In spite of all that's going on in our culture right now, with images of angels that look more and more like Barbie dolls by the minute, the biblical angels remain elu-sive, enigmatic, alien. They come not so much from another place "up there" as from another sphere of reality altogether. When angels appear, it means that the kingdom of God has irrupted into this earthly orb. Angels have no other function than to do God's bidding. They are our fellow creatures, but they are very different from us because their existence is exclusively shaped by the will of God. As such, they themselves disappear into the infinitely larger reality that is God himself. In this sense, it might be better not to talk about angels at all, lest they become a substitute for the worship of God. That's what the first chapter of the epistle to the Hebrews warns against. In that New Testament book, we have a lovely glimpse of God the Father instructing the angels as to what they should do when Jesus is born: "When [God] brings the first-born

---

2. The extracanonical books tell of other angels with names: Raphael, Uriel.

into the world, he says, 'Let all God's angels worship him, [for his] throne
. . . is for ever and ever; the righteous scepter is the scepter of thy kingdom'"
(Heb. 1:6, 8).

When an angel in the book of Revelation appears to John, John starts
to fall down on his knees, but the angel brings him back up again with stern
words: "You must not do that! I am a fellow servant with you and your brethren the prophets, and with those who keep the words of this book. Worship
God" (Rev. 22:9).

So today we are not here to worship Saint Michael, but to reflect upon
what Saint Michael represents. I have taken two texts: the first is from our
first reading today, from Revelation. Saint John writes: "War arose in heaven.
Michael and his angels fought against the dragon. . . . And the great dragon
was thrown down" (Rev. 12:7, 9).

The book of Revelation, much misunderstood, is nevertheless vitally important for the life and witness of the church. "All the powers and forces of the
universe [are] conceived as an embattled host."[3] The struggle is between God
and his great Enemy. In this imagery, each commander has an army; Satan's
troops are angels who, like their leader, are fallen.[4] Michael the archangel is
the general in charge of the "heavenly host" under the commander in chief,
who is Christ the Lord. This vast, cosmic struggle involves all human beings
in some way, but we are not aware of it except by faith. Many people today do
not believe in Satan, so they do not believe in this titanic unseen struggle, but
once in a while someone will confess belief in Satan.

During the genocide in Rwanda, *Time* magazine put a quotation instead
of a photograph on the front cover. It was a statement by a missionary serving
in that country during those unspeakable events: "There are no devils left in
Hell; they are all in Rwanda."[5] During World War II, Lutheran pastor Dietrich
Bonhoeffer and his brother Klaus were both imprisoned by the Nazis. Dietrich
was hanged, becoming one of the great Christian martyrs of the twentieth
century. We have no details of his last days, in which he may have been tortured, but we know of his brother Klaus under torture. He wrote in a letter, "I

---

3. Nineteenth-century preacher Alexander MacLaren, preaching on Revelation.

4. See Jude 6; II Pet. 2:4. This begs the question about why God would allow the angel-
messengers whom he created to rebel against him. There is no clear answer to this; however,
the imagery does help us to conceptualize the impossibility of respecting the mystery and
power of evil without explaining it. In any case, the fallen angels do not operate outside the
permissive will of God. (See my chapter on hell in my book *The Crucifixion: Understanding
the Death of Jesus Christ* [Grand Rapids: Eerdmans, 2015].)

5. *Time*, May 16, 1994.

am not afraid of being hanged, but I don't want to see those faces again . . . so much depravity. . . . I'd rather die than see those faces again. I have seen the Devil, and I can't forget it."[6]

A true grasp of Christian faith requires us to understand what we are up against. A central message of the New Testament is Christ's conquest of the alien powers. Paul's proclamation that Jesus will destroy even the last enemy (I Cor. 15:24–26), John's message that "the ruler of this world" is cast down by the cross of Christ (John 12:31), and the depiction of the victorious Lamb of God in Revelation all add their dimensions to the portrait of the Messiah as the victor over radical evil. However, none of this will mean anything to us if we do not have a clear-sighted grasp of the power, the malignity, and the cleverness of the Enemy. There are many aspects of this that we should understand. In the epistle to the Romans, Paul writes of "the evil that lies close at hand" (Rom. 7:21) within each human being. But the Scriptures also point us to the reign of Powers who take hold of entire groups of people. Paul calls these Powers by the names of Sin and Death. These Powers cannot be accounted for simply as the product of individual guilt.

I have in my file cabinet a folder of newspaper clippings half an inch thick about corporate executives, good respected citizens, who have nevertheless done great harm because they could not or would not see that what was superficially good for their bottom line might be very bad for the community as a whole. To pick out only one example, a clipping from August 8 of this year: "Tobacco industry documents show that cigarette makers took part for years in a sweeping campaign to influence and undermine the World Health Organization's anti-smoking efforts world-wide. . . . In a statement, an official of Philip Morris did not dispute the report's contents."[7] I am not targeting Philip Morris in particular. Many fine American corporations have allowed employees to work in dangerous conditions, have supported ethnic discrimination, have knowingly engaged in false advertising. Quite a few officers of these companies have been leaders in their churches.[8] The point is that there is something loose in the world that is bigger than we are, that estranges us

---

6. Quoted in Eberhard Bethge, *Dietrich Bonhoeffer: A Biography*, 2nd ed. (Minneapolis: Fortress, 2000).

7. Barry Meier, "W.H.O. Says Files Show Tobacco Companies Fought Anti-smoking Efforts," *New York Times*, August 1, 2000. Meier wrote scores of articles exposing the greed and dishonesty of the tobacco industry between 1989 and the present, when his focus shifted to e-cigarettes.

8. Bernie Ebbers, CEO of WorldCom, now serving twenty-five years in prison for defrauding investors, was a Sunday school teacher at his Baptist church.

from our best selves, that catches us up in its grip. Saint Paul called it the Power of Sin.

I recently received a letter from a thoughtful Christian businessman:

> Having spent the past 6 years in a family business has provided a new perspective on faith and life. The issues that I face daily have tempered my own self-righteousness and have demonstrated to me over and over how easy it is to choose the expedient, the profitable, and the less than good. Daily I face decisions that come without instructions on what is right, and I have to decide in partnership with family members and employees who hold different beliefs and ideas. I am caught with a responsibility for the welfare of 40 people who work for our company.

This is a man who takes Christian faith seriously. He recognizes the battle that he is in; he knows that he must operate in shades of gray much of the time; and he has looked the power of greed in the face. He has also learned that the Powers of Sin and Evil can affect the church.

I have other files in my cabinets. One is related to the recent $2.25 million embezzlement by Ellen Cooke, the official who had virtually unlimited power and access at "815," our Episcopal Church headquarters in New York. From all accounts, Mrs. Cooke was a person of such formidable presence that, although she was widely disliked, no one had ever challenged her. An article in the *Living Church* stands out from the others. It was written by a person who observed events closely after the news of the crime began to emerge. She tells a story that was apparently unknown to all but a few until the article was published. According to her information, there was a whistle-blower at 815, a woman who had worked for the Episcopal Church for fifteen years. She was the controller, not the presiding bishop or the president of the House of Deputies, not the internal auditor or external auditor, not a member of the Finance Committee or the Audit Committee. In spite of her position some rungs down the ladder, this woman saw what was going on and dared to protest. She was "mysteriously and quietly removed" from her job. As events unfolded, and as others began to take credit for her actions, she was all but forgotten. This was a person who was willing to step into the front lines in the battle against wickedness in high places. I do not know her, but she is a hero of faith.[9] The battle for justice and

---

9. Kathryn Anschutz, "Where Credit Is Due at 815," *Living Church*, April, 6, 1997. Ms. Anschutz also deserved credit for the clarity of her ethically probing article. The name of the

righteousness is fought without *and within* the church. No one of us can ever take our innocence for granted. There are two kinds of evildoing: the kind that is done directly and the kind that is done because "good" people do not protest. The devil loves nothing more than good people not protesting.

Our second text this morning is from Saint Paul's letter to the Philippians: "It has been granted to you that for the sake of Christ you should not only believe in him but also suffer for his sake, engaged in the same conflict which you saw and now hear to be mine" (Phil. 1:29–30). Paul was in prison when he wrote those words. He knew he might be killed some day, and indeed he eventually was, executed in Rome by order of the emperor Nero. Yet Paul had long since come to terms with his precarious existence. He knew that he was fighting on God's cosmic battlefield. He knew also that he was fighting under the banner of the cross, which meant suffering for Christ's sake. But that is the sign of Christian warfare; it does not inflict suffering on others, but bears suffering for the sake of the other, as our Lord suffered for our sins on the cross. *It has been granted to you that for the sake of Christ you should not only believe in him but also suffer for his sake.* If anyone says he is a Christian because he believes but thinks he does not have to be engaged in the conflict, that probably means he is giving aid and comfort to the Enemy. There is no neutrality in Saint Michael's war.

It takes extra effort for us to remember that Christian warfare is not fought with conventional weapons. I wonder if any of you have watched the remarkable PBS series *A Force More Powerful*. It is about nonviolent movements in the twentieth century. I had one objection to the program; it emphasizes Gandhi but says almost nothing about the deep *Christian* roots of some of the movements, especially in the American civil rights movement. It is often said that Martin Luther King was largely influenced by Gandhi, but recent students of his life have shown that that was not true, that his profound commitment to nonviolence was essentially biblical.[10]

At any rate, one of the most striking moments in the television program, to me, was the interview with John Seigenthaler, former publisher of the Nashville newspaper that was covering the 1960 sit-ins. He looked back with awe at the rigorous training of the young black students who were so committed

---

whistle-blower is Barbara Kelleher Bunten, and, to quote Ms. Anschutz, "no one, with the exception of Ms. Bunten, had the courage to come forward. . . . She did not have a 'personal chancellor' or a 'council of advice' to look to for [support]. She did not ask for thanks or reward or even recognition in doing what was simply the right thing to do."

10. See, for instance, Richard Lischer, *The Preacher King* (Oxford: Oxford University Press, 1997).

to nonviolence. He described the hate that erupted around them as they sat quietly at the lunch counters, not answering back or showing any anger. He said, "Covering the story was like being a war correspondent. It was clear that there was a war on. We [journalists] could see that the weapons of nonviolence were stronger than those of violence."

Another witness said, "In a nonviolent action, all can participate—children, women, elderly"—even the disabled. There are no elites in God's army. There are no special uniforms or equipment or medals for the leaders. The humblest person can be the bravest. You don't have to be young and strong to be a soldier in the army of Jesus Christ. Here is an example. Virginia Durr and her husband Clifford were upper-class white Alabamians who lost most of their friends and most of his law practice when they threw their weight into the civil rights movement in the '60s. They were perhaps best known for bailing Rosa Parks out of jail. When Virginia Durr died a couple of years ago, her obituary contained some lines from a letter that Rosa Parks wrote upon her death and sent to her family. She wrote, "I will miss you, old soldier." Isn't that extraordinary! Two elderly white-haired women, neither of whom had ever picked up a gun in their lives, but field commanders in the army of the Lord.

In 1980 I attended a meeting to honor some older women who had rendered distinguished Christian service.[11] Among them was Victoria Booth Demarest, a granddaughter of General Booth, who founded the Salvation Army. Victoria was about ninety at the time and had to be helped to the podium by her daughter. As she spoke, however, the years fell away and you could see her valorous spirit emerging. She did not speak of herself; she spoke of her own mother, Catherine, who was the first person to take the Salvation Army outside England. "My mother was my general," she said. "My greatest dream was to be my mother's assistant." She told us a story about her mother when she first came to Paris. The Parisian officials were exasperated with Catherine Booth, who persisted in hanging around with the lowest elements of society. They said, "Mme. Boot, you must have police protection. We cannot answer to the British government if you are killed." To which the mother of young "Victoire" said fiercely, "I can't have your police protection, I won't have your police protection, your police protection would drive away my audience. I preach Jesus Christ. He asks convicts and criminals to come to him. *I have protection that you know nothing about.*"

11. These details are taken from my mostly *verbatim* notes made at a national gathering of self-identified "liberal evangelical" women (where are they now?) in Saratoga Springs, New York, June 26, 1980.

Dear people of Saint Michael's: You also have protection that the world knows nothing about. Wherever the Christian soldier faces the powers of evil, the angelic host fights for you on high. If you stand up for what is right, Saint Michael is standing with you. No matter how humdrum your life may seem, you are nevertheless playing your part in the cosmic battle. Every selfish impulse resisted, every act of kindness, every testimony to Jesus, every act of resistance to evil is part of the coming triumph of God. Let one of our greatest hymn writers say it for us: "Am I a Soldier of the Cross?"

> Sure I must fight if I would reign;
> Increase my courage, Lord;
> I'll bear the cross, endure the pain,
> Supported by thy Word.

> Thy saints, in all this glorious war,
> Shall conquer, though they die;
> They view the triumph from afar,
> And seize it with their eye.

> When that illustrious day shall rise,
> And all thy armies shine
> In robes of victory through the skies,
> The glory shall be thine.[12]

Amen.

---

12. Isaac Watts (1674–1748), "Am I a Soldier of the Cross?"

God's Apocalyptic War

Incarnation Camp and Conference Center, Ivoryton, Connecticut
Eastertide, April 1985
In memory of J. Christiaan Beker

JOEL 3:9–16

Many people who don't know the Bible have heard this prophecy from the book of Isaiah:

> They shall beat their swords into plowshares,
>   and their spears into pruning hooks;
> nation shall not lift up sword against nation,
>   neither shall they learn war any more. (Isa. 2:4)

One reason for the fame of this text is that it is engraved in large letters on the wall across the street from the United Nations. There it sits, like a mock-

---

The context for this sermon was unusual. It was preached at the conclusion of a Grace Church (New York City) parish weekend at Incarnation Camp in Ivoryton, Connecticut. These twice-yearly events were well attended by young adults. We had many speakers of distinction for these weekends. The speaker for this particular weekend was J. Christiaan Beker, professor of New Testament at Princeton Theological Seminary and author of *Paul's Apocalyptic Gospel, Paul the Apostle: The Triumph of God in Life and Thought*, and, of especial interest for this group, *Suffering and Hope*. Those were the themes of his addresses.

The people present (whose real names have been changed, for the sake of their privacy) were sophisticated New Yorkers and relatively new to Grace Church, but many of them were already deeply engaged with the Scriptures and were familiar with the Advent themes of conflict, darkness, militant witness, and expectant waiting for the coming of Christ in the last day.

Chris Beker's teaching was unsettling for some of those present. His persona was passionately intense and his hyper-Pauline apocalyptic approach disturbing for some. However, for a significant number of others, his teaching and presence were unforgettable, even life-changing.

ery, while the nations continue to lift up their swords and shake their nuclear arsenals at one another.

Here is another verse, less well known, which says exactly the opposite. This one is from the prophet Joel:

> Proclaim this among the nations:
> Prepare war,
>> stir up the mighty men.
> Let all the men of war draw near,
>> let them come up.
> Beat your plowshares into swords,
>> and your pruning hooks into spears;
>> let the weak say, "I am a warrior." (Joel 3:9–10)

The usual way of domesticating this contradiction in Scripture is something along the lines of yet another famous passage, in Ecclesiastes: "For everything there is a season—a time to be born and a time to die; a time for war and a time for peace" (Eccles. 3:1, 2, 8). But this, surely, is wrong. For the passage in Joel is not about "a time for war" in the temporal sense, as for instance a point in history when the president or the Congress declares a state of national emergency and calls for special military preparations in order to beat back godless Communism, or anything of that sort. This passage from Joel is not directly about "the nations" at all. It is about *God's apocalyptic war.* All of human history strains forward toward a time when the Lord of Sabaoth, the Lord of Hosts (and remember, that means a military host—an army—not an angelic choir), will take the field in a final battle against the enemies of his ultimate purpose. The prophet Joel describes it:

> Multitudes, multitudes,
>> in the valley of decision!
> For the day of the Lord is near
>> in the valley of decision. (Joel 3:14)

Cosmic phenomena testify to this climactic final intervention of Yahweh:

> The sun and the moon are darkened,
>> and the stars withdraw their shining.
> And the Lord roars from Zion,
>> and utters his voice from Jerusalem,
>> and the heavens and the earth shake. (Joel 3:15–16)

This sort of writing in the Old Testament comes relatively late. We don't find it in the early days when there was still every reason to hope that the people of Israel would love God and keep his commandments and live long in the land that the Lord their God was giving them (Exod. 20:6, 12). We find it much later in the history of Israel, when it was no longer possible to believe that things would be so simple. The discrepancy between what is and what ought to be, the "severe contradiction between legitimate expectations and reality," became acute in the period after the Babylonian exile.[1] Where was God? Why did he not act? Why were the enemies of God's people permitted to reign, so that the great name of YHWH was dragged in the dust behind the victorious chariot of the pagan conqueror? To use the language of the New Testament Apocalypse, why was the beast allowed to make war on the saints (Rev. 13:7)?

As these questions became more urgent, the apocalyptic testimony began to develop, slowly at first, then with increasing intensity. There will be a day, there will be a time, when the Lord will "roar from Zion":

The day of the Lord is near
in the valley of decision.

And on that day, the weakling will become strong and say, "I am a mighty man of war": "For consider your call, brothers and sisters; not many of you were wise according to worldly standards, not many were powerful . . . but God chose what is weak in the world to shame the strong, God chose what is low and despised in the world, even things that are not, to bring to nothing things that are" (I Cor. 1:26–28).[2]

In God's apocalyptic battle, where the archangel Michael leads the heavenly host into the final fray against the dragon (Rev. 12:7), the people of God have a role that evokes this kind of language: "Onward, Christian soldiers / Marching as to war . . .":

Prepare war . . .
Beat your plowshares into swords,
and your pruning hooks into spears;
let the weak man say, "I am a warrior."

1. J. Christiaan Beker, *Paul's Apocalyptic Gospel* (Philadelphia: Fortress, 1982), 23.

2. Years after this sermon was preached, I published a book about Tolkien's *The Lord of the Rings* in which I sought to show that the little people—the hobbits—in the saga illustrate what Paul is speaking about here. (*The Battle for Middle-Earth* [Grand Rapids: Eerdmans, 2004]).

Now listen to words spoken many years later on the same subject. From Saint Matthew's Gospel, chapter 24:

> As Jesus sat on the Mount of Olives, the disciples came to him privately, saying, "Tell us . . . what will be the sign of your coming, and of the close of the age?" And Jesus answered them, "Take heed that no one leads you astray. . . . You will hear of wars and rumors of wars; see that you are not alarmed; for this must take place, but the end is not yet. For nation will rise against nation . . . and there will be famines and earthquakes . . . all this is but the beginning of the sufferings. Then they will deliver you up to tribulation, and put you to death; and you will be hated by all nations for my name's sake. . . . And because wickedness is multiplied, most people's love will grow cold. But the one who endures to the end will be saved." (Matt. 24:3–13)

This call to the church is repeated with drum rolls and trumpet fanfares in the book of Revelation: "This is a call for the endurance and faith of the saints" (Rev. 13:10).

The imagery in the apocalyptic literature is complicated and disputed. I don't pretend to have any grasp of the details. What we see, though, in all the apocalyptic texts, is the motif of the double calling of the church: active resistance and patient endurance. Active resistance, because the Beast is truly evil. Patient endurance, because only God can choose the time for his final appearance.

The *active resistance* of the church is summoned up in images like this:

> Prepare war!
> Beat your plowshares into swords!

and in pictures like this: "I saw . . . those who had been beheaded for their testimony to Jesus and for the word of God, and who had not worshiped the beast or its image" (Rev. 20:4). And in this vision: "They have conquered . . . by the blood of the Lamb and by the word of their testimony, for they loved not their lives even unto death" (Rev. 12:11), and in Jesus's words: "You will be hated by all nations for my name's sake" (Matt. 10:22; 24:9).

The *patient endurance* of the church is depicted in Revelation: "I know you that have but little power, and yet you have kept my word and have not denied my name" (Rev. 3:8). And in Jesus's words: "Because wickedness is multiplied, most people's love will grow cold. But the one who endures to the end will be saved." But most of all, we hear it in Saint Paul's words: "Now hope that is seen is not hope. For who hopes for what he sees? But if we hope for what we do not see, we wait for it with patience" (Rom. 8:24–25).

And so, the vocation—the calling—of the church in "these last days" (Heb. 1:2) is indeed to take up arms against the enemy in the warfare of the victorious Lamb; but the church's manner of waging war is in the nature more of "take up your cross" (Mark 8:34) than of "take up your sword," let alone "take up your AK-47." Paul quotes Psalm 44, verse 22:

"For thy sake we are being killed all the day long;
we are regarded as sheep for the slaughter." (Rom. 8:36)

But, he continues, "In all these things we are more then conquerors through him who loved us" (Rom. 8:37).

In the New Testament the swords and spears become "the faith and endurance of the saints." Paul writes, "Let us then cast off the works of darkness and put on the armor of light" (Rom. 13:12). I don't need to tell you that the armor of light is not bulletproof vests or cruise missiles or nuclear submarines. The armor of light does not belong to this age. It does not belong to the enemy's territory at all. It does not belong to the sphere Paul calls "the flesh" (Rom. 8 and throughout his letters). It belongs to the sphere called life in the Spirit (Rom. 8:5). The law of the sphere of the flesh is "the law of Sin and Death." Paul writes, "The law of the Spirit of life in Christ Jesus has set me free from the law of sin and death" (Rom. 8:2). And the movement of this life in the Spirit is the movement that Paul has in mind when he says, "the night is far gone, the day is at hand" (Rom. 13:12). This is a movement entirely determined by the God who approaches us from the future—a future that lies wholly within his control.

Salvation is nearer to us now than when we first believed. (Rom. 13:11)

The day of the Lord is near
    in the valley of decision. (Joel 3:14)

Jesus said, "You also must be ready, for the Son of Man is coming at an hour you do not expect." (Matt. 24:44)

The creation waits with eager longing for the revealing of the children of God. (Rom. 8:19)

Can you feel the heartbeat of these passages? It is the same heartbeat that throbs in that last great utterance of the Bible: "He who testifies to these things says, 'Surely I am coming soon!' Amen. Come, Lord Jesus!" (Rev. 22:20). The church's life is lived in the tension between the Amen and the Come, between the already and the not-yet, between the resurrection of Jesus and the resurrection of the dead.

"The end is not yet" (Mark 13:7). We live, as cannot be said too often in Advent, in the Time Between (W. H. Auden calls Advent "the Time Being"), the time of waiting and the time of hope, the time of enduring patiently and resisting the "works of darkness" in the power of the One Who Comes (*ho erchomenos*—Rev. 1:8).

The sign of life in the Time Between—make no mistake—is suffering. How can it be otherwise? The Christian church is the vanguard of God's conquering future, inserted into "this present evil age" (Gal. 1:4). "We are not contending against flesh and blood, but against the principalities, against the powers, against the world rulers of this present darkness, against the spiritual hosts of wickedness in the heavenly places" (Eph. 6:12).

We, the church, are the paratroopers dropped behind enemy lines. We, the church, are the resistance fighters in the territory occupied by the Enemy. We, the church, are the beleaguered guerrillas waging a war of liberation against ferocious odds. We are the landing troops securing a beachhead while being fired upon from massive fortifications. "We are afflicted in every way," Paul writes; "while we live we are always being given up to death for Jesus' sake" (II Cor. 4:8, 11). This giving up of ourselves, this bearing of the cross, these waves of assault upon the enemy's defenses will continue to cost us even our very lives as long as the "last enemy" (I Cor. 15:26) remains unvanquished; but "the sufferings of this present time are not worthy to be compared with the glory that is to be revealed" (Rom. 8:18).

There is a priest in the Soviet Union named Dmitri Dudko. I read about him in *Time* magazine a couple of years ago. The Soviet government has tried to hush him up with police interrogations and banishment to an obscure village. But his weapon is the Word. He persists in preaching powerful sermons that are printed and distributed by the *samizdat*, the literary underground. The courage required to deliver such sermons is almost inconceivable to us. ("Let the weak man say, 'I am a warrior.'") Father Dudko mocks the totalitarian beast: "The atheists have nothing but physical force to make you shut up. But physical force shows their impotence."

In true Russian Orthodox style, he evokes the Easter message: "We are forced to ponder the resurrection of the dead by those who perished in the two world wars, by those who perished in concentration camps and other torture chambers. They were a countless multitude . . . the Resurrection unmasks all human injustice and restores justice."[3]

> Multitudes, multitudes,
>   in the valley of decision. (Joel 3:14)

Wickedness is multiplied and most people's love will grow cold. (Matt. 24:12)

This is a call for the endurance and faith of the saints. (Rev. 13:10)

They have conquered by the blood of the Lamb and by the word of their testimony, for they loved not their lives even unto death. (Rev. 12:11)

A clipping in my files describes the trial of a Roman Catholic bishop in Zimbabwe (formerly Southern Rhodesia). Donal Lamont was an Irish Roman Catholic missionary bishop in Zimbabwe during the turbulent last years of British rule, when Zimbabwe was still Rhodesia. In 1976 he was sentenced to ten years in prison by the colonial government for years of criticizing it for various abuses of human rights. For instance, he refused to report the whereabouts of guerrillas who had come to a church mission for medicine. At the time of his sentencing, he said calmly, "I expected it, and I expect to go to prison. It is of great benefit to the church. Not to be a martyr in the technical sense, but as one who bears witness." (Apocalyptic literature such as Revelation is the Scripture of the martyrs [in Greek, *martus* means "witness"].) He continued: "The church has been in existence for nearly 2000 years. Tyrants and others have acted against Christians during those years. They have arrested them. They have killed them. They have proscribed the faith. Those tyrants belong now to the flotsam and jetsam of forgotten history—and the Church of God remains, an agent of justice, peace, love, and reconciliation. If they take

---

3. All of this is especially poignant in view of the presence of J. Christiaan Beker, a Dutchman, who lived through the horrors of World War II as a young teenager taken from his parents to a labor camp. (The story is told in an introductory prologue to his book *Suffering and Hope: The Biblical Vision and the Human Predicament*, 2nd ed. [Grand Rapids: Eerdmans, 1994].) The subsequent record concerning Father Dudko is clouded. In his later years, he—like the Russian Orthodox Church in general—made peace with the Stalinist regime. See his obituary, *New York Times*, July 1, 2004.

on the South African Council of Churches, let them just know they are taking on the Church of Jesus Christ."[4]

Where does this kind of courage come from? It comes from hope. Not human hope—another kind of hope, the kind that Paul attributes to Abraham, who "hoped against hope [divine hope over against human hope]," placing his trust in "the God who raises the dead and calls into existence the things that do not exist" (Rom. 4:17–18). This is the hope that continues to empower, over these two millennia, the promise of Jesus: "Surely I am coming soon" (Rev. 22:20).

There is a cosmic battle being waged. The power of Sin and the power of Death threaten to overpower not only our individual selves but also the whole of human society. Chris Beker is right; there is no "private village," no "danger-free zone." Global suffering impinges on private suffering. Apartheid, totalitarianism, torture, famine and starvation, the gap between the rich and the poor, the plight of the mentally ill, homelessness, the traffic in drugs, pornography, child prostitution—all these "works of darkness" force us to face not only the private but also the public questions. There is no person in New York City who is not required every day to "pass on the other side" (Luke 10:31) when seeing homeless derelicts. This is a great evil.

In God's coming apocalyptic war, the church wears the armor of light against the works of darkness. This can mean many things. Drawing from your own testimonies during this weekend, it can mean David Johnson struggling to love his enemies during years of day-in, day-out legal battles, always with the danger of his superiors saying, "You're too soft." It can mean Reg Carpenter hanging on to Romans 8 for dear life during six months of living on the ragged edge; Janice Carter continuing to think of the pain of others during the time of her own pain; Ellen Montgomery's rich life in the family of God during a period of drastic personal crisis; Rob Walters lifting up his voice, in season and out of season, in indignation and against injustice and poverty, even in his own times of depression.[5] Though he would not want me to call attention to him by saying so, Chris Beker wears the armor of light in the passionate struggle against the works of darkness—almost swallowed up sometimes, like Jeremiah, but never

---

4. The original clipping in my file with the full quotation has vanished, but numerous sources report on the bishop's heroic witness. See, for instance, Michael T. Kaufman, "Rhodesian Bishop Is Jailed 10 Years," *New York Times*, October 2, 1976. A book, *Speech from the Dock* (Essex, UK: Kevin Mayhew LTD, in association with Catholic Institute for International Relations, 1977), tells the extraordinary story of the bishop's resistance in detail.

5. These members of Grace Church in New York were present in the congregation at the parish weekend at Incarnation Camp in Ivoryton, Connecticut. I have changed the names.

making peace with oppression, and never ceasing to cry out in protest to God. Against the relentlessly upbeat forms of popular Christianity in America, we affirm the pain of living in the sphere of Sin and Death, and we acknowledge that we live only and always in hope. "Who hopes for what he sees? But if we hope for what we do not see, we wait for it with patience" (Rom. 8:24–25).

No, we do not yet see the great day when "the Lord roars from Zion." We do not yet see the day when "nation will not lift up sword against nation, neither will they learn war any more." The words on the wall at the United Nations are a mockery. They are a mockery, that is, in every respect but one:

The trumpet shall sound, and the dead shall be raised incorruptible, and we shall be changed. (I Cor. 15:52)

Behold, he is coming with the clouds, and every eye shall see him, every one who pierced him. (Rev. 1:7)

Every knee should bow . . . and every tongue confess that Jesus Christ is Lord, to the glory of God the Father. (Phil. 2:10–11)

In the final apocalyptic war of God, the impossible will come to pass, and every promise will be fulfilled: "I am the Alpha and the Omega," says the Lord, the beginning and the end, "who is, and who was, and who is to come" (Rev. 1:8). We are about to receive the body and blood of the Lord. Saint Paul tells us the meaning of the Eucharist: "We show forth the Lord's death *until he comes*" (I Cor. 11:26).

The last words of the Bible are *Amen, erchou kurie Iesou* (New Testament Greek for "Amen, come, Lord Jesus"). The eucharistic prayer of the early church was in Aramaic, the language Jesus spoke: *Maranatha*: "Come, Lord Jesus." He comes at the end of the ages to do away with "Sin, Death, and the devil" and to reign forever as Lord. He comes in the bread and wine of the Eucharist to draw us all into himself. Let us say it now, all together:

Maranatha—Come, Lord Jesus.

What Is Your Battle Station?

Christ Episcopal Church, Charlottesville, Virginia
Advent 2001

ISAIAH 11:1–6; REVELATION 19:11–16

In my files of clippings, I have a photo from the newspaper of a bishop wearing a helmet. Why is he wearing a helmet? Is it because he is inspecting a construction site? Is he perhaps taking batting practice? Or maybe it isn't a helmet at all, just a rain hat. No, the bishop is wearing a helmet because he knows that he may be shot. He is Samuel Ruiz Garcia, the Roman Catholic bishop of a diocese in Mexico that includes Chiapas, where there are a great many poor Indians. He has been teaching them that they do not need to continue passively accepting the discrimination and mistreatment that have been their lot for centuries. He has been preaching equality of all human beings in the sight of God. This drives the local government crazy. A couple of years ago, Bishop Ruiz and another bishop barely escaped from an ambush on a dirt road. They were not injured, but three Bible teachers suffered bullet wounds. Bible teachers! Can you imagine being shot for teaching the Bible? Well, yes, we can imagine it very well, knowing what we know about the narrow escape of the young American aid workers in Afghanistan.[1] Now that they are home, they have a different enemy—the talk show host who ridicules them as "Jesus freaks."

Think about the early days of the Christian church. A good many of the leaders of the early Christian movement were persecuted or put to death in some way. Paul and Peter were both executed by Nero. When Christianity is working as it is supposed to, it is subversive. We are all talking about good and evil in America these days. The New Testament talks about it too, but in a very particular way. When Jesus, the Son of God, came into the world, he did

---

1. This was in the news in November 2001. As noted in another sermon in this book ("Righteous Deeds Like Filthy Rags"), many experienced overseas missionaries were furious at the young women and their sponsoring group for their naïveté.

not step onto an empty stage. He entered a world that was already occupied by a hostile power. We do not become Christians in a vacuum. Somebody else was here ahead of us who had to be pushed out; he is actively trying to get his space back.[2]

There is a great deal of battle imagery in Scripture. God is actually called *a man of war* in Exodus, meaning that he is strong enough to defeat all the horses and chariots of Egypt in order to free his people Israel. Here is a prophecy of the coming of Israel's Messiah from the book of Isaiah:

> There shall come forth a shoot from the stump of Jesse,
>   and a branch shall grow out of his roots.
> And the Spirit of the Lord shall rest upon him. . . .
> With righteousness he shall judge the poor,
>   and decide with equity for the meek of the earth;
> and he shall smite the earth with the rod of his mouth,
>   and with the breath of his lips he shall slay the wicked.
> Righteousness shall be the girdle of his waist,
>   and faithfulness the girdle of his loins.
> The wolf shall dwell with the lamb,
>   and the leopard shall lie down with the kid,
> and the calf and the lion and the fatling together,
>   and a little child shall lead them. (Isa. 11:1-6)

This is a remarkable passage in which we learn that *the Messiah will make war in order to make peace.* To bring about his kingdom where, in the famous image, "the lion will lie down with the lamb," God must obliterate everything that stands against that peace. His Anointed One will do battle against his enemies, and unlike so many wars today where a disproportionate amount of the suffering is borne by women, children, and the elderly, the defenseless of the earth will suddenly find themselves on the winning side. This is God's word spoken through the prophet Isaiah:

> With righteousness he shall judge the poor,
>   and decide with equity for the meek of the earth.

2. These ideas are found in Yale theologian Miroslav Volf's book, *Exclusion and Embrace: A Theological Exploration of Identity, Otherness, and Reconciliation* (Nashville: Abingdon, 1996), 293ff. As a native Croatian, Professor Volf is especially qualified to speak about these matters.

That is the message that the Bible teachers were teaching down in Mexico when they got shot.

There are certain characteristics that identify the presence of the Enemy of God, who is called Satan. If there is great disparity between rich and poor, if there is indifference and smugness among the affluent, if there is lack of respect for human life in any form, if corruption and abuses are tolerated, the devil is very happy. Whenever people are comfortable with things as they are, there is lots of room for the Enemy of God's purposes. When Christians are baptized, they are welcomed into the army of witnesses that God is creating to stand against Satan until Christ comes again. That is part of our baptismal vow. Whenever a child or person is baptized, a piece of Satan's territory is being reclaimed. Did you ever think about that? If you have been baptized, you are a beachhead for God. He has cleared a portion of the enemy's territory and has put you into it. You yourself are part of God's new creation.

It is very easy to think of the language of new creation as benign and non-threatening. We tend to forget that in order to make a new creation, God has to drive out the powers that messed up his first creation. Jesus did not come into a neutral world. Martin Luther wrote his famous hymn "A Mighty Fortress Is Our God" to describe the situation. This world is "with devils filled," and Satan continually "threatens to undo us"; yet "we will not fear, for God has willed his truth to triumph through us." If God has willed his truth to triumph through us, that means that we really are his troops in this world. That is part of what it means to be a baptized Christian.

But what strange weapons God uses! According to the Old Testament imagery, he slays the enemy with his Word. He smites the opponent with his breath, or spirit (same word in both Hebrew and Greek). He wears a special belt or girdle for the battle: "Righteousness shall be the girdle of his waist, and faithfulness the girdle of his loins." This imagery is picked up by the New Testament book of Revelation, with some notable additions:

> Then I saw heaven opened, and behold, a white horse! He who sat upon it is called Faithful and True, and in righteousness he judges and makes war. . . . He is clad in a robe dipped in blood, and the name by which he is called is The Word of God. And the armies of heaven, arrayed in fine linen, white and pure, followed him on white horses. From his mouth issues a sharp sword with which to smite the nations, and he will rule them with a rod of iron. . . . On his robe and on his thigh he has a name inscribed, King of kings and Lord of lords. (Rev. 19:11–16)

These passages give us some idea of the imagery that the biblical writers use to describe what the book of Revelation calls the War of the Lamb. It all sounds very bellicose, but there is a paradox about it, because the blood on the robe of the Lamb of God is not the blood of his enemies, but his own blood and the blood of his followers who have given up their lives for his name.[3] Again, the weapons of the rider on the white horse are very surprising; "from his mouth issues a sharp sword with which to smite the nations." Please notice this: his Word is the only offensive weapon that he has or needs—just as the Word of God, the message of the gospel, is the only offensive weapon that the helmet-wearing Mexican bishop uses. Christ's followers are to depend solely on that Word. The only defense they have is "the testimony of Jesus," the testimony of his life and death for them and their confession of faith in him. "They have conquered by the blood of the Lamb and by the word of their testimony, for they loved not their lives even unto death" (Rev. 12:11). Why was the early church persecuted like this? Was it because they confessed a simple faith in a simple teacher of religion? Indeed it was not. It was because the confession of the cross of Christ was immediately perceived by the Roman government as a threat to its primacy and security.

Paul, the apostle, more than any other New Testament writer, picks up these themes. It isn't possible to understand Paul without thinking of him as he thought of himself, as a soldier of the cross, a general on the front lines. He envisions the whole human race caught up in a cosmic struggle. His letters are written in the context of vast, malign forces arrayed against the Messiah, bent upon destroying Christ's mission to save the world. Paul warns us what we are up against: "We are not contending against flesh and blood, but against the principalities, against the powers, against the world rulers of this present darkness, against the spiritual hosts of wickedness in the heavenly places" (Eph. 6:12).

That's the situation we find ourselves in, whether we recognize it or not. At the time of our baptism, we were enrolled in the army of Christ. But now listen to this. We were not sent out into the world defenseless and unarmed. We were not sent out to fight in our own strength. We were not sent out with human weapons at all. God clothed us in new garments when we were baptized. He gave us his Spirit. He gave us his weapons. He gave us his armor, the

---

3. This has often been interpreted otherwise by those who assume that this is the blood of Christ's enemies, but I hold with the view of Caird, Mangina, and many others who argue that the blood represents either the blood of the Christian martyrs or Christ's own blood. G. B. Caird, *The Revelation of St. John the Divine* (New York: Harper and Row, 1966), 191–95, 243–44; Joseph Mangina, *Revelation* (Grand Rapids: Brazos, 2010), 221–22.

armor that Christ wears himself. "Therefore take the whole armor [panoply] of God, that you may be able to withstand in the evil day. . . . Stand therefore, having girded your loins with truth, and having put on the breastplate of righteousness, and having shod your feet with the equipment of the gospel of peace; besides all these, taking the shield of faith, with which you can quench all the flaming darts of the evil one. And take the helmet of salvation, and the sword of the Spirit, which is the word of God" (Eph. 6:13–17).

Many Christians have heard about this armor of God in a vague sort of way, but few of us have grasped its actual meaning. The armor that God has given you to fight your battles, our battles, the church's battles is *God's own armor.* Think of the firefighter who passes on his helmet to his son. God has been clothed in this armor since before the creation; it is part of him. It was worn by him in the Passover and the exodus. It was proven by him before the walls of Jericho, in the court of Ahab and Jezebel, in Nebuchadnezzar's fiery furnace. The belt of truth is not philosophical or scientific truth; it is Jesus Christ, who said, "*I am* the Truth." The breastplate of righteousness is not your righteousness or mine; it is Christ's righteousness. When you put on the shoes of peace, it is not you who are making peace; it is God. The shield of faith is given to you by him, by the one who answers the prayer, "I believe; help my unbelief." All these weapons are given to you by the one who forged them. In no sense are they your own achievement. We do not earn the right to wear the armor of God; it is given to us. Todd Beamer knew that when he was preparing to rush the hijackers on Flight 93; he was heard to say, "Jesus, help me."

I wonder what you are confronting in your life. Very rarely are we called upon to perform deeds so astonishing that they become legendary. But all of us, every single Christian and every Christian community, are engaged in the struggle with the enemies of God. Each one of you is placed on the battleground somewhere. Are you under pressure from forces outside your control? Are you being called upon for patience that you do not think you have? Are you perhaps wondering if there is anything you can do to be more useful to God in your community and church? Are you struggling with some secret temptation or sin? Is there a burden of sorrow that you carry? Is there something more that you want to do and be?

Then take to yourself the armor of God. When we are in need of patience, God clothes us with the patience of Christ himself. When we are emboldened to speak out against prejudice, he puts the sword of the Spirit into our hand. When we are battling pain and doubt, he comes alongside us with the shield of faith—not our faith, but the never-failing faithfulness of Christ granted to us. When we make our stand for life instead of death, he protects us with the helmet of salvation—not any sort of human salvation or victory, but *his* salvation, *his* victory.

> When you were baptized into Christ, you have put on Christ. (Gal. 3:27)

> Let us then cast off the works of darkness and put on the armor of light. . . . Put on the Lord Jesus Christ, and make no provision for the flesh, to gratify its desires. (Rom. 13:12, 14)

Put on Christ! He is as near to you as a breastplate. He surrounds you with his strength. He embraces you with his love. His faithfulness will overcome your doubt. He will go before you to break down the walls of hostility (Eph. 2:14). "His power is made perfect in your weakness" (II Cor. 12:9). He equips you to remain his faithful soldier and servant unto your life's end. In his crucifixion, the devil has already done his worst. In his resurrection, the powers of hell have already been overcome. In spite of all appearances, they have already lost. The Right Man is on our side.

Amen! Come, Lord Jesus.

The Coming of the Lord
(Last Sunday of the Church Year:
The Feast of Christ the King)

King of Kings and Lord of Lords

Christ Episcopal Church, Westerly, Rhode Island
Feast of Christ the King 2009

II SAMUEL 23:1–5; PSALM 132:11;
REVELATION 1:7; JOHN 18:33–38

When I was in seminary in the 1970s, the whole idea of *kingship* in Christian thought was being called into question. We weren't supposed to be thinking about kings. To begin with, kings were men, and we were being called away from the idea of men ruling over women. But then, the whole idea of "ruling" was suspect in the time of the Woodstock Nation. Everything was supposed to be egalitarian and communal. Children are brought up on Barney: "I love you, you love me, we're a hap-py fa-mi-lee." Everybody's equal; everybody gets a prize. No more rulers, no more lords, no more kings.

Then along came the *Lion King* movie and the *Lion King* musical. Children and their parents everywhere have been thrilled by the story of the lordly lion. Kings, apparently, were not going away. In 2004, the Oscar for Best Picture was given to *The Return of the King*. It's pretty funny, actually; the power of certain symbols is so deeply ingrained in the human psyche that no amount of political correctness is going to make much headway against them.

To this day, however, a significant number of people in the churches still refuse to call Jesus of Nazareth by the title "Lord." There was a controversy about this in the *Living Church* magazine just a couple of years ago. "Lord" (*kurios*) has the same essential meaning as "king" (*basileus*)—they both mean "ruler." When we refer to Jesus Christ as Lord and King, we're expressing faith in Jesus Christ as the Son of God who was, and is, and will be the ruler of the universe; as we heard in our second reading today, he is "the Alpha and the Omega, who is and who was and who is to come, the Almighty."

OK, but we're still being told that these passages are a big problem. There's a major movement in the mainline churches and parts of the academic world to strip away all these transcendent descriptions of Jesus and to present him as a teacher, healer, rabbi, sage, spiritual leader, and ultimate moral exemplar.

This movement isn't new, but we're seeing a new version of it. It's taken hold in the churches without people even noticing that it's happened. I hope you'll cut me some slack here and not take this personally—I'm speaking about what I read, hear, and see in the church at large. It's a trend all across the traditional Christian denominations, and no one is untouched by it.[1]

In our readings today, appointed for Christ the King Sunday, we hear some radical claims about the Kingship of Jesus the Messiah. We need to remember first of all that the whole Hebrew-Christian thing is anchored in the Word of God. No one can be forced to *believe* the Bible, but it's not right to try to make it say what it clearly doesn't say. If we want to read the Bible as the religious thoughts of human beings, we can certainly try to do that, but if that's what we do, we ought to realize that we're ignoring the entire foundation that the church's Book is built on. You can see this foundation clearly in the first lines of the farewell words of King (oops, there's that word!) David. He is "the sweet psalmist of Israel" who says:

> "The Spirit of the Lord speaks by me,
>> his word is upon my tongue.
> The God of Israel has spoken." (II Sam. 23:2–3)

The central claim of this passage is the central claim of the entire Scripture: "The God of Israel has spoken"—and if he pleases (and he does so please), he can speak through human beings.

Now before we go on, we need to bear in mind that King David, with all his enormous sins, was the person with whom God had established an eternal covenant. We find this also in today's passage from II Samuel, "[The Lord] has made with [David] an everlasting covenant" (23:5). We find the same thing in today's psalm:

> The Lord swore to David a sure oath
>> from which he will not turn back. (Ps. 132:11)

What was that "sure oath"? We find it in II Samuel when the Lord says to King David, "Your kingdom shall be made sure for ever before me; your throne shall be established for ever" (II Sam. 7:16). According to the promise of God

---

1. There's also a strong body of opinion that sees Jesus almost exclusively as a political revolutionary. He was a political revolutionary, all right, but not in the way that's often meant.

himself, then, it is through King David and the line of King David that the Messiah is born.

Now if we read this merely as a pious legend, a story like other stories, even the best of stories, it loses its meaning. Its meaning rests in the claim of King David that

"the Spirit of the Lord speaks by me,
    his word is upon my tongue.
The God of Israel has spoken."

We talked about this last night, how the entire Christian enterprise stands or falls on these words: "The God of Israel has spoken." If we fool around with that, it all falls apart. Nobody has to *believe* that God has spoken, but it's not unreasonable to ask, at the very least, that Bible readers acknowledge that this is the way the Bible means to be read. The very first verses of the very first chapter of the Bible establish it: "And God said, 'Let there be light': and there was light." That's creation by the Word.

So, according to the Word of God, there came a man named Jesus from Nazareth in provincial Galilee. He was poor and had no standing in the world, but he preached the kingdom of God and attracted a lot of notice. It's hard for us to grasp the nature of the commotion that surrounded Jesus because we don't live in the circumstances of that time, but we can try to understand how the Jewish people had been living, for centuries, through defeat, exile, disappointed return, various rebellions, further decline, and foreign occupation, waiting, waiting for the promised king of David's line. That's the reason that Jesus is so often called "Son of David" in the Gospels. Here's a typical example: "A blind and dumb demoniac was brought to [Jesus], and he healed him, so that the dumb man spoke and saw. And all the people were amazed, and said, 'Can this be the Son of David?'" (Matt. 12:22–23).

After a brief flurry of popularity, the religious and secular authorities alike took great offense at him and saw to it that he was eliminated. After his horrible, degrading death by public torture, his discredited followers, starting out in Jerusalem and then spreading out all over the Mediterranean, delivered the news that this crucified man was the Lord and King of the universe. *What?* That's what we should be saying: *What?* Again, we don't have to *believe* what the New Testament says, but we should at least acknowledge that this is what it says: "God has made him both Lord and Messiah, this Jesus whom you crucified" (that's Peter, preaching right after Pentecost—Acts 2:36). This message is a scandal, as Paul repeatedly says; it's an offense (*skandalon*) against all reason and common sense—a crucified Lord.

As a preacher of the gospel for a great many years, I testify that this message makes less sense to me now than it did when I got started. It is all so irreligious, so unspiritual, so unreasonable. But that is precisely the point that Paul makes when he says that the gospel of the crucified Lord is a scandal to Jewish people and foolishness to gentile people. "Crucified, dead, and buried . . . raised again on the third day." We say that every Sunday, but this is a good time to think about it anew.

The Advent season begins next week. Most Episcopalians, like most people, think of Advent as the time of getting ready for Christmas. But this is a mistake. For centuries Advent was known as the season of the last things. If you don't believe me, notice the Advent hymns when you sing them. They aren't about the birth in Bethlehem at all. Almost all of them are about the second coming. We just read about that: "Behold, he is coming with the clouds, and every eye will see him, every one who pierced him; and all tribes of the earth will wail on account of him. Even so. Amen" (Rev. 1:7).[2]

It is the last day, when "the kingdom of this world has become the Kingdom of our Lord and of his Christ, and he shall reign for ever and ever." Does that sound familiar? It should; it's the "Hallelujah" chorus, and the words are from Revelation.[3]

Now we come to today's Gospel reading from John: "Pilate . . . called Jesus, and said to him, 'Are you the King of the Jews?' . . . Jesus answered, 'My kingship is not of this world; if my kingship were of this world, my servants would fight, that I might not be handed over; . . . but my kingship is not from the world.' . . . 'For this I was born, and for this I have come into the world, to bear witness to the truth. Every one who is of the truth hears my voice.' Pilate said to him, 'What is truth?'"

This dialogue sets the kingship of Jesus into the sharpest possible contrast to "the kingdom of the world." This man who is in so many ways a human being just like us has also something about him that is uncanny. He can't be made into a religious sage without deleting large parts of the New Testament. He is, as he says here, from another world. The Christian church calls this the incarnation: the descent of God from the eternal realm of uncreated light into

---

2. Charles Wesley's great Advent hymn, "Lo, He Comes with Clouds Descending," is based partially on this text from Revelation.

3. Rev. 11:15. The title "Lord" is used interchangeably for God and for Christ throughout the New Testament.

the violence, darkness, sickness, and death of this world. The Lord Jesus says this in John 8:23—"You are from below, I am from above; you are of this world, I am not of this world."

Pontius Pilate, the Roman governor, could not be more uncomprehending. "What is truth?" he asks, as if Jesus had posed a philosophical question. At the University of Virginia, there is a gateway arch with these words on it: "You shall know the truth, and the truth shall make you free." Those are the words of Jesus in the Gospel of John (8:32), but the university has taken them out of context. In the world of the university, "the truth" is an abstraction. But this isn't what Jesus's words mean at all. Here is what he says: "If you continue in my word, you are truly my disciples, and you will know the truth, and the truth will make you free" (8:31–32), and "if the Son makes you free, you will be free indeed" (8:36). Pilate is just like us when we want to read the Bible as if it were science or philosophy. He has the Truth standing right in front of him and doesn't recognize it, because he doesn't recognize the Son of God.

I'm not likely to preach to you here in Westerly again. I must take these few moments to bear witness to the Truth, that is, to Jesus Christ the King of kings and Lord of lords. If we choose to think of him as less than this, we should be aware of what we are doing. Whom do we want to be ruler of our lives? Whom do we want to be ruler of this world of Sin and Death? Let's answer the first question first. Whom do we want to be ruler of our lives? That's easy to answer. We want *ourselves* to be rulers of our own lives. I am the master of my fate, I am the captain of my soul.[4] Yeah. That's the American way. Then why hasn't your career gone the way you had hoped? Why is your marriage troubled? Why aren't your children doing what you want them to do?

Second question: Whom do we want to be the ruler of this world of Sin and Death? But maybe you don't think of the world that way. Maybe you think of it as white sails on Long Island Sound. Maybe you think of it as hitting the perfect golf shot. Maybe you think of it as Norman Rockwell's Thanksgiving. I know a man who is famous for being cheerful and optimistic about everything, always upbeat, always ready with a solution for problems, very successful in his lifelong career, valued and respected. On the eve of his daughter's wedding, his son took a fatal overdose of drugs.

I saw him months later, not knowing. His face was shadowed. He had been through something. I inquired. He told me what had happened to his family. Here's what he said to me: "We are not in control of our lives. Who would plan for his son to OD on the night of his sister's wedding?" Then he said, "I

---

4. The reference is to the poem "Invictus" by William Ernest Henley.

went back to the baptism service in the Book of Common Prayer.[5] I saw that in baptism, the child becomes God's. My son belongs to God. Nothing can change that. This thing is between him and God. I can let it go."[6]

That's what it means to trust in God as the ruler of Death.

Every baptism is a victory over Death.[7] "The Lord swore to David a sure oath from which he will not turn back." Baptism is the action of God in this world to ratify his "everlasting covenant" in the lives of each of his beloved children. It is the action of Jesus Christ as Lord and King over all the demonic powers. It is the action of God in the tortured death of his Son where, on the cross, he drew into himself all the wickedness and all the pain and all the sorrow in the world and, in the resurrection, conquered it—conquered it because he came from the world where death has no dominion and he returned to the world where death has no dominion. From that dominion, he rules as the living Lord: his dominion is Light; his dominion is Truth; his dominion is Life—*for the mouth of the Lord hath spoken it.*

*   *   *

[Therefore] fight the good fight of the faith; take hold of the eternal life to which you were called when you made the good confession in the presence of many witnesses. In the presence of God who gives life to all things, and of . . . our Lord Jesus Christ . . . the blessed and only Sovereign, the King of kings and Lord of lords, who alone has immortality and dwells in unapproachable light. . . . To him be honor and eternal dominion. Amen. (I Tim. 6:12–16)

---

5. He went to the old 1928 Prayer Book, interestingly.

6. Immediately after we parted, I wrote down his words to make sure I had them right.

7. "Do you not know that all of us who have been baptized into Christ Jesus were baptized into his death? We were buried therefore with him by baptism into death, so that as Christ was raised from the dead by the glory of the Father, we too might walk in newness of life" (Rom. 6:3–4).

We Will Be There

Saint John's Church, Salisbury, Connecticut
Christ the King Sunday 1996 (Stewardship Sunday)

MATTHEW 25:31-32

The front page of last Monday's *Berkshire Eagle* featured an amazing story. It told of a couple in Great Barrington, John and Libby Moritz. In January 1992, all of their three children, aged eight, nine, and eleven, were killed in an automobile accident as they were being driven home from school. In November of that same year, the mother and father of those children, motivated by the desire to turn their grief to work for other children, founded an organization called Hearts of the Father Outreach, Inc. "Since then, they have sponsored an orphanage in Mexico, another in Grenada, established a scholarship program in Kenya with another on the way in India, started a feeding program in the Philippines and distributed shoes in Guatemala. They are buying a 71-acre farm in Berne, NY, to be converted into a foster home. . . . The couple have devoted their lives to this cause. They finance their ministry partly with their own money, partly through contributions. In the summer, John Moritz tends to his swimming pool business in Sheffield. In the off-season, they travel to the orphanages and programs they sponsor."

What caught my eye especially, in view of the reading from Matthew's Gospel today, was the beginning of the article: "Prepare to feel a little guilty. It's not that John and Libby Moritz would want anybody to feel guilty. It's just that if you want to compare good-deed checklists with them, yours will probably come up short."[1]

Today is Stewardship Sunday at Saint John's, but far more important, it is the Sunday called Christ the King. It's a wonderful day to preach about stewardship. The Lord Jesus Christ is Lord and King over all creation! There is no other day in the Christian calendar quite like this one. On this last Sunday of

1. Article by Timothy Q. Cebula, *Berkshire Eagle*, November 18, 1996.

the liturgical year, we look both backward and forward. We look back on the completed story of the earthly ministry of Jesus as we have followed him all year from Christmas to Holy Week to Easter to Pentecost. But more, as the first Sunday of Advent approaches, we look forward on this day to the second coming of the Lord, the future time when, as Saint Paul writes, "Every knee will bow . . . and every tongue confess that Jesus Christ is Lord" (Phil. 2:10–11).

And so, in today's Gospel reading we find Jesus teaching his disciples for the last time before his arrest and death. Jesus said, "When the Son of man comes in his glory, and all the angels with him, then he will sit on his glorious throne. Before him will be gathered all the nations, and he will separate them one from another as a shepherd separates the sheep from the goats."

Let's pause for a moment and allow this incredible statement to sink into our minds and hearts. Here is a man who was born into a poor family, who went to no university, who owns nothing, who has no bank account, no resume or portfolio, no job or house, no title or rank, a man who is about to be judged guilty and not fit to live by the highest religious and political tribunals of his time, and here he is saying that he is going to come again, personally, at the end of the world, to determine the fate of all human beings who have ever been born. It should make our brains crunch just to think about it. This man Jesus is about to go on trial for his life before the judges of this world, but according to the Gospels, Jesus tells his disciples that he himself is actually the Judge. All the peoples of the world will be gathered before him. It will be the final, ultimate, conclusive trial of the world, and the crucified One will be the Judge. And what's more, you're going to be there, and I'm going to be there.

On that last day when the Son of Man "comes again in glory to judge the quick and the dead," he will not be a little baby in a manger anymore. He will be surrounded with all the unmistakable accoutrements of majesty and dominion. He will be attended by numberless legions of angels, the heavenly host. He will sit on his throne of glory, and at his feet, spread out before him, will be all of human history in unimaginable completeness. Napoleon will be there; Julius Caesar and Genghis Khan and Joan of Arc will be there; Martin Luther and Columbus and Pol Pot will be there. Let's allow this awesome spectacle to penetrate our consciousness. Let's not be sidetracked by woodenly literal-minded questions like, How can all those trillions of people be in one place? What language will be spoken? When is this going to happen? These speculations are irrelevant. What we are intended to feel is not intellectual curiosity but the overwhelming gravity and solemnity of the picture of the whole world called to judgment before the throne of Christ. Saint Paul echoes it in Romans when he says, "We shall all stand before the judgment seat of God" (14:10).

The impression burned into our hearts today by the passage from Matthew is this: on that climactic and final day, *we will be there*.

Jesus the Lord will be the judge, and no one else. To him "all hearts are open, all desires known, and from [him] no secrets are hid."[2] The picture given is of a shepherd looking out over a flock of sheep, dividing them just as the prophet Ezekiel says in today's Old Testament lesson: "As for you, my flock," thus says the Lord God: "Behold, I judge between sheep and sheep, rams and he-goats." The sheep he will put at his right hand. To them he speaks words of incomparable, stupendous consequence: "Come, O blessed of my Father, inherit the kingdom prepared for you from the foundation of the world." The goats he will place at his left hand, and to them he speaks terrible words, words that chill the heart: "Depart from me, you cursed, into the eternal fire prepared for the devil and his angels."

To the "sheep" on his right hand he will say, "I was hungry and you gave me food, I was thirsty and you gave me drink, I was a stranger and you welcomed me, I was naked and you clothed me, I was sick and you visited me, I was in prison and you came to me." The response comes back, "Lord, when did we do all those things?" And the King shall answer and say unto them, "Verily I say unto you, inasmuch as ye have done it unto one of the least of these my brethren, ye have done it unto me."

We have heard these famous lines many times. Here they are on these donation boxes piled up here in front of our church. They are often quoted glibly and superficially. Usually in such cases the people doing the quoting are judging someone else, or perhaps justifying themselves, thinking of themselves as more charitable than somebody else. That's pretty hard to do when we compare ourselves with John and Libby Moritz of Great Barrington. I remember a friend of mine, an affluent woman living a very comfortable life, who presented herself as a very ardent Christian. She defended herself from guilt by saying, "I don't think God wants me to be Mother Teresa." Can we really get ourselves off the hook that way? Imagine you and me on judgment day, saying, "Well, Lord, in November 1996 I put a box of Cheerios and a jar of peanut butter in a box at Saint John's." If even that *Berkshire Eagle* reporter knows that our good-deeds checklist is going to come up short, Jesus is certainly going to know it. As a character in a Barbara Pym novel says, "The trouble with doing good works is that one can never be said to have done one's share."[3] In the final analysis, all we can say is, "Lord, have mercy on me, a sinner" (Luke 18:13).

2. 1979 Book of Common Prayer, 355.
3. *An Academic Question.*

Notice the response of those on Jesus's *right* hand when they are told that they are about to inherit the kingdom. They are amazed. They didn't even know that they had ministered to the hidden Christ among the "least" of these his brethren. "Lord," they say. "When did we see thee hungry and feed thee?" Those who are vindicated in the judgment are those who are not even aware that they have done any good works. Notice also the response of those on the left hand. They are not aware either. Apparently, they expected to be commended. It looks as though there are going to be surprises for everyone. He who congratulates himself on having done enough is precisely the one who has not. He who thinks himself safe is in the greatest danger. The man who trembles to think of himself before the judgment seat is closer to the kingdom of heaven than the one who complacently assumes he is on the side of the angels.

The coming of Jesus Christ as judge of the world calls every single person's existence into question. There is no human merit anywhere to bail us out. We cannot rely on any known good deeds; the complete astonishment of the redeemed and the shattered confidence of the condemned are clear evidence of this. The works of mercy done by those on the right hand were spontaneous acts performed without any thought of reward. They do not even remember doing them: "Lord, when did we see thee?" Many years ago I was a smug, self-satisfied member of a congregation that prided itself on its good works. We were all quite sure that we were sheep, not goats. The goats were all on the other side of town, in the conservative, racist, hawkish church. I have since learned how insidious this is. The parable of the last judgment is not about totaling up one's own good deeds, whether politically correct or incorrect. It is about serving Christ the Lord. The originality of Matthew's Gospel is its unique stress on two things at once: the cosmic divinity of Jesus, and at the same time, his identification with the lowest and the least among human beings. That combination is what makes the parable of the last judgment so powerful. Without the titanic figure of Christ as the final arbiter of the destiny of all creation, the teaching would simply deteriorate into moralistic pabulum along the lines of "He knows if you've been bad or good, so be good for goodness' sake." This is not what the parable means. The division of the sheep and goats is not based on who is good and who is bad. It is based on serving and honoring Christ by serving and honoring those who are in need.

Today is the day for us to decide what we are going to do about our pledges to Saint John's Church. As we said last week, Jesus talked about money all the time. In literally countless ways, he made it known that we can either serve God with our money or be enslaved by it all our lives. "You cannot serve God and money," he said (Matt. 6:24; Luke 16:13). What we decide to do with our money will be the strongest possible indication as to who is king in our lives. Most of us go through our lives spending our money on this and that, sometimes on necessities like utilities and insurance, sometimes on luxuries like big cars, trips, spas, clubs, cosmetic surgery, lavish interior design. Then, if we have anything left over, we give a few dollars here and a few dollars there to church and charity. Thus we indicate clearly who and what is king in our lives. Every Christian stewardship leader will tell you that the way to acknowledge Christ on the throne of our lives is to decide about our giving *first, before* we spend our money on other things. That's why the concept of pledging is important. It should represent a significant *proportion* of what God has given us. As we heard last week in the parable of the money in trust, it should be our return on his investment.

In fund-raising (as opposed to stewardship), donors are usually ranked in order of the size of their gift. I am by no means impervious to this technique. I love to see my name among the patrons. It makes me feel like a big shot. Here's an example. Four years ago, in a weak moment, I made a pledge to the new Seiji Ozawa Hall at Tanglewood. I made the pledge because I love Tanglewood. However, I did not determine the *amount* of the gift based on my love for Tanglewood or any other high-minded reason. I selected an amount based on the fact that it was the smallest amount I could give and still have my name on the plaque in the completed Ozawa Hall.

You may say there is nothing wrong with this. No, but it is at the opposite end of the spectrum from Christian giving. Christian giving does not glorify the giver; it glorifies Christ. It acknowledges him as King of kings and Lord of lords. We will not be ranking our gifts at Saint John's by dollar amounts. What counts is the thankfulness to God, the praise of Christ that accompanies the gift.

Our parish needs our money. If we get our finances on a solid footing, we can begin to move out in mission and service. If we do not, we will have to continue spending our money on ourselves. I cannot believe that is what you want the future of Saint John's to be. I believe we have more of a vision of Christ the King than that. Salisbury has a tradition of generosity, and generosity is powerful. If we can get our parish budget into shape this year, by next year we can begin to respond to the Lord's presence in the world in ways that we have not yet begun to imagine. Jesus did not hesitate to promise heavenly rewards to those who responded to him with joy and thankfulness. This is the only true reason for Christian giving—gratitude to God and praise of Christ.

If this stewardship message makes you feel guilty, angry, judged, or manipulated, I suggest you not give a single cent. If you are giving in order to buy favor with God and man, I suggest you think again. Our financial gifts should not be coerced. They should not be a means to personal glory. They should come in response to the King in awe and wonder, amazement and gratitude, rejoicing that he alone is Lord of our destinies. He cares so much for the least, the last, and the lost that he is willing to die even for such poor specimens as you and me, covering our unrighteousness with his righteousness, offering his life to save us from death, the Judge judged in our place. He has compensated for our too-short list of good deeds by his one great deed. Now by his indwelling Spirit he will make us into those who will someday hear the blessed words: "Come, O blessed of my Father, inherit the kingdom prepared for you from the foundation of the world."

Amen.

When the Man Comes Around

Trinity Episcopal Church, Columbus, Georgia
First Sunday of Advent 2003

LUKE 21:34–35; I PETER 4:7, 12, 17

There is never any problem finding Advent in the newspapers. Last Wednes-day I found my themes on the front page of the second section of the *New York Times*. In the middle of the page is an article about the brutal war in Chechnya, where Russia has been deliberately targeting civilians for years. At the bottom of the page is an article about the new Museum of Southern Art in New Orleans, with quotations from Shelby Foote: "Southerners . . . are very much aware that they are party to a defeat. . . . We know that life can take some dreadful downturns. That lends a special tone to our lives." And on the top of the page is an Advent text from an unlikely source—or, depending on your point of view, not unlikely at all. A huge memorial service was recently held in Nashville for the late, great country music singer and devout Christian Johnny Cash. Here is what the article says: "His determination to recognize *life's darker side* has become a symbol and a reproach to a country music busi-ness that now depends on blandly inoffensive songs geared to radio-station formulas."[1]

Life's darker side: that's Advent. The season arises out of darkness; that's what gives it its special character. For several weeks before the first Sunday of Advent, the Scripture readings begin to sound ominous. When you know to start looking for it, you'll notice it beginning to happen after All Saints' Day. The readings begin to have a noticeable "edge," as we say. There is an unmis-takable note of urgency, and the message is one of impending judgment. I

---

1. Jon Pareles, "A Nashville Tribute to Johnny Cash," *New York Times*, November 12, 2003.

This sermon sets the stage for the location in historic time: two years after 9/11, with the Iraq War under way.

remember reading something about Václav Havel, the poet-playwright who became the leader of the "Velvet Revolution" in Czechoslovakia and then president of the Czech Republic. Havel is one of the very few great public thinkers of our time; almost anything he says is striking. Speaking about the theater, where much of his heart has been throughout his career, he said that the role of the theater is not to be soothing or instructive but to remind people that "the time is getting late, that the situation is grave."[2]

That's very similar to the mood of this season. Indeed, it's a good way of describing the entire framework of the New Testament. For the Christian, the time is always getting late; the situation is always grave; ultimate matters press in upon us. The pre-Advent and Advent seasons are more attuned to this than any other time of the church year. As you may know, the medieval church designed the four Sundays of Advent around the themes of the four last things: death, judgment, heaven, and hell—in that order, so that the subject of hell was preached on the Sunday just before Christmas Eve.[3] That was no accident. The idea was—and is—to show how the light of the birth of Christ appeared against a backdrop of darkness, depravity, and despair.

So, as we prepare to enter the Advent season, the church hunkers down. The Episcopal Church in America has been known for being really scrupulous about observing Advent; it's one of the best things about us. We don't decorate the church during Advent; we don't sing carols; we don't move to Christmas until the eve itself. Advent is a time for making a fearless inventory of the darkness. This is a call for character and courage, because we would prefer bland sentimentality and cheerful inoffensiveness.

At no time is there a greater contrast between what the church teaches and what is going on all around us. The messages coming at us at this time of year are so preposterous that the only proper response for Christians is either to laugh or to cry. As always, we are being urged to find happiness in shopping. Every shop window is already festooned. Peace comes in a box, whether from Tiffany or Target. And all the while, the bodies are coming home in bags. Last week on the Don Imus radio talk show, Andy Rooney was a guest. Mr. Rooney is a much more serious person than one would know from his cameos on *60 Minutes*. Imus asked him why in his opinion President Bush wasn't going to any of the military funerals. Rooney said that it was "a political decision that

2. Václav Havel, *Disturbing the Peace: A Conversation with Karel Hvížďala* (New York: Vintage Books, 1990), 199.

3. Professor Karl Froelich of Princeton Theological Seminary was my consultant about this. I have noted elsewhere in this volume that Richard A. Norris taught me this, and instituted a series of sermons for Advent on these topics at his parish in New York City.

Bush made, or that was made for him—he doesn't want to be associated with death."[4]

Exactly. We don't want to be associated with death. Indeed we do not. We want soothing messages; upbeat messages; bland, inoffensive messages. We don't want to have our noses pushed up against reality. Two years after September 11, we in New York are almost back to normal, it seems, going about our daily lives almost as though there were no war, as though terrorism were back in the place where it belongs—over there in the incomprehensible Middle East, not over here.

The entire thrust of this season at the end of the church year is designed to bring us face-to-face with reality—reality about sin and death, reality about the human race, reality about God. Something ultimate has entered our world, something or Someone that calls us to attention, calls us out of our daily pre-occupations and our routine points of view. That is what this season with its special biblical readings is designed to reveal. The collect for the first Sunday of Advent is taken from Paul's letter to the Romans, where he says, "You know what hour it is, how it is full time now for you to wake from sleep. For salvation is nearer to us now than when we first believed; the night is far gone, the day is at hand" (Rom. 13:11–12).

I have been preaching during the Advent season for twenty-eight years, and I have never had to look far afield to find signs of the times, signs of crisis to fit the season. Every year there is some sort of shadow looming over our society. Advent 2001—less than two months after the Twin Towers so horribly collapsed—was particularly soul-wrenching, of course. Yet in a way that was a more deceptive time than this for understanding the message of this season. It was easy then to slip into the language of a battle against evil.

Now, two years later, matters are not so clear-cut. It is generally agreed that we have squandered the international goodwill that was ours for a few months after 9/11. Within our own body politic, we are sharply divided by opinions about the Iraq War and about the president's intentions. Newspaper columnists are pointing out some interesting trends. Nicholas Kristof of the *New York Times* has been hammering away at the blindness of the Democratic Party, which does not seem to realize that virtually all the very numerous Christian conservatives in the United States have become Republicans. Kristof has

4. Although Imus was a somewhat ridiculous figure, he was trying to be serious (part of the time) and occasionally had serious guests. Andy Rooney was one of the regulars for a while. Imus revered him, called him "Mr. Rooney," and asked him only serious questions. Mr. Rooney (whom I knew personally) liked that and thought that Imus was intelligent. My husband listened to the Imus show in those days when it was much better than it later became.

been pleading for the mainline churches to get back into the mix after decades of decline. The *Wall Street Journal* has been issuing call after call for the "media elite" to stop sneering at Christian faith in America and to recognize its importance. I couldn't agree more. But there is something very disturbing going on. The rhetoric of good versus evil has intensified, and many people in our country seem to think that there can be no question about the goodness of America.

To give an example, there is a very intelligent conservative columnist named David Brooks who has just started writing for the *New York Times*. I think he is an absolutely terrific writer and social commentator, but a new column came out a few days ago that shocked me deeply. In this column, he describes some of the horrific things that Saddam Hussein's henchmen have done. Yes. This needs to be said over and over. But then he talks about the role of America in a way that seems to me to be completely wrong. He says, "It is our responsibility to recognize the dark realities of human nature while still preserving our idealistic faith in a better Middle East. The murderers . . . can not be permitted to beat the United States of America."[5]

What is wrong with this? Just one thing. Brooks does not allow any room for understanding that Americans, too, are part of the dark reality of human nature. Human nature is universal. That is why the first epistle of Peter says, "The end of all things is at hand. . . . Beloved, do not be surprised at the fiery ordeal which comes upon you to prove you. . . . For the time has come for judgment to begin with the household of God" (I Pet. 4:7, 12, 17).

The themes of judgment and repentance are strongly emphasized in this season, and they are applicable to the church first of all—*the time has come for judgment to begin with the household of God.* This motif is not being heard in the religious rhetoric coming down from the White House. You would think that the only people who needed to repent were Islamic terrorists (and perhaps the French).[6]

On September 11, 2001, the archbishop of Canterbury, Rowan Williams, was at Trinity Church, Wall Street, right next to the World Trade Center. He could easily have died that day. He lived to write a little book called *Writing in the Dust*. He says this: "Bombast about evil individuals doesn't help in under-

5. David Brooks, "A Burden Too Heavy to Put Down," *New York Times*, November 4, 2003. I may have misjudged David Brooks here. I had just started reading him. Now, fourteen years later, Brooks, who is Jewish, is beloved by many Christians, including me, for his deeply appreciative writing about religious perspectives with a strong dose of Augustine. The column referred to here does read, today, as a bit naive about what Americans might be capable of.

6. This was the era of "freedom fries" and cartoons depicting the French as weasels.

standing anything. . . . Without that self-questioning, we change nothing. It is not true to say, 'We are all guilty'; but perhaps it is true to say, 'We are all able to understand *something* as we look into ourselves.'"[7] Looking into ourselves, recognizing our own potential for evildoing, rendering solemn thanks to God for his justice and mercy—that is what this season is about.

In the chapter of Luke's Gospel appointed for today, Jesus has a warning for his disciples and for all who belong to him: "But take heed to yourselves lest your hearts be weighed down with dissipation and drunkenness and cares of this life, and that day come upon you suddenly like a snare" (Luke 21:34). At the time of the Reformation, the Reformers did away with the concept of purgatory for reasons that were crucial at the time. Purgatory was thought to be a realm where people went to be "purged" of sin before admission to paradise. The concept was thought to be unbiblical, besides being subject to all sorts of corruption and exploitation. There is now good reason for building it back in again, because it preserves the idea that there is not one among us who does not need to be finally and fully separated from our sin as the wheat is separated from the chaff.[8] Contrary to much that is taught by the churches these days, we are not simply "accepted" by God just as we are, none of us. As various biblical passages make plain, we must be purged and purified by the judgment of God. As T. S. Eliot wrote, we must be "redeemed from fire by fire."[9]

The refiner's fire of which the prophet Malachi speaks at the very end of the Old Testament (Mal. 3:2–3) may sound terrifying, and of course in a sense it is; but when it's understood as the second coming of our Lord Jesus Christ, it will be the salvation of us all "when the Man comes around." Johnny Cash testified to this with his reordered life and with his songs. T. S. Eliot also wrote that "human beings cannot face very much reality,"[10] but with tremendous courage the Man in Black taught many people how to look reality in the face. This was never more true than at the very end of his life. Another article about him tells how he kept on coming to the recording studio every day after his beloved June died, even though he was almost blind and in a wheelchair. He said, "I'm not going to do all the things that people normally do when they lose their life partner. I'm not going to go out and spend money or chase girls. I'm just going to work every day."

7. Rowan Williams, *Writing in the Dust: After September 11* (Grand Rapids: Eerdmans, 2002), 21–22.

8. Jesus's parable of the wheat and the tares (Matt. 13:24–30), though not appointed reading for Advent, is perfectly suited to the themes of the season.

9. T. S. Eliot, "Little Gidding," *Four Quartets*, in *The Complete Poems and Plays* (New York: Harcourt, Brace, and Co., 1952), 144.

10. T. S. Eliot, "Burnt Norton," *Four Quartets*, 118.

He recorded an amazing number of new songs not long before he died. Here is the description from the article; the reporter is listening to a tape of one of these songs: "A voice, singing, came through the earpiece: 'I never thought I needed help before/ Thought that I could get by by myself.' The voice was that of Johnny Cash . . . [his] voice cracked and wavered with each word, at times falling out of tempo and time as if fighting against extinguishment. Yet it continued, slow, determined, choking back emotion: 'But now I know I just can't take it any more/ And with a humble heart on bended knee/ I'm begging you please for help.' That was recorded two months after June's death, two months before his own death on September 12."[11]

"Take heed to yourselves lest your hearts be weighed down with dissipation and drunkenness and cares of this life, and that day come upon you suddenly like a snare; for it will come upon all who dwell upon the face of the whole earth." When the Man came around for him, Johnny Cash was ready. He had already passed through the judgment and emerged on the other side. May it be so for us all. In the midnight hour, as we with humble hearts on bended knees beg the Lord for his help, a thrilling cry is heard. In our closing Advent hymn we will join our voices to that of the watchman in the night, with faith, with hope, with confidence, and with joy.

Rejoice, rejoice, believers, and let your lights appear!
The Bridegroom is advancing, and darker night is near.
The Bridegroom is arising, and soon he will draw nigh;
Up! Watch! in expectation! At midnight comes the cry.

See that your lamps are burning, replenish them with oil,
Look now for your salvation, the end of sin and toil.
The marriage feast is waiting, the gates wide open stand;
Rise up, ye heirs of glory, the Bridegroom is at hand.

Our hope and expectation, O Jesus, now appear!
Arise, thou Sun so longed for o'er this benighted sphere.
With hearts and hands uplifted, we plead, O Lord, to see
The day of earth's redemption, and ever be with thee.[12]

---

11. Neil Strauss, "Johnny Cash's Legacy of Emotions, on CDs," *New York Times*, November 27, 2003.

12. Hymn by Laurentius Laurenti (1660–1722), translated from German by Sarah B. Findlater (1823–1907).

Who Are Those Wailing People?

Trinity Episcopal Church, Columbus, Georgia
Second Sunday of Advent 2003

MALACHI 3:2–3; LUKE 3:7

Here at Trinity Church we are observing Advent. People who are unfamiliar with the Episcopal Church are somewhat baffled by the peculiarities of Advent. Why don't we have any Christmas decorations around the church? Why aren't we singing Christmas carols? And why do we have to have John the Baptist two Sundays in a row, with his startling demeanor and even more startling message? Today's Gospel reading from Luke stops one verse short. If you go on just one more verse you hear this from John: "You brood of vipers! Who warned you to flee from the wrath to come?" (Luke 3:7). I've always wanted to design an Advent calendar. You would open up one of those cute little windows and there would be John the Baptist glaring at you, saying, "You brood of vipers!"

In ten days of teaching here at Trinity Church, we have been emphasizing the unique character of this season. We have explained that Advent is not really the season of preparation for Christmas. It is the season of preparation for the second coming of Christ. The aura of the last days hangs over Advent. John the Baptist is the central personage of the season because he is the singular figure who stands at the juncture of the ages, the one who, *even before his conception,* was called forth by the divine purpose to declare the apocalyptic arrival of God on the world scene.[1] John is held in utmost reverence by all four Evangelists. He is the last and greatest of the Hebrew prophets, but far more important, *he is the first person to belong to the arriving age of the kingdom of God.*[2] In the

1. The predestination (yes) of John the Baptist is told in detail in chapter 1 of Luke's Gospel.

2. The scholarly discussion about whether John closes off the Old Testament succession of prophets or belongs entirely to the messianic age is fascinating, but much too complicated to go into here. Virtually all scholars agree, however, that he is the unique herald of

243

ministry of John the Baptist, the entire prophetic tradition arrives at its goal as he electrifies the people with his proclamation that the time is fulfilled, the day of the Lord is about to dawn, the Messiah is about to appear. No wonder they all went flocking to the river to be baptized, before the judgment of God came down upon them. The preaching of John carries with it to this very day the urgent sense that the decisive moment is about to happen. This is the mood of Advent.

Let's think for a moment of the Collect for Purity that we read at the beginning of every Eucharist: "O Lord to whom all hearts are open, all desires known, and from whom no secrets are hid . . ." We rattle that off every Sunday, but if we stop to think about it, it's pretty scary. It makes me think of the millions of documents that Saddam Hussein kept on all his perceived enemies, a colossal assortment of information on people's every move. The person from whom no secrets are hid is a person that we would likely hate and fear. Even in our own free society, we don't want people around us who are "judgmental." We don't *want* all our desires to be known. We don't *want* our hearts to be exposed. We want our secrets to *remain hidden*, thank you very much. A friend of mine said that her idea of hell would be to have to sit through a video of every detail of her own life.

Advent is the season for reflection upon these matters. There is more dissonance in the church's message at this time of year than at any other— even more than in Lent, I think, because the contrast between the authentic Christian gospel, on the one hand, and sentimental holiday religiosity on the other is never sharper than during this season. More than any other time in the church's calendar, Advent forces us to look at the dark side of ourselves. Last Sunday we spoke of the integrity of Johnny Cash, who never changed his gritty themes to suit the typical radio-station format. Indeed, two days ago I saw a review of a new recording of his "grim" version of "The Little Drummer

---

the dawning age to come, the kingdom of God. Matthew, Mark, and Luke all insist, each in his own way, that John is the promised reappearance of Elijah, the one who would arrive at the end-time to usher in the day of the Lord. In John's Gospel, the Baptist denies that he is Elijah, but although that Evangelist tells John's story in a different way, as is typical of the Fourth Gospel, John's indispensable role is emphasized, if anything, even more strongly. It is therefore very important to understand John the Baptist's *location* as the one who stands on the very edge of God's dawning new day—the distinctive Advent note. That is why Jesus says, "Among those born of women there has risen no one greater than John the Baptist" (Matt. 11:11). The next part of that saying, "yet the one who is least in the Kingdom of God is greater than he," is especially addressed to the "little ones." In Matthew, Jesus characteristically refers to his disciples this way (Robert H. Gundry, *Matthew* [Grand Rapids: Eerdmans, 1982], 209).

Boy." Johnny Cash is a sort of John the Baptist for today. We pampered mall-shoppers do not expect to hear a "grim" Christmas song, but our medieval forebears were made of tougher material. They sang the Coventry Carol, with this verse:

Herod the King, in his raging,
chargèd he hath this day
his men of might, in his own sight,
all young children to slay.[3]

This is not the sort of message that we in our era would expect to hear so close to Christmas.[4] Those who love the special themes of Advent may seem downright perverse to those who do not. Twenty-four years in the ministry tells me that people who don't like to hear about judgment are those who fear it most. Sometimes the people who protest that others are "judgmental" suffer acutely from the same disease themselves without realizing it. It would be funny if it weren't so serious; the circle of judgment goes round and round, so that we judge others for being judgmental. Awareness of some sort of bar of judgment—whether it be the judgment of one's fellow human beings, the judgment of history, or the judgment of God—is a deeply embedded human psychosocial fact. The question is, where does final, definitive judgment ultimately reside?

Today the first lesson is from the prophet Malachi. Many of you will recognize it from Handel's *Messiah*. You can hear the leaping flames in the music: "But who can endure the day of his coming, and who can stand when he appears? For he is like a refiner's fire and like fullers' soap; he will sit as a refiner

---

3. This is a carol from a pageant regularly performed in the city of Coventry in the early sixteenth century. It is much misunderstood today; in the pageant, this was not sung to the infant Jesus. It was sung by a chorus representing the mothers of the babies who are about to be murdered by King Herod (Matt. 2:16–18). There is a mistake in the Episcopal hymnal; the hymn is appropriate for Holy Innocents Day, which is *December* 28 (the Fourth Day of Christmas), not *January* 28. The Twelve Days of Christmas therefore include a massacre— the darkness is still with us in "this present evil age." Interestingly, there is another hymn for Holy Innocents ("In Bethlehem a Newborn Boy") with quite good words, written in the twentieth century—but I have never heard it sung.

4. Even the more sentimental nineteenth century would sometimes come through with an apocalyptic message, like this one by the admirable Christina Rossetti (1830–1894) from her nativity hymn called "In the Bleak Midwinter"—

Our God, heaven cannot hold him nor earth sustain,
Heaven and earth shall flee away when he comes to reign.

and purifier of silver, and he will purify the sons of Levi and refine them like gold and silver, till they present right offerings to the Lord."

We have referred to this passage over and over these past few days in the Advent teaching here at Trinity. Those of us who have been studying together in a small group have agreed, I think, at least in theory, that none of us can expect to come before God just as we are. The gospel message is often presented as "Jesus accepts you just as you are." This is true, up to a point. Yet it is not the complete story. There is more to it than that. Something has to be *done to* us; we have to be purified and refined before *any* of us can present ourselves, in the words of Saint Paul, "as a living sacrifice, holy and acceptable to God, which is your spiritual worship" (Rom. 12:1).

But the danger of this sort of proclamation is that we are all likely to be thinking not of ourselves but of someone else. As we go out of church we are already thinking of *someone else* who needs to be cleaned up, not me. The "sons of Levi" may need to be purified, but not *our* children. Some other group of people needs to be refined, not *my* group. This is our problem and our challenge. Do not think that the preacher in the pulpit is in any different case from anyone else. As you sit in your pew and as I stand here before you, each of us is equally addressed by the word of God: "Who can endure the day of his coming, and who can stand when he appears? For he is like a refiner's fire and like fullers' soap"—like lye soap that burns terribly while it scrubs away impurities. If we think that we are going to be able to pass through our Christian lives without significant pain, we have not yet understood the way of the cross. Everybody seems to love the "Battle Hymn of the Republic"—all those "glory, glory, hallelujahs"—but how many of us stop to reflect on the line, "He is sifting out the hearts of men before his judgment seat"? Abraham Lincoln knew that meant sifting the North as well as the South.[5]

Most of you are too young to remember that the marriage service in the Book of Common Prayer used to contain this charge: "As ye shall answer before the dreadful day of judgment when the secrets of all hearts will be disclosed." Well, those words are gone now. But sweeping the words under the bed hasn't changed anything. The reality of judgment is still there, and it is still dreadful to contemplate. The secrets of all hearts will be disclosed before God.

But something has happened. *Something has happened.* John's preaching sets it in motion. With the announcement of John, the world begins to turn on its hinges. The final reckoning is going to take place. The Judge of all the

---

5. This very week, a monument was unveiled in Duluth, Minnesota, to commemorate the lynching of three black men in the 1920s (*New York Times*, December 2003).

universe steps on the scene. With every bit of earnestness that I can muster, I ask you to imagine this picture and to think of the secrets of your heart. Not someone else's secrets, but your own—your secrets that you will bring before the throne of God. The Judge confronts us. But it is not as we feared. The face of the Judge is marked with infinite compassion and infinite suffering. His hands and feet are torn by spikes driven in by violent blows. His brow is pierced by the crown of thorns, and his expression bears the tokens of utmost humiliation. The judgment has already happened. It has taken place in his own body. The Son of God has borne it all himself. The Judge who is to come has given himself to be judged in our place, "to save us all from Satan's power when we were gone astray."[6]

As our concluding hymn today, we are going to sing a hymn by Charles Wesley, perhaps his greatest.[7] If we place ourselves within it, as Wesley means us to do, we will understand everything.

As we sing the first verse, we imagine ourselves actually seeing the second coming of the Lord:

Lo, he comes with clouds descending, once for our salvation slain;
Thousand thousand saints attending swell the triumph of his train;
Alleluia! Alleluia! Christ the Lord returns to reign.

The second verse is in another key altogether. The glorious vision of the second coming does not bring instant joy. As the viewers recognize the judge to be Jesus, fear seizes many souls. Everyone who participated in his death begins wailing in distress and terror:

Every eye shall now behold him, robed in dreadful majesty:
Those who set at naught and sold him, pierced and nailed him to the
   tree,
Deeply wailing, deeply wailing, shall the true Messiah see.

Who are these wailing people? We recognize ourselves. These people are you and me. *All* of us sinners "set at naught and sold him." We do it every day. We

6. From "God Rest Ye Merry, Gentlemen."

7. On the first Sunday in Advent 2014, I attended worship at Saint Thomas Fifth Avenue. As far as I know, there is no church anywhere that does the Advent liturgy better. After the service I stood on the front steps with the rector, Andrew Mead, and we both found ourselves agreeing that, taking words together with the superb *Helmsley* tune, it is the greatest of all hymns.

set him at naught constantly. We sell him for our own pleasure, for "the devices and desires of our own hearts."[8] It is our sin that nailed him to the tree. Here is the key insight of the hymn and of the Advent season. We cannot draw a line between the righteous and the unrighteous with ourselves on the good side.

The third verse is the charm. In the third verse, it is revealed to us that we are redeemed in spite of ourselves. Looking more closely at the celestial body of the Lord, we see that he still has the mark of the nails:

> Those dear tokens of his Passion still his dazzling body bears;
> Source of endless jubilation to his ransomed worshippers;
> With what rapture, with what rapture gaze we on those glorious scars.

The narrative force of the hymn brings us through tears of self-recognition to blazing, ecstatic joy as we recognize the Savior who has ransomed us from Sin and Death. Fear of the judgment melts away as we see the One who has come to be our advocate and defender, the One who is on our side, who stands not against us but for us.

This morning I have one concern and one concern only—to bring before you the person of our Lord Jesus. We were unworthy, but he counted us worthy. We deserved judgment, but he gave us mercy. We were slaves to sin and death, but he brought us over into righteousness and life. How can we not love him with every fiber of our being?

Be assured that *the day of his coming* means that he will not allow us to remain as we are. Even now he is already beginning to refine us into his image and likeness. The advent of divine judgment means that we do indeed find ourselves in urgent need of a complete overhaul, but the final act of the drama is resurrection and the passage into eternal life. The trajectory of the first Sunday of Advent is completed by transforming praise, as we join our voices with those who have gone before us in the name of Christ and those who will come after us in the name of Christ, joining our voices to those of the angels and the archangels and all the company of heaven:

> Yea, Amen! let all adore thee, high on thine eternal throne;
> Saviour, take the power and glory; claim the Kingdom for thine own.
> Alleluia! Alleluia! Thou shalt reign, and thou alone.

---

8. The phrase is from the General Confession for Morning Prayer in the Book of Common Prayer.

Advent Begins in the Dark
(Advent I)

Advent Begins in the Dark

Saint John's Church, Salisbury, Connecticut
First Sunday of Advent 1996

ISAIAH 64:5–7

Every year, Advent begins in the dark. Today's reading from the prophet Isaiah sets the stage:

> In our sins we have been a long time, and shall we be saved?
> We have all become like one who is unclean,
>> and all our righteous deeds are like a polluted garment. . . .
> . . . Thou hast hid thy face from us,
>> and hast delivered us into the hand of our iniquities. . . .
> Be not exceedingly angry, O Lord,
>> and remember not iniquity for ever. (Isa. 64:5–9)

Today's psalm repeats the theme:

> O Lord God of hosts,
>> how long will you be angered?
> You have fed your people with the bread of tears. (Ps 80:4–5)

In any given Episcopal congregation at this time of year, you will have two groups of people. One group, seeing the purple hangings and hearing the lessons about sin, judgment, and the wrath of God, will say, "Oh, good, it's Advent." The other group will say, "Where are the Christmas decorations? Why aren't we singing Christmas carols?" It takes some practice to get used to Advent. Once you do, though, you will never want it any other way. The more the world outside lights its trees, the more sparkle and glitter it throws about, the more it sings "Have yourself a merry little Christmas," the more you will want to immerse yourself in the special mood of Advent. No other

Western denomination does Advent as conscientiously as we do. It is one of the most important, most cherished contributions that the Episcopal Church has made to Christian worship. Advent teaches us to delay Christmas in order to experience it truly when it finally comes. Advent is designed to show that the meaning of Christmas is diminished to the vanishing point if we are not willing to take a fearless inventory of the darkness.

Now, don't get me wrong. Episcopalians have long since learned to lead a double life during December. Outside these church doors, I carry on about Christmas as much as anybody. I become positively intoxicated by the seasonal offerings. I can't get enough wreaths, lights, presents, carols, holly, panettone. I bid on four different trees at the Noble Horizons Christmas tree festival. But at the same time, even as the season outside gets more exuberantly festive, those who observe Advent within the Christian community are convicted more and more each year by the truth of what is going on inside—inside the church as she refuses cheap comfort and sentimental good cheer. Advent begins in the dark.

Isaiah depicts the silence and absence of God in today's reading: "Thou hast hid thy face from us." The biblical readings are set for us, but they are filled out each year by contemporary voices that add their own notes. Here is an example. A few months ago, a funeral was held in Belgium for one of the little girls who was slowly and systematically starved to death in a dungeon by a man so perverted that he was disowned by his own mother. At the Catholic funeral, the priest's hand trembled violently as he recalled the passionate prayers said for the children all over Belgium. In a voice of intense anger, he said, "*Is the good Lord deaf?*"[1] That is an Advent question, perhaps *the* Advent question.

Here is another Advent text from the newspaper. A woman told of praying for her husband's safety the night before he took off on Pan Am Flight 103, which exploded over Lockerbie, Scotland. After his death in the explosion, she said her view of God had changed. "I don't dislike him," she said. "I'm not mad at him. I'm afraid of him." That idea, too, belongs to Advent. It is the season of the wrath of God.

Many people do not like to hear these things during the Christmas season. That is understandable. We would rather build fantasy castles around ourselves, decked out with angels and candles. Indeed, I read yesterday that Americans now spend several hundred million dollars a year on scented candles, often marketed as "spiritual" aids. This is precisely the sort of illusion about spiritual health that the church, in Advent, refuses to promote. The sea-

1. Christopher Dickey, "The Death of Innocents," *Newsweek*, September 2, 1996.

son is not for the faint of heart. During the trial of Susan Smith, who drowned her little boys, several commentators observed that our fascination with the case had to do with our displacement of our own darkest impulses onto this unfortunate young woman, upon whom we could then lock the door. It requires courage to look into the heart of darkness, especially when we are afraid we might see ourselves there. Isaiah says that even our best selves are distorted and unclean: "Even our righteous deeds are like a polluted garment." The authentically *hopeful* Christmas spirit has not looked away from the darkness, but straight into it. The true and victorious Christmas spirit does not look away from death, but directly at it. Otherwise, the message is cheap and false. Instead of pointing to someone else's sin, we confess our own: "In our sins we have been a long time." Advent begins in the dark.

Last Sunday in the Bible class, the questions were asked: If God has truly come in Jesus Christ, why do things remain as they are? Why do so many terrible things happen? Where is God? These are the Advent questions. The church has been asking them from the beginning, going all the way back to the first century AD when the Gospel of Mark was being put together. The early Christians were facing a crisis. Voices within and without the community were saying, "Where is the King? Show us some evidence! He said he would return, but there is no sign of him. The world has not improved. Where is God?" And in its perplexity, the young church told and retold a story to herself, a story once told by Jesus of Nazareth—the parable of the doorkeeper: "It is like a man going on a journey, when he leaves home and puts his servants in charge, each with his work, and commands the doorkeeper to be on the watch. Watch therefore—for you do not know when the master of the house will come, in the evening, or at midnight, or at cockcrow, or in the morning—lest he come suddenly and find you asleep. And what I say to you I say to all: Watch" (Mark 13:34–37).

We can still feel the tension in the atmosphere of the parable. Were it not for the master, the household would have no reason for existing; yet he is away. The expectation of his return is the driving force behind all the household activity, yet often it seems that he will never come. Everybody has been told to be in a state of perpetual readiness, yet sometimes it seems as though it has all been a colossal mistake. Strangely, however, in spite of all this, the Christian believer will experience the urgency and stress in the text as a sign of its continuing truth. The heartbeat of the parable remains strong, even accelerated, just as the drama of salvation accelerates in Advent. The atmosphere of crisis is the story of the life of the Christian community in the Time Between for two thousand years.

If you were to say to me at the end of this sermon that I have not answered the Advent questions, I would have to say you are right. We do not know why God delays so long. We do not know why he so often hides his face. We do not know why so many have to suffer so much with so little apparent meaning. All we know is that there is this rumor, this hope, this expectation, that the Master of the house is coming back. The first Sunday of Advent, as you can tell from the hymns, is not about the first coming of Jesus, incognito in the stable at Bethlehem. It is about the second coming, "in glory, to judge the quick and the dead." It is about the final breaking in of God upon our darkness. It is about the promise that against all the evidence, there is a God who cares. Where is God? Until he comes again, he is hidden among us, "the wounded surgeon," the bleeding Victim, the One who hung on the tree, accursed for our sake.[2] It is this hiddenness that gives Advent its special character. The church's life in Advent is hidden with Christ until he comes again, which explains why so much of what we do in this night appears to be failure, just as his life appeared to end in failure. If Jesus is the Son of God, he is also the One who, as we learned last Sunday, identifies himself with "the least, the last, and the lost,"[3] who takes their part, who is born into the world as a member of the lowest class on the social ladder and identifies himself with our human fate all the way to the end, as he gives himself up to die the brutal, shameful, and dehumanizing death of a slave.

This is not the end of the story. It is the beginning of the end. As many theologians have pointed out, the church lives in Advent, the Time Between, *The Time Being*, as Auden calls it. We stand in a dark place, no question about it; but all the faculties of the faithful are straining toward the watchman who stands on the heights with his face toward the dawn—one of the most wonderful of all biblical symbols. Watchman, tell us of the night! In a very deep sense, the entire Christian life in this world is lived in Advent, between the first and second comings of the Lord, in the midst of the tension between things the way they are and things the way they ought to be. "I don't dislike God. I'm not mad at him. I'm afraid of him." Like many other Pan Am 103 families, the woman who fears God and lost her husband has given herself in service to others who have lost their loved ones in air crashes. She has not clutched at the scented candles, but has followed her calling to go out among others who suffer. In the words of the Advent collect, "now in the

---

2. "The wounded surgeon plies the steel . . .": T. S. Eliot, "East Coker," in *Four Quartets*, in *The Complete Poems and Plays* (New York: Harcourt, Brace and Co., 1952), 127.

3. This phrase is borrowed from Robert Farrar Capon.

time of this mortal life" she has "cast away the works of darkness and put [on] the armor of light."

I asked my mother yesterday to tell me why, in our family when I was growing up, we did not decorate our house until Christmas Eve. I knew the answer, of course—we were conscientious Episcopalians—but I wanted to hear what she would say. She surprised me. She said, "I think Christmas should come in a burst." Exactly. Auden writes, "Nothing can save us that is possible." The human race cannot expect to receive any lasting comfort from the world. The comfort that we so desperately need must come from somewhere else—in a burst of transcendent power breaking upon our ears from beyond our sphere altogether.

It was evoked for us last night in the Bach concert when the thrilling voice of the Evangelist sang, "And suddenly . . . (*Und alsbald*)!" That's why we are singing, today, "Sleepers, wake! A voice astounds us!" The news of God's entrance into the world ruled by sin and death is nothing less than astounding. After a long and agonizing silence that seemed never to end, the voice at last is heard in the wilderness: *Prepare ye the way of the Lord.* To each and all on this first Sunday of Advent, we bring this announcement: God will come, and his justice will prevail, and he will destroy evil and pain in all its forms, once and forever. To be a Christian is to live every day of our lives in solidarity with those who sit in darkness and in the shadow of death, but to live in the unshakable hope of those who expect the dawn.

"I don't dislike God. I'm not mad at him. I'm afraid of him." *And the angel said unto them, Fear not.*

Amen.

The God Who Hides Himself

Grace Church, New York City
First Sunday of Advent 1987

ISAIAH 63:7–64:12

Every year, Advent begins in the dark. It begins in a world where—day before yesterday—Christian missionary couples and their children were hacked to death with axes, in Zimbabwe. It begins in a world where a little girl is hit in the face and in the head, many times, again and again and yet again until she is dead—not in Zimbabwe, but two and a half blocks from Grace Church. Advent begins once again in the contemplation of the spectacle at Grand Central Terminal, which becomes more and more startling and upsetting each year as winter approaches—affluent, well-dressed, and above all *purposeful* commuters striding across the concourse while at their feet lies an ever more numerous, ever more desperate multitude of the purposeless, the wretched, the filthy, the deranged, the lost.[1] Advent begins in the dark.

Advent begins with the recognition that human progress is a deception. The preacher doesn't have to spend more than five minutes gathering examples. It's all right there, in this morning's paper.

In the Rutledge family, however, things are decidedly better than they were in Advent 1986. This makes me, personally, feel very grateful, thankful, and hopeful. Working at Grace Church is wonderful; my husband is very happy in his splendid new job; our daughter, who was so sick, graduates from college in two weeks; we are renovating the bedrooms of our house.[2] Speaking for myself, I feel very "up." What, then, is the point of concentrating on these

1. This was in 1987. Today, after an extraordinary restoration, Grand Central Terminal gleams from end to end, from polished floor to starry ceiling. The wretched and lost of the city are still with us in great numbers, but they are no longer in the terminal or visible to the well-dressed throngs.

2. As the congregation knew, the previous year had been a terrible one for our family. Our daughter received her diploma late because of the lost months.

256

bleak Advent themes? The Christmas lights are coming on all over the city; why does the church insist on beginning Advent in the dark?

An image comes to mind, another image of Grand Central. Since I'm a commuter, I probably spend more time there than most of you do. There have been several major changes in the last five years. The restoration of the great central space is very impressive, a real joy to behold, but the waiting room with benches, which used to be a nice place to sit and wait for trains, is now 100 percent taken up by derelicts and homeless people. There is now a very busy café and bar on the second-level gallery, overlooking the concourse. It is therefore possible, if you want to spend four dollars for a drink, to sit high above the homeless people, surrounded by Christmas trees and lights, completely oblivious to the misery below.

It is very tempting for the church to consider itself lifted out of the general wretchedness to a higher level of existence. Much of the theology that is taught in mass-market inspirational paperbacks and on television would encourage us to do so. The theology of blessing—accept Christ as your personal Savior, receive answers to your prayers, find assurance of salvation, be free from AIDS, feel good about yourself and the world—seems to be the message of much of popular religion nowadays in America. It is a Christianity of the second-level gallery, from which one need only descend (with a pleasant alcoholic buzz) to catch the suburban train home. If one is feeling especially expansive, there is always the possibility of donating a dollar to a homeless person along the way, thereby feeling even better about oneself. (Russell Baker, who, like all major humorists, is a first-class social critic, wrote the other day that in New York, with all its seven-dollar movie tickets and twenty-nine-dollar power breakfasts, the only time that a single dollar had any significance was when it was given to a beggar.)[3]

The church's very ancient liturgical traditions call the theology of blessing sharply into question. A theology of the church as a society of the second-level gallery can't stand up to scrutiny in the season of Advent. For the church first of all, for the people of God who thought they had been guaranteed prosperity, for the chosen ones first of all, Advent begins in the dark.

This year, the opening lesson of the first Sunday of Advent is a passage from the book of the prophet Isaiah that has been called "the most powerful psalm (liturgical poem) of communal lamentation in the Bible."[4] The setting is one of apparent despair and hopelessness. God has withdrawn himself from his

---

3. Double these amounts for year 2018.
4. Claus Westermann, *Isaiah 40–66* (Philadelphia: Westminster, 1977), 392.

people. They have returned home from exile in faraway pagan Babylon, only to find terrible conditions back in Israel. Isaiah describes it:

> Thy holy cities have become a wilderness,
>> Zion has become . . . a desolation.
> Our holy and beautiful house,
>> where our fathers praised thee,
> has been burned by fire,
>> and all our pleasant places have become ruins.
> Wilt thou restrain thyself at these things, O Lord?
>> Wilt thou keep silent, and afflict us sorely? (Isa. 64:10–12)

Why does the church begin Advent this way? What is this supposed to mean for us at Grace Church? Our holy and beautiful house has *not* been burned by fire. My pleasant place in Westchester, far from being a ruin, is being made bigger and nicer. God has been wonderfully good to us. Where does this biblical lament fit in?

Isaiah writes,

> We have become like those over whom thou hast never ruled,
>> like those who are not called by thy name. . . .
> For thou hast hid thy face far from us,
>> and hast delivered us into the hand of our iniquities.
>> (Isa. 63:19; 64:7)

Here is the powerful Old Testament theme of the God who has hidden himself. We begin Advent with this message. Where is he? the prophet cries out. "O Lord, where are thy zeal and thy might? Thy compassion [is] withheld from me" (63:11, 15).

The clue to the meaning of this lesson for those of us who do not personally feel overwhelmed by the silence of God is found in that word "communal"—a "communal lamentation." Unlike American Christianity, the Bible is not individualistic, but thoroughly social in its orientation. When the church groans with Isaiah, "Thou hast hid thy face far from us," it speaks as a corporate body with a common lot. If one suffers, all suffer.

Suffering communities have always understood this. Solidarity is indeed an apt name for the Polish labor movement. In resistance movements like Solidarity, like the American civil rights struggle, like Black Sash in South Africa, there is no place for individuals looking down from the second tier.

Instead, those who are better off stand shoulder to shoulder with those who suffer. No one is free until all are free. No one is safe until all are safe. No matter how "up" I may feel personally, my place as a Christian in the larger scheme of things is not to bask in the continual sunshine of God's presence, but, in repentance and prayer, to come alongside those who bewail the seeming absence of God. Pascal wrote, "Every religion which does not affirm that God is hidden, is not true."[5]

I, for one, was shaken to my foundations by the story of the barbarity in Zimbabwe. Here were young missionary couples, teenage children, a toddler, and an infant—tied up in their own homes and hacked to death with axes. They were the only farmers in the whole area who did not have elaborate fences, floodlights, security systems, and watchdogs. They had no fences at all; God was their protection. Where was he? Where was his zeal and his might? One can perhaps understand that an adult missionary knowingly accepts the risks he takes. But children? Hacked to death? Advent summons us to lament on behalf of all the victims in the world—the children in Zimbabwe and on West Tenth Street and in P. W. Botha's South African prisons, the despairing farmers of Nebraska and the destitute miners of West Virginia, the homeless in Grand Central and the patients dying of AIDS at Bellevue. On the first Sunday of Advent, the church does not sit on the second level enjoying herself, but is summoned to identify herself with victims everywhere. On behalf of them, we cry out with Isaiah,

> Wilt thou restrain thyself at these things, O Lord?
> Wilt thou keep silent, and afflict us sorely?

I suggest, now, that we look again, in our imaginations, at that bar on the second level. Many people there seem to be having a genuinely good time, but there is a man who is alone and clearly has had too much to drink. There is a middle-aged woman who is talking a little too loudly and flirting a little too frenetically. There is another, older man, also alone, staring blankly into space. There are some young people, too young to be in a bar, smoking and looking stoned. There is a couple in their late twenties, having a bitter argument. All is not well on the second level. Isaiah writes,

---

5. Blaise Pascal, *Pensées*, no. 584, available at https://www.gutenberg.org/files/18269/18269-h/18269-h.htm. The full thought is, "God being thus hidden, every religion which does not affirm that God is hidden, is not true; and every religion which does not give the reason of it, is not instructive. Our religion does all this: *Vere tu es Deus absconditus*."

In our sins we have been a long time, and shall we be saved?
We have all become as one unclean,
   and all our righteous deeds are like filthy rags. . . .
There is no one that calls upon thy name. . . .
For thou hast hidden thy face from us,
   and hast delivered us into the hands of our iniquities. (Isa. 64:5–7)

The fortunate and the "religious" people are not set apart in a position of privilege. The proper stance for *everyone*, this first Sunday in Advent, is confession of sin and repentance—everyone, not just killers in Zimbabwe and child murderers on West Tenth Street. The proper stance for *all* Christians today, not just the homeless and wretched, is "Wilt thou restrain thyself at these things, O Lord? Wilt thou keep silent?" Advent begins in the dark.

This, however, is not the whole story. It is notable that all these complaints against God are made to his face. This is one of the most arresting features of biblical faith. Even when God appears to be absent, the community goes on addressing him, protesting to him. Isaiah's lament begins with an affirmation of who God is, and a list of all the great things he had done for the people in the past. The lament carries within it, in spite of its apparent hopelessness, a kind of hope against hope, a kind of expectation, a kind of insistence that God has got to *do* something. That is the mood of Advent as we begin in the dark.

Be not exceedingly angry, O Lord,
   and remember not iniquity forever.
Behold, consider, we are all thy people. (Isa. 64:9)

In spite of God's apparent hiddenness, the memory of what God has done in the past continues to activate hope for what he will do in the future. This is the movement of the Advent season. The God who hides himself is still the God of the covenant. He is absent and present at the same time (*Deus absconditus atque praesens*).

How is God present at the murder of children? You will get no easy answer to that question today. Rather, let us turn to the witness of Beulah Mae Donald, whom most of you will have recently read about. She is the woman whose son was chased through the nighttime streets and hanged by the Ku Klux Klan. Where does this poor, black woman, living alone and getting along in years, get her faith in God from? Her faith in God is what got her through; she testifies to that constantly. Her faith in God enabled her to look one of the killers right in the eye and say, "I forgive you." Where does that kind of strength come from?

Where was God when the young man was hanged? Where was God for the families of Zimbabwe? Where was God for the child murdered just around the corner? I cannot answer those questions. The biblical affirmation is that God is present even in his apparent absence. What I can say for sure is that God is present in Mrs. Donald's faith. Like so many people, in the black community, like the people of Isaiah's community, she had heard the stories about the mighty acts of God and about his invincible love for his people, and she believed those stories and she believed that "God is always like himself," as Calvin says—his nature cannot turn against itself. The sufferings of God's people come before him; he has said so. He may hide himself, but it can never be forgotten that he was once present in power and that he will be again. That is Advent—the time between.

God hides God's *self.* This paradox pervades the Bible. Strange and offensive as it seems, God's hiding of himself is in order to make himself known. When God's presence is taken for granted, it is no longer real presence. Samuel Terrien writes, in an astonishing sentence, that the presence of God is "a surging which soon vanishes and leaves in its disappearance *an absence that has been overcome.*"[6]

"An absence that has been overcome." That is what the church believes about God. A religion that talks about God being obviously present all the time is not true. That would be a religion that had taken God for granted, that had tried to appropriate God for its own ends. The lament of Isaiah teaches us something different. The church cannot possess or control the presence of God. Only God is in control of his own presence. It is faith that teaches us that God is to be trusted, in spite of appearances.

What the church holds on to, by grace through faith, is two things: we hold on to *memory,* and we hold on to *hope.* We *remember* the great things that God has done for us, and we hold on to a *hope* that amounts to a certainty, because God has made promises and it is an inalienable part of God's nature that he keeps his promises.

Beulah Mae Donald remembered, hoped, and believed. The only face visible to her was the face of the devil, but she trusted the God whom she knew, even though he had hidden himself. Then there were some white lawyers, and others, who were willing to come down from that second level and

---

6. Samuel Terrien, *The Elusive Presence* (New York: Harper and Row, 1978), 476 (emphasis added).

stand alongside her. Mrs. Donald was no mere passive sufferer. Her fortitude and determination made it possible to win a decision in court that has broken the back of the Klan. That is why she is in the news today. There is work to be done, work in resistance to the powers of darkness, work to be done in expectation of the coming of the Lord—and even the secular readers of the *New York Times* will respond to it.

Where is God when it is dark? The church proclaims that he never hides himself to no purpose. Somewhere, somehow, in spite of all appearances, his vindication awaits the proper moment. At the heart of the Advent season is the proclamation that God did not remain where he was, high above the misery of his creation, but came down, incognito, into the midst of it. Nor did he come down merely to sympathize. Even incognito, Jesus of Nazareth had power to heal every disease and drive out every demon. He had power to do this at every level—he came not only to the poor and wretched of the earth but also to the lonely people on the upper level, in the bar, and to the commuters and suburbanites who spend their dollars mostly on themselves. To each and all, we bring this announcement: God will come, and his justice will prevail, and he will destroy evil and pain in all its forms, once and forever. To be a Christian is to live in expectation of that fulfillment. The life of the church, lived in solidarity with those in darkness, carries with it the embodiment of a certainty: when he comes again, it will be the God of mercy and no one else, and it will be morning.

Amen.

The Doorkeeper

Christ's Church, Rye, New York
First Sunday of Advent 1975

MARK 13:33-37

There's a sense in which the history of the Christian church can be described as a history of thoroughgoing confusion about who we are and what we are called to do. It's not a very edifying spectacle. We can all make long lists of the various wrong ideas that the church has had about herself—sometimes the church has been a form of government called a theocracy (they tried that up in Massachusetts Bay), sometimes an instrument of war and inquisition, sometimes a socially restricted club, sometimes a museum, sometimes a guardian of public morality, sometimes—most times—a defender of the status quo. In America, the church has been from the beginning a partner of the cultural setting. Going to church has been part of the American way of life. This is still so on Christmas Eve and Easter; it is still so to some extent in the South and in smaller towns. But all of you are aware, I'm sure, that it won't be so much longer. The church in America is soon going to be having a major crisis of identity, if it isn't having it already.[1]

I'm seeing a good deal of evidence of this crisis of identity now that I'm an ordained minister of the church. Everywhere I go, people ask me, "What is going to happen to the church? Why is there such a startling drop in church membership? Does the church have any relevance to modern life?" When non-churchgoing people ask these questions, they are sometimes merely curious, more often derisive, sometimes aggressively hostile. When churchgoers ask me these questions, however, I often think I can detect a note of heartfelt, life-threatening anxiety. Have we been deceived all these years? Can the church survive? Should the church survive?

Two weeks ago, there was an article in the *Wall Street Journal* headlined

---

1. More apparent in 1975 than I would have thought from the perspective of 2018.

"Crime Wave Hits Churches. Jewels, Gold Stolen. Clergymen Hire Guards, Bolt Doors." The reporter tried to ascertain, through interviews, why churches all of a sudden were becoming targets for burglary and vandalism. A police officer was asked why thieves looted churches. This was his reply—"Why do they rob churches? Why not? There's nothing sacred about religion or churches any more."

The world is knocking more insistently on those church doors than it has in a long, long time; and those who knock are not always "our kind." Some are thieves and murderers. Many are desperately poor and starving. Many are members of other races. Some are handicapped, some are jobless, some are refugees. Some are prisoners. Some are Communists. Some are political terrorists, and some are their victims. Who knocks? Shall we open? Some knock on the doors of the church for help. Some knock hoping for an answer, a response, a piece of bread, a place to sleep, a kind word, a shred of hope. Others knock in anger. Some come to negotiate; others come to demand; others come to seize and destroy. Still others knock on the door for the purpose of sending it crashing to the ground, to clear the path, to rid the landscape of a nuisance, to eliminate irrelevances like churches so that the work of the world may be done. What is the response of the church to those who knock? Shall we pretend we do not hear? Shall we lock the doors? Shall we install a security system? Shall we give pass keys—and who will we give them to? To members only? To the ones who are baptized? To the ones who come every Sunday? To the ones who pledge money? Shall we keep our lights on, or will it attract the attention of marauders? Who are we, within these doors, and what do we do here? What sort of life are we called to live? What is the church?

It is dark early at this time of year, and that reminds us of a darkness in our world. The rules are becoming harder and harder to follow because fewer and fewer people know what the rules are, anymore. There is Christmas tinsel in the streets and Christmas music on the radio, but there is a cheapness at the core. The clock on the bank says it is day, but the hands on the church clock point to midnight.

It is Advent—the deepest place in the church year.

Advent—for the world, it is a time of counting shopping days before Christmas. Advent—for the church, it is the season of the shadows, the season of "the works of darkness," the season in which the church looks straight down into its own heart and finds there—the absence of God.

Now. Come back with me into the very first century AD when the Gospel of Mark was being put together. The young Christian church is going through a crisis of identity. It, too, hears knocking upon its doors. It hears mocking laughter outside, voices saying, "Where is your King? You thought he was coming back, but he has not returned. You have made a very stupid mistake. How can you live without your Lord? He has abandoned you—for this, you want to risk your lives?"

And in its perplexity, the young church repeated a story to itself, a story once told by Jesus of Nazareth. It is one of the so-called "crisis parables." It is the Gospel for the first Sunday in Advent, the parable of the doorkeeper. Jesus said: "Be alert, be wakeful, for you do not know when the moment comes. It is like a man away from home: he has left his house and put his servants in charge, each with his own work to do, and he has ordered the door-keeper to stay awake. Keep awake, then, for you do not know when the master of the house is coming. Evening or midnight, cock-crow or early dawn—if he comes suddenly, he must not find you asleep, and so what I say to you, I say to all—keep awake!" (Mark 13:33–37).

Do you see the picture? Here is a great household with many family members and many servants. There is a master, who established the household in the first place and gave it its reason for being; he is the one who gathered its members and assigned a place to each. It is he who put the whole operation in motion, who gave shape and direction to its existence. The master is now away, but his orders are that there is to be a watch at the door, a constant alert. This is the command to the doorkeeper—"Stay awake"—but what he has said to the doorkeeper he says to everyone: "Keep awake." This state of readiness is to be maintained through the ceaseless vigilance of each family member and servant, each in his own work, until the master returns.

Perhaps you begin to feel the tension in the atmosphere of this parable. Were it not for the master, the household would have no reason for existing; yet he is away. The expectation of his return is the moving force behind all the activity that takes place; yet no one knows when the return will be. Everybody has been ordered to keep awake; yet the days and months and years pass, and still he does not come. Over and over again, the household repeats to itself the charge that it was given—"If he comes suddenly, he must not find us asleep." The heartbeat of the parable is strong and accelerated—it is a parable of crisis. It is the story of the church, living in a crisis for two thousand years.

The church calendar is not the same as the world's calendar. The Advent clock points to an hour that is later than the clock on the bank. There is knocking at the door! Take heed, watch—your Lord and Master may be standing at the gates this very moment. Keep awake, for if he comes suddenly, he must not find you asleep. "A thousand ages in his sight are like an evening gone."[2]

---

2. Isaac Watts, "Our God, Our Help in Ages Past."

There is no way for the church to adjust its calendar to the world's calendar. The church is not part of American culture, and never should have been. The church keeps her own deep inner rhythms. New Testament time is different from the world's time; Saint Paul says, "My friends, the time we live in will not last long. . . . For the whole frame of this world is passing away" (I Cor. 7:29, 31). New Testament time is a million years compressed into a single instant— and the time is *now*. "The hour cometh and now is" (John 4:23). There is no way to alleviate the overwhelming tension produced by the Advent clock; the only way to be faithful is to be faithful at each moment. "Keep awake, for you do not know when the master of the house is coming."

The church lives in Advent. That is to say, the church lives between two advents. Jesus Christ has come; Jesus Christ will come. We do not know the day or the hour. If you find this tension almost unbearable at times, then you understand the Christian life. We live at what the New Testament depicts as the turn of the ages. In Jesus Christ, the kingdom of God is in head-on collision with the powers of darkness. The point of impact is the place where Christians take their stand. That is why it hurts. That's why the church has to take a beating. This is what Scripture tells us. No wonder there are so many who fall away; the church is located precisely where the battle line is drawn. The knocking at the door is the noise of the struggle. That's why the church may not—may not—lock its doors. Whether we take that literally or figuratively, we must take it seriously. At any moment, the master himself may be the one who knocks—and we do not know what guise he will come in. What we do know is that he said, "Inasmuch as ye have done it unto one of the least of these my brethren, ye have done it unto me" (Matt. 25:40).

It is the Advent clock that tells the church what time it is. The church that keeps Advent is the church that is most truly herself. The church is not supposed to be prosperous and comfortable and established. It is Advent—it is dark and lonely and cold, and the master is away from home. Yet he will come. Keep awake. He came among us once as a stranger, and we put him on a cross. He comes among us now, in the guise of the stranger at the door—perhaps with a face of the wrong color, or manners that are not of the best. He will come in the future, not as a stranger, but as the King in his glory, and "at the name of Jesus every knee shall bow" (Phil. 2:10). "The coming of the Lord is at hand," says Saint James. "Behold, the judge is standing at the door" (James 5:8–9). Keep awake, then . . . if he comes suddenly, he must not find you asleep.

What does it mean to keep awake? Here's a story.

I was in Grand Central Terminal getting ready to take the train home to Westchester. I missed a train and had a few minutes to kill. In a fit of would-be generosity, I decided to buy a nice sandwich and a soft drink for one of the derelict people that hang around the terminal. I bought these items and went over to the phone booths, where many of the needy and homeless people sit on the seats in the booths. I approached the first one and offered the sandwich: "Would you like something to eat?" He shook his head roughly. I went to the second phone booth and repeated my question and my offer. The second person refused, rudely. I was beginning to feel like a complete fool, standing there with this unwanted sandwich. I began to think, well, the hell with these ungrateful people. Then suddenly, a very quiet voice from the fourth or fifth booth came to me: "I would like something." I presented the sandwich to the little woman in the booth with a profound sense of having been rescued.

Who was the giver in this little story and who was the receiver? Who was the benefactor? Who was more awake than whom? The roles were reversed, and the situation changed completely. I was abashed and ashamed of my self-importance. My Lady Bountiful image was shattered. I have never been quite the same since; I have approached charity—I hope—with a more humble spirit. The Lord came to me in a most unexpected guise.

The Lord has come—he will come. The life of the Christian church is located and lived at the intersection of those two advents. And in the meanwhile—"the Time Being," as W. H. Auden calls it—we stay awake, like the doorkeeper, by watching for signs of his presence in the most unlikely places and the most unlikely people. It will take us by surprise every time, but we will be ready to recognize him when he makes himself known. But you will remember this also: there is a place where he *always* comes to meet you. He has promised us his presence in the sacrament of communion. Here, the doorkeepers may receive refreshment for the next watch, for in the body and blood of the Lord, he has guaranteed his presence not only in the unforeseeable future, but "now in the time of this mortal life."[3] "Come unto me, all ye that labor, and ye shall find rest" (Matt. 11:28). Fellow doorkeepers, fellow watchmen, we are Advent people. Together we receive his very self for this Advent life. We may return to our posts with gladness, having been fed and upheld by the One Who Comes.[4] Rejoice, rejoice! Emmanuel shall come to thee, O Israel.

Amen.

---

3. A phrase from the collect for the first Sunday in Advent, and from other collects.

4. In the book of Revelation, one of the names of Christ is "the one who comes" (*ho erchomenos*).

The Advent Life for Nonheroic People

Grace Church, New York City
First Wednesday in Advent 1986

ROMANS 13:11–14

On the first Sunday of Advent—three days ago—the *New York Times* book review section featured an article about the latest biography of Martin Luther King Jr. There is nothing particularly new in the review, but the way that the reviewer has put it together is a grabber—especially for the first Sunday of Advent.

It can be argued that Advent, more than any other season of the church year, is immediately relevant to our concrete lives as individuals, to the concrete life of the church under stress, and to the concrete headlines in the newspaper. The reason for that is that Advent tells us about our own lives as Christians, here and now. Advent is where we live, work, play, laugh, struggle, and die. Advent is the Time Between—between the first coming of Christ and the second coming, between darkness and dawn, between the kingdoms of this world and the kingdom of our Lord and of his Christ. It is not the time of fulfillment; it is the time of waiting. It is not the time of seeing face-to-face; it is the time of seeing "through a glass, darkly" (I Cor. 13:12). It is not the time of triumphant victory; it is the time of bearing the cross. That is the title of the King biography—*Bearing the Cross*. The book spares no detail in its description of King's "sacred and profane" life, his Advent life lived on the edge between his "inner demons" and his calling to be a great moral and religious leader. As the reviewer says, we see King in "the grandeur of his courage and the frailty of his humanity."[1]

---

1. Howell Raines, "Driven to Martyrdom," review of *Bearing the Cross*, by David Garrow, *New York Times Book Review*, November 30, 1986, http://www.nytimes.com/books/99/02/07/nnp/garrow.html. Raines was a very sympathetic reviewer. Most reviewers thought the book a failure, but that changes nothing about the points in this sermon.

Let's listen again carefully to the wonderful text from Romans for the first Sunday in Advent. Saint Paul writes:

> You know what hour it is, how it is full time now for you to wake from sleep. For salvation is nearer to us now than when we first believed; the night is far gone, the day is at hand. Let us then cast off the works of darkness and put on the armor of light; let us conduct ourselves becomingly as in the day, not in reveling and drunkenness, not in debauchery and licentiousness, not in quarreling and jealousy. But put on the Lord Jesus Christ, and make no provision for the flesh, to gratify its desires. (Rom. 13:11–14)

Notice first of all "what time it is." It is still night, though the night is "far gone." It is not day yet, though the day is "at hand." Salvation has drawn nearer and nearer, but it is not yet fully arrived. We are to cast off the works of darkness, conducting ourselves "as if it were day," even though it is not yet light and the "works of darkness" assail us on every side. It is Advent, the Time Between. It is your life that is being spoken of, and my life, right here, right now. As the collect for the first week of Advent puts it, "give us grace to cast away the works of darkness and put on the armor of light, *now in the time of this mortal life.*"

Martin Luther King contended with two different types of "works of darkness." There were the external evil of segregation, racial hatred, sheriffs, police dogs, jail sentences—and he hated going to jail; but there was also the inner torment of his obsessive sexual adventuring, which he knew was wrong, which he knew was a profound threat to his moral authority, which he knew the FBI was documenting. Did Martin Luther King "cast off the works of darkness and put on the armor of light"? In some ways, yes, in some ways, no—in his public life, yes, in his private life, not so much. He was a larger-than-life example of *simul peccator et iustus* (saint and sinner simultaneously), and he remained so until he was killed. He did not "put off" reveling and drunkenness, debauchery and licentiousness. And yet—and yet the power of his life seized his biographer David Garrow, long after he was dead. Mr. Garrow said that it was the depth of King's Christian faith that allowed him to go through seven hundred interviews and seven years of writing the book. "Realizing how deep a faith motivation he had really gave me a much deeper understanding of what this man was about and made him a more fundamentally powerful and moving figure for me."

In the Gospel for today Jesus says, "Watch, therefore, for you do not know on what day your lord is coming. . . . You must be ready, for the Son of Man is coming at an hour you do not expect." Jesus refers to himself, and he refers to the last day of final judgment. Watchfulness and readiness are the hallmarks of the Advent life. "Put off the works of darkness—put on the armor of light—salvation is nearer than when we first believed."

Was Martin Luther King ready for the coming of the Son of Man? Are you ready? Am I ready? In some ways, yes. In some ways, no. Then "who can abide the day of his coming, and who shall stand when he appears?" (Mal. 3:2). David Garrow, King's biographer, traces the source of his heroism and his perseverance to his experience when he was twenty-six, already a national celebrity and the recipient of numerous death threats. Sitting at the kitchen table in the middle of the night, unable to sleep, he thought of giving up, of turning aside. Then, as King himself tells it, "I heard the voice of Jesus saying still to fight on. He promised never to leave me, never to leave me alone. No never alone. No never alone. He promised never to leave me, never to leave me alone."[2]

Do you think Jesus kept his promise? Do you think that he left Martin King alone at the end because he did not give up his sin? Did God leave the Israelites alone when they continued to follow after false gods? Has God abandoned the church because the church has committed abominations? Will Jesus forsake you because you are still a sinner? Will he forsake me? Do you have any doubt about the answers to these questions?

In our own Advent life, we who are saints and sinners at the same time must find a way to believe and proclaim two seemingly paradoxical things at once:

- "We shall all stand before the judgment seat of God" (Rom. 14:10).
- "Nothing will be able to separate us from the love of God which is in Christ Jesus" (Rom. 8:39).

Both of these Scriptures are true. And both of these things are also true:

- God hates the works of darkness, God will root out the works of darkness, God will not permit the works of darkness to endure.
- God will not allow the works of darkness to swallow up his children forever. We will be judged for our sins, and there will be left of them neither root nor branch (as Malachi says); "but for those who call on the name of Jesus the Sun of Righteousness will rise with healing in his wings."

2. Quoted in Howell Raines, "Driven to Martyrdom."

Both of these things are true:

- As sinners we will be judged and condemned.
- As God's children justified in Jesus Christ, we will be delivered in the final judgment, and indeed in a sense are delivered already.

The joyous news of this salvation is the anvil where the Sun of Righteousness is forging our armor of light even now in the time of this mortal life.

But note that Martin Luther King, while a great sinner, was also a great hero. You and I, on the other hand, are great sinners and no great heroes at all. What of us?

But it is precisely to us, ordinary nonheroic Christians in the pew, that the ringing words are addressed: "now in the time of this mortal life." I was absolutely amazed today to see in the paper that the number of young people volunteering to do good deeds in the city is actually *increasing*. A young woman who volunteered in response to a radio appeal is quoted in today's *Times*: "I just want to do something to help. I don't want to put in tremendous time and energy—I know I don't have that kind of commitment. But I can work one day collecting food or clothing for the homeless. The problem is so visible and overwhelming. To be able to live with myself, I have got to do something."

Not much, you may say, not much at all. Not Martin Luther King giving up his whole life. But something. Not a work of darkness, for sure. One tiny link in the chain mail of God's light.

Every step we take in this world is a step toward either darkness or light. Every harsh word, every mean act, every vengeful thought is a part of the works of darkness. Every act of forgiveness, every small act of charity, every temptation resisted is a piece of the armor of light.

Salvation is nearer to us now than when we first believed. Watch—discern the signs, call them for what they are, speak against the darkness, bear the cross, praise God for the hope of his marvelous light. And "rejoice, rejoice, believers," in the hope of glory—"peace on earth and mercy mild, God and sinners reconciled."

"Never to leave me, never to leave me alone. No never alone. No never alone. He promised never to leave me, never to leave me alone."

Amen.

The Armor of Light
(Advent II)

On Location with John the Baptist

Saint John's Church, Salisbury, Connecticut
Second Sunday of Advent 1996

MARK 1:1–3

Here's an Advent text from the daily news. All the radio stations in Belgrade are controlled by the despotic Milošević government except one, and that one is being jammed. The only way that protesting Serbs can get any news of their own movement is by listening to this station. According to a recent report, one man told a reporter that he picked up the radio signal by standing in the water in his bathtub holding the antenna: "My whole family comes in to listen." We Americans complain all the time about "the media," forgetting that freedom of information is the backbone of a democratic society. In Belgrade today, members of "the media" are heroes. One of them is named Miomir Grujic, a blind disc jockey with a passionate following. "Good evening, zombies," he said the other night as he opened his show. "Good evening, zombie town. Is there life out there? Do you cower in fear and anger? Be alive."[1] This is as good an Advent message as one could wish for. In one of the classic biblical texts for Advent, Jesus says to his disciples, "Watch therefore—for you do not know when the master of the house will come, in the evening, or at midnight, or at cockcrow, or in the morning—lest he come suddenly and find you asleep. And what I say to you I say to all: Watch" (Mark 13:35–37).

Keep awake! Be alive! Those radio reporters may not know it, but they are Advent watchmen. Wherever people are willing to come out from the paralysis caused by fear and anger to active participation, there is the Advent spirit. Wherever there are voices in the darkness speaking out for light, there is the Advent hope. Wherever there are people willing to face

---

1. Chris Hedges, who reported this, was a war correspondent doing important work in Belgrade when he filed this story: "Jammed Belgrade Radio Defies the Buzz of Power," *New York Times*, December 3, 1996.

danger for freedom, there is the Advent frontier. The work of God is located there.

This sermon is about **location**. It is about the location of the Christian church in a world largely given over either to self-indulgent pleasures or to repressive brutality. If we understand our location, we will understand Advent, and if we understand Advent, we will understand what it means to be a Christian.

All around the globe today, Christian churches who use the common lectionary are observing Advent. For two Sundays, this one and the next, the spotlight will be on John the Baptist. This is one of many reasons for the peculiarity of the season. Like John the Baptist, Advent is out of phase with its time, with our time. It encroaches uncomfortably upon us, making us feel some degree of dissonance with its stubborn resistance to the usual round of shopping and wrapping and baking and partying. I have never seen a picture of John the Baptist on any Advent calendar, yet he is the foremost figure of Advent.

Here are the opening words of Saint Mark's Gospel: "The beginning of the gospel of Jesus Christ, the Son of God. As it is written in Isaiah the prophet, 'Behold, I send my messenger before thy face, who shall prepare thy way; the voice of one crying in the wilderness: Prepare the way of the Lord, make his paths straight.' John the baptizer appeared in the wilderness, preaching a baptism of repentance for the forgiveness of sins."

All four New Testament Evangelists agree: there is no good news, no *gospel* of Jesus Christ, without John the Baptist. John's whole life was lived with but one purpose; he was born, a man of destiny, to declare the imminent arrival of the coming Messiah. This voice crying in the wilderness, this "lantern which shone in front of the Son of God,"[2] is extraordinary in many ways, but most of all for the single-mindedness with which he pursued his mission even to death, for John the Baptist feared no man, not even Herod the king, and no woman either, not even Herod's wife, who in the end arranged to have his head cut off. But let us take note: this firebrand who recognized no superior was utterly submissive before the One whose coming he lived and died to illuminate. "John said to them, 'One is coming who is mightier than I, and I am not fit to untie the thong of his sandal'" (Luke 3:15–16).

To be the witness, to point away from himself to Jesus Christ—this is the destiny of John, and in these things, he is a model for every Christian preacher.

There is very little in John's character or his history to appeal to the modern sensibility. If people today think of him at all, it is usually as a head on a

2. A phrase of John Calvin's.

platter.[3] I have preached about him during Advent for twenty-one years, yet I find him each year to be more uncanny and intractable than ever. After two thousand years, he still stands there, irreducibly strange, gaunt and unruly, lonely and refractory, utterly out of sync with his age or our age or any age. Even Elijah is positively lovable and cuddly in comparison. John's character, however, was never the central focus, even for the early church. Though his person is remarkable by any standard, it is not his person that marks him out; it is his *role*. No, not even his role; we would more accurately say his *location*.

In order to **locate** John, we need to go back into the Old Testament, to some famous words in the book of the prophet Malachi: "Surely the day is coming; it will burn like a furnace, . . . says the Lord God Almighty. . . . But for you who revere my Name the sun of righteousness will rise with healing in its wings. . . . Behold, I will send my messenger, who will prepare the way before me. . . . Behold, I will send the prophet Elijah before that great and terrible day of the Lord comes" (Mal. 4:1–5).

These words about Elijah are the very last words of the Old Testament. The Hebrew Bible does not end this way. When the Christian church put together the Old and the New Testaments, they shifted the order of the Hebrew books, making Malachi last. This is very important, and it is the most important difference between the Hebrew Bible and our Old Testament. The intertestamental period, between the time of the close of the Old Testament and the time of the opening of the New, is very interesting for understanding the gospel of Christ. Jewish expectation was focused on the figure of Elijah the prophet, who had not died but was taken up to heaven in a chariot of fire. When Elijah came back, it was believed, that would be the sign that the end of the world was at hand. And when we read the description of John the Baptist in Mark and realize it is the same as the description of Elijah in II Kings 1:8, we begin to understand what is going on here. John the Baptist is the new Elijah, standing at the edge of the universe, at the dawn of a new world, the turn of the ages. That is his **location** as the sentinel, the premier personage of this incomparable Advent season—the season of the coming of the once and future Messiah.

John's divinely ordained location in the world, according to the New Testament, is on the frontier of the ages as God arrives in his world to turn it away from its past of sin and bondage toward a future of promise and freedom. John's function is to proclaim the coming reversal of the downward spiral of

---

3. John the Baptist was well known in his own time. We have much more evidence of him from nonbiblical sources than we do of Jesus, whose entire history is known to us only from the New Testament.

THE SERMONS: THE ARMOR OF LIGHT

human history, to deliver the message of the invading Son of God. He cries, "Already the axe is laid to the root of the trees; every tree therefore that does not bear good fruit is cut down and thrown into the fire" (Matt. 3:10). "Bear fruit that befits repentance" (3:8).

The whole purpose of John the Baptist is to announce the beginning of the end. His appearance on the banks of the Jordan River means that the kingdom of God has begun. The wickedness of this world is truly doomed; the Lord of the universe is about to step on the stage of world history to reverse its course. For those in the know, the import of John the Baptist as Mark's opener could not be more clear: when Elijah comes back, *the next person to appear will be God, and it will be the first day of the age to come.*

The Evangelist Mark, in his uniquely brusque and staccato but highly artful style, is telling us that the arrival of the Messiah is immediately preceded by the work of John the Baptist, whose single-minded life and horrendous death at the hands of the powers and principalities are a preview of Jesus's own death. What a strange story we Christians have to tell! It is in the suffering and death of God's servants at the hands of despots and tyrants that God's new rule is made manifest.

Here is another Advent story. In November, four Catholic priests ministering in Zaire were beaten, hacked, and shot to death by Hutu militiamen. These four missionaries had spent more than a decade in the country. Their staff had fled to safety a few days before. The priests chose to stay at their posts among the people they had come to serve. Local peasants reported that the attackers killed them by degrees with machetes before shooting them. The cries of one priest resounded some distance away: "Dear God, we are about to die. Have pity on our souls." Their bodies were thrown into a well they themselves had dug a few months before to provide water for refugees.[4] This barbarity revolts us, truly; and we should pause to honor these martyrs. However, such atrocity should not surprise us. These Christians were like John the Baptist. They paid the price for holding their positions on the frontier where the goodness of God's coming age opposes the rulers of this present evil age (Gal. 1:4). They stayed in their location in order to bear witness to the One whose coming John the Baptist lived to illuminate.[5]

---

4. Reported by Tunku Varadarajan, *Times* (London), November 16, 1996.

5. A similar, more recent story is the well-known refusal of the monks of Tibhirine to leave their post in the Atlas Mountains when threatened by Islamic terrorists in spite of the monks' deep love for the Muslim people among whom they lived. All the monks were killed except two, who were able to hide. Their severed heads were later found. An excellent book, *The Monks of Tibhirine*, by John Kiser (New York: St. Martin's Press, 2002), tells the story behind the highly praised film *Of Gods and Men* (2010).

Now it is for you and me to reflect, this Advent season, on our own positions. Where are you and I located along that frontier? Where do we stand on the great divide between this age of despotism, disease, and death and God's coming kingdom of truth, liberty, and love? Our lives are not very dramatic compared to the stories we have just heard. No one is asking us to confront dictators or gunmen with machetes. But the Advent warfare is conducted on many fronts. I think of a businessman who refuses to go along with corrupt company policies even though it would benefit him financially; he is holding his position on the Advent frontier. I think of a woman who came to see me to tell me that she was not going to leave her marriage in spite of the keen temptation to be happier with someone else. I think of social workers and teachers who remain content with their salaries, parents who insist on limits even when it makes the children intensely angry, accountants and builders and researchers who hold the line against declining standards—these are Advent people, holding their positions in spite of personal losses. They are on location with the One who is to come,[6] the One whom John announced at the price of his own life.

"This present evil age" (Gal. 1:4), as Saint Paul called it, is an age in which routine horrors take place. There are widely publicized horrors like the murder of small children, and there are unnoticed horrors like people in our own country sick and dying from lack of access to advantages that you and I take for granted. The only cure for such an age is the intervention of God. That is what John the Baptist was sent to announce. The coming of Jesus Christ marks the beginning of the end of this old age of corruption and death. "The end is not yet" (Mark 13:7), but it has begun.

Who is getting ready for Christmas? Last week on NBC News there was a story about the big retail season. A woman was interviewed standing in the aisles of F. A. O. Schwarz with her children. She said, "We are going to be able to spend about $1,500 more this year." Is that the way to get ready for Christmas? I think of a couple I know, in fact several couples I know, who this very week are sitting down together to plan the year-end gifts they will give to worthy causes instead of buying lavish presents. Who is getting ready for Christmas, the woman in the store, or the couples with their budgets and their lists of charities? Bear fruit that befits repentance (Matt. 3:8).

For all of us who are here today, getting ready for our worldly Christmas, let us make a place in our hearts for that strange, lonely sentinel on the fron-

---

6. "The One who is to come" (*ho erchomenos*) in Greek is one of Jesus's titles in the book of Revelation.

tier of the ages, still pointing away from himself to the One who is to come, identifying for us the place we are to stand. We're not zombies here at Grace Church. Let's be alive and alert! Whenever we do the right thing in spite of its cost, we are doing what Christian soldiers do; we are standing our ground. It may not be a very big piece of ground, but it is the one God has given us to hold, and it will be part of God's new world in the Great Liberation. Let the news go forth: God is on the move. He is creating a new humanity. You and I belong to it. Let us honor the Master by holding our piece of territory, and by remembering the needs of "the least of these his brethren" (Matt. 25:40). "Rejoice, rejoice, believers, and let your lights appear!"[7]

Amen.

7. Hymn text by Laurentius Laurenti (1660–1722), translated by Sarah B. Findlater (1823–1907). Parenthetically, I am struck by the significant number of nineteenth-century women who either wrote or translated hymn texts.

Advent at Ground Zero

Christ Episcopal Church, Charlottesville, Virginia
Second Sunday of Advent 2001

MALACHI 3:18–4:1

Advent: never has this exceptional season been better timed to meet the situation at hand than it is this year. Three months after the eleventh of September, Advent is a preparation for Christmas in the war zone. Advent says Christmas is not for sissies. Advent says—flatly contradicting the Christmas song—all your troubles are *not* going to be "miles away." Advent says this world is full of darkness, and it was into "such a world as this," not fairyland, that the Son of God came.[1]

Advent is the season that forbids denial. It brings into the open all the turbulent emotions we have been feeling since September 11. When that American Airlines plane full of Dominicans went down just out of JFK last month, there was not a functioning person in the United States who didn't have a moment of panic. Three weeks ago, unbelievably, we had anthrax up in rural New England where I go to get away from it all. We don't quite know how to conduct ourselves; we want to help out the economy by shopping, but when Sarah Jessica Parker, no less, says she doesn't feel like buying anything for Christmas, you know that the merchants of America must be feeling anxious. Advent is perfectly in tune with these moods. Advent has long been the season that embodies the anxieties and fears that force themselves upon us, citizens of a world in danger.

Around the world, we see a universal human phenomenon. We deal with insecurity by dividing up the world into good and evil. Everyone has been in overdrive doing this since the eleventh of September. It would be absurd if

---

1. A verse from a much-loved Christmas carol sung by the King's College (Cambridge) Chapel Choir says that Christ has laid aside his divine glory, that he "[has] come from highest bliss / down to *such a world as this*." "See amid the Winter's Snow," text by Edward Caswall.

it weren't so deadly serious. Here is Osama bin Laden in his cave, separating humanity into two groups: the faithful and the infidels. Here we are on the other side of the globe, talking about civilization versus barbarism. I don't mean to equate the two sides in this instance. The point is that the human tendency to make these absolute distinctions is universal. And, of course, we always—always!—place ourselves on the side of the good guys.

The lectionary readings for the Sundays just before Advent seem to be making these same distinctions. Malachi, for instance: "You shall distinguish between the righteous and the wicked, between one who serves God and one who does not serve him. For behold, the day comes, burning like an oven, when all the arrogant and all evildoers will be stubble; the day that comes shall burn them up, says the Lord of hosts" (3:18–4:1).

That sounds like Osama bin Laden, don't you think? The righteous are going to stamp out the wicked, reducing them to ashes. That's too close for comfort right now—very scary stuff. This is the sort of passage that we read just before Advent, every year. And then there is John the Baptist, Mr. Advent himself. We just heard from him. "He said therefore to the multitudes that came out to be baptized by him, 'You brood of vipers! Who warned you to flee from the wrath to come?'" (Luke 3:7). John's message was hardly one of inclusion and tolerance: "[The Messiah's] winnowing fork is in his hand, and he will clear his threshing floor and gather his wheat into the granary, but the chaff he will burn with unquenchable fire" (Matt. 3:12).

That leaves us with a huge question: Who is wheat and who is chaff?

Affluent white Episcopalians have not embraced the theme of judgment—at least they didn't before September 11. We have tended to think of God exclusively as loving, merciful, kind, forgiving, and embracing. The trouble with that is that it makes God sound like a pushover. Perhaps we are newly receptive right now to the Old Testament presentation of God as a warrior who defeats evil. But not just the Old Testament! The New Testament is full of warlike imagery also, not only the image in Revelation of Christ as a conqueror on horseback, but also Paul's conception of the Christian life as conflict, and the challenging language of Jesus himself. The biblical imagery shows God as the great arbiter of all things who brings justice and righteousness upon the earth. We have heard much talk of this since September 11. When we unexpectedly find ourselves facing ferocious enemies, we change our minds about things: suddenly we are glad to remember that God judges evil. We are delighted to hear that we are going to tread down the wicked under the soles of our feet.

But who exactly are "the wicked"? Who is wheat and who is chaff? Opinions change. As the whole world knows by now, one of the great shifts in public consciousness since September 11 resulted from the stories about the bond traders going down the stairs of the World Trade Center and the firemen going up. Before the attack, people in the financial markets, software specialists, and other technocrats were considered most valuable people—masters of the universe, if you will. Now it is the firemen who are the heroes. The *New Yorker* magazine cover showed children dressed like firemen for Halloween. Women are going down to the site to fling themselves at firemen. A cartoon shows a mother saying to her little girl, "Why do you want to marry a doctor? Why not a fireman?" In view of all this, it is probably a good thing—a reality check—that a disappointing episode took place a few weeks ago when angry firefighters, demonstrating at the World Trade Center site, insulted and punched their fellow heroes, the police. Mayor Giuliani, world champion fan of the FDNY, declared that they had committed sin, if you can believe that. Today's heroes are tomorrow's sinners. Idolizing people is never a good idea. There is an underside to everyone.

A few days after the 9/11 attack, the great paleontologist Stephen Jay Gould wrote an op-ed piece about his experiences at ground zero. Professor Gould is respected all over the world. He knows everything there is to know about the natural sciences; about human nature, not so much. He tells a genuinely moving story about volunteers giving out food to the rescue workers, but then he falls into a common mistake. He writes that "Good and kind people outnumber all others by thousands to one. The tragedy of human history lies in the enormous potential for destruction in rare acts of evil, not in the high frequency of evil people."[2] This is a very naive view of humanity. Let me give just one example. I used to go to an Italian restaurant in New York City. The very popular owner was an incredibly friendly, exuberant man who created a warm, hospitable environment for his customers. There is no doubt in my mind that he would be first in line to donate food to rescue workers. However, as a pastor, I was in a position to know for a fact that this man regularly beat his wife, sometimes in front of their grandson.

Is that man evil or good? Is he wheat or is he chaff? All the great writers know that the line between the two is blurred in all of us. In *Following the Equator*, Mark Twain wrote, "If the desire to kill and the opportunity to kill came always together, who would escape hanging?" A reviewer wrote of novelist Muriel Spark (author of *The Prime of Miss Jean Brodie*) that she does not "campaign for the goodness of one character as against the evil of another," but is interested

2. Stephen Jay Gould, "A Time of Gifts," *New York Times*, September 26, 2001.

in "the dark formations that lie within."[3] In a recent book called *The Fragility of Goodness*, Tzvetan Todorov asks why the Jews of Bulgaria were not sent off to the death camps (I didn't know that, did you?) and discovers that the reasons were mixed, not purely altruistic by any means. The author concludes, "we can never draw a straight line and consider ourselves completely innocent."[4]

So then, why does the Bible constantly say things like this: "You shall distinguish between the righteous and the wicked, between one who serves God and one who does not serve him" (Mal. 3:18)? Isn't that, in fact, one of the themes of the Bible? Isn't it one of the themes of Advent, this distinction between the godly and the ungodly?

Well, yes and no. Yes, because the meaning of life is serving and honoring God. That is what our worship this morning represents. But no, because there are "dark formations" in each one of us. And no, because none of us serve and honor God as we really should. All of us are in rebellion against God in one way or another. As C. S. Lewis wrote, "Fallen man is not simply an imperfect creature who needs improvement: he is a rebel who must lay down his arms."[5] Saint Paul makes this very clear in his letters to his churches. We must be disarmed by God. That's the theme of Advent. God is on the move to disarm us all—as Isaiah tells us in today's first lesson:

> They shall beat their swords into plowshares,
> and their spears into pruning hooks. (Isa. 2:4)

This will not happen without judgment. But note this: the judgment of God is not just judgment on someone else. There's a very important verse in the first epistle of Peter: "The time has come for judgment to begin with the household of God; and if it begins with us, what will be the end of those who do not obey the gospel of God?" (I Pet. 4:17).

That puts the matter in the right perspective. God's judgment will be exactly fair and right, and we can count on him to establish justice and righteousness in the earth, as the psalm says; but the judgment does not take place in a remote location, over in Tora Bora, as if the evil people were all far removed from us, the righteous. *The time has come for judgment to begin with the household of God*, and that means you and me.

3. Andrew O'Hagan, "Double Lives," review of *Aiding and Abetting*, by Muriel Spark, *New York Review of Books*, April 26, 2001.

4. Chris Hedges, "They Saved the Jews, but Few Were Heroes," *New York Times*, May 26, 2001. This article was about Tzvetan Todorov, the Bulgarian historian of ideas.

5. C. S. Lewis, *Mere Christianity* (New York: Macmillan, 1943), 59.

I don't want to be misunderstood here. Osama bin Laden and his network of terrorists must be stopped. Period. It looks as though that grim task will be the work of our generation. But America must not lose its soul in the process, and Christians must help to see that that does not happen. There is something built into American society, and I believe it is because of Christian influence, that helps us to understand that there is no sharp line to be drawn between the wicked and the righteous. It is the openness and generosity of our society, our respect for each individual, our commitment to human rights, that makes us the envy of the world. If we lose this, we lose everything that we are fighting for. Some people in high places are saying that suspected terrorists do not deserve the protection of the American Constitution. But that is exactly what we don't want to do, get into talk about the deserving and the undeserving. The very definition of grace is "favor shown to the undeserving." That's what makes it "amazing grace." If it were favor shown to the deserving, it wouldn't be amazing. We need always to have before us the lesson from the epistle to the Romans: "There is no distinction; all have sinned, all fall short of the glory of God" (Rom. 3:22–23). Wars must be waged with resolve, but resolve is not incompatible with Christian humility.

The lesson from Malachi states that the righteous are going to trample the wicked under their feet. This is tricky. We *want* to trample the wicked, we are *delighted* to trample the wicked, but we want to be able to define who the wicked are. That's where Jerry Falwell and Pat Robertson went wrong. They wanted to blame the abortionists, the lesbians, the feminists, and the ACLU. "I point my finger in their face," said Mr. Falwell, imagining himself to be Elijah no doubt, with no indication whatever that he himself also is under God's judgment. Ultimately, it isn't for us to decide who is a good person and who isn't. "Vengeance is mine, I will repay, says the Lord" (Rom. 12:19). Our appointed task is to fight evil itself, not to divide up the world into good people and bad people. I went to a Presbyterian church in New York City on the Sunday after the attack. The pastor, a noted preacher, was remarkably direct in his sermon about the rage that he felt about what had happened. He was in a passion about it, as a matter of fact. It was a very warlike sermon. But he said something very important along the way. He said, "I don't hate the terrorists. *I hate what they have done.*" That's where the line should be drawn. It isn't that this clergyman was soft on terror. You could tell that he wished he were young enough to sign up for combat duty himself. But he drew the distinction in the right place—not between people or groups of people, but between what Saint Paul calls Adam and Christ, the old human being and the new.

True Christians continue to have a lot of the old Adam in them all their lives. We don't understand that very well; we compare one Christian to another based on our superficial impressions of their supposed goodness, but we can't really compare one person to another in that way because none of us knows what sorts of inner pressures another person is under, or how that person would behave under certain conditions. The test of a true Christian is not degrees of goodness, but quite simply the love of Jesus Christ—his love for us, our love for him, shining through in spite of everything.

If one thing is clear in the aftermath of September 11, it is that the people who went immediately to the top of the list of those most admired were those who gave their lives for others. Madonna, Michael Jordan, Britney Spears, the *People* magazine "sexiest man of the year" will always have their fans, but they will never be able to evoke the tidal wave of emotion that arose around the world and that will never be forgotten. The firefighters' deeds and the sacrifice of the passengers on Flight 93 have already passed into legend. And note: they were not giving their lives for Americans only. They were giving their lives just for people, human beings of every stripe, without regard for whether they were deserving or undeserving. In that respect, their actions reflect Jesus Christ, who placed himself in the space between the human race and the onslaught of Satan, and in so doing took upon himself the sin of the whole world. He, the Son of God in person, became the Judge judged in our place.

Today I have one concern and one concern only—to bring before you the person of our Lord Jesus. How can we not love him with every fiber of our being? We were unworthy, but he counted us worthy. We deserved judgment, but he gave us mercy. We were slaves to sin and death, but he gave himself to release us into life and righteousness. He is remaking us into his image and likeness. The advent of divine judgment means that we do indeed find ourselves in urgent need of a complete overhaul, but the final act of the drama is resurrection and a passage into eternal life. In this sense, the oppressive threat of condemnation has already been lifted. The theme of judgment will follow us—*must* follow us—all the days of our life in this world, but there is a true sense in which the sentence has already been passed and has been fully absorbed into the crucified body of our Lord Jesus Christ. Therefore, as the Fourth Gospel tells us, the Lord himself has promised us: "Truly, truly, I say to you, those who hear my word and believe him who sent me have eternal life; they do not come into judgment, but have passed from death to life" (John 5:24).

Amen.

God's Cut-and-Fill Operation

Saint Michael and Saint George Episcopal Church,
Saint Louis, Missouri
Second Sunday of Advent 1993

ISAIAH 40:3–5

Our text this morning is a famous passage from Isaiah:

> A voice cries:
> "In the wilderness prepare the way of the Lord,
>   make straight in the desert a highway for our God.
> Every valley shall be lifted up,
>   and every mountain and hill be made low;
> the uneven ground shall become level,
>   and the rough places a plain.
> And the glory of the Lord shall be revealed,
>   and all flesh shall see it together,
>   for the mouth of the Lord has spoken." (Isa. 40:3–5)

I think most music lovers will prefer the King James Version, because it's the text for the opening tenor solo in Handel's *Messiah*: "The voice of him that crieth in the wilderness, Prepare ye the way of the Lord, make straight in the desert a highway for our God. Every valley shall be exalted, and every mountain and hill shall be made low: and the crooked shall be made straight, and the rough places plain: And the glory of the Lord shall be revealed, and all flesh shall see it together: for the mouth of the Lord hath spoken it."

Prepare ye the way of the Lord. Because of the musical *Godspell*, this verse is known even to popular, secular audiences. But when a biblical text becomes popular, it loses its bite. The offense of the original text is muted when it's set to music for flower children to bop down the theater aisle. *Godspell* is a wonderful show, but it is not the whole story. The effect of the words is light and amusing in the musical; when they ring out from a tenor throat at a thrilling pitch as they do in *Messiah*, we respond in quite a different way.

Advent is the season when the church makes a strenuous effort to recover some of the sovereign recalcitrance of the original biblical message. This Sunday and next belong to John the Baptist, who is not an easily manageable figure. The opening lines of Mark's Gospel bring him on the stage in such an abrupt and peremptory fashion that it's startling. Here is this alarming man straight out of the desert, wearing animal skins and eating insects, and that, Mark says, is "the beginning of the gospel of Jesus Christ, the Son of God." Among the four Gospels, Mark's version of the story is the most stark and dramatic, but all four Gospels agree that there is no gospel story without John the Baptist at the opening. Christmas does not come in the church without these two Sundays in Advent that focus on the message of John.

I can't count the number of times that I've preached about John the Baptist, and yet, though I find him more and more fascinating, I also find him more and more uncanny and intractable. Jesuit scholar John L. McKenzie once commented that John has never been fully understood, and, after two thousand years, he still stands there, gaunt and unruly, utterly out of sync with his age or our age or any age. Even Elijah is cuddly in comparison.

Like John the Baptist, the season of Advent is peculiar. It's out of phase with the times. People who are new to the Episcopal Church are puzzled by Advent; if they come to the services in December, they expect Christmas decorations and music, and they are put off to find them missing. Advent encroaches upon us in an uncomfortable way, making us feel somewhat out of sorts with its stubborn resistance to anything remotely resembling the season of shopping and decorating and wrapping and partying. Like everyone else, I am not beyond domesticating Advent, up to a point. I have a cute little Advent calendar on my office door with cute little windows that open and show cute little pictures. What I have not yet found is an Advent calendar with a window that opens to show a picture of John the Baptist—preferably saying, "Repent ye!"

We may laugh at this, but many Episcopalians who are fond of Advent wouldn't have it any other way. We love Advent in the same way that we love a lot of the language of the old Prayer Book where we referred to ourselves as "miserable offenders," and said solemnly together in the General Confession, "There is no health in us."[1] There's a very important sense in which the confession of sin is good news for us, and there are still a few Episcopalians of

---

1. This was 1993. The number of Episcopalians who remember this has now shrunk considerably.

a certain age who understand that. In the same way and for the same reason, the message of John the Baptist is much better for us than the message of all those catalogues that you and I have been hauling out of our mailboxes by the fistful. That's why you're here today; in some part of yourself you know that you need to be here in our worship today more than you need to be out buying presents. "Prepare ye the way of the Lord."

Mark's deceptively simple Gospel is, as we now know, extraordinarily artful. He introduces John the Baptist in his abrupt way because he has a profound theological purpose. The appearance of John on the world stage means that the turn of the ages has come.

How do we know this? To understand what Mark is up to, we have to know the Hebrew Bible—the Old Testament—much better than most of us do today. To locate John the Baptist in the history of salvation, we have to know that Mark is presenting him in the context of the prophet Elijah's return. Many of you know that Jewish families set a place at the Passover table for Elijah. When Elijah returns, the day of the kingdom of God is about to dawn. The role of John the Baptist is to prepare us for the appearance of God's own self in the person of the Messiah.

What is the proper response of the human being when God suddenly appears? My mind goes to the words of that favorite Christmas hymn so beloved by aspiring sopranos everywhere: "O Holy Night." What is the proper response when God appears? *Fall on your knees!*

John the Baptist stands at the edge of the universe. Advent looks, not to the birth of a baby, but to the long-anticipated day of the Lord when the old age of Sin and Death will pass away. The new day of the righteousness of God is coming and is founded in eternity. The old aeon is ruled by the spirit of rebellion against God; in the coming kingdom of God there will be no need to rebel, because there will be "perfect freedom."[2] God sent John the Baptist into the world at the appointed time to announce the imminent arrival of such a deliverance. *Fall on your knees!*

A voice cries:
"In the wilderness prepare the way of the Lord,
    make straight in the desert a highway for our God."

There is a twist in this passage from Isaiah. Most people don't notice it. First we are told, "Prepare the way of the Lord," as though we were going to do it

2. The Collect for Peace, Book of Common Prayer, p. 57.

ourselves, and then in the next breath the prophetic voice announces that the Lord is going to prepare his own way. "Every valley shall be exalted, and every mountain and hill shall be made low: and the crooked shall be made straight, and the rough places plain . . ."

My grandfather was professor of history at the University of Virginia. When I was a child, our family drove each year from Franklin, Virginia, to Charlottesville, where we always spent a few summer weeks with my grandparents. These were very exciting trips for my sister and me in the 1940s in our little sedan with our father driving 35 miles an hour all the way because of gas rationing. The ride took us out of the flat Tidewater into the Piedmont, where you could actually see hills. We used to call the state road from Richmond to Charlottesville "Two-More-Hill-Street" because every time you got to the top of a hill there would be two more hills ahead of you, and the little two-lane highway rose and fell like a ribbon across their contours. Eventually we would see the Blue Ridge Mountains in the distance, and then we would know we were almost there.

Then one year there was a new road. Nobody warned the two little Parker girls about the new road. The new road was four lanes, and faster, and we got to Charlottesville a lot sooner, but it was a great disappointment to us. There were no hills! Where had the hills gone? My father patiently explained. The new highway was flat instead of hilly because the machines had cut through the hills and filled up the hollows. That was the first time I had ever heard of "cut-and-fill." Every valley had been exalted and every mountain and hill made low; the crooked had been made straight and the rough places plain, but I didn't like it one bit. I never enjoyed the trip to Charlottesville as much after that.

In many of the world's cities, the affluent people live in the hills overlooking the common herd below. In New York City, where I work, the penthouse serves the same function. Human nature being what it is, a lot of our enjoyment in life comes from having things that others don't have. Part of the fun of traveling first class, I imagine, is that curtain that separates you from the lower orders in the back of the plane. Well, one of the themes of the Bible is that God is going to tear down that curtain and flatten the hills. Mary, the mother of the Lord, says so when the angel tells her that she will bear a son; in the great canticle called the Magnificat, she says, "God has put down the mighty from their seats, and has exalted the humble and meek" (Luke 1:52). Uh-oh. Sounds as if it's going to take all the fun out of the trip.

Preparing the way for the coming of the Lord Jesus Christ is not going to be so easy for you and me. It means laying ourselves open to God's great leveling operation. It means relinquishing our most cherished strategies and defenses. It means living every day in anticipation of God's work of cutting and filling. It means being ready at all times to relinquish one's own special privileges in the world on behalf of those who might be very different from oneself.

I don't need to tell you how hard this is for us. We don't like admitting that we need radical surgery. The New Testament Greek word for this is *metanoia*, repentance. It doesn't just mean being sorry. It means a change of life. It means reorientation toward a different goal—the kingdom of God. It means a whole different way of being. It doesn't mean loss of self-esteem—quite the contrary. Repentance is for the strong. Perhaps you have noticed this. The person who steps forward and takes responsibility is the leader, not the weakling. People who are insecure are either unable to repent, out of fear, or are forever saying, "I'm sorry! I'm sorry!" in such a reflexive way that it becomes meaningless. John the Baptist preached a baptism of repentance. Our entrance upon the Advent life means taking a good long look, not at *someone else's* deficiencies and faults, but at *our own*.

The final words of the Christian Old Testament are quite amazing. The Hebrew Scriptures are arranged so that the prophetic literature is in the middle, but the Christian Old Testament has the prophets at the end. The last book is Malachi, and the next-to-last verses foresee a "great and terrible day," the day of judgment and the second coming of the Lord. It will be a time when all that has been wrong will be set right. The example that Malachi gives is astonishing. At the last possible moment, he turns away from the language of wrath and flames to something very unexpected. This is the way the Old Testament ends: "Behold, I will send you the prophet Elijah [that would be John the Baptist]. . . . He will turn the hearts of parents to their children and the hearts of children to their parents, so that I will not come and strike the land with a curse."

The worst thing in the world, the prophet seems to be saying, is estrangement within families. It is given as the sign of the final judgment of God, his worst curse upon the human race. If you are a young person here today feeling miserable about your parents, if you are parents here today worried about your children, then this message is for you. God does not desire this situation. His will is for reconciliation. Family breakdown is a sign of the old age of Sin and Death. Reconciliation between parents and children is the sign that the kingdom of heaven is at hand.

Maybe you don't have these kinds of problems yet in your family, but every family, over generations, will have some kind of wrenching, heartbreaking trouble. In every case, the fracturing of the most basic human connection is the antithesis of what God intends for his people. And reconciliation, when it happens, is one of the clearest of all indications that God is at work. Therefore, the most important way that we can participate in the life of God is to seek reconciliation.

Reconciliation is hard work. It requires daily repentance. For a number of years, I have had two distinguished psychoanalysts as teachers. I asked both of them a fundamental question: What is the most important ingredient in a strong marriage? They gave the same answer. One of them is a secular Jew, so I was very surprised to hear him say, "The most important ingredient is asking forgiveness."

I wouldn't be able to count the number of times I've seen relationships break down because one or more family members—and that includes members of the church family—refused to repent, refused to see that they had anything to be sorry about. On the other hand, I have seen rainbows of grace when a family member acknowledges fault and asks forgiveness. Just saying the words—sincerely and earnestly saying them—"Will you forgive me?" can be transformative. Saying the General Confession on Sunday is a very good thing, but it can become rote. What is not rote is looking straight down into your very own personal, individual failure and acknowledging it to your spouse or your children. At that point we really come to know what it means to *fall on our knees*. God has put down the mighty from their seats once again.

The great comfort of the Christian gospel is that such acts of repentance are part of God's great cut-and-fill operation. They are part of the great plan of redemption. When husbands and wives, parents and children, brothers and sisters seek reconciliation with one another, confessing their faults and asking forgiveness, it is a sign that God is on his way, that the curse is being lifted. Such seemingly small actions are part of the eternal plan of God for the salvation of the world. We are not doing it; he is doing it; that's why we can trust the unfolding of his purpose and find our own place in it. This is what it means to prepare the way of the Lord; make straight in the desert a highway for our God.

This is the Advent life, full of hope; and as God has promised us, the trip is still going to be fun.

Amen.

The Axe at the Root of the Trees

Grace Church, New York City
Second Sunday of Advent 1983

MATTHEW 3:1, 7–10

It would be hard to say which is more alien to our contemporary ideas of getting ready for Christmas, the season of Advent or the figure of John the Baptist. All around the world, today, words are being read in the churches that seem ill-suited, to say the very least, to the anticipated holidays. "You brood of vipers! Even now the axe is laid to the root of the trees!" How would you like to get that on a Christmas card? But there it is; this is the second Sunday of Advent, and this is John the Baptist's day.

This unlovable figure is very much out of sync with our times, yet he is the foremost figure of Advent. This Sunday and next Sunday feature him as the main character of the season. The spotlight is on him for two weeks. This is one of many reasons for the peculiarity of the season. Like John the Baptist, Advent is out of phase with its time, with our time. It encroaches upon us in an uncomfortable way, making us feel somewhat uneasy with its stubborn resistance to Christmas cheer. To be sure, we have done a pretty good job of domesticating Advent; I'll never forget going to a church of another denomination a few years ago and seeing a poster that they had in the hallway—it cheerfully proclaimed, with an appropriate illustration, "Advent is a red balloon!"

I will be snooty and say that it was not an Episcopal church, and it even had the seasonal color wrong! But I am by no means beyond this sort of thing myself—every year I used to buy Advent calendars for my children with cute little doors that open and show cute little pictures. I have yet to find an Advent calendar that has a picture of John the Baptist. We really don't know exactly *what* to do with him; he doesn't fit into anything.

But here he is, for two whole weeks, by the river, dressed in the fashion of the wilderness and assaulting the crowds that come out to hear him: "You brood of vipers! Who warned you to flee from the wrath to come? . . . Already the axe is laid to the root of the trees" (Matt. 3:7, 10).

John the Baptist sets the tone for the first weeks of Advent, and in all four Gospels he sets the tone for the proclamation of Jesus Christ. Jesus arrives on the scene precisely at the moment John says, "Every tree that does not bear good fruit will be cut down and thrown into the fire." This is apocalyptic language, and it signifies the arrival of God. When Jesus appears, the message of John has come true—"The kingdom of heaven is at hand." Even if we thought we could fit baby Jesus into our scheme of things at Christmastime, there is no way to get rid of the recalcitrant figure of John the Baptist announcing "the wrath to come."

I have an Advent wreath in my dining room just like many of you, but it does occur to me from time to time that the soft, romantic glow of candlelight fails to do justice to the conflagration announced by John. The extremely odd thing about Advent, in spite of its reputation as a season of preparation for Christmas, is that its emphasis really does not fall on the coming (Latin, *adventus*) of Jesus as a baby in Bethlehem, but rather on the coming of Jesus as the Judge of all things at the end of all time. The overwhelming presence of John the Baptist in the lectionary in this season drives the point home; his announcement of the imminent arrival of the Messiah comes thirty years after Jesus's birth, and is intended to summon the people to repentance in preparation for Jesus's adult ministry. John does not proclaim Jesus as a captivating infant smiling benevolently at groups of assorted rustics, potentates, and farm animals; instead he cries out, "One is coming after me that is mightier than I. . . . His winnowing fork is in his hand and he will clear his threshing floor, gathering the wheat into his barn and burning up the chaff with unquenchable fire" (Matt. 3:11–12).

If this were not enough evidence, the characteristic liturgical petition of Advent is *Maranatha*—come, Lord Jesus! It is certainly not a prayer for Jesus to come again as a helpless baby; it is the longing cry of God's people for him to return in power and glory, when "every knee will bow and every tongue confess that Jesus Christ is Lord" (Phil. 2:10–11). All but one or two of our Advent hymns—you can look in the front of the hymnal yourself if you don't believe me—are oriented toward the second advent, the second coming of Jesus.[1]

Why do all four Evangelists introduce their Gospels with John the Baptist? What is the purpose of making everyone's hair stand on end during Advent? I've been thinking a good deal about these matters. It has occurred

---

1. This refers to the 1982 Episcopal hymnal.

to me that the image of Jesus as the cosmic Judge who will ultimately come again to put an end to all sin and wickedness forever is not so frightening to the poor and oppressed of the earth as it is to those who have a lot to lose. If your loved one is going to buy you a Christmas present at the Trump Tower, or if you're hoping to receive a miniature Pembroke table for your dollhouse for $3,800 from Neiman Marcus, you might not be so crazy about the idea of Jesus coming back before Santa Claus gets here. Heck, I don't even want him to come back right now, and I'm only getting a Krups dual-automatic coffeemaker! But suppose I were a Christian in prison in the Soviet Union? Suppose I were a black person in South Africa directed to pack up my meager belongings and take them to a so-called homeland that wasn't my home and that wouldn't offer me dignified employment? Suppose I was elderly and handicapped in the South Bronx and had just been robbed and terrorized for the third time? In that case, I might say *Maranatha* (Come, Lord Jesus!), and really mean it.

Even today, John the Baptist's lonely, austere style of life bears witness to a reality that is coming, a reality that will expose all worldly realities, all earthly conditions, all human promises as fraudulent and transitory. His appearance on the scene at this time of year exposes our pretensions for what they really are. Never have we needed him more! For here in this city we are in a culture where a big decision is whether or not to get a face-lift, while around the world people do not know if they will be able to eat or work or worship or see their children grow up.

When John the Baptist—probably the most single-minded person who ever lived—said, "Repent, for the kingdom of heaven is at hand," his whole being, his entire existence, was on fire with the reality of the One Who Comes. He was in the grip of what I've been calling apocalyptic transvision—that vision given to the church that sees through the appearances of this world to the blazing power and holiness of the coming of the Lord. John the Baptist is the ultimate embodiment of the apocalyptic character of Christian faith—faith that is oriented not to the past but to the future, not to the repetition of religious exercises but to the person of the Messiah, not to arrangements as they are but to an utterly new authority and dominion.

In the most extraordinary way, John is truly our contemporary; he stands at the very precipice of the collision of two forces, at the juncture where the world's resistance to God meets the irresistible force of the One who is coming—"the axe is laid to the root of the trees." There he is, and there he will be until the trump sounds, forever summoning us to rethink and reorder our lives totally, orienting ourselves to an altogether new perspective—the perspective of God. Have you recently considered the call to look at ourselves the way God sees us? Does God care if I have a matched set of Gucci luggage? Will God judge me by the degree of recognition given to my name when it appears in the playbill, or on the letterhead, or in the list of trustees and patrons? Will he even judge me by my performance as a mother, or a husband, or a friend, or a neighbor? What will he judge me by?

Repent, for the kingdom of heaven is at hand.

Bear fruit that befits repentance.

Every tree that does not bear good fruit is cut down.

The criterion of judgment is the fruit that is characteristic of repentance. Is there anyone here who needs to be reminded that repentance does not mean just being sorry? Have you ever had the experience of having a person say "I'm sorry" once too often, so that you explode with anger and frustration and say, "I'm sick and tired of hearing that you're sorry! I don't want you to be sorry! I want to see some changed behavior!" Repentance does not mean being sorry. The Greek word *metanoia* means to turn around, to reorient oneself in another direction. It means to receive a new start altogether.

If I am told, over and over, to repent, to change, to orient my life to God, nothing will ever happen. I will cling to the Gucci luggage—not that I could afford it!—and the earthly status symbols more desperately than ever. I don't need to hear exhortations to repent. I need power from outside myself to make me different.

That extraordinary French mathematician and theological thinker Blaise Pascal wrote, "Comfort yourselves. It is not from yourselves that you should expect grace; but, on the contrary, it is in expecting nothing from yourselves, that you must hope for it."[2] Exactly. That is the place where a repentant person takes up his or her position on the frontier of the ages. No previous commitment or identity will have any ultimate meaning; no human ancestry or allegiance, no ranking or claim, will be of any consequence, for, as John the Baptist instructed the religious elite, "Do not presume to say to yourselves, 'We have Abraham as our father'; for I tell you, God is able from these stones to raise up children to Abraham" (Matt. 3:9).

2. Blaise Pascal, *Pensées*, no. 516, available at https://www.gutenberg.org/files/18269/18269-h/18269-h.htm.

Now do you see? A power from outside is coming, a power that is able to make a new creation out of people like us, stones like us, people who have no capacity of ourselves to save ourselves. The power that is coming is not our power—not the power of our deeds, or our inner strength, or our spiritual discipline, or our faith, *or even our repentance.* It is God's power that gives good deeds and inner strength and spiritual discipline and faith and repentance. We are able to repent and bear fruit because he is coming.

We cannot trust any of the powers of this world to make us children of Abraham. We cannot presume to say to ourselves that we have better genes, or better morals, or better theology, or better attitudes, or better humility, or better repentance. It is God who is making children of Abraham—making people new for his kingdom—making them out of stones.

What does it all mean?

It means any number of things. It means that you are being changed and I am being changed. It means that we Christians are going to be weaned away from our possessions and oriented toward being everlastingly possessed by the love of God. It means that we will become less interested in receiving personal blessings for ourselves and more interested in making Christian hope known to those who "sit in darkness." It means that we will become more and more thankful as we become less and less self-righteous. It means that we will gradually become less preoccupied with our own privileges and prerogatives and gradually see ourselves more and more in solidarity with other human beings who, like us, can receive mercy only from the hand of God and not because of any human superiority. These changes have political consequences as well as individual ones. Repentance will mean seeking after the good of all, not just the comforts of a few; and the knowledge of the coming of the Lord means that there will be hope—in the light of his power—of his intervention in the affairs of nations, that the efforts of the peacemakers will somehow, miraculously, be blessed.

I said at the beginning that the Advent spotlight was on John the Baptist—specifically, on his preaching. Now it's time to revise that description. John is the model Christian preacher and witness. By the grace of God alone, all Christian preachers stand in the line of this strange, unattractive man. The spotlight, you see, is not on the preacher. Nor is the spotlight on John. John himself is the spotlight. Have you ever seen a spotlight? Probably not, unless you've been backstage. You don't actually see the spotlight. What you see is the beam of light and the object that is illuminated. John himself disappears; his preaching is the beam, and the light falls upon Jesus only. Yet even this simile fails us, because, as the Fourth Evangelist writes, "There was a man who came from God; his name was John. . . . He himself was not the light; he came only as a witness to the light" (John 1:6, 8).

The witness is from God; the light is from God; the preaching is from God—all for the purpose of revealing Jesus—Emmanuel, God-with-us. This preaching, too, is from God. The preacher is nothing; the Word is everything. Jesus is everything. He comes; he comes at the end of the ages and he comes in the hearts of all human beings who even now relinquish all human claims in the face of the God who is coming in power.

Rejoice!
Rejoice!
Emmanuel shall come to thee, O Israel.

Amen.

The Armor of Light

Trinity Episcopal Church, Hartford, Connecticut
Second Sunday of Advent 2000

PHILIPPIANS 1:6; ROMANS 13:11–14

The city of New Orleans, where I have just spent a week, has a new D-Day museum. It has occasioned a lot of thought. Almost everyone I talked to who had seen it were asking themselves, "Is there anything today that we would die for, the way those young men died on those beaches?" Is anything worth that much to us? That's a good question to ask ourselves, this second Sunday of Advent. What would we die for? I wonder if this strange election season has anything to teach us.

Advent is the season in which we wait to see what God is going to do. At the risk of misunderstanding, we may say that it is the passive season, the wait-and-watch season, the season in which the emphasis is very clearly upon God's action and not our own. The Advent symbol is the watchman who waits all night in his watchtower to see what will happen when the sun comes up. Thus Jesus says, "Watch therefore—for you do not know when the master of the house will come, in the evening, or at midnight, or at cockcrow, or in the morning—lest he come suddenly and find you asleep. And what I say to you I say to all: Watch" (Mark 13:35–37). The fact is that watching and waiting can be active and constructive.

For example, the willingness of the American people to wait, this last month, has been a sign of health in the republic. In fact, the *New York Times* reported yesterday that the only people in the world who didn't seem to be worried about America were the Americans. There has been an upsurge of interest in our political system, signifying a new alertness, a new watchfulness, if you will. Another symbol of Advent is the lighted candle, symbolizing expectation and hope. This is the attitude of the watchman who does not know exactly what will happen or when it will happen, but he knows *that* it will happen.

It is customary to say that the Advent season is one of preparing for the coming of Christ. John the Baptist sounds the call in today's Gospel: "The voice of one crying in the wilderness, Prepare ye the way of the Lord" (Luke 3:4). A renowned theologian wrote, however, that "it is impossible to state too clearly that only the coming Lord Himself can make ready the way for His coming. . . . The end [the goal] of all preparation of the way of Christ must lie precisely in perceiving that we ourselves can never prepare the way."[1] That theologian was Dietrich Bonhoeffer, who knew something about waiting and watching; he spent the last eighteen months of his life in a Nazi prison.

This way of watching has been called the *via negativa*, the negative way, or the dark night of the soul. It means relinquishing, yielding, giving over, making way. Again, although this may sound passive, it really isn't. Bishop Desmond Tutu has spoken about this. He says that during the years of struggle against the cruel system of apartheid in South Africa, he was frequently accused of cowardice, of timidity, of not fighting. He was given strength by God, all those years, not only to continue to be nonviolent himself, but also to persuade many of his own people to be nonviolent in spite of the most dire provocation. During the American civil rights movement, the young black students underwent intense training in nonviolence preparatory to the lunch-counter sit-ins. Their leaders conducted practice sessions where they dumped ketchup on the students, blew smoke in their faces, called them "nigger" and worse. One student protested that he didn't think he could sit there and take it; he wanted to fight back. The leader said, "You are fighting back. Nonviolence is the best way of fighting back." Another student was told, "You are not strong enough to be nonviolent."

It is very interesting that all during this election struggle, many commentators have suggested that the loser will be the winner.[2] There is a vestige of Christian theology here. If one of the candidates steps aside with a noble speech of self-sacrifice for the good of our democracy, that will be a memorable moment in American history. Even the most hardened cynics seem to realize this. The problem is that neither candidate seems willing to take this step, and according to the recent *New York Times* polls, neither party thinks it should be the one to stand aside. The polls show our people to be divided almost equally down the middle, along partisan lines. It is a sobering time. Will there be a sign of God's activity amidst the hurly-burly of legal maneuvering and increasing rancor? Will God raise up leaders who

1. Dietrich Bonhoeffer, *Ethics* (New York: Simon and Schuster, 1955), 140.
2. George W. Bush and Al Gore were deadlocked as the nation waited for a recount.

have the ability to bring us together? We shall see; we will wait, we will watch and pray and hope.

In the meantime, the Christian church has its vocation to consider. Advent, more than any other season of the year, is tuned to Christian life in this world as it is lived between suffering and hope. The note sounded in the hymns, prayers, and readings is one of imminent anticipation. The sudden appearance of John the Baptist out of the desert signals it. Saint Paul captures it in chapter 13 of Romans, a text that has always been closely associated with this season: "You know what hour it is, how it is full time now for you to wake from sleep. For salvation is nearer to us now than when we first believed; the night is far gone, the day is at hand. Let us then cast off the works of darkness and put on the armor of light" (vv. 11–12).

This is the special atmosphere of Advent, a sense that something portentous is approaching us. We are not approaching it. This is not our journey to God but God's journey to us. "The kingdom of God is at hand"; "your redemption is drawing near"; "salvation is nearer to us now than when we first believed"—all these are Advent texts. Something is about to arrive. The hymns of Advent signal it: "Sleepers, wake! A voice astounds us!," "The watchman on the height is crying 'Awake, Jerusalem, arise!,'" "Watchman, tell us of the night, what its signs of promise are," and "Up! Watch in expectation! at midnight comes the cry!" All this comes from Scripture. I think you can feel the urgency, the sense that something or someone is coming. And that, after all, is what the word "advent" means: "coming." Salvation is nearer to us now than it was; the kingdom of God is at hand.

Sometimes you will hear it said that the early church made a mistake, that they thought Jesus was coming back any minute. Now we know they were wrong (it is said), so we really don't need to take these passages seriously, or we interpret them in terms of Christ's presence coming into each human heart. More recently, the church has been willing to rethink this. We realize that people act differently if they are convinced that there will be a definitive future action. A prisoner who knows he will be freed is a very different person from one who knows he will never get out. A group of hostages who know that the SWAT team is on its way is a very different group from the one that has no hope of rescue. If you know that your chemotherapy really might heal you, you can tolerate it a lot better than if it is just a last, desperate measure. Advent is like that. In this season, the church celebrates two things: God has already acted definitively on our behalf, and God will act definitively in the future to bring his purposes to pass once and for all. That is what it means to watch and wait for the second advent of Christ, no matter how long it takes.

So maybe instead of talking about what we would die for, we should be asking what, in light of Christ's coming, we should live for. Not many of us are going to be Dietrich Bonhoeffer or Martin Luther King or Stephen Biko (the South African antiapartheid leader who died in the custody of the state police). For most of us, the call will not be to die, but to live for something. What then is this *armor of light* that Saint Paul writes about?

We find this armor in several places in the New Testament. Here is Ephesians 6: "Be strong in the Lord and in the strength of his might. Put on *the whole armor of God*, that you may be able to stand against the wiles of the devil" (vv. 10–11). And in I Thessalonians, Saint Paul writes, "You are not in darkness, brothers and sisters, for that day to surprise you like a thief. For you are all sons of light, daughters of the day; we are not of the night or of darkness. So then let us not sleep, as others do, but let us keep awake and be sober. . . . Let us . . . put on the breastplate of faith and love, and for a helmet the hope of salvation" (5:4–6, 8).

When I was in New Orleans, I noticed a significant number of red, white, and blue bumper stickers around town. They had just one word on them: "eracism." This was a single word formed out of two words, "erase racism." This was a campaign started by just one person, a woman who owns a local bookstore who wanted to do something about the New Orleans racial problem. She offered herself to the community to help facilitate conversations between blacks and whites, and the bumper stickers are used by citizens as signs of support. Now, I know everybody makes fun of bumper stickers, and for all I know, the whole program may have been a failure as the world counts failure, but if I were an African American, I think it might give me a little boost to see a bumper sticker like that. It would be a lot better than seeing a Confederate flag bumper sticker. My sister, who lives in Columbia, South Carolina, never went on a march for anything in her life—she's not the type to do that—but when the mayor of Charleston led a march to Columbia to protest the flying of the Confederate flag over the state capitol directly across from her church, she joined it for the last mile. Was that a meaningless thing to do? Not in God's economy it wasn't. Little things like bumper stickers and marches might sometimes be part of the armor of light.

We are given courage to put on this armor by God himself. It is his work, not ours. That's what Paul says today in Philippians: "He who began a good work in you will carry it on to completion in the day of Christ Jesus" (1:6). The Prayer Book says that all our works are "begun, continued, and ended" in God.[3]

3. A Collect for Guidance, Book of Common Prayer, p. 832.

God begins good works in us, continues them in us, and will complete them in us. The Christian battle is God's, not ours. This gives us the confidence and boldness to do things that might seem very small but nevertheless have their place in the greater cause.

As a student of the American Revolution, I'm struck by all the little things that were done by "little people" that made a difference: the women called "Molly Pitchers" who brought water to the troops; the innkeeper who told Jack Jouett to go warn Thomas Jefferson; the Marblehead fishermen who rowed George Washington across the Delaware; the woman who threw a piece of her underwear out of the window to muffle the oars of the boat that carried Paul Revere. Those who have enlisted in God's army each have a part to play, a piece of armor to wear, a trust to keep—and there is no task so small that God cannot use it for his great plan.

There was a striking series on television recently—*A Force More Powerful*. It was a chronicle of all the nonviolent resistance movements around the world in the twentieth century. One of its messages was that in a nonviolent battle, everyone can play a part—children, the elderly, disabled people. I have been waiting many years to tell the story of Marie and Joseph Rentall of Ridgewood, Queens. This seems like a good time to tell it. When I first came to New York City to work as one of the clergy staff at Grace Church in Manhattan, one of my greatest privileges was to visit the Rentalls in their home. It took an hour and two subway changes to get out to deepest Queens, and the same to get back, but it was one of the most wonderful experiences you can imagine. Marie and Joseph were not husband and wife, but brother and sister, both in their eighties. She had been a schoolteacher all her life, greatly beloved. She and her brother had lived in the family home in Ridgewood ever since they were born. You could see the love in the family; you felt it off the walls and radiating out of the pictures of the Rentall parents and grandparents. Joseph was developmentally disabled. He had been cared for all his adult life by his sister Marie. The love and devotion between the two of them were something rare to behold. When I visited, I would bring communion, and then afterward Marie would serve a tea that was the equivalent of lunch and dinner put together. Joe would be dressed in a suit, tie, white shirt, and polished shoes. You could tell that Joe had been surrounded by love all his life. It was palpable.

But now here is the point. Marie gave me a Bible verse to carry with me for the rest of my life, and now I am giving it to you. The verse is from I Samuel chapter 30. The context is a victory just won in battle. King David and his forces have wiped up the field with what was left of the Amalekites and the Philistines, and they have taken a great deal of loot. A fierce dispute arose, because some of David's soldiers had fought two battles in two days while others, who were weaker, perhaps wounded and otherwise exhausted, had not been able to fight but one battle. The stronger soldiers did not want to share any of the looted goods with the weaker ones. King David spoke to them in words that Marie Rentall, Spirit-filled reader of the Bible that she was, applied to her brother. She quoted from the King James Version, so I'm going to read that first, and then we'll hear it from a newer translation: "Then said David, Ye shall not do so, my brethren, with that which the Lord hath given us, who hath preserved us, and delivered the company that came against us into our hand. . . . As his part is that goeth down to the battle, so shall his part be that tarrieth by the stuff: they shall part alike. And it was so from that day forward" (I Sam. 30:23–25). And from the Revised Standard Version: "But David said, 'You shall not do so, my brothers, with what the Lord has given us; he has preserved us and given into our hand the band that came against us. . . . For as his share is who goes down into the battle, so shall his share be who stays by the baggage; they shall share alike.' And from that day forward he made it a statute and an ordinance for Israel to this day."

The Word of God! As the apostle writes in the epistle to the Hebrews, it is living and active. It gave life to Joseph and Marie Rentall; it gave life to me; it gives life to you. Beloved people of Trinity Church, you are already wearing a piece of the armor of light because you are committed to staying in the city of Hartford. You are already participating in the Lord's campaign. You have already discovered that when you put on the armor of light you may find yourself alongside a person very different from you—a disabled person, or a poor person, or a person of another ethnic background—but it will be your privilege, it will be your joy. It will be God's sign to you that he himself is preparing the way for the coming Son of God: "For salvation is nearer to us now than when we first believed; the night is far gone, the day is at hand. He who began a good work in you will carry it on to completion in the day of Christ Jesus."

Amen.

Bearing Witness on the Brink
(Advent III)

Advent on the Brink of War

The National Cathedral Church of Saint Peter and Saint Paul,
Washington, DC
Advent III 2002

ISAIAH 64–65

Here is an Advent story. It comes from a recent *New York Times* article about the just-released audiotape from the South Tower of the World Trade Center. The voices of the firefighters are clearly heard. The article describes the calm, professional way that the men were going about their job. It quotes a lot of what they were saying as they climbed from floor to floor, calling for specific tools, calling for more men, describing the conditions in their technical shorthand. The reporter writes, "Nested in the code language of the tape . . . are powerful human dramas." Some of the firefighters, we know, climbed as high as the sky lobby of the South Tower, on the seventy-eighth floor. Scores of people, many of them severely injured, had been stuck there for nearly an hour; those who escaped later described the lobby as "a desolate vista of the dead, the dying, and the trapped." At 9:48 a.m., Fire Chief Orio J. Palmer arrived with men from Ladder Company 15. The reporter asks us to imagine what it must have meant to the people who had been desperately waiting for rescue when they saw before them a fire chief, a fire marshal, and their men. *"In their final two minutes, they could behold the promise of deliverance."*[1]

End of article. At 9:50 a.m., the South Tower collapsed. The voices on the tape were never heard again.

Why is this an Advent story? Because the promise and the deathblow arrived at the same time. The moment of deliverance and the moment of anni-

---

1. Jim Dwyer, "In Rescuers' Voices, Tape Reveals Gripping Histories," *New York Times*, November 12, 2002.

This sermon was preached one year and two months after the 9/11 attacks on the World Trade Center.

hilation are overlaid, like two slides placed one on top of the other so that you see them both at once. The season of Advent is like that. Judgment and mercy arrive at the same time. War and peace are announced by the same voice.

Portions of the prophet Isaiah are always read during Advent. The reading you heard this morning is a message of coming deliverance:

"For behold, I create new heavens and a new earth. . . .
Be glad and rejoice for ever
    in that which I create. . . .
They shall not labor in vain,
    or bear children for calamity;
for they shall be the offspring of the blessed of the Lord,
    and their children with them. . . .
The wolf and the lamb shall feed together. . . .
They shall not hurt or destroy
    in all my holy mountain, says the Lord." (Isa. 65:17–18, 23–25)

It's important to remember, however, that prophetic messages of hope encompass passages of judgment. Indeed, the book of Isaiah ends with judgment. The context for the prophecies of restoration is prophecies of destruction. Or is it the other way round? Let me try to illustrate. We cannot have Isaiah's rhapsodic vision of a new creation without the chapter that goes just before it, a section that is also related to Advent. The people are begging God not to be silent, to show his presence to them—even if it has to be in judgment:

O that thou wouldst rend the heavens and come down . . . !
When thou didst terrible things which we looked not for,
    thou camest down, the mountains quaked at thy presence. . . .
Behold, thou wast angry, and we sinned;
    in our sins we have been a long time, and shall we be saved?
We have all become like one who is unclean,
    and all our righteous deeds are like a polluted garment.
We all fade like a leaf,
    and our iniquities, like the wind, take us away. . . .
    All our pleasant places have become ruins.
Wilt thou restrain thyself at these things, O Lord?
    Wilt thou keep silent, and afflict us sorely?

                         (Isa. 64:1, 3, 5–6, 11–12)

You see what I mean about the overlap of condemnation and mercy? Isaiah laments God's absence in the midst of proclaiming his presence. All the works of the Hebrew prophets are like this; passages of severe judgment are interleaved with passages of divine promise. In some prophets, judgment predominates; others emphasize promise; but all of them in one way or another proclaim this apparent contradiction. The ending of Shakespeare's *King Lear* comes to mind; no play has ever presented a more terrifying spectacle of cosmic judgment, yet there are some who believe that in the very moment of Lear's death, as he holds his daughter's corpse, he sees her resurrection.[2]

The greatness of this season, and the reason some of us cherish it more than any other, is related to its uncompromising view of the human situation. There is some irony in this. Here we are in this spectacular building this morning, surrounded by beauty, reading words of comfort, hearing a message that the warfare of Jerusalem is accomplished. What could be more bitterly ironic than that? There is no peace in Jerusalem today; and it was little more than a year ago that just across the Potomac, the Pentagon was in flames. Now it is widely believed that we are on the brink of a new war.

I've just been reading a new book about Abraham Lincoln's Second Inaugural Address. I recommend this book very highly; the title is easy to remember—*Lincoln's Greatest Speech*.[3] The Second Inaugural is one of the most distinguished works of Christian theology ever written, and I mean that quite seriously. It has this very plain sentence: "And the war came." Lincoln struggled to understand the war for four years, struggled with every fiber of his being. He seems to conclude that "the war came" with an independent life of its own, precisely as a judgment of God on *both South and North*. The book, *Lincoln's Greatest Speech*, shows that Lincoln was addressing a real audience of real people—wounded soldiers, bereaved parents and widows, freed slaves, politicians of every stripe, and the man who would kill him in four weeks—all of whom know that the war is almost over and that the South is going to lose. That's what makes this address so amazing. There is no gloating; there is no bombast; there is no self-righteousness; there are no recriminations. There is no hint that the South is wicked and deserves to be defeated. On the contrary,

---

2. "Look there! Look there!" These words can be, and have been, interpreted in various ways. Many think that Lear was deceived. However, the professor who taught Shakespeare in the honors program in my college many years ago believed that the play ends with cosmic redemption through sacrificial love, with many specific biblical echoes.

3. Ronald C. White, *Lincoln's Greatest Speech* (New York: Simon and Schuster, 2002). This book is featured, with a cover photo of Lincoln, in the most recent issue of *Smithsonian* magazine.

he suggests in his powerful prose that "[God] now wills to remove [the offense of slavery]. . . . He gives to both North and South, this terrible war, as the woe due to those by whom the offense came."[4] Do you see how remarkable this is? "The offense came" by both South *and* North! He calls upon *both* sides to shoulder the blame and to acknowledge that "as was said three thousand years ago, so still it must be said, 'the judgments of the Lord are true and righteous altogether'" (Ps. 19:9).

Four days from now, the second installment of the *Lord of the Rings* movie will hit the theaters. Viggo Mortensen, the actor who plays Aragorn in the *Lord of the Rings* films, was deeply disturbed by the widely popular post-9/11 interpretation of the movie *The Two Towers* as a story of good people and their cause versus evil people and demonic forces, particularly in America after the attacks. He wrote an impassioned preface to the official book concerning the making of the film in which he said that Gandalf, the Elves, and other wise figures in the story were "conscious of good and evil in neighbors, strangers, adversaries, and most important, themselves."[5] Tolkien himself said repeatedly in his personal letters that humanity will always need to be on the lookout for the evil that lies within, undermining any sense of personal righteousness that we might develop as we fight for a cause.

It seems to me that that's a pretty good set of reflections to come out of the entertainment industry. I am not advertising the movie particularly; the book by J. R. R. Tolkien is the thing. It is much clearer in the book that the War of the Ring is a purely defensive war, fought only as a last resort because the enemy has already begun to penetrate and overrun the peaceful lands of Middle-Earth.[6] Our situation with regard to Iraq is not so clear. I do not know what we should do about Iraq. What we do know is that followers of Jesus Christ will always want to remember that the true and righteous judgments of the Lord are applicable to *every* side of every conflict. At yet another funeral in Israel two weeks ago, Benjamin Netanyahu said that we are in the midst of "a war of worlds."[7] Yes, we are—or, if you prefer, a "clash of civilizations"[8]—but if we are following Lincoln's biblical wisdom, we will not be so certain that our

4. Lincoln's syntax is actually more conditional and complex. I have simplified the tenses of the verbs for oral delivery.

5. Viggo Mortensen, introduction to *The Lord of the Rings: The Two Towers—Visual Companion*, by Jude Fisher (Boston: Houghton Mifflin, 2002) (emphasis mine).

6. Two years later, Eerdmans published my book *The Battle for Middle-Earth*.

7. Michael Wines, "Mourners at Israeli Boys' Funeral Lament a Conflict with No Bounds," *New York Times*, December 2, 2002.

8. This now-famous phrase was coined by Samuel Huntington of Harvard.

own side is always unblemished. Our two greatest presidents, Washington and Lincoln, both in their time called America to self-examination, humility, and repentance. It is hard to imagine any president doing that today. It is therefore the vocation of the Christian church to do it. That is what Advent is for. As we read in the first epistle of Peter, "The time has come for judgment to begin with the household of God" (I Pet. 4:17).

Oddly, of all the seasons of the year, Advent preaching is the easiest, at least in my opinion. Why is that? It is because Advent is about a world in darkness, and it is not at all difficult to show that this is a world of darkness, certainly not at this period in our history. Advent is therefore a season in which we help one another to face up to the truth about the human race in general and also the truth about ourselves. Another book has just come out from a well-known war correspondent, Chris Hedges. He writes to remind us of the darkness within ourselves. He writes that his book "is not a call for inaction. It is a call for repentance." "The myth of war is essential to justify the horrible sacrifices required in war, the destruction and the death of innocents. [This myth] can be formed only by denying the reality of war, by turning the lies, the manipulation, the inhumanness of war into the heroic ideal."[9]

Chris Hedges questions the "moral certainty of the state in wartime . . . a dangerous messianic brand of religion, one where self-doubt is minimal." It will be seen right away that Abraham Lincoln in the Second Inaugural categorically rejected this kind of religion and called the nation away from moral certainty about itself toward a future of "malice toward *none*" and "charity for *all*."

Why would God allow such a man to be killed at the moment when the nation, and especially the defeated South, needed him most? That is an Advent question to which there is no answer in this world. Death was at work even as Lincoln spoke; the face of his assassin, John Wilkes Booth, can be seen in the photograph taken on the day of the great speech. We can be certain, however, that Lincoln, had he known, would have repeated the psalm again: "The judgments of the Lord are true and righteous altogether."

9. Chris Hedges, *War Is a Force That Gives Us Meaning* (New York: Public Affairs, 2002), 3, 17. Hedges earned a master of divinity degree from Harvard and is now an ordained Presbyterian minister and visiting lecturer at Princeton University. He was a renowned war correspondent for twenty years. A controversial figure, Hedges has nevertheless won awards for his book *War Is a Force That Gives Us Meaning* (a highly ironical title). He styles himself a "Christian anarchist" of the Dorothy Day school. Another of his books is entitled *I Don't Believe in Atheists*. He teaches a course through Princeton University in which the class is composed of half prisoners and half Princeton undergraduates (He is a lover of the classics and, by the way, does not agree with me about *King Lear*.)

That leads us to the largest question, a question that includes all the other questions. This is the key to the whole enterprise. Looking back at the actor Viggo Mortensen's remarks, admirable as they are, we see that there is something missing in them. *He writes as if there were no God.* He writes as though the "war between worlds" was up to us. In that case, truly, we would indeed "*always* have to contend with destructive impulses in ourselves and others," for without intervention from another sphere of power, there is no way out. The real question for this season, and for every season, is this: *Is there a living God who acts on behalf of his creation?* Is there a righteous God who is working his purposes out in and through the griefs and atrocities of the human drama? Is there a God who can make good on his promise of deliverance in our last hour?

Abraham Lincoln thought so; J. R. R. Tolkien thought so; the prophet Isaiah not only thought so but knew so. How did he know? Was he more gifted, or more spiritual, or more far-seeing than other people? And how can we, here in this congregation today, in the nation's capital, in a time of dire uncertainty, trust what this prophet of Israel says?

That is a matter of faith. The whole prophetic literature of the Bible depends upon the essential, foundational claim *that God has spoken.* The prophets of the exile were no more gifted or spiritual or prescient in themselves than anyone else, but against their own inclinations they had been impressed into the Lord's service, summoned into the presence of God to hear the divine counsel and to bring the Word of the Lord to the people.[10]

And the Word of the Lord said,

"Be glad and rejoice for ever in that which I create. . . .
I will rejoice in Jerusalem,
　　and be glad in my people;
no more shall be heard . . . the sound of weeping
　　and the cry of distress.
No more shall there be . . .
　　an infant that lives but a few days,
　　or an old man who does not fill out his days. . . .

10. We are not being naive here about the authorship of what we have today as the book of Isaiah. In the context of the entire canon, however, "second" and "third" Isaiah clearly stand in the tradition of the first Isaiah, and every one of the Old Testament prophets without exception was commandeered into the Lord's service. *They did not volunteer.* Therefore their words come down to us as the living voice of the living God. See Brevard S. Childs, *The Struggle to Understand Isaiah as Christian Scripture* (Grand Rapids: Eerdmans, 2015).

They shall not hurt or destroy
    in all my holy mountain, says the Lord." (Isa. 65:18–25)

"Every valley shall be exalted, and every mountain and hill made low;
the crooked straight, and the rough places plain.
And the glory of the Lord shall be revealed, and all flesh shall see it
        together,
for the mouth of the Lord has spoken it." (Isa. 40:4–5)

Amen.

The Bottom of the Night

Saint John's Episcopal Church, New Milford, Connecticut
December 15, 2012

PSALM 115

A Sermon for the Ordination of Jack Gilpin in the Third Week of Advent. This sermon and this ordination took place the morning after the massacre of schoolchildren in Newtown, Connecticut, one town over from New Milford.

Follow, poet, follow right
To the bottom of the night.
                    —W. H. Auden, "In Memory of W. B. Yeats"

The moment I heard about the massacre at the Sandy Hook elementary school yesterday, I called Jack. A black midnight pall has been cast over his momentous day, and there is not one person here who does not acknowledge that. As Jack said to me on the phone last night, the problem of how to conduct an ordination in the face of an atrocity in the very next town is as nothing compared to the anguish of the parents and families who have lost their precious little ones. The lament of Jeremiah comes to mind:

> Why is my pain unceasing,
>   my wound incurable,
>   refusing to be healed? (Jer. 15:18)

In the church, this is the season of Advent. It's superficially understood as a time to get ready for Christmas, but in truth it's the season for contemplating the judgment of God. Advent is the season that, *when properly understood*, does not flinch from the darkness that stalks us *all* in this world. Advent begins in the dark and moves toward the light—but the season should not move too quickly or too glibly, lest we fail to acknowledge the depth of the darkness. As our Lord Jesus tells us, unless we see the light of God clearly, what we call light is actually darkness: "how great is that darkness!" (Matt. 6:23). Advent bids us take a fearless inventory of the darkness: the darkness without and the darkness within.

I mentioned something along these lines to Jack, and he said, simply, "This is what I signed on for." He understands that Christian ministry means living with the anguish and the inexplicability of this mortal life, not reaching too quickly for easy answers. The divine light breaks in upon us of its own will, independently of our wishes and desires. We must wait, and that means suffering.

Here is part of what the great poet W. H. Auden wrote about Advent:

Ice condenses on the bone,
Winter completes an age.
. . . .
The evil and armed draw near
The weather smells of their hate
And the houses smell of our fear;
Death has opened his white eye. . . .[1]

And T. S. Eliot writes in the same vein:

The white flat face of Death . . .
And behind the face of Death the Judgement
And behind the Judgement the Void . . .
Emptiness, absence, separation from God.[2]

1. W. H. Auden, "For the Time Being: A Christmas Oratorio," in *The Complete Poetry of W. H. Auden* (New York: Random House, 1945).

2. T. S. Eliot, *Murder in the Cathedral*, in *The Complete Poems and Plays* (New York: Harcourt, Brace and Co., 1952), 210. In the dramatic scene in the cathedral immediately following the lament of the chorus quoted above, Thomas Becket, the soon-to-be martyred archbishop of Canterbury, makes a heroic speech to the priests who are trying to protect him. He declares that his decision to face his murderers is taken "out of time" and that he has "fought the beast" and has (already) "conquered . . . by suffering." Whether this is an accurate depiction of the historical Thomas's historical quarrel with Henry II is not the point here. Eliot has a profound sense of the precarious, temporary nature of human time and the eschatological reality of God's time, a major theme of Advent.

I finished writing this sermon—so I thought—before the calamity at the Sandy Hook school. As you can imagine, I have struggled with the thought that I should write a completely new sermon. Instead, I have made some small but significant adjustments to what I already prepared. This message, ultimately, is about God. In the final analysis, there is no *human* answer whatsoever to the problem of evil. We can only continue to insist upon the reality and power of God in spite of all the evidence to the contrary.

So we turn to Jack Gilpin and his two vocations. I'm sure many of you have seen Jack on television, but my husband and our daughters have had the special privilege of seeing Jack performing on stage (the highest form of acting), always with the greatest delight and admiration. So I'm thinking now about the connection between acting and preaching.

Jack and Anne were prominent among many actors (and would-be actors) who were part of the congregation at Grace Church in New York City in the 1980s and '90s. Some of them, in addition to the Gilpins, were very successful—one appeared several times in important roles on Broadway, one won a Tony, one has continued to appear in Hollywood movies, several still act in regional theaters, and so forth. So, as you can imagine, Scripture readings in the worship services at Grace Church were memorable. However, there was one hurdle that had to be overcome (Jack will remember this). Before the actors became great readers of the Bible, they had to learn to stop acting!

The best way I can explain this is to refer to a passage written by Dietrich Bonhoeffer, the great Christian pastor and theologian who was executed by the Nazis. This is from his book called *Life Together*, and it's about the proper way to read aloud from the Bible. I'd like to read you a paragraph. I hope it will be edifying not only for those who read Scripture but also for those who listen to it being read.

> How shall we read the Scriptures? . . . It will soon become apparent that it is not easy to read the Bible aloud for others. . . . It may be taken as a rule for the right reading of the Scriptures that the reader should never identify himself with the person who is speaking in the Bible. It is not I that am angered, but God; it is not I giving consolation, but God; it is not I admonishing, but God admonishing in the Scriptures. I shall be able, of course, to express the fact that it is God who is angered, who is consoling and admonishing, not by indifferent monotony, but only with inmost concern and rapport, as one who knows that he himself is being addressed. It will make all the difference between right and wrong reading of the Scriptures if I do

not identify myself with God but quite simply serve Him. Otherwise I will become rhetorical, emotional, sentimental . . . or coercive and imperative; that is, I will be directing the listeners' attention to myself instead of to the Word. But this is to commit the worst of sins in presenting the Scriptures.[3]

One of the things that I always noticed about our actors at Grace Church was that when they were just getting started as lay readers, they would emote. They would act out all the roles, including that of God. But as soon as they were given this passage from Bonhoeffer, they immediately—to a person—caught on, and they never made that mistake again. The actors became the best readers we had—not for the reasons you might think, not because they read dramatically or gestured theatrically, but because even when they learned not to act, they knew how to use their voices—and their posture—to communicate. They knew it from their training; but even more, I think they knew it by instinct. Instinct is God-given, and not everyone has it. It's part of what makes a really good actor.

But another aspect of being an actor is being able to take direction. An actor who couldn't take direction would never have a chance. Our actors at Grace Church were very much more ready to take direction from Dietrich Bonhoeffer than many other nonactor readers that I've known, who tended to push back. This reminds me of the story in Luke's Gospel about Jesus and the centurion who had a beloved slave. The slave was sick and at the point of death. The centurion sent friends to tell Jesus that he didn't have to come in person:

> "Lord, . . . I am not worthy to have you come under my roof. . . . Say the word, and let my servant be healed. For I am a man set under authority, with soldiers under me: and I say to one, 'Go,' and he goes; and to another, 'Come,' and he comes; and to my slave, 'Do this,' and he does it." When Jesus heard this he marveled . . . and turned and said to the multitude that followed him, "I tell you, not even in Israel have I found such faith." And when [they] returned to the house, they found the slave well. (Luke 7:6–10)

This is not a story about slavery, or military leadership, or even healing. Rather, it's a story about the power of the word of Jesus, and the authority of the word

---

3. Dietrich Bonhoeffer, *Life Together*, trans. John W. Doberstein (New York: Harper and Row, 1954), 56.

of Jesus. It's a story about faith in Jesus Christ as the very Word of God. Taking direction from the Word of God is the very heart and soul of Christian faith, and certainly the heart and soul of ordination to the Christian ministry.

We have read Psalm 115. Here is the first verse again:

Not to us, O Lord, not to us,
　　but to thy name give glory.

The senior professor of New Testament at Princeton Theological Seminary, Beverly Gaventa, was a student at Union Theological Seminary, where Jack studied, at the same time that I was.[4] When I saw her again at Princeton a few years ago, I asked her what she was working on, and she said she was writing a commentary on the book of Acts. Knowing that Acts has been called "the most disputed book in the New Testament," I asked her somewhat warily, "What approach to Acts will you be taking?" I was thinking of stuff like, is it historically trustworthy? what about its depiction of Paul? what sort of community was it written for? is it Jewish or Hellenistic? what genre is it? and so forth. What's your angle on Acts?

Professor Gaventa said something revolutionary. She said, "It's about God."

It's about God. In other words, the Acts of the Apostles is misnamed. It's not about the actions of the *apostles*. It is about the actions of *God*. Now this may seem obvious to you, but it isn't. More often than not, the Bible isn't taught today as if it were about God. It's taught as a repository of human religious thinking. It's presented as an interesting and important document about human spiritual development. It's treated as a collection of human imaginings about God. But this is precisely what the Bible is *not*. The Bible demands to be understood as the revelation of the one true God who is really God. This doesn't have to be *believed*, of course, but it requires that we hear it the way it means to be heard, whether we believe it or not. It means to be understood as the Word of God. Not the dictated-directly-from-heaven Word, to be sure, but the true and living Word of God nonetheless.

The professor who taught Shakespeare when I was an undergraduate gave me a great gift for which I have been grateful all my life. He taught his students that Shakespeare is vast, colossal, inexhaustible. Shakespeare, he insisted, is

4. After spending most of her academic career at Princeton Theological Seminary, Beverly Gaventa was named as the Distinguished Professor of New Testament at Baylor University.

bigger than any of us, bigger than all of us put together. He instilled in us a respect, indeed a reverence, for Shakespeare's plays, and this evoked a corresponding humility in us. We were assigned various critics to read, but in the end, he used to say, "the critics are all bad"—including himself. The plays were indeed the thing. Only by submitting ourselves to the texts for months and years on end would we ever approach wisdom—by entering the world of the plays, by giving ourselves up to their shaping power, by allowing Shakespeare to reconfigure our horizons and open our eyes to new realms of understanding. This is totally different from the way Shakespeare is taught now. Students are encouraged to think of themselves as competent to interpret the text as they think best before they have allowed the text to have its way with them.

Jack, I don't know much about how you have developed as a biblical interpreter since we were together during those great days at Grace Church when the congregation was full of people who went on to become theologians and professors of Bible and ordained clergy all over the map, in the Grace Church diaspora. I do know this: you have always been in the Lord's sights. I know that you have pursued this course without flinching for many years. After all, you graduated from Union Seminary fifteen years ago. By now you are old enough to play Woodrow Wilson without makeup.[5] We don't know how many years you will have to use your gifts in the service of the Lord's church. But we do know a few things. We know that God is one who calls. Why he calls some and not others we do not know; it is part of his inscrutable will. But the entire biblical enterprise depends on the premise that *God calls* people, and not just ordained people, either. As the psalmist writes, "Our God is in the heavens; he does whatever he pleases."

The first lines of Psalm 115 are the theme of this sermon:

> Not to us, Lord, not to us,
>   but to thy name give glory.

After this the psalmist asks, anxiously,

> Why should the nations say,
>   "Where is their God?"

Where, indeed? Where was God yesterday morning? Why didn't he *do* something? We have to acknowledge that there is no ready answer to that. The ques-

---

5. He was in rehearsal for a play about Wilson at the time, playing the role of Wilson.

tion that Advent asks is, "How long, O Lord?" *How long* before all that is wrong with this world is made right? The lament of Jeremiah continues this way:

> Wilt thou be to me like a deceitful brook,
>> like waters that fail?

Is God deceitful? Has he abandoned us? Indeed, is there a God at all?

The response of Psalm 115 to these questions is not answers. Instead of answers we get revelation, a revelation of the God who alone is powerful, the God who alone creates, the God who alone is able to right wrongs. The psalm mocks all the nongods that human beings worship:

> Their idols are silver and gold,
>> the work of men's hands.
> They have mouths, but do not speak;
>> eyes, but do not see. . . .
> They have hands, but do not feel;
>> feet, but do not walk. (Ps. 115:4-7)

The gods that human beings create and worship have no power. They make false promises that they cannot keep. Instead, the people of God are summoned to faith in the true God:

> O Israel, trust in the Lord!
>> He is [your] help and [your] shield. . . .
> You who fear the Lord, trust in the Lord!
>> He is [your] help and [your] shield. (Ps. 115:9-11)

*   *   *

Jack, will you please rise?

This is your calling: as never before, we need to help our people understand that *it's about God*. This is an age that is drifting further and further away from faith in the God of Abraham, Isaac, and Jacob, further and further away from faith in the God and Father of our Lord Jesus Christ. It's an age that prefers to pretend that it can create its own god. Therefore, when calamity strikes, there is no one home.

In the time that God gives you to lead the people of Saint John's in New Milford, the abundant gifts he has given you will help you to teach that the

God of the Bible is truly God. You will continue to take direction from the Bible, live in the world of the Bible, give yourself up to the shaping power of the Bible, and allow the Bible to continue to reorient your horizons. Thus you and your flock will grow more deeply into trust in the Lord, who is your help and your shield.

There will never be easy answers. Sometimes it will seem that there is no answer at all except what appears to be emptiness, absence. But this is what the servants of God have always known. As one of our Union Seminary professors, Kosuke Koyama, wrote, "Jesus Christ is not a quick answer. If Jesus Christ is the answer he is the answer in the way portrayed in crucifixion."[6]

Where was God yesterday? We see him only in the way Dietrich Bonhoeffer described him, as one who let himself be pushed out of the world onto the cross.[7] But the power that is God's alone is the power that raised the crucified Christ from the tomb. That power is the power that is able, in the words of Saint Paul, "to raise the dead and call into existence the things that do not exist" (Rom. 4:17). That power, Jack Gilpin, is the power poured into you by the Spirit . . . and it is the power poured into the whole church, and that means all those here today to uphold you. And so . . .

> Follow, poet . . . [follow, preacher] . . . follow right
> To the bottom of the night,
> With your unconstraining voice
> Still persuade us to rejoice.[8]

"And to [God] who by the power at work within us is able to do far more abundantly than we can ever ask or imagine, to him be glory in the church and in Christ Jesus to all generations, for ever and ever. Amen" (Eph. 3:20–21).

---

6. Kosuke Koyama, *Mount Fuji and Mount Sinai* (London: SCM, 1984), 241.

7. Dietrich Bonhoeffer, *Letters and Papers from Prison*, enlarged ed. (New York: Macmillan, 1972), 360.

8. W. H. Auden, "In Memory of W. B. Yeats," in *The Complete Poetry of W. H. Auden*, 51.

Grace in a Violent World

All Saints Episcopal Church, Princeton, New Jersey
Third Sunday of Advent 1998

MATTHEW 11:12

There are a lot of things wrong with the Episcopal Church, but one thing we have traditionally done well is Advent. Theologically speaking, Advent is not really the season of preparation for Christmas. It is the season of preparation for the second coming of Christ. The aura of the last days hangs over Advent. John the Baptist is the central personage of the season because he is the unique figure who stands at the juncture of the ages, the one who, even before his conception, was called into being by the divine purpose[1] to declare the apocalyptic arrival of God on the world scene. John is held in utmost reverence by all four Evangelists. He is the last and greatest of the Hebrew prophets, but far more important, he is the first person to belong to the arriving age of the kingdom of God.[2] In the ministry of John the Baptist, the entire prophetic tradition arrives at its goal as he electrifies the people with his proclamation that the time is fulfilled, the day of the Lord is about to dawn, the Messiah is about to appear. "Even now," cried John, "the axe is laid to the root of the trees" (Matt.

---

1. This is told in detail in chapter 1 of Luke's Gospel.
2. The scholarly debate about whether John closes off the Old Testament succession of prophets or belongs entirely to the messianic age is important, but much too complicated to go into here. It is virtually unanimous, however, that he is the unique herald of the dawning age to come, the kingdom of God. Matthew, Mark, and Luke all insist, each in his own way, that John is the promised reappearance of Elijah, the one who would arrive at the end-time to usher in the day of the Lord. It is therefore very important to understand John the Baptist's location as the one who stands on the very edge of God's dawning new day. That is why Jesus says in today's reading, "Among those born of woman there has risen no one greater than John the Baptist." The next part of the saying, "yet the one who is least in the kingdom of God is greater than he," is a challenge to those who hear the message to follow John on the way of Jesus, who refers to his disciples in this Gospel as "little ones" (Robert H. Gundry, *Matthew* [Grand Rapids: Eerdmans, 1994], 209]).

3:10). Everyone knew what that meant. No wonder they all went flocking to the river to be baptized, before the judgment of God came down upon them. The preaching of John carries with it to this very day the urgent sense that the decisive moment is about to happen. This is the mood of Advent. Our second lesson for today, from the epistle of James, reflects this same urgent expectation: "Establish your hearts, for the coming of the Lord is at hand. Do not grumble, brothers and sisters, against one another, that you be not judged, for behold, the Judge is standing at the doors" (James 5:8–9).[3]

The Judge is standing at the doors! Our natural reaction to this is one of extreme discomfort. The most hated man in America right now seems to be Kenneth Starr.[4] Why is this so? Let's think for a moment of the Collect for Purity that we read at the beginning of every Eucharist: "O Lord to whom all hearts are open, all desires known, and from whom no secrets are hid . . ." The person from whom no secrets are hid is, I think, a person whom we are likely to fear and hate. In our present culture, one of the worst things one can be is "judgmental." Mr. Starr seems to epitomize everything that is judgmental: snooping, prying, exposing, condemning. We don't *want* all our desires to be known. We don't *want* to get caught. We want all our secrets to remain hidden. Would we really want to sit through a video of every detail of our personal lives? That would come as no revelation to the God "to whom all hearts are open, all desires known, and from whom no secrets are hid."[5]

Advent is the season for reflection upon these matters. There is more dissonance in the church's message at this time of year than at any other— even more than at Lent, I think, because the contrast between the authentic Christian gospel, on the one hand, and sentimental holiday religiosity on the other is never sharper than during this season. More than any other time in the church's calendar, Advent forces us to look at the dark. Advent is about what the Hank Williams song calls "life's other side"; "Lost love and soiled virtue . . . the road to salvation fraught with the temptations of Satan."[6] In today's lesson this third Sunday of Advent, we meet John the Baptist, not on the banks of the Jordan with adoring multitudes thronging around him, but on death row, in

3. The New Testament epistle of James is not apocalyptic like John the Baptist, but it is noteworthy how it continues to preserve the urgency of the expectation of the Judge precisely as the motivating nerve center for the Christian's ethical conduct, especially toward the poor.

4. Kenneth Starr was the special prosecutor in the matter of President Clinton and Monica Lewinsky. He was widely regarded as obsessively puritanical.

5. Book of Common Prayer, the Collect for Purity.

6. Narration accompanying the Hank Williams song in the sound track of *Family Name*, a film by Macky Alston.

the dungeon of King Herod. As the rector pointed out in his sermon last week, John dared to speak the truth to the powers and principalities. The John who speaks to us today met a violent death at the hands of those worldly powers. This is not a message that one would expect to hear so close to Christmas, and some may find it offensive. Once you get used to Advent, however, you wouldn't want it any other way. It is the very strangeness of Advent that makes it so compelling. It sets before us the contradiction of the Christian gospel. If the kingdom of heaven is at hand, as John the Baptist says, then all our other kingdoms are called radically into question, including my own private kingdom, and yours.

Those who love the special themes of Advent may seem downright perverse to those who do not. Twenty-four years in the ministry tell me that people who don't like to hear about judgment are those who fear it most. Sometimes the people who protest that others are judgmental suffer acutely from the same disease themselves without realizing it. This past Wednesday, that peerless observer of human nature, Francis X. Clines, wrote an article in the *Times* about the impeachment hearings that could serve as an Advent text. The article refers to judgment a couple of dozen times. Sean Wilentz, the Princeton University historian, "unapologetically pronounced judgment on members" of the Judiciary Committee who were in turn sitting in judgment on the president. "History will track you down and condemn you for your cravenness," thundered the professor. Elizabeth Holtzman referred to Mr. Starr as the "Grand Inquisitor." The Reverend Robert Drinan, a former congressman who voted to impeach Nixon twenty-four years ago, accused the Republicans of vindictiveness and "vengeance." "'Did you use the word "vengeance"?' Congressman George Gekas furiously demanded of the priest. Father Drinan said, 'I'll leave it to God to judge that.' The lawmaker shot back, 'Then maybe God's messenger should not prejudge.'"[7] From such little vignettes we learn that casting judgment upon others precisely for being judgmental is an inescapable human trait, and, even more important, we see that the appeal to a bar of judgment—whether it be "history" or "God"—is deeply embedded in the human consciousness.

Much as I admire the Advent lectionary, there is a point at which it, too, flinches from the full strength of the undiluted message, as though the revision committee had finally said to itself, "Too much judgment!" Take for example the passage from James. The lectionary begins with verse 7 and includes only

---

7. Francis X. Clines, "Day of Furious Crossfire," *New York Times*, December 9, 1998. All of this is about President Bill Clinton's lying about his affair with Monica Lewinsky, which dominated the news for months.

three verses. That's a little bit of a cop-out. They could just as easily have begun six verses earlier:

> Come now, you rich, weep and howl for the miseries that are coming upon you. . . . Your gold and silver have rusted, and their rust will be evidence against you and will eat your flesh like fire. You have laid up treasure [of the wrong sort] for the last days. Behold, the wages of the laborers who mowed your fields, which you kept back by fraud, cry out; and the cries of the harvesters have reached the ears of the Lord of hosts. You have lived on the earth in luxury and in pleasure; you have fattened your hearts in a day of slaughter. You have condemned, you have killed the righteous man. (James 5:1–6)

That comes immediately before the reading for today. It puts a rather different face on the saying that *the Judge is standing at the doors*, doesn't it? Do you think it might have any relevance to you and me, here in America, the most prosperous country in the world? What about our migrant workers and our overseas sweatshops and our millions who are without health insurance, while we rush about buying expensive baubles for Christmas? Jesus sent a message to John in prison, "Go and tell John what you see and hear . . . the poor have the good news proclaimed to them." The Messiah has come to place himself squarely on the side of those who are without status or resources in this world, "for theirs is the kingdom of heaven" (Matt. 5:3).

There is another problem with the lectionary today. It stops short of the ending of the Gospel passage. It omits the two last verses. Here are the words of Jesus as we find them in Matthew: "From the days of John the Baptist until now the kingdom of heaven has suffered violence, and men of violence take it by force. For all the prophets and the law prophesied until John; and if you are willing to accept it, he is Elijah who is to come. He who has ears to hear, let him hear" (Matt. 11:12–13).

This verse about violence has had a number of different interpretations. I'm sure there are some Flannery O'Connor fans in the congregation this morning. As you know, she entitled her second novel *The Violent Bear It Away*.[8] She was using the old Catholic Douay Bible, which (mis)translates the verse as follows: "From the days of John the Baptist until now the Kingdom of heaven

---

8. The title of her book proved to be as problematic as is John the Baptist. She was informed that a small-town Georgia bookseller had referred to the book as *The Bear That Ran Away with It*. She herself liked to refer to it as *The Violent Bear*.

arrives violently, and the violent bear it away." "The kingdom of heaven," she wrote, "has to be taken by violence or not at all. You have to push as hard as the age that pushes against you."[9] She also wrote, "my subject in fiction is the action of grace in territory held largely by the devil."[10]

Mistranslation or not, Flannery surely got it right in the essential respects. The violent episodes in her stories are always invasions of God's grace. This present age pushes against us so hard that we cannot resist unless there is some sort of divine raid on our defenses. We are so bent upon having things our own way, the world's way, that we are likely to experience the drastic love of God as foreign. Even John the Baptist was assailed by doubts. He did not understand Jesus's style of warfare. He had expected the advent of God in fire and whirlwind, with God swinging a scythe across the earth, overturning the thrones of the wicked. He had not expected to end up in the wicked king's prison. How could Jesus be the Messiah when he was so lowly, so vulnerable, when his followers were in so much trouble?[11] From his prison, he sent a message to Jesus: "Are you the One who is to come, or should we look for another?"[12] Jesus replied, "Blessed is he who takes no offense at me."

The world will take offense at Jesus. Many will react violently to him and to those who truly follow him. That is why there are ten new statues over the front entrance of Westminster Abbey. They are not statues of kings and queens and prime ministers. They are of Dietrich Bonhoeffer and Martin Luther King and Bishop Oscar Romero and seven other martyrs of the twentieth century who suffered violence for the sake of the kingdom, as John did. This is the contradiction of Advent. As Victor Preller preached to us so unforgettably on Christ the King Sunday, the way of the conquering Messiah is the way of his suffering. Advent tells us that Christmas is not really Christmas if all we are thinking about is a nice little baby. The baby will grow up, and all the violence that the rulers of this world can devise will expend itself upon his broken, bloody, naked body. As Flannery O'Connor wrote, "Grace . . . operates surrounded by evil."[13]

---

9. Flannery O'Connor, *The Habit of Being* (New York: Farrar, Straus and Giroux, 1979), 275, 229.

10. Flannery O'Connor, *Mystery and Manners* (New York: Farrar, Straus and Giroux, 1961), 118.

11. Eduard Schweizer, *The Good News according to Matthew* (Atlanta: John Knox, 1975), 256.

12. *Ho erchomenos*, the One who is to come, is a messianic title ascribed to Jesus in the book of Revelation.

13. O'Connor, *The Habit of Being*, 144.

From the time of John the Baptist until now the kingdom has suffered violence. The shadow of the cross falls across the manger.

Do you sometimes find life hard and disappointing? You are right. Does it sometimes seem to you that the best people are the ones who suffer the most? You are right about that too. This present evil age pushes against us. "The road to salvation is fraught with the temptations of Satan." The devil will not go without a battle. Since the territory is largely held by Satan, the action of grace will often be more like guerrilla warfare than gentle persuasion. Hence the dissonance of Advent and the jarring notes sounded by John the Baptist.

In the last day of God, King Herod and Pontius Pilate are going to be judged. President Clinton is going to be judged. Ken Starr is going to be judged. America is going to be judged, and not just by "history." And listen: you and I are going to be judged. The inmost secrets of our hearts will be disclosed.[14] We are not strong enough or virtuous enough, neither the worst of us nor the best of us, to resist our demons. Well might we fear the judgment, all of us.

But something has happened. John's preaching sets it in motion.[15] With the announcement of John, the world begins to turn on its hinges. The final reckoning is going to take place. And so the Judge of all the universe arrives upon the scene. But it is not as we thought. The face of the Judge is marked with infinite suffering. His hands and feet are torn by spikes driven in by violent blows. His brow, pierced by the crown of thorns, bears the tokens of utmost humiliation. The judgment has already happened. It has taken place in his own body. The Son of God has borne it all himself. The Judge who is to come has given himself to be judged in our place "to save us all from Satan's power when we were gone astray."[16]

The news of judgment and the news of salvation arrive at the same time. That is precisely what the prophet Isaiah proclaims in our first reading for this third Sunday of Advent. The bad news and the good news arrive at the same time, and there can be no doubt as to which one is victorious over the other: "Strengthen the weak hands, and make firm the feeble knees. Say to those who are of a fearful heart, 'Be strong, fear not! Behold, your God will come *with vengeance, with the recompense of God. He will come and save you.*'"

Amen.

14. This phrase appeared in the marriage service in the Book of Common Prayer until 1976.

15. Jesus himself says that John the Baptist is Elijah. Everyone knew that the reappearance of Elijah meant that the end-time had arrived. After Elijah, there is no one left to appear except God.

16. From "God Rest Ye Merry, Gentlemen," traditional eighteenth-century English Christmas carol.

A Better Bet

Grace Church, New York City
Third Sunday of Advent 1994

HABAKKUK 1:2, 13; 2:1, 4; LUKE 3:1–2; ROMANS 1:16–17

Welcome to our Sunday morning worship service this third Sunday in Advent! In a typical congregation at Grace Church during the Advent season, I would imagine that about half of you are accustomed to the peculiar themes of Advent and half of you are not. If the preacher starts talking about wickedness and judgment and hopelessness, half of you will smile knowingly to yourselves and think, "Oh, good, it's Advent again," and half of you will be wondering what in the world is going on in this church so close to Christmas, and where are the poinsettias? Well, this message is addressed to both halves of you today, whichever one you belong to. One of the distinctive things about the Episcopal Church is that we don't observe Christmas until it gets here. This is a great thing, once you get used to it. Advent is the time for getting ready for Christmas in the truest sense.

Advent is the time for meditating upon the condition of the lost world and the lost people in it, the same world that received its Lord and King two thousand years ago. It is the time for looking with unblinking eyes at the evil around us, just as our old friend John the Baptist, the main man of Advent, looks unblinkingly at the crowds of people who come to him as to a guru in California, and calls them a brood of vipers who had better flee from the wrath to come. The gurus in California, not to mention the Tarot card readers and psychics over in the Village, are not likely to say that, are they? They know as well as the next person that a message of judgment is not happily received. But we aren't asked to receive the message of John the Baptist in individual isolation. The great wisdom of the Advent season immediately preceding Christmas is that we are invited all together to prepare ourselves for the Lord's coming by gathering intentionally as a community to hear the truths about the human condition that are hard to bear. This is our corporate task this Advent season, and our privilege—to listen for these truths in the context of our faith.

You never know where you might see an Advent message. Last week I found one in an unlikely spot, in that magazine devoted mostly to the celebration of celebrity, *Vanity Fair*. Annie Leibovitz, in between photo sessions with David Geffen, Steven Spielberg, and O. J. Simpson's defense attorney, went to Rwanda to take pictures inside the bloody churches where hundreds of people were massacred. Sandwiching these photos in between stories about models and movie stars seems a tasteless enterprise, but the words accompanying the photos gave them their proper content. The article, written by David Rieff (Susan Sontag's son), is entitled "God and Man in Rwanda." (Mr. Rieff uses the politically incorrect generic term "man." I shall follow his lead throughout.) It begins like this: "The story goes that a French priest in Rwanda who had survived the massacres of the spring of 1994 was asked whether his experiences had shaken his faith in God. 'Absolutely not,' he replied. 'But,' he added matter-of-factly, 'what happened in this country has destroyed my faith in mankind forever.' . . . In Rwanda these days, even an atheist has a hard time pushing away the thought that God is a better bet than man."[1]

In Advent, more than any other season of the Christian year, the prophets of ancient Israel come into their own. Their theme is the judgment of God upon the wickedness of the human race. The prophets knew exactly what that French priest was talking about. They, too, had lost their faith in mankind. They had no hope in human progress. They did not see any improvement in people's behavior. Everywhere they looked there were signs that human nature seemed to be irredeemably corrupt. They preached, they pleaded, they threatened, they cajoled, they wept for the people's sins, and still the children of Israel were unresponsive and unrepentant. Where was God in this situation? The prophets could not imagine how there could be anything ahead for the people except abandonment and condemnation, otherwise known as the wrath of God. The Requiem Mass from the early Middle Ages contained a section called the *Dies Irae* (the wrath of God), from the prophet Zephaniah:

> A day of wrath is that day,
> > a day of distress and anguish,
> > a day of darkness and gloom. (Zeph. 1:15)

1. David Rieff, "God and Man in Rwanda," *Vanity Fair*, December 1994.

It has been set to music by no less than Mozart and Verdi, among others. No one would want to have the *Dies Irae* sung at their funerals today![2]

The great poets have not been as afraid to talk about the wrath of God as we are. Think, for instance, of Robert Frost and Emily Dickinson, both of whom can be (and have been) read as though they were treacly nature poets, when in fact their subjects are the terrible things in life. Advent is the time for thinking in the biblical language of Emily Dickinson, who wrote, "I saw no Way—The Heavens were stitched."[3] This poet imagines herself as

> A Crescent in the Sea—
> With Midnight to the North of Her—
> And Midnight to the South of Her—
> And Maelstrom—in the Sky.[4]

These fearsome images have their counterparts in the prophetic and apocalyptic portions of Scripture that are so central to the Advent season. Overarching all these thematic passages is the sense that even God's wrath would be preferable to God's absence. Miss Dickinson again:

> Of Course—I prayed.
> And did God Care?
> He cared as much as on the Air
> A Bird—had stamped her foot.[5]

She calls him "a God of Flint"[6] and writes,

> I know that He exists.
> Somewhere—in Silence—
> He has hid his rare life
> From our gross eyes.[7]

2. For a portion of the text of the *Dies Irae*, see above, the sermon "Silver and Gold on the Last Day."

3. Emily Dickinson, "I Saw No Way—the Heavens Were Stitched," in *Complete Poems of Emily Dickinson*, #378.

4. Emily Dickinson, "Behind Me—Dips Eternity," in *Complete Poems of Emily Dickinson*, #721.

5. Emily Dickinson, "Of Course—I Prayed," in *Complete Poems of Emily Dickinson*, #376.

6. The phrase occurs in Emily Dickinson, "Just Once! Oh Least Request," in *Complete Poems of Emily Dickinson*, #1076.

7. Emily Dickinson, "I Know That He Exists," in *Complete Poems of Emily Dickinson*, #338.

W. H. Auden, the poet of Advent par excellence, writes at the outset of his *Christmas Oratorio,*

> We are afraid of pain but more afraid of silence; for no nightmare
> Of hostile objects could be as dreadful as this Void.
> This is the Abomination. This is the Wrath of God.[8]

Advent is a season for looking more deeply into the questions of existence than we do at any other time. Here is Robert Frost's poem "Desert Places":

> They cannot scare me with their empty spaces
> between stars—on stars where no human race is.
> I have it in me so much nearer home
> To scare myself with my own desert places.[9]

For a long time now, this congregation has been known for its willingness to face up to these hard matters. It is a form of repentance to do so. The Lord has seen fit to give us this high privilege and this solemn responsibility. Many of us lost our faith in mankind a long time ago. In Advent, where faith in mankind comes to an end, the message of Christmas begins. When there is no Way from here to eternity because the heavens are stitched, that is the time when the prophets of Israel begin to speak.

There are two little prophetic books, very short, next to each other in the Old Testament. Both are associated with Advent. The source of the *Dies Irae* passage is Zephaniah. The other book is that of Habakkuk. This prophet lays it on the line with the Lord:

> Lord, how long shall I cry for help,
>   and thou wilt not hear?
> Or cry to thee "Violence!"
>   and thou wilt not save? . . .
> [Why] art [thou] silent when the wicked swallows up
>   the man more righteous than he? . . .
> I will take my stand to watch,

---

8. W. H. Auden, "For the Time Being: A Christmas Oratorio," in *The Collected Poetry of W. H. Auden* (Random House, 1945), 411.

9. Robert Frost, "Desert Places," in *Complete Poems of Robert Frost* (New York: Holt, 1949), 386. Frost is responding to Pascal here ("The infinite spaces frighten me").

and station myself on the tower,
and look forth to see what [the Lord] will say to me. (Hab. 1:2, 13; 2:1)

You'll recognize in these lines the Advent image of the watchman who, recognizing that there are no human answers to his questions, stations himself on the frontier to watch for the coming of the Lord. Against all human expectation, the prophet announces that the Lord is about to break his silence.

At this point I bring against myself the charge implicit in David Rieff's words, "In Rwanda these days, even an atheist has a hard time pushing away the thought that God is a better bet than man." Is this the reason that I believe in God, because I have come to the end of my tether and cannot bear to face the truth about God's absence?

This has been my year to deal with the strongest challenges to my faith that I have ever had to face. I didn't plan it that way; it just happened. Last spring I read Freud's *The Future of an Illusion*, which is the most powerful argument against religious faith that I know. This past week I read something else. In the latest copy of the *New York Review of Books*, there is an essay-review from the pen of the illustrious professor of classical literature at Oxford and fellow of ultra-elite Balliol College, Jasper Griffin.[10] He writes a brilliant assessment and critique of the apocalyptic literature that Jim Kay and I are teaching on Sunday mornings at ten. Though its tone is withering, it's a scintillating exercise in intellectual rigor and, as such, commands attention. His conclusion is that the ancient Hebrews and early Christians, while deserving admiration for their tenacity and imagination, ultimately prove themselves to be on a fool's errand, having invented the story of salvation and the resurrection of the dead in order to preserve the notion of an all-powerful, redeeming God who will come in spite of a massive accumulation of evidence to the contrary. At the time of the Babylonian exile, "the devout were driven into a corner," he writes. "Earthly prospects looked uniformly dark." In response, Professor Griffin continues, the Hebrew prophets come up with their "touchingly transparent piece[s] of wish-fulfillment." Touchingly transparent! This sort of patronizing comment from a major intellectual is much more devastating than outright scorn. I wrote in the margin, "Who can go on believing after reading this?"

10. Jasper Griffin, "New Heaven, New Earth," *New York Review of Books*, December 22, 1994.

Listen to the words of Zephaniah that follow the *Dies Irae* passage, and ask yourself what evidence the prophet could possibly have for making these audacious promises:

> Sing aloud, O daughter of Zion;
>   Shout, O Israel!
> Rejoice and exult with all your heart,
>   O daughter of Jerusalem!
> The Lord has taken away the judgments against you,
>   he has cast out your enemies.
> The King of Israel, the Lord, is in your midst;
>   you shall fear evil no more. (Zeph. 3:14–15)

The passage is beautiful, and much admired, but how can it be true? There is not a shred of evidence, only wishful thinking, isn't that so?

When Habakkuk goes up into his metaphorical watchtower, the answer of the Lord comes to him: "The righteous shall live by faith." Do you recognize that? This text has had a second life in the church, of incalculable importance, having been picked up by Saint Paul in the epistle to the Romans. But what sort of answer is this to the questions about the intractable wickedness of the human heart and the apparent absence of God, which is the theme lying at the heart of the Advent season? Is faith ultimately nothing more than a human strategy for coming to terms with the meaninglessness of existence? Is that something to live by? Why not choose the truly courageous human stance of the Stoics, who at their best advocated living with unflinching moral courage and dying with consummate serenity—or committing suicide at the end as an act of ultimate self-affirmation in the face of an implacable destiny?[11]

Christian faith says something very opposite to this, but are we just deluded? Are we just willing victims of an illusion, perpetrators of the most imaginative piece of wish-fulfillment that the world has ever seen?

It is in the face of just such accusations that Saint Paul planted his feet squarely in the midst of the intellectuals of Athens and the mystagogues of Corinth and the imperial might of Rome and said, "I am not ashamed of the

11. My revered professor of English literature at Sweet Briar College, Lawrence Nelson, always said that Stoicism was the only system of belief to rival Christianity. I have never found any reason to disagree with that. It's better by degrees of magnitude than Christianity's other rival, gnosticism. Unfortunately, gnosticism will always be wildly popular whereas Stoicism is for the very few and the very elite.

gospel; it is the power of god for salvation to those who have faith, to the Jew first and also to the Greek. . . . *For it is written, 'He who through faith is righteous shall live'*" (Rom. 1:16–17). See how Paul takes Habakkuk and makes it the heart of the gospel?

Where does this kind of confidence come from? Where does this kind of faith come from? Even in America, one of the most religious countries in the world, it is getting harder and harder not to be embarrassed to believe in God simply because he is a better bet than man. We are not talking here about the kind of faith in God that gets politicians elected. We are talking about the real thing, the kind of faith that changes lives and creates a new situation. In the face of death, Christians talk about resurrection. In the face of evil, Christians go on trusting in God. In the face of scorn, Christians are not ashamed of the gospel. Why not? I have asked myself these questions a thousand times.

I hope that what I say next will surprise you a little bit. I believe in the gospel because of words like these: "And it came to pass in those days, that there went out a decree from Caesar Augustus, that all the world should be taxed" (Luke 2:1), and because of words like these: "Now in the fifteenth year of the reign of Tiberius Caesar, Pontius Pilate being governor of Judea, and Herod being tetrarch of Galilee, and his brother Philip tetrarch of Iturea and of the region of Trachonitis, and Lysanias the tetrarch of Abilene, Annas and Caiaphas being the high priests, the word of God came unto John [the Baptist] the son of Zacharias in the wilderness" (Luke 3:1–2).

It's not important that Luke got some of these details wrong. What's important is that Jesus of Nazareth was a historical person who lived in a specific time in a specific place under specific governors and officials whose names we know. In the ancient Near East, at the time we are talking about, dying and rising gods were a dime a dozen. They died and rose again all the time. Every time the green shoots came pushing out of the earth in the spring, here came Osiris and Tammuz and Adonis and Attis. Now *that's* wishful thinking for you.

Jesus was different. There are a thousand arguments against believing he was the uniquely begotten Son of God, and there are a thousand reasons not to believe that he was raised from the dead, but none of them is convincing to Christian faith. Who could have made Jesus up? Who could have invented the resurrection of a man who was "crucified under Pontius Pilate"? The idea of a resurrection is preposterous enough, but not as preposterous as the idea of a crucified Messiah. To believe that it is all illusory, you have to believe that resurrection was a tidy idea invented by the disciples of a crucified man so that they could go out and meet their deaths proclaiming him to the entire world. People who believe that will believe anything; they will even believe that mankind is inherently good and progressing nearer and nearer to perfection every day. You will see that I am turning the tables on the skeptics here, because I am not ashamed of the gospel; it is the power of God for salvation.

Look. You and I are probably not going to win any arguments with our sophisticated friends about this. I spend a good deal of my time trying to convince the unconvinced. Very possibly none of them will ever change their minds. But that's not my responsibility. That's up to God. My responsibility and yours, my vocation and yours, is to bear witness. God is a better bet than man.

There *is* a message of God's wrath, yes; but God's wrath is far better than God's absence. In the first epistle of Peter we read, "The time has come for judgment to begin with the household of God" (4:17), and that means that you and I are to step forward and be first in line, on behalf of the whole world. If this were not so, our faith would truly be monstrous, because it would be the self-identified good people (us) setting ourselves up against the people of whom we do not approve. In that case, Jasper Griffin would be right to accuse us. But he has misunderstood. The Christian faith has not been invented in order for us to claim for ourselves a powerful God who will push the delete button on all our enemies. The Christian faith is, rather, grounded in the story of that One who, against all human reason, emptied himself of his glory and came into our desert places, midnight to the north of him and midnight to the south of him, to stand under the wrath of God in place of the murderers of Rwanda and us sinners inside these four walls today. He has not "hid his rare life from our gross eyes." "No one has ever seen God; the only Son, who is in the bosom of the Father, he has made him known" (John 1:18).

If it were not for the crucifixion of Jesus, I for one could not continue. The cross is the sign that God has not remained silent when "the wicked swallows up / the man more righteous than he." For Jesus, the man more righteous, gave *himself* to be swallowed up instead of the wicked, and in so doing, has won the victory over all our desert places. Where faith in mankind comes to an end, the message of Christmas begins. W. H. Auden says it for us. The same poet who begins in Advent with the wrath of God concludes on Christmas Day:

. . . After today,
The children of men
May be certain that
The Father Abyss
Is affectionate
To all its creatures.
All, all, all of them.
Run to Bethlehem.[12]

12. Auden, "For the Time Being," 441.

Beyond the Valley of Ashes

Christ Church, Greenwich, Connecticut
Third Sunday of Advent 1999

ISAIAH 40:3–4; LUKE 1:13, 16–17

A new opera based on F. Scott Fitzgerald's *The Great Gatsby* opens at the Met this week. Reading various articles about it got me thinking about the famous last sentence of that celebrated novel: "So we beat on, boats against the current, borne back ceaselessly into the past." As always with great fiction writing, there is a world of suggestion here, much more than I can grasp, but going back a few sentences we do find clues. We read that the future, "year by year recedes before us," and that Jay Gatsby's dream is "already behind him." As I reread these pages, I felt the tension and undertow of the Advent themes. Advent is a season in which the past and the future seem to collide with one another. No other time of the church year presents us with so much contradiction. I'm not thinking so much of the contrast between the shopping mega-frenzy and the church's summons to hushed reverence. Rather, on this particular morning of Advent lessons and carols, I am thinking of the tension between looking back and looking forward, and above all the question, *looking forward to what?*

The closer we get to Christmas, the more tempted we are to retreat to the cozy, imagined world of our childhood. "I'm dreaming of a white Christmas, just like the ones I used to know." Just like the ones I used to know—those are the operative words. The suggestion is that the dream is behind us; the way to happiness is to return to that idealized past. Sentiment and nostalgia play a major role in our Christmas observances. We bring out the ornaments we loved as children, we display little nineteenth-century towns with snow-covered roofs, we collect figures of carolers dressed in the style of Dickens's London. There is nothing wrong with this—I do some of it myself—but it does illustrate

---

This is a slightly revised version of a sermon previously published in *Help My Unbelief* (Grand Rapids: Eerdmans, 1998).

our tendency to romanticize the past. Popular Christmas music is popular precisely because it trades on this basic human tendency to sentimentalize. "Have yourself a merry little Christmas," goes the song, evoking the "olden days, happy golden days of yore."

Advent is exactly the opposite of all this. Nostalgia and sentiment play no part in the season. There were no golden days of yore. Advent refuses to dwell in a past that never was. Advent is about the future. It isn't a season of remembering something that happened a long time ago; it is a season of preparation for the great coming day of the kingdom of God. I went through the Advent section of our Episcopal hymnal to make sure I hadn't made a mistake. There are twenty-four hymns in the Advent section. Twenty-three of them are about the second coming of Christ.[1] The one we just sang is by Charles Wesley, one of the greatest hymn writers of all time. "Come, thou long expected Jesus," it begins. The proximity of Advent to Christmas leads us to think this means Jesus's coming as a baby. But the hymn ends:

> By thine own eternal Spirit
> Rule in all our hearts alone;
> By thine all-sufficient merit
> Raise us to thy glorious throne.

The hymn doesn't take us back in time to pretend we are first-century Jews waiting for a Messiah who has not yet shown up. Advent, more than any other season of the church year, looks forward to the *return* of the one who was

> . . . born a child, and yet a king;
> Born to reign in us for ever
> Now thy gracious kingdom bring.

You will notice this when we sing our last hymn today, "O Come, O Come, Emmanuel." This venerable hymn is not about a baby in a manger. It is an extended eight-part prayer about an event still in the future.[2]

---

1. Hymn #69 in the 1982 Episcopal hymnal, "What Is the Crying at Jordan?," is a twentieth-century carol focused on the coming of the living Christ in the present, but its words are classic Advent: "Dark is the season, dark our hearts, and shut to mystery." It was written by an established poet, Carol Christopher Drake (b. 1933). One of her poems, "Immigrant" (1956), can be found at Poetry Foundation, https://www.poetryfoundation.org/poetrymagazine/browse?contentId=27143.

2. The original Latin text of *Veni Emmanuel* can be traced definitively from at least the

O come, Desire of Nations, bind
in one the hearts of all mankind;
Bid thou our sad divisions cease,
and be thyself our King of Peace.

These are the works of the last day. Peace in the world as we know it is only hints and suggestions of the true peace in the world to come.

Here again, though, we are capable of deceiving ourselves endlessly. There are many strange things going on around the world in the name of peace. Last Sunday an article in the *New York Times* described some truly bizarre scenes in the little Palestinian city of Bethlehem as it prepares for the new millennium. The Palestinian Muslim leader Yasir Arafat has cleverly commandeered the event, staging a big rally in Manger Square, proclaiming Bethlehem as "the city of Jesus, the city where it all began," and concluding, "in the name of God, in the name of Palestine, I declare open the celebrations of the third millennium." A Peace Center has just opened in Manger Square; a local man said to a reporter that peace, for him, was "the Palestinian flag in the square and the Israelis gone."[3] In another context, it could just as well have been an Israeli speaking; the point is that peace, in this world, is often a euphemism meaning that the enemy has been displaced. This is not peace.

The Kosovars are now in the process of doing to the Serbs what the Serbs did to them; it will mean a Serb-free Kosovo, but it doesn't mean peace. Just because people have withdrawn into gated communities doesn't mean peace. Cleaning all the homelessness off the streets doesn't mean peace. Recently I visited a church so split by the issue of homeless people that people literally won't sit down and talk to each other. Right here in Greenwich people are fighting about the disposal of compost. The world-transforming peace that the angel declared to the shepherds is found only in bits and fragments now. Its eternal fulfillment is to be found only in the future of God.

We are mistaken to look for peace behind us, in an idealized past. As Scott Fitzgerald shows with such artistry in his novel, the past is a destroy-

---

ninth century, but is likely to be much earlier. Its ascriptions and petitions are sometimes referred to as the Great "O" Antiphons of Advent. Each verse is based on an Old Testament image of the coming Messiah. The Latin text as we know it today(in English translation) is much more recent. It first appeared in the eighteenth century in the Psalteriolum Cantionnum Catholicarum (Cologne, 1710). For more information, refer to the Advent liturgy at the end of this volume.

3. Deborah Sontag, "Eager Palestinians Seek New Millennium's Fruits," *New York Times*, December 5, 1999.

ing current, ready to swallow us up in futility. The reader is drawn into the radiant atmosphere of the novel, only to see it collapse upon itself. The symbolism of light and darkness, so central to the Advent season, is in play throughout the story. The dream world of Jay Gatsby is a world of light. Fitzgerald's book is celebrated for its glowing images of Gatsby's illuminated house, lawns, and garden. It is all deeply ironic, for immediately adjoining the mansion and bay on Long Island Sound is a valley of ashes where nothing can grow, an image of our illusions and their ultimate end, the place where Gatsby's dream dies. Similarly, we humans try to create artificial worlds of light at Christmas, hoping to stave off the darkness. Advent summons us to do exactly the opposite: to renounce the easy consolations of artificial light in order to recognize the Coming One, who said, "I am the Light of the world" (John 8:12).

I hope you understand that I am not saying don't have a Christmas tree. The Rutledge family loves our Christmas tree. The evergreen tree is not such a bad symbol of the living hope we have in Christ. Even in the very midst of the Christmas story itself, however, the expectation of the *second* coming is dominant. Let us listen again to the words spoken by the two angels in the readings that you just heard this morning. The first is the announcement of the birth of John the Baptist:

> The angel said to him, "Do not be afraid, Zechariah, for your prayer is heard, and your wife Elizabeth will bear you a son, and you shall call his name John. . . .
>
> > And he will turn many of the children of Israel to the Lord
> > > their God,
> > and he will go before him in the spirit and power of Elijah,
> > to turn the hearts of the fathers to the children,
> > and the disobedient to the wisdom of the just,
> > to make ready for the Lord a people prepared."
> > > > (Luke 1:13, 16–17)

If you know your Bible, you will recognize these references to Elijah and the turning of the hearts of the children to the parents as the last words of the Old Testament, the final section of the prophet Malachi, where *the focus is entirely on the future coming* of the Lord, the event to end all events. Charles Wesley has wonderfully incorporated portions of Malachi into his beloved Christmas hymn "Hark! The Herald Angels Sing":

Hail the heaven-born Prince of Peace,
Hail, the Sun of righteousness;
Light and life to all he brings,
Risen with healing in his wings.

We think of these as Christmas words, but because they are from Malachi, they are more closely related to Advent and to the second coming. Similarly, the angel Gabriel speaks to Mary:

"Do not be afraid, Mary, for you have found favor with God. And behold, you will conceive in your womb and bear a son, and you shall call his name Jesus.

He will be great, and will be called the Son of the Most High;
and the Lord God will give to him the throne of his father
David . . .
and of his kingdom there will be no end." (Luke 1:30–33)

These words are familiar to us and we associate them with the nativity, but if we take another look, we will see that they are not about an infant at all, but an adult King, one whose kingdom lies still in the future.

Some of you here today are young: you are Jay Gatsby's age. Your dreams are still alive. God rest you merry, and I mean that with all sincerity. Others of you are middle-aged but perhaps still deceived into thinking that it doesn't get any better than the good life in Greenwich, Connecticut. More power to you too. Sooner or later, though, every person here in this church today will find himself or herself following one of two interpretations of life. Either you will come to a point where it will be clear to you that life is full of disappointment, or you will settle into a pattern of denial, bluster, and false optimism. These latter manifestations belong to the world of the past. They may appear to give light, for you can fool yourself and others for quite a while, but in fact they are the "works of darkness." In the world of denial and illusion, the future "year by year recedes before us." We are "borne back ceaselessly into the past" where we can only brood over the loss of a childhood that never was.

What then? In such a wilderness, what rescue? Out of such a past, what hope of the future? Listen again to the words of the prophet Isaiah:

"In the wilderness prepare ye the way of the Lord,
    make straight in the desert a highway for our God.

Every valley shall be lifted up,
  and every mountain and hill be made low;
the uneven ground shall become level,
  and the rough places a plain.
And the glory of the Lord shall be revealed,
  and all flesh shall see it together,
  for the mouth of the Lord has spoken." (Isa. 40:3–5)

Here is the forward thrust of Advent, the countervailing motion that lifts the boats clear, the heralding announcement of the arriving God. The note that is struck is sounded from the future. We are not looking backward sentimentally to a baby; we are looking forward to the only One in whom the promise of peace will some day be fulfilled. Trusting in that promise, we can do things we thought we could not do. Relying on him, we can change our habits, confront our addictions, forgive our enemies, curb our spending, challenge our society, raise our pledge, lower our defenses, stand up for justice, speak the truth—not all of these things at once, to be sure, but *even one* break from past patterns of sin will be in its way a sign of Christ's coming. Because God is out ahead of us, we know that the cover-ups, the denials, the lies and frauds and pretenses are part of the old world that is passing away. We are not trapped in our mistakes and delusions. God is enlisting us on the side of his future.

Listen to the first lines of the Advent hymns: "Hark, a thrilling voice is sounding!"; "Lo, he comes, with clouds descending!"; "Sleepers, wake! a voice astounds us!"; "Rejoice, rejoice, believers!" As the electrifying message reaches our ears, we recognize that we are hearing something entirely new in religion. God is on the move toward us, not the other way round. In the very midst of our confusion and incapacity, we are met by the oncoming Lord. In our valley of ashes, we are seized by hope. In the graveyard of dreams, the Holy Spirit breathes life from the dead. In the place where illusions die, the Sun rises upon us, and *of his kingdom there will be no end.*

Emmanuel shall come to thee, O Israel.

Amen.

Waiting for the Dayspring

Saint Matthew's Episcopal Church, Bedford, New York
Third Sunday of Advent 2005

LUKE 1:76–79

Last week I went to visit a friend who is in the very early stages of Alzheimer's disease. She is still perfectly lucid and able to express herself. She said both her parents had had the terrible affliction and she was reconciled to it. Her biggest problem, she said, was her husband's attitude. She said, "You know Steve. Things have worked out for him in his life. He has had everything pretty much the way he wanted it. Now he's faced with something that isn't what he wanted. He gets really angry now. That never used to happen."

That's an Advent story. Here is a sermon text to go with it. This is from the first chapter of Luke's Gospel, the canticle called the Benedictus, the song of Zechariah. Zechariah was the father of John the Baptist, and this is his welcome to his baby son: "Thou, child, shalt be called the prophet of the Highest: for thou shalt go before the face of the Lord to prepare his ways; To give knowledge of salvation . . . whereby the dayspring from on high hath visited us, To give light to them that sit in darkness and in the shadow of death" (Luke 1:76–79 KJV).

Every year in Advent, John the Baptist gets two whole Sundays to himself. He has music composed for him, too. Today's anthem is commonly used on the second or third Sunday in Advent: it is a setting of a passage from John's Gospel.[1] John the Baptist testifies, "I am not the Messiah. . . . I have been sent before him. . . . He must increase, but I must decrease" (John 3:28–30). The

---

1. The anthem, familiar to many Episcopalians in recent years, is "The Record of John," by Orlando Gibbons (1583–1625), and the words are from the interrogation of John the Baptist in John 1:19–20. In this passage John refuses three times to accept a high title for himself (John 1:19–21). "They said to him then, 'Who are you? Let us have an answer for those who sent us. What do you say about yourself?'" John quotes from Isaiah: "I am the voice of one crying in the wilderness, 'Make straight the way of the Lord'" (1:22–23).

prophet's whole life was dedicated to the purpose of disappearing into the light of the One Who Is to Come.[2] Many of us who are called to preach have taken John the Baptist as our patron saint. He said, *"I am a voice."* A voice: that is all. Nothing more. The preacher likewise hopes to disappear into the Word of God, to become a voice testifying to the Word made flesh, Jesus the Son of God. We must decrease; Christ must increase.

But now we must recognize that this fire-breathing prophet, so very much the center of the Advent season, brings a message that is not at all what most people associate with Christmas. John's importance is not related to baby Jesus. John sees Jesus as an adult.[3] He was destined to spend his entire life devoted to the single mission of announcing the arrival of the Messiah, and to prepare the people for his coming. For this devotion, he was locked in a dungeon and then brutally executed by the king and the first lady of Judea. Such is the cost of telling truth to power.

In all three Synoptic Gospels (Matthew, Mark, and Luke), John's message has two parts: *First,* an uncompromising condemnation of the people for their sin—their greed, heedlessness, dishonesty, neglect of the poor, and above all, their easy assumption that God is on their side (Matt. 3:9; Luke 3:8). Does that sound at all familiar? And *second,* he brings a fiery call to repentance and baptism for the remission of sin. Episcopalians have been known to look down on backwoods preachers for hellfire-and-damnation sermons, but we had better watch out that we are not being contemptuous of the great prophet who rules over the Advent season in the name of the One Who Comes.

The Fourth Gospel, of John the Evangelist, usually presents things a bit differently. In this Gospel, John the Baptist is the one who identifies Jesus by announcing, *"Behold, the Lamb of God who takes away the sin of the world."* This central affirmation is a particularly distinctive part of the message of John the Baptist. Yet Sin plays no part in the run-up to Christmas as we know it in our culture today, and most people, even in the churches, have no idea what

---

2. This is a title given to Christ in the book of Revelation, *ho erchomenos* in Greek, the One Who Is Coming, "who is and who was and who is to come, the Almighty" (Rev. 1:8).

3. His only connection to the baby Jesus that we know of is that wondrous moment when Mary, after the visit of the angel Gabriel, goes to tell the news to her cousin Elizabeth, who is already five months pregnant with John. Saint Luke tells us that when Elizabeth heard the greeting of Mary, the babe leaped in her womb; and Elizabeth was filled with the Holy Spirit, and she exclaimed with a loud cry, "Blessed are you among women, and blessed is the fruit of your womb! . . . For behold, when the voice of your greeting came to my ears, the babe in my womb leaped for joy" (Luke 1:42–44). This remarkable incident unforgettably illustrates for us how John's vocation was determined for him even before he was born.

a Lamb of God might be except that it sounds sweet and fuzzy. In fact, John's salutation is a reference to Jesus's sacrificial death. In his death, Christ makes himself the substitute for the lambs that were slaughtered in the Old Testament rites, becoming the "full, perfect and sufficient sacrifice, oblation and satisfaction" for sin.[4] We don't hear about this kind of Lamb on Christmas cards. That's why we need Advent.

John's father, Zechariah, glorified the mission of the coming Messiah in these words:

> ". . . the dayspring from on high hath visited us,
> To give light to them that sit in darkness and in the shadow of death."

Now this doesn't mean "darkness and the shadow of death" in the general sense that "everybody has to die sooner or later." The images are much more textured than that. Darkness and the shadow of death are poetic images for our tragic, fallen human condition. "Dayspring" is also a poetic image, another name for the Messiah.[5] "Dayspring" means something far more than just "dawn." It means the primordial source of day, God himself—the One who in the beginning said, "Let there be light." So when we read that the light dawns for those who suffer darkness and death (and that means all of us), it means that God is going to restore his original creation—but this time without the temptation of the serpent.

I have been listening to Advent carols on my CD player, and one of them is called "Jesus Christ the Apple Tree." I have known this carol for many years, but I never gave much thought to why Jesus is called an apple tree until just last week when it became clear to me. I was thinking about my friend with Alzheimer's and her angry husband. I was thinking about the sadness of human life and how much disappointment and loss there are in it. Suddenly I realized that Jesus is called the apple tree because he will undo the disobedience of Adam and Eve, who ate the forbidden apple in the garden of Eden. In the death and resurrection of Christ, a great reversal has occurred. The original paradise is restored, only this time the "apple tree" will bring life instead of death. In the new creation that the Lamb of God brings, there will no longer be any possibility of making the wrong choice, and therefore no possibility of Sin anymore.[6]

4. From Thomas Cranmer's Prayer of Consecration, Book of Common Prayer.

5. One of the verses of "O Come, O Come, Emmanuel" begins "O come, thou Dayspring from on high."

6. Saint Augustine of Hippo called this *non posse peccare*—it will no longer be possible to sin. That will truly be freedom, of a sort never before known.

That is the promise of God in Jesus Christ. The lesson we heard this morning from Isaiah about the new Jerusalem is a lavish picture of this promise fulfilled: "I will rejoice in Jerusalem, and be glad in my people; no more shall be heard in it the sound of weeping and the cry of distress."

But before we sing "Jerusalem, my happy home" at the end of this service, we need to meditate deeply on *the darkness and the shadow of death* that we find ourselves in right now, as individuals, as a community, as a nation. The meaning of the season is not arguing about whether nativity scenes can be set up in the town park. The meaning of the season is *understanding why and how we sit in darkness* and *recognizing that we need to repent of our sinful nature.* "On Jordan's bank the Baptist's cry" tells us that's what Advent is for. The Messiah is on his way.

Another friend, much younger, sent me an email. She has been grieving for her husband, who died unexpectedly in his early fifties. She wrote, "Holidays are a challenge for me. . . . My husband loved Christmas, and his birthday was December 22. Advent is my favorite time: I love the darkness and the anticipation of promise to be fulfilled." That's a wonderful phrase: "the darkness and the anticipation of promise to be fulfilled." This is one of the best descriptions of the atmosphere of Advent that I've ever heard. And notice—she loves the season. Even with her wounds still raw and unhealed, she loves the darkness. It reminds her of the contrast between *what is* and *what is promised*.

I feel sure that every single person in this congregation this morning has given some thought to the fact that we American parents have allowed our children to become incredibly spoiled. An article in the *New York Times* a few days ago described a new development: not only are children today acting more rudely and disruptively than ever, but also and more ominously, their parents seem to think it's cute. I am a doting grandparent, and I know from personal experience how hard it is to deny my grandchildren anything. Yet even as I am giving in, I know it is the wrong thing to do. Advent is about delayed gratification. Advent teaches us to wait. Advent shows us how to be empty, living in the anticipation of promise to be fulfilled—emphasis on the word "anticipation."

The prophecies of Isaiah have always been associated with the Christmas season. In today's reading we hear of the messianic age, the new Jerusalem. But there is something dangerous to our health when we take such a passage out of its context. If you look in your Bible when you go home, you will see that this series of glorious promises in chapter 65 is immediately preceded by words that sound more like John the Baptist. This is the word of God to his people:

[You are] a rebellious people,
who walk in a way that is not good,
    following their own devices;
a people who provoke me
    to my face continually. . . .
They are a smoke in my nostrils,
    a fire that burns all the day. . . .
. . . "I will repay . . .
    their iniquities and their fathers' iniquities together, says the Lord."
                            (Isa. 65:2–3, 5–7)

If we ignore passages like this—in other words, if we jump straight to Christmas without observing Advent—we will fail to understand the nature of the grace of God that comes to us even though we "provoke God to his face continually." Advent teaches us to recognize this grace, to turn aside from our own devices, and to wait in the darkness with patience for the promised time of fulfillment.

To be sure, Christmas is itself the time of fulfillment. The promised Messiah has appeared on earth. Yet the manner of his coming—in poverty, in obscurity, in humility—points ahead to the destiny that he will suffer on the cross.[7] The husband who has always had his life exactly the way he wanted it is actually very unfortunate. He has no understanding of the suffering of others, and he has not developed empathy for those who have not had it so easy. He has never thought of himself as one of those who sit in darkness and in the shadow of death. Therefore, although he has been a churchgoer all his life, the Dayspring is for him only a figure of speech, not a living reality, and he has no reserves for his suffering wife.

This morning, the third Sunday of Advent, the preacher brings news of a living reality that changes everything. The Dayspring has come; the Dayspring will come. Whatever your own personal darkness, it has been and will be overcome. If you are not patient, God will yet grant you patience. If you are not charitable, the Savior will create charity in you. If you are not forgiving, the Lord will work a wonder of forgiveness in you. The darkness has been overcome, and it will be overcome.

---

7. At the Cloisters in Manhattan there is a great masterpiece of Flemish art, a painting of the annunciation. As the angel speaks to the Virgin, a little ray of light slips through the window, carrying with it the image of the Child being conceived, and the newborn infant *is already carrying his cross.*

There is always an element, in Advent, of "not yet." Not yet, but it will come. It will come because *he* will come. That is the promise given to us by God himself. The One who comes to be our Judge is the One who is the Lamb who takes away the sin of the world. The Dayspring *has* come and *will* come "to give light to them that sit in darkness and in the shadow of death" (Luke 1:79).

Behold, God creates a new heaven and a new earth.

Amen.

The Glory of Lebanon

Grace Church, New York City
Third Wednesday of the Advent Season 1983

ISAIAH 35:1–10; MATTHEW 11:2–15

In last Saturday's *New York Times*, there's a story about the Lebanese community in Danbury, Connecticut. The occasion was the eve of the Feast of the Immaculate Conception, Mary the mother of Jesus being "Our Lady of Lebanon" to the Maronite Catholics. "The parishioners of St. Anthony Maronite Catholic Church prayed out loud for relatives left behind in Lebanon. 'We pray for peace in Lebanon and peace for the whole world,' said one. 'We pray for the young American they're keeping prisoner,' said another."[1]

One by one the parishioners walked up to the Reverend Ronald N. Beshara and lit a candle from the one he held in his hand. After yet another week of grim news from Lebanon, the hearty celebration was filled with mourning for what many fear is a dying land. "There is no Lebanon any more," said the president of the Lebanon-American Club here. Father Beshara and other pastors in Danbury said the continuing violence has brought some members of the community close to despair. "Many people come asking me why does God allow this to happen," he said, "and I tell them that people there may think they are fighting over religion, but they are not living according to the Christian faith if they do so."

And from the first lesson, taken from the book of the prophet Isaiah:

The wilderness and the dry land shall be glad,
    the desert shall rejoice and blossom;
like the crocus it shall blossom abundantly,
    and rejoice with joy and singing.
The glory of Lebanon shall be given to it. (Isa. 35:1–2)

---

1. Susan Chira, "Lebanese in Danbury Mourn for Homeland," *New York Times*, December 10, 1983.

Now, of course, there are two ways to read about geographical places in the biblical literature. They are real, on-the-ground realities, and that is an important factor in understanding the "earthed" nature of the Judeo-Christian faith. After all, Jesus was crucified "under Pontius Pilate" in a specific province of the historical Roman Empire. But at the same time, the places mentioned often have a symbolic or transcendent significance, as here. We need to keep both in mind all the time, as we need to do in the case of Jerusalem today.

I have never been to the actual country of Lebanon, but I have always heard that it is beautiful. In biblical times, it was celebrated for its splendor—its mountains, its seacoast, and its legendary cedar trees ("the cedars of Lebanon"). Parishioners of the church in Rye where I used to be on the staff lived in Beirut years ago, and they described it as a gorgeous, sophisticated city. They can hardly bear to think of it anymore. It is completely ruined now, they say.

Why does God allow such destruction and war in his world, year in and year out? What are we to say about the sorrow, the waste, the vengefulness that fill our newspapers day after day?

From our second lesson, taken from the Gospel according to Saint Matthew, we read of what John the Baptist asked Jesus, when John was in prison: "Now when John heard in prison about the deeds of the Christ, he sent word by his disciples, and said to [Jesus], 'Are you the one who is to come, or shall we look for another?'" (Matt. 11:2–3).

As my colleague's sermon illustrated for us on Sunday, John the Baptist was full of doubts about Jesus, because he was not the kind of Messiah that John or anyone else had expected. John could not understand why nothing messianic and grand was happening. John could not understand why Jesus wasn't doing anything revolutionary or cataclysmic. John did not understand why God was not inaugurating his powerful kingdom with apocalyptic splendor then and there.

Jesus gave John a strange answer. These are his words to the messenger: "Go and tell John what you hear and see: the blind receive their sight and the lame walk, lepers are cleansed and the deaf hear, and the dead are raised up, and the poor have good news preached to them. And blessed is he who takes no offense at me" (Luke 7:22–23). Now, this is a reference to the prophet Isaiah. If there's one thing we can be sure of, it is that John the Baptist knew the prophet Isaiah by heart. Jesus certainly knew that John would have recognized the reference immediately. Jesus's quotation is a paraphrase of the famous prophecy from Isaiah:

The eyes of the blind shall be opened,
  and the ears of the deaf unstopped;
then shall the lame man leap like a hart,
  and the tongue of the dumb sing for joy. (Isa. 35:5–6)

When Jesus gave this answer to John, he must have counted on the fact that John would instantly understand what he was saying. In his response, Jesus is saying to John that, yes, the messianic hour has actually arrived. He is saying that the time foretold by the prophet has actually come true *in my ministry*. The time of God's liberation is here. The signs of the in-breaking kingdom of God are occurring, *because I have arrived*. Jesus refers John the Baptist to the great eighth-century prophet, knowing that John, more than any other human being, would understand that in Jesus's seemingly enigmatic words, the decisive event of salvation history is being described. Who would know this if not John the Baptist? John, the sentinel at the turn of the ages, stands on the brink of the old world, looking into the future of the new age of God. Who would know better than John that Jesus means to say that the death knell of the old aeon has sounded?

But please note: there is still a very odd quality about Jesus's answer to John. In spite of its clear reference to the messianic age as foretold by the prophet Isaiah, it is still inconclusive, unless one has eyes to see and ears to hear. Think about it for a minute. Yes, it is true that Jesus did heal the sick. Yes, it is true that Jesus did give sight to the blind. Yes, it is true that Jesus made the deaf hear. But how many? Only a very few, in the total number. Only a blind man here and a lame man there. He did not heal all the sick or raise all the dead; there were only a few, a token number. And so, the signs remain ambiguous. The signs of the kingdom still have a hidden quality about them, because only a few are healed and only a few are made to see. Jesus's answer is still inconclusive.

Now this morning, while I was standing in the hall, I heard a group of parishioners planning the food distribution for this weekend. On Saturday, the Evangelicals for Social Action will distribute a sizable quantity of food that has been donated to needy families and elderly people on the Lower East Side. These people in the hall, whom I overheard, were speaking about the distribution to take place, in which Grace Church people will assist.

They were talking about the real suffering they had encountered as they had gone to visit some of the people who had applied for this food distribution. One woman begged that no cardboard boxes be brought because the rats would get into them. The Evangelicals for Social Action have so many requests for food that they cannot possibly handle them. Right here in our own neighborhood, very nearby, people are lonely, people are hungry, people are desperate. They do not know this message: that the lame are being made to walk, and the blind are being made to see. What is the good news in that for them? The ESA volunteers felt angry and frustrated that they have so much and that others have so little. The system seems all wrong. How can we speak of good news for the poor from our lofty position of comfort and plenty?

John the Baptist said, "Are you really the one who is to come?"

We're beginning to doubt it. Things are not happening. "Shall we look for someone else?" Why does God allow this to happen?"

I suppose you've heard me say this a hundred times already, but I believe it must be said over and over, for the encouragement of us all. The signs of the kingdom remain hidden. They were hidden in Jesus's time, and they are hidden now. That, in part, is the reason that Jesus said, "Blessed is he who takes no offense at me." We did not want or expect that kind of a Messiah—a Messiah who would be so obscure and so humble, and in the end, so rejected. We expected power; we expected victory; we expected triumph. But as Jesus clearly indicated to John by quoting Isaiah, the decisive moment has come just the same. The signs of the kingdom prophesied by Isaiah have taken place in Jesus's ministry, he says, thereby placing himself at the center of the proclamation. Even as Jesus says those things, we must acknowledge that they were taking place only in a few places, and only with a few people; they were, and they remain, hidden signs. Signs for those who have eyes to see and ears to hear, for those who will not take offense, but not signs that everyone can properly interpret.

When the ESA group takes the food down to the Lower East Side on Saturday, it will scarcely make a dent in the great, vast, miserable condition of the world's hunger. We might have skeptics among us saying, "Is that all? What good will it do?" But it is a sign; it is a hidden but nonetheless tangible sign of the kingdom of God breaking through.

Think about that Lebanese congregation in Danbury, Connecticut. They are people just like us—no better, no worse. (I say this because I sometimes tend to sentimentalize certain ethnic groups. I tend to think of them as being especially nice or friendly or romantic. When you really get to know different people from different countries, they're just like us—neither better nor worse.) Think of those ordinary Lebanese Christians with their little candles and their questions and their sorrow and their despair and their prayers. That is the true "glory of Lebanon" today—the hidden sign of God's faithfulness to that little band of Christians.[2]

---

2. In the recent history of the Middle East, the Maronites in the country of Lebanon have not been stellar performers. That is beside the point here.

The mystery of God's activity in the world is that the tiny signs of faithfulness and love and mercy and hope, the tiny signs enacted by the Christian community, are the pointers to the glory that will come when the Lord takes his power to himself. This is not the way I would have done it; it is not the way you would have done it. No wonder we take offense. You and I would have made it obvious, so that it would have stunned everybody and made argument and questioning irrelevant. But the glory of Lebanon, which one day will break over the universe in a crescendo of song from the angels and archangels and all the company of heaven—that glory is secreted for the time being in the small deeds and the little prayers of the church of God. That is the way that God planned it, for reasons that we shall someday understand in the kingdom of God.

"Tell John what you see"—a few are healed, a few are fed, a few hear the good news. Signs of the kingdom, signs of his power—because you see, in the Isaiah passage, it is God who is doing it all. "Strengthen the weak hands and make firm the feeble knees," says the Lord—you must imagine a group of ragged exiles, staggering and stumbling back through the desert. Where does the strength for the weak hands and feeble knees come from to make it back home? *It comes from God*: "Behold, your God will come. He will come and save you. Be strong. Fear not. The redeemed of the Lord shall return, and come to Zion with singing—everlasting joy shall be upon their heads; they shall obtain joy and gladness, and sorrow and sighing shall flee away."

The true "glory of Lebanon" is given by God, and it is hidden, with joy, in the deeds and the prayers of his church.

Amen.

The Sign of Immanu-el

Virginia Theological Seminary, Alexandria, Virginia
December 14, 1990

ISAIAH 7:14

There are a few verses of Scripture that have achieved a kind of independent immortality apart from their context, even in the secular world. I am always amazed and perplexed at how, every Christmas, thousands upon thousands of New Yorkers attend dozens of performances of Handel's *Messiah* and come away as unmoved by the words as they were thrilled by the music.

For many a Christian believer, on the other hand, it seems as though God must have known all along that he was going to raise up this prodigiously gifted composer (and his close-to-genius librettist, Charles Jennens) to set some of his Word into a music drama and thereby implant it permanently in the imagination of even the most determinedly irreligious moderns. For many of us, pagan and Christian alike, the famous verse imbedded in the seventh chapter of Isaiah has become forever associated with the weighty solemnity of the contralto voice announcing: "Behold, a virgin shall conceive and bear a son, and shall call his name Immanuel—God with us."

All the more reason to find the original context of the verse—part of the Old Testament reading for today, the second Friday of Advent—to be startling and challenging.

I would imagine that I am not the only person here who has had to go through a lot of mental gymnastics on account of this verse. I remember vividly the days, twenty or thirty years ago, when I was told that the word was not "virgin" at all, but simply "young woman," and that no particularly miracu-

---

A brief homily delivered at the Eucharist during a meeting of SEAD (Scholarly Engagement with Anglican Doctrine). I was the only nonacademic at this meeting. This was intended as a small testimony to the reconciliation of biblical interpretation in the academy with living faith. The chapel at Virginia Seminary is called Immanuel Chapel.

lous event was implied. As in the case of everything else I was told in those days about interpreting Scripture, I attempted to acquiesce, in order to be an up-to-date, scholarly, responsible child of the advancing and advanced twentieth century. And, to be sure, to this day I would not argue that the Hebrew word is unambiguous. However, what has happened to me in the interim has to do partly with a new respect, threshed out over decades, for the way the early Christians read the Hebrew Bible, and partly with the fact that, as I have become (I hope) a more sophisticated interpreter, I have at the same time become a more simple believer, as ready to assent with my mind as to acquiesce with my heart before the scene at the manger in Bethlehem.[1] What a thoroughly unexpected blessing it was for simple faith to discover, a few years ago, that so rigorous a scholar as Raymond Brown, after years of exhaustive research, had concluded that there was indeed an irregularity about the birth of Jesus that goes back as far as we can trace the traditions.[2]

But to return to our Old Testament setting. There are few sections of Scripture that are more unabashedly political than Isaiah 7. The sign of the child called Immanu-el is given in a context that is as concrete and localized as the events transpiring in Kuwait and Iraq today. The idea that God is with his people in the person of an infant is deemed, in that wonderfully no-nonsense way of the Old Testament, to be relevant to the circumstances of invasion and siege, shifting alliances and military strategy, peace and war. The prophet Isaiah was to go out to meet King Ahaz at a particular spot on the road, as concrete as if it were Exit 23 on I-95, in order to tell him that, in spite of everything, Yahweh had not abandoned him—and that, appearances notwithstanding, the kings and armies of foreign nations were Yahweh's possession as surely as was the kingdom of Judah.

The juxtaposition of Old Testament lesson and New Testament Gospel for today seems peculiar at first glance, but as always, there is an inner connectedness that seems to me this morning to be as truly marvelous as it must have been to the early Christians, who were making daily discoveries about the messianic meanings to be gleaned from the Hebrew Bible. It is in Jesus's words to the disciples on the eve of his death that we find that astonishing duality so

---

1. Paul Ricoeur has called this, famously, "the second naïveté."

2. R. E. Brown, *The Birth of the Messiah* (Garden City, NY: Doubleday, 1977), appendix 6, pp. 518–42. I highly recommend this whole section as a premier example of Brown's work when he was beginning to move away from his training in the historical-critical method into a more literary way of interpreting the Scripture. He maintains his scrupulous methods of examining every possible historical and critical issue as thoroughly as possible, yet moves beyond into a mode of interpretation that lends itself to preaching, faith, and witness.

characteristic of the Advent season. The one who is about to be handed over to condemnation, torture, and public execution is the same one who says to his disciples the night before, "I assign to you, as my Father assigned to me, a kingdom, that you may eat and drink at my table in my kingdom, and sit on thrones judging the twelve tribes of Israel" (Luke 22:29–30).

It never ceases to stagger the imagination: the utter audacity of the Advent proclamation that the baby in the manger is the reigning Messiah, that the crucified Jesus will come again in glory to judge the living and the dead, that the one who is to be delivered up is the one who will dispose of all earthly power and authority with imperial ease, being King of kings and Lord of lords. The Word of God that holds and shapes the future is the same Word who implanted prophecies in the testimony of his people Israel for the comfort of those who still travel through the wilderness. The wonder of it is that, for us whose calling it is to live and bear witness in the time between the times, it is still an hour in which God says *I am not against you: I am with you*—a time in which it is yet possible to discern in the midst of events, as Timothy Garton Ash wrote last year during the liberation of Eastern Europe, that "somewhere, an angel has just opened his wings."

Amen.

King of the Last Things
(Advent IV)

Hell

Grace Church, New York City
Advent 1993

Some of you have been curious about the hymns I would choose on this night when the subject, hell, has been so widely advertised. The fact is that I have never had an easier time picking hymns. All I had to do was look through the Advent section of the hymnal. Here are some words that one finds in the Advent hymns: "shadow," "exile," "fear," "darkness," "gloom," "captive," "misery," "decay," "bondage," "torment," "grave," "doom," "judgment," "ancient curse," "dread foe," "Satan," "sin," "evil," "death," "**hell**." You get the idea.

You might think, oh, well, this is *Advent*. But if you look sharply, you will notice that these themes persist into the Christmas season. It is truly remarkable that the season of our Lord's birth has evoked, over the centuries, a large number of carols and hymns based on these motifs. You might particularly notice this at Christmas Eve services when choirs often sing early music, or early words set to modern music. Only in more recent centuries has the focus been on shepherds, sheep, camels, mangers, stars, and other child-friendly motifs. I have recently purchased the latest hot ticket in early music, a CD from Anonymous Four called *On Yoolis Night*. It's a collection of medieval Christmas carols and motets. Glancing through the texts, I note these additional terms: "guilt," "hostility," "offences," "danger," "malice," "crimes," "punishment," "treachery," "falsehood," "vileness," "horror," "dregs of foulness," "heretical fraud," "malignant bond," "the devil's power," "the Judgment Day." Can you imagine? Modern Americans are not used to thinking of Christmas this way. We don't want our nice pretty holiday spoiled by these morbid subjects. In

---

This was the last in a series of Advent sermons on the four last things: death, judgment, heaven, hell—in their traditional order. The sermons were given on successive Wednesday evenings in Advent 1993. Some—not all—of the names of parishioners are changed.

fact, we have a notable capacity for overlooking such things altogether; we are so enchanted with the music that we forget to listen to the words. The King's Singers' version of the Coventry Carol is a good one because it is so harsh and dissonant that one simply cannot avoid the fact that it tells a story about the massacre of babies.

The wisdom of earlier centuries was sometimes greater than ours, though that is hard for us to believe. The medieval church had an Advent tradition of focusing on what were called the four last things during the four weeks of Advent, in this order: death, judgment, heaven, and hell. This meant that hell was the subject in closest proximity to the birth of Jesus. This was no accident. Here at Grace Church we are following this custom on Wednesday nights this year, believing that there is an important reason for the old tradition.

A member of Grace Church gave me a book three weeks ago; newly published, it is called *The History of Hell* by Alice K. Turner. It has lots of text and spectacular illustrations, but it is interesting to note that Ms. Turner issues a lighthearted disclaimer at the beginning; she writes, "I do not believe in Hell; I could hardly attempt this book if I did. . . . [My book is] a real history of an imaginary place."

I find that an amazing statement. The reason that Advent preaching is so important in the Christian church is that it is the time in our calendar when we take sin and evil seriously (that's why we don't bring out our Christmas decorations until Christmas Eve). It astonishes me that a thoughtful person could write a whole book about hell and then toss the subject off so lightly. I myself think hell is one of the realest things I know.

Now let's not have any misunderstanding. I will not be talking tonight about hell as a place of eternal fire and everlasting physical torment. Even Billy Graham has given up that idea, as he says in a recent *Time* magazine interview. I somewhat agree with Ms. Turner here, who says that the descriptions of hell in Matthew, Mark, and Luke are "colorfully hyperbolic repetitive rhetoric" used to make a point. I am not very interested in the concept of hell as a place of unceasing fiery torture, which I believe to be extrabiblical. Most of the mythology that clings to the subject of hell came along in postbiblical times. For instance, there is a widespread belief that the Bible depicts the saints taking delight in the torments of the damned. That is not true; those admittedly gruesome passages come later in church history, with Tertullian and others.

What is hell, then?

I believe what I am going to say is compatible with the New Testament and with the facts of life in this world. Hell is not a *place*. It is a *domain*. It is the domain of evil, the sphere where wickedness rules. It is, I believe, necessary to posit the existence of hell as a way of acknowledging the reality and power of radical evil. By "radical evil," I mean evil that has an existence independent of the sum total of human folly. Radical evil is aggressive, clever, willful, diabolical—that is to say, it has a personality, an intelligence, a purposefulness all its own, which explains why we personify it as the figure of Satan. Flannery O'Connor, who has written about the devil as memorably as anyone, says that he, or it, "is not simply generalized evil, but an evil intelligence determined on its own supremacy."[1]

I believe, as I said before, that hell is one of the realest things I know. It has been described in philosophical terms as "the absence of good." That's true so far as it goes, but it does not go anywhere near far enough. It's too abstract. Auschwitz was not just the absence of good. Pol Pot's genocide in Cambodia was not just the absence of good. The massacre of the population of El Mozote in El Salvador, many of whom were evangelical Christians, was described in the *New Yorker* last month; this massacre was not just the absence of good, but an example of demonstrable evil in which the United States government and the *Wall Street Journal* and other organizations participated by covering it up, by lying about it, by refusing to believe the testimony of scores of witnesses and photographs.[2] But the *Wall Street Journal* is a fine Christian paper, is it not, with all sorts of good articles that I cut out and put in my files? But that is just what I mean. Radical evil is loose in the world, and it finds many well-meaning people and institutions to serve its purposes. That is what the New Testament means by the "principalities and powers." Satan has gotten hold of the principalities and powers so that a tobacco company executive, for instance, will testify with a straight face, "To my knowledge, it's not been proven that cigarette smoking causes cancer."[3] That is a good example of the nature of evil as idiotic, vulgar, and stupid. No one has outdone C. S. Lewis in

1. Flannery O'Connor, *Mystery and Manners* (New York: Farrar, Straus and Giroux, 1961), 168.

2. My book *The Crucifixion*, published more than thirty years after this sermon, goes much further into this discussion about *privatio boni*. It is in the chapter called "The Descent into Hell." *The Crucifixion: Understanding the Death of Jesus Christ* (Grand Rapids: Eerdmans, 2015).

3. Infamous statements such as these were repeatedly made by tobacco company executives, beginning with a meeting of tobacco company CEOs in December 1953 at the Plaza Hotel in New York City. The purpose of this meeting was to refute the accumulation of scientific evidence about cancer and smoking. Their efforts were rewarded by continued tobacco consumption, which did not begin to drop until the 1980s. A thoroughly researched description of all this can be found at http://tobaccocontrol.bmj.com/content/21/2/87#article-bottom.

portraying the obscene, coarse stupidity of evil. His descriptions of the devil in *Perelandra* are the most memorable that I have read in this regard. Here is no glamorous Satan like Milton's in *Paradise Lost*. I have not been able to see *Schindler's List* yet, but I gather that one of its virtues is in depicting the Nazis, not as the dashing, impeccable villains we are accustomed to from a thousand movies, but as coarse, mindless, and gross.

We have not said anything about hell as a place to which one goes after death. I want to be sure to establish the idea that hell is not a *place* at all, but a *realm*. It is the domain of wickedness, of stupidity, of despair, of hopelessness. You will remember the famous words over the gate to Dante's Inferno: "Abandon hope, all ye who enter here." To have no hope is truly to be in hell. How can anyone not believe in hell who has known a person who has committed suicide? I believe that most people who kill themselves do so because they are experiencing hell; they have lost hope; darkness reigns over them. That is why the Samaritans and other agencies that undertake suicide prevention are making a Christian witness, whether they know it or not; it's a way of doing battle against the reign of darkness. It's a way of signifying that death is not the last word.

I think of the Advent collect: "Almighty God, give us grace that we may cast away the works of darkness and put upon us the armor of light, now in the time of this mortal life, in which thy son Jesus Christ came to visit us in great humility; that in the last day, when he shall come to judge the quick and the dead, we may rise to the life immortal." Here is the Advent theme of the link between this life and the life to come, the link that will finally and decisively be made in the day of judgment. On that day there will be only one Ruler, only one Lord; Scripture is quite clear and unambiguous about that. The Judge of all the cosmos will not be Satan. Radical evil will have no status in the last day. "Death will have no more dominion" (Rom. 6:9).

Until that day comes, we must believe in the "hideous strength" of the realm of wickedness.[4] We must believe in it because of that little two-year-old boy in England who was dragged off and beaten to death and left on the railroad tracks by two children not much older than he. We must believe in hell because there is no other way to take seriously the nature and scale of evil in the world. We must believe in hell because there is no other way to do justice to the victims of darkness. We must believe in hell because, without it, Christian faith is sentimental and evasive, unable to stand up to reality in this world. Without an unflinching understanding of the radical nature of evil, Christian faith would be nothing but a suburban bedtime story.

4. The last volume of C. S. Lewis's space trilogy is *That Hideous Strength*.

Will hell, conceived as a *domain*, not a *place*, persist into eternity? The book of Revelation, which is a major source for these motifs, speaks somewhat mysteriously of the "second death" in a lake of fire. Again, not even Billy Graham understands this literally; he says the fire is "possibly an illustration of how terrible it's going to be [to be separated from God]." I think we can say this much for sure, based again on the book of Revelation with its "Hallelujah Chorus": the Messiah is going to reign for ever and ever. The devil is *not* going to reign for ever and ever. It is not for nothing, therefore, that we read the passage from Romans 8 earlier in the service: "For I am sure that neither death, nor life, nor angels, nor principalities, nor things present, nor things to come, nor powers, nor height, nor depth, nor anything in all creation will be able to separate us from the love of God in Christ Jesus our Lord."

Why is hell brought into such close proximity to Christmas in the liturgy of the church? Once again we will find answers in the Christmas hymns. Here is a translation from the Latin of one of the motets from *On Yoolis Night*: "When time had run its course, the Father . . . sent from the heavenly throne his only begotten son . . . that in this fleshly abode he might vanquish the devil." Over and over again you will find it, if you are alert; the meaning of Christmas is that God has entered the lists against the Prince of Darkness. You will hear this on Christmas Eve at Grace Church. Satan has met his master.

Our Gospel lesson tonight was one of the classic lessons for Advent, the story of the wise and foolish virgins. You remember that the story tells of a wedding with ten bridesmaids. Five were ready and five were not. When the bridegroom arrives, the five bridesmaids who have their lamps burning are admitted to the feast. The other five have the door shut in their faces, and hear these terrible words: "Truly, I say to you, I do not know you" (Matt. 25:12).

Last week we had a sermon on heaven. One way of understanding hell, surely, is that it is the opposite of heaven, which is typically depicted in Scripture as a wedding banquet. Last Friday night Susan Leckrone was married to David Copley. After their honeymoon and a few more weeks of furlough, they are going back to Liberia to continue the work they have begun in resisting the devil by ministering to the children who have been traumatized by the civil war there. This wedding was one of the great events of recent years at Grace Church. Many, many people were present, some of them coming from considerable distances, who had not been here for years—people I had thought I might not see again. I did not realize how many there were until I began distributing communion. It was simply astonishing to look out and see the people who were coming forward. I was overwhelmed. It seemed like a little foretaste of the kingdom of God. It was as if the saints past, present, and future were being gathered for the marriage feast of the Lamb. There were so many of them from so many different eras at Grace Church that I could hardly believe it. I began to imagine that I was seeing other dear people too, people who had died, faces from the church triumphant joining with us "who toil below." Then suddenly I saw the radiant faces of James and Susan Clark.[5] It would be a great surprise to them to learn that they were serving tonight in this sermon as illustrations of the kingdom of heaven. When they were members here, Susan and I had some run-ins. When they left, I was sad that there had not been more of a reconciliation. When I saw their glowing faces as they came to the altar rail, an amazing thing happened to me. It was as if the past had been simply erased. We were two sinners rejoicing in the same salvation, the same deliverance. For a few minutes, at least, I felt I knew what heaven was going be like. Everything unhappy will be purged away. It will be God's doing, not ours. We will be new creatures, children of the day. All our unlovable traits will be gone forever. Reconciliation will be complete; for the mouth of the Lord has spoken it. "And they will come from north and south, and from east and west, to sit at the marriage feast of the Lamb" (Luke 13:29; cf. Rev. 19:9).

There is no music in hell; there is only hideous discordance. There is no dancing in hell. There is no joy in hell. There is no hope in hell. Above all, there is no love in hell. But the day will come when the divine laughter will ring through heaven like Papageno's glockenspiel in *The Magic Flute*, and the devil, like the villain Monostatos in the opera, will dance to the Lord's tune before he is overthrown forever.

> And there [will be] war in heaven, Michael and his angels fighting against the dragon. . . . And the great dragon was thrown down, that ancient serpent who is called Satan, the deceiver of the whole earth, he was thrown down. . . . Then the seventh angel blew his trumpet, and there were loud voices in heaven, saying, "The kingdoms of this world have become the Kingdom of our Lord and of his Christ, and he shall reign for ever and ever." (Rev. 12:7, 9; 11:15)

Amen.
Hallelujah!

---

5. Not their real names.

God on the Move

Saint John's Church, Salisbury, Connecticut
Fourth Sunday in Advent 1996

LUKE 1:26–33

Who is the sexiest man in the Bible? Put your money on King David. He's got it all. He's a real man's man, and a woman's man too: handsome, glamorous, magnificent in statecraft, a lion on the battlefield, a brilliantly gifted musician and poet, a flamboyantly physical presence yet deeply introspective and prayerful, a man of action and a man of contemplation . . . just recounting these traits makes me go weak in the knees.

Yet, as you know, David's family was a mess. One of the most heartrending lines in all literature, as William Faulkner knew well, is David's anguished cry upon hearing the news of his treacherous son Absalom's defeat and death: "O my son Absalom, my son, my son Absalom! Would I had died instead of you, O Absalom, my son, my son!" (II Sam. 18:33). An unusual number of people in Salisbury and Lakeville have lost their sons—I count at least seven—but David's cry for Absalom rings down the ages with unusual force because when Absalom died he was trying to kill his father and usurp the crown. Into such a household the prophet Nathan speaks the words we hear today: "The Lord declares to you [his servant David] that the Lord will make you a house. When your days are fulfilled and you lie down with your fathers, I will raise up your offspring after you, who shall come forth from your body. . . . I will be his father, and he shall be my son. . . . I will not take my steadfast love from him. . . . And your house and your kingdom shall be made sure for ever before me; your throne shall be established for ever" (II Sam. 7:11–16).

Thus we learn that God's unconditional promise of an eternal kingdom is made to David in the very midst of all the ambiguity and pain of human life. God did not wait until David got his family straightened out before he made the promise. God's unconditional promise came to David in spite of himself.

One of the most excruciating passages of literature that I have ever read is about a Christmas dinner. It is in William Styron's novel—his best by a long way, in my opinion—called *Lie Down in Darkness.* The family whose desperate and doomed lives make up the plot of the novel gather around the table. It is gorgeously laid with the family silver, linens, and crystal (this takes place in Tidewater Virginia). The dining room is gleaming with candlelight and festooned with evergreens. The mother has outdone herself with the food. Everyone is trying to be nice, trying not to say the wrong thing, trying to be happy. But bit by bit, the pain and torment in the family relationships are exposed and the dinner ends in catastrophe. The power of the scene lies in the contrast between the polished perfection of the holiday table and the unendurable anguish in the hearts of the participants. I don't for a minute mean to suggest that everybody's Christmas dinners are like that. But I think you know what I mean. Things don't work out the way we want them to. At the heart of human life there is an incapacity to make things turn out right.

As Advent draws to its close, the special nature of the season summons us to sober reflection on the nature of a world without a Savior. It is no coincidence that the promise of an everlasting throne was given by God to a man who had even less control over his own household than does the present queen of England. The mercy of God does not depend on human virtue for its fulfillment. The mystery of the Advent season lies precisely in its location, placed as it is between the *now* of human failure and disappointment and the *not-yet* of God's coming kingdom. When we are young, our lives seem full of possibility, but that sense of hopefulness inevitably begins to wind down. Here is something I wrote in an Advent sermon only nine years ago: "I am fifty years old, I am in excellent health and I feel as if I have at least fifty more years and great deeds ahead of me." How quickly a decade passes! Somehow those great deeds seem to be receding further and further into the realm of things that may never come to pass. Those are Advent thoughts.

The final chapter of King David's life is as pathetic as the rest of his life is titanic. He has become so feeble that he cannot leave his room, and he shivers constantly. His servants and family pile covers on him, to no avail. Finally, in desperation, they resort to a stratagem appropriate to an Eastern potentate—they put a young woman into bed with him to keep him warm. This may sound exciting, but since he has become impotent, it is not even the last flickering of a once-brilliant flame, but a pitiful dying away into ashes—precisely the kind of death we all dread.

It is said that we do not truly know ourselves until we are alone at three o'clock in the morning. When John Updike was fifty-five, a decade or so ago, he wrote an article about a trip he made alone to Finland in bad weather. He was famous, he was rich, he was successful, he was besieged by admirers everywhere, but on this particular trip he found himself alone in his sterile hotel room in a country whose language was utterly inaccessible to him, struggling with sleeplessness, jet lag, and a nameless dread. He went out on his rainy hotel balcony in the middle of the night and looked at the sleeping town. "Nothing moved," he wrote, "not even the clouds moved—yellow layers of nimbus that seemed the hellish underside of some other realm. I had never before been this far north on the planet . . . the precariousness of being alive and human was no longer hidden from me by familiar surroundings and the rhythm of habit. I was fifty-five, ignorant, dying, and filling this bit of Finland with the smell of my stale sweat and insomniac fury."[1]

Very often as I read the papers I feel as if nothing is moving and that there is a dull yellow cloud over the world that gives the whole landscape an infernal aspect. Salisbury and Lakeville Main Streets are magical at this time of year, but the sign identifying the Mental Health Center reminds us that not all is well. Peace talks around the world are stalled. Acts of terrorism and violence know no season. Refugees in Africa go this way and that way, yet nothing improves for them. There are exponentially more poor children in America today than there were a few years ago. When the Wednesday noon Eucharist was over last week, some of us stood around in the aisle afterward and talked about how much bad news there often was at Christmas.

As you will remember, after King David's death there was one more brilliant chapter, the reign of his son Solomon. After that the house of David collapsed into ashes like David himself. The united monarchy was divided and conquered, first by the Assyrians and then by the Babylonians. The children of Israel were carried off and humiliated in foreign lands where they did not know the language, where nothing moved and the yellow underside of the clouds cast a hellish glow over the world.

> By the waters of Babylon,
> there we sat down and wept. (Ps. 137:1)

How truly odd, then, that Nathan's prophecy to David should have been preserved and treasured. Ordinarily, a prophecy that did not come true would

---

1. *New Yorker*, September 28, 1987. In fairness to Mr. Updike, the Finnish episode has an upbeat ending. Through a series of small events that Mr. Updike perceives as the grace of God, he returns to the USA with a grateful sense of having survived and even of having regained some sense of mastery.

be tossed on the scrap heap, too embarrassing to keep. Why was it told and retold? Had not the promises of an eternal kingdom turned to ashes? Had not the joyful celebrations of freedom ended in bondage? There had been no progress. If it was not the Babylonians, it was the Romans; the people were still slaves. Nothing had moved.

Yet Israel held on to the prophecy of Nathan, for one reason and for one reason only: it was said to have come not from man, but from God. It was said that *the Lord* had spoken to the prophet Nathan. God is not dependent on human success. Independently of anything David had said or done, God had made a decision to be merciful to his people through the line of David. The focus had shifted away from human arrangements to the initiative of God. This is the meaning of the word "annunciation" in the Bible: *Thus saith the Lord,* stand aside and watch what I am about to do![2] "In the sixth month God sent the angel Gabriel to a virgin named Mary, 'Behold, you will conceive in your womb and bear a son . . . and the Lord God will give to him the throne of his father David, and he will reign over the house of Jacob for ever; and of his kingdom there will be no end'" (Luke 1:26–33).

What is an angel? I have a postcard of a carving from the door of the cathedral in Köln (Cologne), in Germany. It depicts the moment of the angel's appearance to the shepherds. The lead shepherd is shown recoiling violently, as though he had received a sudden, terrific blow. That's exactly right. Angels are not pretty or cute. Angels are powerful, and there is nothing more frightening than power when you don't know if it is against you or for you. As Emily Dickinson suggested, angels are bisecting messengers, cleaving between truth and falsehood, life and death, mercy and judgment. That's why the first words of the angels in the Bible are almost always "Fear not." You can try that test if you read the cover story about so-called angels in *People* magazine this week.[3] We have a lot of notions about angels these days that surely don't come from the Bible. No wonder the epistle to the Hebrews, in the New Testament, warns us about worshiping angels. An angel is only an angel if he reveals something of the presence and power of Jesus Christ.

Once a month I meet with the clergy of the Northwest Corner. I am very fond of this group of faithful people. Last Thursday we spent some time discussing the biblical passages for today. We asked each other whether we believed in the angel and the Virgin or not. There were various points of view. Here is mine. I believe the Bible teaches us that the world of human beings

---

2. I got this last clause from a commentary but have unfortunately lost the reference.
3. "Touched by Angels," *People*, December 19, 1996.

has been under a hellish cloud since the fall of Adam and Eve, whenever and whatever that was. I believe the Bible shows that human history without God is a story of human wickedness going round and round on itself. Depending on how you count, there are either eighty or ninety wars going on around the globe at this moment; humanly speaking, nothing has moved. All the technology and science in the world have not been able to stop people from hating each other and killing each other. All the psychotherapy and Prozac that we can throw at the problem has not been able to make the Christmas dinner turn out right. If the Christmas dinner turns out right, it is not our doing; it is the grace of God.

At Dorothy Warner's funeral, we had a fascinating counterpoint. We heard a reading from Ecclesiastes and we sang "O Come, O Come, Emmanuel." Ecclesiastes is a very important book in the Bible. It is the one that contains the refrain "There is nothing new under the sun" (Eccles. 1:9). This is the biblical book that says, *Nothing moves.* Human history is the same thing over and over—rebellion and violence and fratricide and death, over and over and over. Left to ourselves, the Christmas dinner would end in disaster every time. But we are not left to ourselves. Something has moved. It is not human beings who have moved; it is God who has moved. The "bisecting messenger" has arrived. Is the power for us or against us? This is the announcement: *Emmanuel, God-with-us.* We are not abandoned. The power that created the universe with a word and could equally destroy it with a word is not against us, but for us.

God has moved, not we to him, but he to us. The angel Gabriel has bisected the ghastly yellow clouds. The sons and the daughters will be raised from the dead, and the human family will be restored around the table of the Lord. I cannot tell you why it takes so long and why it costs us so much pain. I can tell you this: we are speaking today, not about human hopes and human wishes and human dreams, but about God. What is happening at Christmas is not from man but from God. That is what the virgin birth signifies.[4]

Hail, Mary, full of grace, the Lord is with thee.

Emmanu-el shall come to thee, O Israel.

Amen.

---

4. The correct term is actually "virginal conception."

In the Bleak Midwinter

Christ Episcopal Church, Cooperstown, New York
December 21, 2016, being the Feast of Saint Thomas, Apostle

JOHN 20:26–29

This sermon was preached for the institution of the Reverend Dane Boston as rector of Christ Church, Cooperstown, New York.

It was very exciting to be invited to preach at this service for your new rector. When Dane invited me, I accepted instantly, without even thinking, but then I began to realize what a compounded blessing it was going to be. First of all, I've loved Cooperstown for many years. To me, it's one of the most attractive towns in the United States, with its literary history, its opera, its museum of my favorite sport, and the loveliest and most poetic of lakes, the headwaters of the graceful Susquehanna. I have dropped into Christ Church anonymously many times and yearned to feel at home here. Now, by the grace of God, I have my opportunity!

But there's something much more important about the wonders of this occasion. First of all, tonight is the shortest and darkest night of the year, the deepest part of the season just before Christmas. Second, it's the feast day of Thomas the apostle, often called "doubting Thomas." We'll soon learn why that's so significant. And third, it's the fourth week of Advent. For the Christian church, it's the most expectant week of the year, saturated with the sense of something uniquely impossible about to happen.

The Advent season offers something remarkable to the church—the calling to live in two places at once. If the church is doing its job, the people of God are going about their December routines in a double sense. We are shopping, decorating, baking, wrapping, and creating as much magic for the children as possible. We are burning candles and putting out multitudes of lights. But in our hearts and in the worship of the church, the Advent season begins in the darkness, in the depths of the night. In the world of darkness, refugees are homeless; families shopping at a Christmas market are run down; the people of Aleppo are hunted from house to house. In our own country, we are divided and wary of one another. It is the midnight of the year. The early church knew what it was doing when it settled on the winter solstice as the date for approaching Christmas.[1]

This is the right moment in the year for the announcement of the coming of the Lord. A few years ago, on the radio, I heard a breathtaking African American spiritual that I had never heard before. It had a question-and-answer format, or, rather, call-and-response:

What month was my Jesus born in? Last month of the year.
What month? January? No . . . February? No . . . March? No . . .
Last month of the year . . .
Born of the virgin Mary.

What does this suggest? It suggests that the clock of human progress and human potential was winding down to zero.

The supreme poet of the Advent season, W. H. Auden, writes,

Cold the heart and cold the stove,
Ice condenses on the bone,
Winter completes an age
. . . .
The evil and armed draw near
The weather smells of their hate
And the houses smell of our fear;
Death has opened his white eye. . . .

The image of the evil and armed, the symbolism of hate and fear, combined with winter cold and ice suggests that the miracle of God's coming occurs

---

1. Actually, as I have more recently learned, there is considerable scholarly disagreement about this. American and British scholars tend to believe that the early church calculated the date of Christmas nine months from the annunciation, already set for March 25 (well argued by Thomas J. Talley, *The Origins of the Liturgical Year*, 2nd emended ed. [Collegeville, MN: Pueblo Publishing, 1986], 87–91). Professor Karl Froelich has explained to me that Continental scholars are more wedded to the *sol invictus* notion (the winter solstice) than English-speaking ones. Talley and others think it unlikely that the early church would have wanted to select the date of a pagan celebration for the birth of the Savior—among other historical evidence.

precisely at the last moment when human hope is extinguished. "Winter completes an age"; he is speaking of the end of the age of false hopes, false promises, false saviors.

The poet continues. He suggests that all our attempts at human self-help and our religious strivings for peace and meaning come to an end:

> Was the triumphant answer to be this?
> The Pilgrim Way has led to the Abyss.

All our religious searching leads to a dead end—the Abyss, the impotence of human wishes, the collapse of human hopes.

You probably know of the famous utterance by Roman gladiators. As they came into the arena to fight to the death for the amusement of the public, they faced the emperor and said, "*Ave, Caesar, nos morituri te salutamus*" (We who must die salute you).[2] Auden uses this by changing it into a refusal to salute worldly power and a turning to another Power from another sphere:

> We who must die demand a miracle.
> How could the Eternal do a temporal act,
> The Infinite become a finite fact?
> Nothing can save us that is possible;
> We who must die demand a miracle.[3]

How could the Eternal do a temporal act? How could the Infinite become a finite fact? Auden is audaciously describing the central mystery of Christmas— the moment when the impossibility of the human condition ("we who must die") is met by the possibility of God—the miracle.

The question of Christmas can be stated very simply as the first line of a Christmas carol: "What child is this?" I'm going to say something now that might cause you to drift off, but stay with me for a minute. Christmas has been called "the feast of Nicene dogma." What? How can *dogma* be a good thing? Many people think it's a bad thing. I just finished reading a very popular, and for the most part very good, book called *Take This Bread*.[4] I loved it for the first two-thirds, but I got pretty much turned off when the author referred to

2. There are several versions of this famous Latin saying. The original is quoted by the historian Suetonius.

3. W. H. Auden, "For the Time Being: A Christmas Oratorio," in *The Collected Poetry of W. H. Auden* (New York: Random House, 1945), 408, 411.

4. Sarah Miles, *Take This Bread* (New York: Ballantine Books, 2007).

the Nicene Creed as a "toxic document" that *her* enlightened church would never use. She did not understand its crucial importance. When the Council of Nicaea met early in the fourth century, their purpose was to determine, once and for all, "What child is this?" Who was Jesus of Nazareth? Was he a man who became a god? Or was he himself God from the beginning? This argument was settled at Nicaea, but the argument is not over; it is still going on in the church.

Was Jesus of *similar* substance with God—was he *like* God (that's *homoiousia* in Greek)—or was he "of *one* substance" (*homoousia*) with God? There's only one letter of difference in the two words, the Greek letter iota. (I'm trying to hold your attention here.) My theology professor used to tell his students that "The truth about the salvation of the human race hung by an iota." What child is this? "The Infinite has become a finite fact." Everything depends on this, or the nativity story is just a child's fable that no thinking adult can believe.

Now we come to the apostle Thomas, whose feast day this is. Peter was the leader of the twelve disciples, and the best known to us today, but in the Gospel of John, Thomas the doubter plays a key role. When Jesus tells his disciples that he's leaving them and that they know the way where he's going, Thomas is the one who protests. Thomas says to him, "Lord, we don't even know where you are going; how can we know the way?" This protest leads to one of Jesus's greatest sayings: "I AM the way . . . and the truth, and the life."

All through the Gospel of John, Thomas is the contrarian. But when the Evangelist John brings Thomas back at the end, it's the climax of the story. John was a master storyteller. He shaped the material he inherited so that Thomas, the one who resisted, becomes the one who tells us finally and completely *who Jesus is.*

Thomas was not with the disciples who first saw Jesus after the resurrection, and he said he didn't believe it. He said he *wasn't going* to believe it till he saw the prints of the nails in Jesus's feet and hands. A few days later, the disciples were gathered together, and this time Thomas was with them. The doors were shut, but Jesus came and stood among them, and said, "Peace be with you." Then he said to Thomas, "Put your finger here, and see my hands; and put out your hand, and place it in my side; do not be faithless, but believing." Thomas answered him, "My Lord and my God!" (*ho kurios mou kai ho theos mou*).

My Lord and *my God.* All commentators agree: this is the highest and most unequivocal confession in the Gospel of John. Thomas no longer calls Jesus "Master." When he calls him Lord and God, the Evangelist has brought his Gospel full circle, back to the prologue, which is the reading for Christmas

Day: "in the beginning was the Word, and the Word was with God, *and the Word was God.*" "Jesus has now returned to the place where he was before the Incarnation."[5] Thomas's confession is the pinnacle of Christian faith. When you sing "O Come, All Ye Faithful" on Christmas Eve, I hope you will find new meaning in the second verse: "Very God, begotten, not created." That's Nicene dogma. That's who the infant is. The Eternal has done a temporal act, the Infinite has become a finite fact. "For us and for our salvation he came down from heaven."

Our hymn at the conclusion of this service is one that I'm sure you all know, but perhaps you don't all know the fullness of doctrine (dogma) that it proclaims. It's a very old hymn, from the early Middle Ages, and was originally in Latin. Each verse sets out what has become known as the Great "O" Antiphons of Advent. The child in the manger is given all the great messianic titles of the Old Testament. (I'd love to expound them all, but I won't stretch out my time that far.) Here, briefly, are the Great "O" Antiphons:

- *Emmanu-el* (in Hebrew, God with us)
- *Sapientia* (Wisdom from on high that proceeds from the mouth of God)
- *Adonai* (the name of God on Mount Sinai, who gives the Ten Commandments to Moses)
- *Radix Jesse* (Root of Jesse, the father of King David, from whose line the Messiah was to come)
- *Clavis David* (Key of David that opens what no one else can unlock)
- *Oriens* (the longed-for Daystar that scatters the darkness)
- *Rex Gentium* (the King of the gentiles and all the nations to the end of the earth)[6]

So when you sing "O Come, O Come, Emmanuel" at the end of our service, recall that Thomas's confession of faith is the summary of *all* the titles and *all* the prophecies and *all* the hopes of the Old Testament: "My Lord and my God." Out of the unrelieved darkness of death, the Daystar arises. Again, in the words of the prologue of John's Gospel, "the light shines in the darkness, and the darkness overcame it not."

"My Lord and my God." I am sure there are many doubting Thomases here tonight. I assure you that I am a doubter myself, many times a week. But

---

5. Rudolf Bultmann, *The Gospel of John* (Philadelphia: Westminster, 1971), 695.

6. The Great "O" Antiphons are described in the "Service of Lessons and Carols for Advent" in the final section of this book.

here are the words of the Lord himself that will be our light in the darkness of doubt. Here is the promise that Jesus himself makes to us. Yes, to us, to this congregation gathered to welcome a new apostolic messenger into its midst. This is what Jesus says to Thomas; listen to him speaking *directly to you*: "Jesus said to him, 'Thomas, have you believed because you have seen me? Blessed are those who have not seen and yet believe'" (John 20:29).

That's you, and that's me. We are the ones who, unlike Thomas and the other disciples, have *not* seen with our eyes like Thomas. We are the ones who have *not* seen and yet, in spite of that lack, receive the Lord's blessing and become believers. The Lord looks through and beyond the disciple Thomas; he looks past the disciples, down the ages and across oceans, and he sees you and me, and he promises his own self to us, to those who have not seen but yet put their trust in him. And so, the Evangelist John writes late in his Gospel these words: "Now Jesus did many other signs . . . which are not written in this book; but these are written [so] that you may believe that Jesus is the Christ, the Son of God, and that believing you may have life in his name."

May it be so. And may the God and Father of our Lord Jesus Christ be with you always.

Amen.

Somewhere beyond Mindless Fluffland

Grace Church, New York City
Fourth Sunday of Advent 1982

LUKE 1:5–30

Everybody knows that Jesus was turned away by an innkeeper, born in a stable, laid in a manger, surrounded by animals, admired by shepherds, sung to by angels. Never mind the fact that half these details aren't in the Bible; no good red-blooded American would be surprised to see his macho neighbor's mantelpiece adorned with angels or his front yard full of plastic sheep at this time of year. A significant percentage of the population will show up in one church or another on Christmas Eve, even in these days of shrinking church attendance, and it's a safe bet that most will be warmed to the heart once again to hear the old familiar details in the old familiar language. "And it came to pass in those days, that there went out a decree from Caesar Augustus . . ." "And there were in the same country shepherds abiding in the field . . ." "And this shall be a sign unto you; ye shall find the babe wrapped in swaddling clothes, lying in a manger." And God help the unfortunate reader who renders the story in any version other than the King James! Nobody wants to hear about any shepherds "out in the fields keeping guard throughout the night"—those shepherds have got to *abide* in those fields and *keep watch* over those flocks. *By night.*[1]

The Gospel of Luke, which contains all these cherished details (contains *some* of them, I should say, because numerous others have been added

---

1. I am grieved to report that, some thirty-four years after this sermon was preached, this passionate attachment to the King James Version has almost disappeared from the earth. There are now a rapidly dwindling number of octogenarians like me remaining who remember or care about the KJV rendering of the story. Jesus is now wrapped in "bands of cloth" instead of swaddling clothes—as if people were too dim to figure out what swaddling clothes might be. Only in *A Charlie Brown Christmas*, the beloved annual Peanuts television program, does the KJV still reign supreme, with Linus's deeply reverent reading of Luke's story, topped off with "And that's what Christmas is all about, Charlie Brown!"

through centuries of pious embellishment), lends itself, unfortunately, to sentimentality. It has had the bad luck to be called "the most beautiful book ever written"—a fate that should never have befallen a New Testament document. More faithful to Luke's intention is the depiction of the shepherds in Hugo van der Goes's paintings on the Portinari Altarpiece, in Florence; three ruffians are portrayed, coarse of face and ungainly of body, with dirty fingernails, crooked teeth, and bad haircuts, very much as real shepherds would actually have appeared—yet, for all that, utterly transfigured by the wonderment on their faces.

It is hard to realize, today, that, just as the great Flemish paintings are devoid of sentimentality, so also are Luke's stories of the birth of Jesus. Perhaps we ought to offer a definition of sentimentality. Bernard Shaw archly said that it was the working up of the greatest possible quantity of emotion on the cheapest possible terms. Flannery O'Connor, in a more sober mood, wrote that "sentimentality is . . . a distortion . . . in the direction of an overemphasis on innocence."[2]

What are the most sure-fire motifs for sentimentalists? Surely these would be the top three: children, cute animals, and motherhood. Hence the universal appeal of Luke's Christmas story, with its baby Jesus, its sheep, and its young Madonna. If sentimentality, as Flannery further wrote, is "an early arrival at a mock state of innocence," then the function of babies, animals, and Madonnas is to convince us that things really are not as bad as they seem, that the human race and the created order really are quite attractive and—well, innocent.

This is not what Luke had in mind. Later on in the Gospel, when Jesus was on his way to Jerusalem and certain death, a woman in the crowd called out to him fulsomely, "Blessed is the womb that bore you, and the breasts that you sucked!" But Jesus replied to her as follows: "Blessed rather are they who hear the word of God and keep it!" (Luke 11:27–28). J. B. Phillips, in his translation, gives that section the subtitle "Jesus Brings Sentimentality down to Earth." And in chapter 8, a message is brought to Jesus that his mother and brothers are waiting outside to see him; Jesus turns to the assembled gathering and says, "My mother and my brothers are those who hear the word of God and do it" (8:20–21). There is no automatic ticket to the state of innocence; mothers and kiddies are no more innocent than anybody else.

Three months before the birth of John the Baptist, eight months and a couple of weeks before the birth of Jesus, a newly pregnant girl named Mary

---

2. Flannery O'Connor, "The Church and the Fiction Writer," from *Mystery and Manners* (New York: Farrar, Straus and Giroux, 1969).

took off in great haste for the hill country where her very elderly and formerly barren cousin Elizabeth was awaiting the birth of her firstborn son, to be named John. Mary had seen an angel and had heard incredible, miraculous news; in the way of all human beings, her first and overriding need was to reach out to the only other person who might understand, the only other person who was mentioned by the angel—"your kinswoman Elizabeth in her old age has also conceived a son; and this is the sixth month with her who was called barren. For with God nothing will be impossible" (1:36–37).

How many countless paintings, Flemish or otherwise, have been done of this scene, called the visitation of Mary and Elizabeth! Of all biblical subjects, it must be one of the most difficult to render, since all that is really going on is invisible. Even the great Giotto could not show the flash of revelation, the child John leaping for joy in his mother's womb, the instantaneous response of Elizabeth as the Holy Spirit filled her with the knowledge of the identity of Mary's baby.

And Elizabeth cried out in ecstatic joy, "Blessed are you among women, and blessed is your child! What an honor it is to have the mother of my Lord come to see me! Why, as soon as your greeting reached my ears, the child within me jumped for joy!" (J. B. Phillips translation). But weren't we just saying that Luke gives no place in his Gospel to sentimentality about mothers and children? Is there anything to distinguish this scene from a million and one gatherings of women at baby showers and Lamaze clinics?

Yes, actually, there is; and that distinction means everything. Elizabeth ends her passionate exclamation with these words: "Blessed is she who believed that there would be a fulfillment of what was spoken to her from the Lord" (1:45). In this way the Evangelist joins the words of the aged Elizabeth, addressing the virgin mother of the yet-unborn Messiah, with the words spoken thirty-three years later by Jesus of Nazareth to the woman in the crowd on the road to Jerusalem: "Blessed rather are they who hear the word of God and keep it!" (11:28).

Elizabeth's cry of supernatural joy has nothing to do with the ordinary human pleasure in contemplating the birth of a child. It is her response to that revelatory kick from John the Baptist, already vitalized by his destiny as "The prophet of the Most High [who will] go before the Lord to prepare his ways, to give knowledge of salvation to his people by the forgiveness of their sins" (1:76–77). No phony innocence here, no sentimental glorification of motherhood, but the announcement of the turning point of world history—the entrance of God himself on the human scene. No Pollyannas here, no "early arrival at a mock state of innocence." As Luke records it, the very first words uttered by John the Baptist, hurled by that fire-breather at the crowds who came to him by the river, are "You brood of vipers! Who warned you to flee from the wrath to come? Bear fruits that befit repentance" (3:7–8).

I think we can safely say that Luke the Evangelist, not to mention John the Baptist, would be utterly scandalized to see the cutesy-cutesy shepherds and sheep and babies and Virgin Marys strewn about the landscape these days. I don't mean to sound harsh; I have a houseful of sheep and angels at Christmas just like everybody else. But we need to know—need to know as a matter of life and death—that these things, in their contemporary sanitized versions, may actually *prevent* us from understanding that (in the words of John the Baptist's father) "The Lord God of Israel has visited and redeemed his people" (1:68). We need to know that this news is able to transfigure the ugliest shepherds, the most birth-damaged babies, the violated pregnant women dead in the ditches of the war-torn countries of this world.

I don't know why sentimentality flourishes more in some periods of history than in others. It certainly has something to do with fear—fear of facing the unpleasant truth. Why should Americans be filled with fear, when we live in a free country with the world's highest standard of living? The *New York Times* shed some light on this yesterday. Mayor Koch pointed out to the City Club that "600 blacks picketed the shelter for the homeless," "2,000 Chinese marched in opposition to the new prison," "2000 Jews demonstrated and protested against the resource recovery plant in Brooklyn." (What the WASPs did, he does not say.) He calls it "the new selfishness." Saint Luke and John the Baptist would have called it the same old selfishness; it would have been no surprise to them. Things *are* as bad as they seem, and we are *not* innocent. Trafficking in cocaine has become an acceptable upper-class thing to do; running red lights is epidemic; organized crime has moved into the Sun Belt . . .

I'd hazard another guess as to why we are able to maintain sentimental illusions about life. In ways that Mary and Elizabeth could not have imagined, we are insulated from disagreeable reality. In his column yesterday, Russell Baker describes how it works. There are two types of TV news in New York, he says; the first is the honest Gabe Pressman type, depicting what seems to be a real city, and the second type is what Baker calls "Mindless Fluffland." He describes how "Pressman's line to the real world" of homeless men sleeping on the floor in Penn Station is constantly being cut off by stories about mink coats and watches made from gold coins. "How are we supposed to respond, sitting in the parlor, when we are jerked without benefit of decompression chamber between these two visions of America? . . . My guess is that most of us don't respond at all. We've been too numbed by television's constant flow of images juxtaposing misery with luxury cars and new improved panty hose."[3]

Whether it be fear or whether it be numbness, sentimentality is preferred to truth, and the most that we really want to know about Christmas is that a pretty girl had a beautiful baby and a nice light shone around them. Let me assure you, the crèche figures on the Rutledge mantelpiece are very easy on the eyes. None of us wants to mess up the Christmas spirit with thoughts of poverty and disease and war and death. A week or so of Mindless Fluffland is exactly what the doctor ordered. Don't bother me with John the Baptist or the new selfishness or the latest debates on the death penalty. Let's pretend that this baby in the straw really is our ticket to innocence—in no way particularly different from other babies.

And yet—and yet. What if it were really so? What if "the hopes and fears of all the years" really were to be met in Bethlehem one night?[4] What if Saint Luke really was telling the truth when he said that *God* had entered the womb of a poor, lowly village girl?

The second Sunday of Advent is John the Baptist's day. Today, the fourth Sunday of Advent, is Mary's day. "Blessed is she who believed that there would be a fulfillment of what was spoken to her from the Lord." Saint Luke's message is clear: Mary is a model of the true disciple. Her greatness does not lie in her intercessions with her son (an utterly unbiblical idea), or even in her giving birth to Jesus; rather, her greatness, according to Luke, is that she heard, believed, and obeyed God. Mary was brought up in the knowledge of God. She knew the Old Testament intimately; the story of God's mighty acts was second nature to her. Luke depicts her, in the story of the visitation, breaking forth into one of the greatest of all biblical hymns, the Magnificat. This is not some vague religious sensibility on Mary's part; Mary has received a message from the God of Israel, the God of Abraham, Isaac, and Jacob, and she knows very well where she stands in relation to that. "Behold the handmaid of the Lord; be it unto me according to thy word" (Luke 1:38).

What if it were true? Is it possible that the wonderment and awe on the faces of the ugly shepherds signify something other than the spectacle of a cute baby lying in the straw? What if there were news, not only for the woman in the mink coat but also for the man on death row, news not only for the fearful but also for the numb, news not only for the homeless but also for those of us who are afraid of the homeless, news not only for the would-be innocent but

3. *New York Times*, December 18, 1982.
4. Phillips Brooks, "O Little Town of Bethlehem."

also for those of us who know ourselves to be frauds? Let John the Baptist kick the message to kingdom come:

> "The day will dawn upon us from on high,
> to give light to those who sit in darkness and in the shadow of death."
> (1:78–79)

Let the self-centered and self-sufficient hear Mary's song:

> "He has shown strength with his arm,
> he has scattered the proud in the imagination of their hearts,
> he has put down the mighty from their thrones." (1:51–52)

Let the proclamation sink in to the ears of the rich and the poor:

> "He has filled the hungry with good things,
> and the rich he has sent empty away." (1:53–54)

There is no automatic ticket to the state of innocence; but what if it were true that Jesus himself is the ticket? There is no such place as Mindless Fluffland, but what if it were true that "no ear may hear his coming, but in this world of sin / where meek souls will receive him, still / the dear Christ enters in"?[5]

With every fiber of my being I hope and pray this morning to convey this message and this hope: the *Son of God* is born of Mary. Listen: many of you, most of you this morning, are already believers. You have already heard and obeyed, like Mary. You know that God is really God, and not some vain, wish-fulfilling projection of ourselves onto an abstract figure in the sky. But on Christmas Eve, the ratio will be reversed. Most of the people in the churches will be—well, what will they be? Some will be sentimentalists, definitely—in search of a childhood innocence that hasn't existed anywhere in the world since Adam and Eve took that apple. Some will be tradition-lovers, seeking reassurance from the repetition of old patterns. Some will be curious, some will be aesthetes, some will be lonely. Some will be drunk—and not all of them from the Bowery, either. But somewhere deep down in each one is a lost and frightened child who has lost its way, who has been rejected by its father, who has been shut out of the party, who is truly afraid—deep down—that ashes

---

5. Brooks, "O Little Town of Bethlehem."

are all it will get for Christmas. Help us, you who believe—help us spread the word, in carols, in bells, in lights, in prayers, in presents, in words and deeds of love, that the Father has come seeking for all his children, that he has a place set at his table with your own name on it, that he will deliver us from numbness and from fear and from guilt so that we will be able to reach out with joy and gladness to those who have not yet heard.

> Blessed be the Lord God of Israel, for he has visited and redeemed his people . . . that we, being delivered from the hand of our enemies, might serve him without fear, in holiness and righteousness before him, all the days of our life.[6]

---

6. The Song of Zechariah (the father of John the Baptist) is also called the Benedictus.

The Magical Reversal

Grace Church, New York City
Fourth Sunday of Advent 1984

LUKE 1:26–38

A few days ago, quite late in the evening—I think it was about 11:45—I was walking with a few friends past a rather scruffy little coffee shop at Fourteenth Street and Third Avenue. Inside, it was brightly lit, although all the customers had long been gone. The lights revealed the various employees of the coffee shop in their jeans and work pants, standing on the counters and on the tables, shouting instructions to each other as they draped a gold tinsel garland across the drab little room. A simple scene, hardly worth noting, hardly worth mentioning—but it stayed in my mind. Why was this motley little group of undoubtedly very tired people hanging a foolish, cheap bit of glitter over the coffee urns and the cash register? Because the customers expected it? Because it would help business? Perhaps; perhaps . . .

What is it? What is it about a rope of tinsel? What is it about a string of lights on a tree? I remember an image from years ago when I found myself, one deep December night just before Christmas Eve, driving through a very depressed, dark, and deserted neighborhood in Stamford, Connecticut. The street-level warehouses and other buildings were barred, bolted, or boarded up. The second- and third-story windows were empty, dingy, black. Bits of trash blew along the sidewalks when the wind stirred. I had seen such neighborhoods many times before, of course, but for some reason, on this particular night, the darkness and emptiness of the streets seemed to me particularly oppressive and disturbing, and I locked my car door, not because I saw anyone, but as if to shut the feelings out. Then, as I approached a deserted intersection, I looked up and saw among all those blank and lifeless windows one tiny string of multicolored Christmas lights, just one little string, hung across just one window, bravely blinking out its message in the dark. Who knows who hung it there? Who knows what forlorn hope, what inarticulate longing, what simple human impulse of cheerfulness or defiance or humor or tenacity or courage caused it to appear in that window? I will never know; but it spoke to this heart, and I have not forgotten it to this day.

In the musical comedy *Mame*, you'll remember the episode where the irrepressible heroine, threatened by some disaster or other and determined not to be defeated by it, rallies her incongruous household—the orphaned nephew, the frumpy unmarried pregnant secretary, the Japanese houseboy—with a spirited rendition of a song called "We Need a Little Christmas Now." The whole musical was pretty forgettable (in my opinion), but I do have this recollection of those assorted characters dancing around, in the middle of what is supposed to be summertime, fighting off depression with a song about how "we need a little Christmas, right this very minute!"

I think there is one thing clear amidst all the protests about the excess and the commercialism and the frenzy and the too-much-ness: even the most jaded, even the most blasé, even the most sated sophisticates in this most worldly of all possible cities will in some way at some point let his guard down, let the truth slip—we need a little Christmas.

I have already started laying plans for next year's Christmas. I'm going to try to persuade my sister to fly my seven-year-old niece and godchild up here so I can take her to *The Nutcracker* at Lincoln Center. Am I going to do this for my niece's benefit? Not really. It's really for me. One of the reasons for the enduring popularity of *The Nutcracker* is that it permits the grown-ups an evening of unadulterated Christmas magic on the pretense of taking the children.

Christmas magic. What is it? Not so much about Christmas trees that grow and snowflakes that dance, though that is an important part of the aura; no, the moment in the ballet that makes this grown woman choke up, year after year, is the part where evil is defeated conclusively and forever, the part where the little boy and little girl, holding hands, begin their magical journey through the enchanted forest, together, unafraid, the danger over and past, the phantoms banished, led and protected by a splendidly luminous star, into a kingdom of joy and delight where no disappointment can ever enter.

Magic is what we want; the illusion of magic puts billions of dollars in motion every December as we give permission to the advertisers and the retailers and the entertainers and the restaurants to let us pretend for a few weeks that there really is such a thing as magic, even though we know, we know there isn't.

One image is all it takes to shatter the illusion; you saw it, as I did, in the paper—two young boys, in Ethiopia, wrapped in ragged blankets, bent almost double with the pain of starvation, their faces contorted into what looked like the most terrible smiles—the gruesome grimace of famine. Where is the magic?

One image is all it takes to break the enchantment—a woman dragging her small boy up the subway stairs, slapping him and cursing him on every step while he, stupefied and powerless, offers no resistance. Where is the magic?

Up at the Cathedral, a much-publicized Peace Tree is decorated with two thousand folded white paper cranes, made by Japanese children. This is all right, I suppose, though everybody knows that there isn't even peace among the members of the Cathedral hierarchy, let alone peace among the nations. I think about the Peace Tree only with an effort; the image that keeps coming before me is the fountain of blood in the cemetery in Tehran. You saw that picture too, I'm sure—red-colored water, looking all too horribly like real blood, cascading over the stones—the latest device to stir a nation to continuing martyrdoms in the holy wars and other acts of terror.

As I look back over my Advent and Christmas sermons of past years, I see how little difficulty I have had finding illustrations of horror. The Ayatollah came to power in Advent; the Jim Jones suicide orgy was in Advent; the Union Carbide disaster was in Advent.[1] Every year, I note, there are the same themes: war, crime, violence, poverty, racial hatreds, totalitarian oppression, religious persecution, torture, selfishness, greed, SIN. What would you like to wager about Christmas next year? What would be the better bet—that at this time next year there will be peace in the world, or that there will be fountains of blood? Which is the better bet?

No; there is no magic. We can send Christmas cards about love and peace all we want, but the human race is utterly incapable of turning itself around. The children who go to see *The Nutcracker* grow up to be victims of disappointment just like all the rest of us. There is no magical kingdom anywhere.

In a world no better and no worse than this one, at another time and in another place, where men and women struggled against poverty and disease

---

1. The Ayatollah Khomeini was the leader of the Iranian Revolution of 1979. Overthrowing the Shah might have been a good thing, but the Ayatollah was an anti-Semitic religious autocrat. He played the Iranian hostage crisis—fifty-two Americans were held hostage for 444 days—for all it was worth, while establishing a rigid regime in which human rights violations were comparable to the Shah's. The charismatic and fanatical Jim Jones led 918 members of his People's Temple (in Jonestown, Guyana) in a mass murder-suicide in 1978. The Union Carbide explosion of 1984 in Bhopal, India, exposed five hundred thousand people to poisonous gases. Eight thousand died within two weeks, and more than that died later, not to mention all the diseases and disabilities that ensued. It is still called the worst industrial disaster in the history of the world.

and greed and disillusionment as we do, in a time when moments of hope and happiness and peace were just as delusory and fugitive as they are today, Saint Luke the Evangelist wrote a magical story.

> In the sixth month [of Elizabeth's pregnancy] the angel Gabriel was sent from God to a virgin [whose] name was Mary . . . and the angel said to her, "Do not be afraid, Mary: for . . . behold, you will conceive in your womb and bear a son, and you shall call his name Jesus. He will be great, and will be called the Son of the Most High, and the Lord God will give to him the throne of his father David . . . and of his kingdom there shall be no end."
>
> And Mary said to the angel, "How can this be, since I do not know a man?" And the angel said to her, "The Holy Spirit will come upon you, and the power of the Most High will overshadow you: therefore the child to be born will be called holy, the Son of God . . . for with God, nothing will be impossible."

An angel, and a virgin. A heavenly messenger, an obscure young woman, a child who will be the Son of God. A beautiful story, an inspiration for hundreds of Old Master paintings, the centerpiece for a zillion manger scenes; but it could not possibly be true. We have seen to that. In Scarsdale, as you know, there is a continuing battle about whether or not a nativity scene can be displayed on public property. One citizen wrote an indignant letter of protest to the village newspaper. She asked "how anything as simple as a Mother, Father, and Child—a once-a-year symbol of peace—could [possibly] offend anyone."[2]

A generic "symbol of peace"! This is what we have done to the message of the angel. We want magic on the screen and over the amplifiers; we want it at Radio City Music Hall and in the Lord & Taylor windows; we want it on the stage and in the streets and in the shopping catalogues, but when the real thing is right there staring us in the face, we refuse to believe it; we try every way we can think of to make it just another pretty story about a nice family with a new baby. Thank God for the Bible! Thank God for God's decision to have his Evangelists and apostles put it down in writing! There is no editorial board, no sociological task force, no concerned citizens' group, no ad hoc committee, no civil liberties union, no department of philosophy and religion anywhere on earth that can tamper with the message of the angel to Mary: "The Holy Spirit will come upon you, and the power of the Most High will overshadow

2. *New York Times*, December 20, 1984.

you: therefore the child to be born will be called the Son of God." We can fiddle around with this text all we want to—we can call it poetry or fantasy or myth or fairy tale or whatever we like—but we need to recognize very clearly that Saint Luke is not fiddling around. Luke has a message of the most momentous consequence that he wants to communicate.

What is the meaning of the message? I planted some tulip bulbs this fall. On the wrapper, I noticed these words: "Bulbs from Holland—Nature's Miracles." Is Saint Luke telling us of a "nature miracle" like the birth of a child? On the Metro-North trains that I ride into the city, there is an advertisement for Frangelico liqueur. It shows a lovable old monk with a brown Franciscan habit and a beatific expression on his face, sniffing at a glass of the liqueur. The writing under the picture says, "The blessings of nature with a dash of divine inspiration." Perhaps that is what the story of the nativity is about! Almost every voice I heard for most of my life said so, and I don't mean just the commercial messages, either. I mean voices from the pulpits of the churches. The blessings of nature with a dash of divine inspiration.

But this is not what God is telling us through his servant Saint Luke. In the story of the annunciation, we are hearing a *novum*, a New Thing. The angel and the Virgin—their story tells us that God is to enter this world directly in the person of his Son, begotten by the power of the Holy Spirit, the same power that brought forth the creation out of nothing in the first chapter of Genesis.

You know, during all those years that I was told, and believed, that the virginal conception of Jesus wasn't important, and didn't really make any difference one way or the other, there was another influence going on in my life that I failed to recognize at the time. There was the Nicene Creed:

> I believe in one Lord Jesus Christ, the only begotten Son of God . . .
> being of one substance with the Father;
> by whom all things were made;
> who for us men and for our salvation came down from heaven,
> and was incarnate by the Holy Ghost of the Virgin Mary . . .

And there was also the little-known second verse of *Adeste Fideles*, which, by some mercy of the Lord, the Episcopal Church still sings:

> God of God,
> Light of Light,
> Lo! he abhors not the Virgin's womb;
> Very God,

> Begotten, not created;
> O come, let us adore him, Christ the Lord.

And there was also the second verse of Charles Wesley's "Hark! The Herald Angels Sing":

> . . . Christ, the everlasting Lord;
> Late in time behold him come,
> Offspring of the Virgin's womb.
> Veiled in flesh the Godhead see;
> Hail the incarnate Deity . . .

And there was also . . . but I won't go on. You see the point. Two thousand years of Christian proclamation testify: we are not talking about a human birth. We are talking about one who was "born as no one else was born";[3] born as a fully human being, yes, absolutely; but begotten directly of the power of God.

This is what we learn from the story of the annunciation. Natural processes could not have brought the Son of God into being, not even with "a touch of divine inspiration." It is beyond the capacity of human parents to produce a child who is God. Humankind cannot bring forth a Jesus, any more than it can bring forth true and lasting peace. Only God can do it. Only God will do it. Only God. Mary was just as helpless as Joseph to make this happen. The human impossibility is overcome by the irresistible power of God.

What is an angel? I don't know. I have never seen one, and I would probably be suspicious of anyone who said he or she had. But in the Bible, these mysterious servants of God play a very important role. Gabriel, with Michael, is one of the two most important. His name, Gabriel, means "Man of God." Gabriel and Michael both appear in the wonderful book of Daniel, in which the coming of the Son of Man is announced, the one whose dominion is an everlasting dominion that will never pass away, and his kingdom one that will never be destroyed (Dan. 7:14). And, according to the intertestamental book of Enoch—listen to this!—Gabriel is the angel whom God placed at the gates of the garden of Eden, the angel who drove Adam and Eve out of Paradise. Now Gabriel returns! This is breathtaking! He returns to announce God's mighty reversal of the sin of the ancestors.[4] He comes to proclaim the

---

3. Karl Barth, *Church Dogmatics* I/2 (Edinburgh: T. & T. Clark, 1956), 185.
4. I have long had a fondness for a medieval Christmas carol with a much-repeated

advent of the one who will save his people from their sins—a Savior, who is Christ the Lord.

This is the magic. This is the real magic. An angel, and a virgin. God has acted. God has intervened. God is the one who rules over the everlasting kingdom that he delivers to his Son. In the announcement of Gabriel to the Virgin Mary, we hear a voice from beyond ourselves, a voice quite literally from out of this world. Only God is able to give true and lasting peace. Only God can create a new kingdom where no evil and no disappointment can ever enter. The news from Saint Luke is that God himself has entered this world. His own blood will be shed in order to guarantee that the fountains of blood will one day come to an end forever. Jesus Christ, the Lord, is our hope. Jesus Christ is our future. Jesus, our Savior, and our God. The little strings of lights in the dark places remain lit, by his grace, in the dark places until he comes again.

Amen.

Latin refrain: "*Nova! Nova!*" (A new thing!), but I could not figure out the next line: "*Ave fit ex Eva*." Two scholars helped me, one a Latin teacher, another a professor of medieval church history. It's a little awkward to translate—"*Ave* becomes from Eve"—but it is a word-play in the Latin, an exercise beloved by the medieval mind. The angel Gabriel says *Ave* (Hail!) to Mary, and in this announcement, the sin of Adam and Eve is reversed: *Ave-Eva*. Wonderful!

A SERVICE OF LESSONS AND CAROLS FOR ADVENT

The Great "O" Antiphons of Advent

Adapted from the Advent services of lessons and carols at Trinity Episcopal Cathedral, Columbia, South Carolina; Christ Episcopal Church, Greenwich, Connecticut; and the College of Corpus Christi and the Blessed Virgin Mary at Cambridge (England).

Organ prelude

The Advent Responsory

Choir, from narthex or transept

> I look from afar: and lo, I see the power of God coming,
>> and a cloud covering the whole earth.
>
> Go ye out to meet him, and say:
>> "Tell us, art thou he that should come to reign over thy people
>>> Israel?"
>
> High and low, rich and poor, one with another,
>> go ye out to meet him, and say:
>>> "Art thou he that should come?
>>> Hear, O thou Shepherd of Israel,
>>>> thou that leadest Joseph like a sheep,
>>>> tell us, art thou he?"
>>> Stir up thy strength, O Lord,

and come to reign over thy people Israel!

Text from an early medieval Roman rite.
Music adapted from a Magnificat by
G. P. da Palestrina (c. 1525–1594)

The Entrance Hymn

"Comfort, Comfort Ye My People"   *Psalm 42*, melody Charles Goudimel;
Johann G. Olearius (1611–1684),
trans. Catherine Winkworth
(1827–1878)

or

"Come, Thou Long Expected Jesus"   *Stuttgart*, Charles Wesley (1707–1788)

The Bidding Prayer

Beloved in Christ, we are met together in this season of Advent to prepare
ourselves in heart and mind for the coming of the Lord Jesus Christ, our Savior and our Judge, to hear in Holy Scripture and sacred song the message of
salvation wrought by him, and to be put in mind of the great day of Judgment.

Let us therefore beseech our Heavenly Father that of his mercy he will
forgive our past deeds, whether they be committed or omitted through weakness, through ignorance, or through willful disobedience; being mindful of
the perfect sacrifice of his Son that bought us once for all on Calvary's tree:
and let us seek his grace to amend our lives, that we may follow the pattern of
his Son's perfect life.

May we now therefore mark in Holy Scripture the tale of the loving purposes of God from the first days of our disobedience unto the glorious redemption brought us by the Advent of the Savior, that we may look expectantly to
the final day when he shall come in glory to fulfill his promise of a redeemed
and transfigured creation.

Let us pray:

The Collect for the First Sunday of Advent

Almighty God, give us grace that we may cast away the works of darkness, and put upon us the armour of light, now in the time of this mortal life, in which thy Son Jesus Christ came to visit us in great humility; that in the last day, when he shall come again in his glorious majesty to judge both the living and the dead, we may rise to the life immortal, through him who liveth and reigneth with thee and the Holy Ghost, now and ever. *Amen.*

Hymn

"Sleepers, Wake!"   *Wachet auf!*, Phillip Nicolai (1556–
                                     1608); trans. Carl P. Daw Jr. (1944–)

The First "O"

O Sapientia

Antiphon
O Wisdom, coming forth from the mouth of the Most High,
Reaching from one end to the other mightily,
And sweetly ordering all things,
Come and teach us the way of prudence.

                         cf. Ecclesiasticus 24:3; Wisdom 8:1

Reading

Proverbs 8:1, 10–11, 21–26, 32–35   The creation and the summons
                                           of Wisdom

Hymn

"O Come, O Come, Emmanuel,"   *Veni Emmanuel*; Latin text,
first two verses   eighth century

The Second "O"

O Adonai

Antiphon
O Adonai, leader of the house of Israel,
who appeared to Moses in the fire of the burning bush
and gave him the law on Mount Sinai:
Come and redeem us with outstretched arm.

cf. Exodus 3

Reading

Exodus 24:12–18; 31:18   The manifestation of the Lord at Sinai
and the giving of the Law

Hymn

"O Come, O Come, Emmanuel," third verse

Reading in Unison

Psalm 119:169–176   The beauty and excellence of God's
commandments

Hymn

"Prepare the Way, O Zion"   *Bereden väg för Herran*, from
Then Swenska Psalmboken (1697);
Frans Mikael Franzen (1772–1847),
adapted Charles P. Price (1920–1999)

The Third "O"

O Radix Jesse

Antiphon

O Root of Jesse, standing as an ensign among the peoples,
Before you kings will shut their mouths,
To you the nations will make their prayer;
Come and deliver us, and delay no longer.

Reading

Isaiah 11:1–10   The Spirit of the Lord rests upon the branch of Jesse's stem

Hymn

"O Come, O Come, Emmanuel," fourth verse

The Fourth "O"

O Clavis David

Antiphon

O Key of David and scepter of the house of Israel;
you open and no one can shut;
you shut and no one can open;
Come and lead the prisoners from the prison house,
those who dwell in darkness and in the shadow of death.

Reading

Isaiah 22:22; 42:6–9   Christ, the key of the house of David,
                                        unlocks the prison of sin and death

Hymn

"O Come, O Come, Emmanuel," fifth verse

The Fifth "O"

O Oriens

Antiphon
O Morning Star,
splendor of light eternal and sun of righteousness:
Come and enlighten those that dwell in darkness
and in the shadow of death.

Choir anthem (or congregational hymn)

"People, Look East"   17th c. French carol tune *Besançon*;
                                        Eleanor Farjeon (1881–1965)

Reading

Isaiah 9:2, 6–7   The light of Christ arises upon a world
                                        in chaos and darkness

Hymn

"O Come, O Come, Emmanuel," sixth verse

The Sixth "O"

O Rex Gentium

Antiphon
O King of the nations, and their desire,
the cornerstone making both one,
come and save the human race whom you fashioned from clay.

Hymn

"Hail to the Lord's Anointed"	*Es flog ein kleins Waldvögelein*; James Montgomery (1771–1854)
or	
"The King Shall Come When Morning Dawns"	*St. Stephen*; Greek text; trans. John Brownlie (1859–1925)

Reading

Isaiah 60:1–7	The nations bring their treasures to the Messiah

Hymn

"O Come, O Come, Emmanuel," seventh verse

The Seventh "O"

O Emmanuel

Antiphon
O Emmanuel, our King and our lawgiver,

the hope of the nations and their Savior;
Come and save us, O Lord our God.

Reading

Isaiah 7:14; 42:1–7   The prophet heralds the birth of
                                        God-with-us

Hymn

"O Come, O Come, Emmanuel," eighth and final verse

The Collect for the Third Sunday of Advent

Stir up your power, O Lord, and with great might come among us; and, because we are sorely hindered by our sins, let your bountiful grace and mercy speedily help and deliver us; through Jesus Christ our Lord, to whom, with you and the Holy Spirit, be honor and glory, now and for ever. *Amen.*

The Lord's Prayer

Advent Vespers Responsory
adapted from G. P. da Palestrina (c. 1525–1594)

Versicle: **We wait for thy loving kindness, O Lord,**
Response: in the midst of thy temple.
Versicle: **Judah and Jerusalem, fear not, nor be dismayed.**
Response: Tomorrow, go ye forth, and the Lord, he will be with you.
Versicle: **Stand ye still, and ye shall see the salvation of the Lord.**
Response: Tomorrow, go ye forth, and the Lord, he will be with you.
Versicle: **Glory be to the Father, and to the Son, and to the Holy Ghost.**
Response: Tomorrow, go ye forth and the Lord, he will be with you.

Hymn

"Lo, He Comes with   *Helmsley*; Charles Wesley (1707–1788)
Clouds Descending"

Blessing and Dismissal

May Almighty God, by whose Providence our Savior Christ came among us in great humility, sanctify you with the light of his blessing and set you free from all sin. *Amen.*

May he whose second coming in power and great glory we await, make you steadfast in faith, joyful in hope, and constant in love. *Amen.*

May you who rejoice in the first advent of our Redeemer, at his second advent be rewarded with eternal life. *Amen.*

And the blessing of God Almighty, the Father, the Son, and the Holy Spirit, be upon you and remain with you for ever. *Amen.*

Organ voluntary

*   *   *

Jared Johnson, the organist-choirmaster of Trinity Episcopal Cathedral in Columbia, South Carolina, made an additional observation about the Great "O" Antiphons that further illuminates the depths of these ancient liturgical texts. Here is what he wrote:

> When using the Episcopal Hymnal 1982 version of "O come, O come, Emmanuel," I often wish we could start at verse two and have the stanzas match the O Antiphons without revealing Emmanuel at the beginning. This would of course present some practical challenges to persuade the congregation to skip verse 1, but it might illuminate the magic of *ero cras* and the time-bending nature of the Antiphons more directly.

The "magic of *ero cras*" is elucidated in this excerpt from the website of the Catholic Resource Center, where Professor Robert Greenberg of the San Francisco Conservatory of Music is quoted as follows:

> The Benedictine monks [possibly as early as the sixth century, certainly by the eighth century] arranged these antiphons with a definite purpose. If one starts with the last title and takes the first letter of each once—Emmanuel, Rex, Oriens, Clavis, Radix, Adonai, Sapientia—the Latin words *ero cras* are formed, meaning, "Tomorrow, I will come." Therefore the Lord Jesus, whose coming we have prepared for in Advent and whom we have addressed in these seven Messianic titles, now speaks to us, "Tomorrow, I will come."

This reflects not only the expectation of the coming of Christ "tomorrow" (Christmas Eve) but also, in keeping with the "time-bending nature" of the Advent season, anticipates the second coming and the consummation of all things in the day of the Lord.

In a fitting conclusion to this book, we respond with the ancient call in the Aramaic language,

Maranatha!

Come, Lord Jesus. (I Cor. 16:22)

Index of Biblical Passages